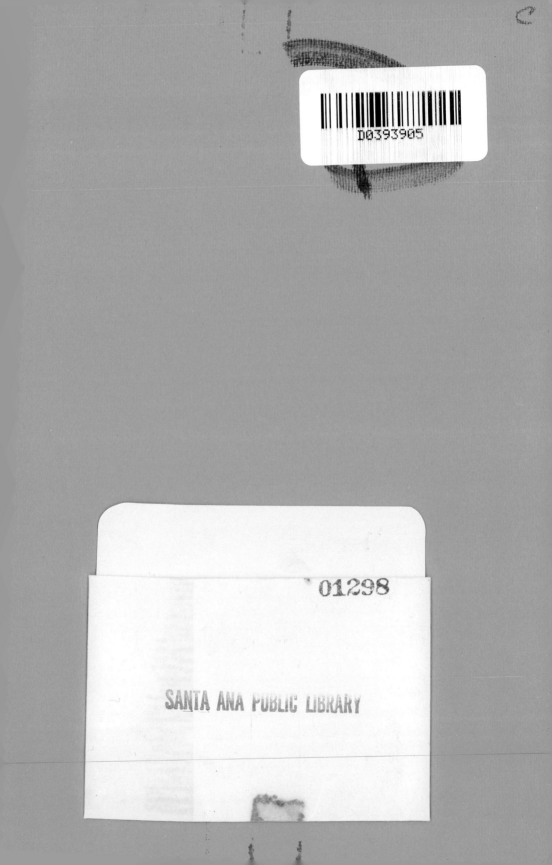

Jean Renoir

Jean Renoir

RAYMOND DURGNAT

University of California Press

Berkeley and Los Angeles

University of California Press
Berkeley and Los Angeles, California

University of California Press, Ltd.
London, England

Copyright © 1974 by
The Regents of the University of California

ISBN: 0-520-02283-1
Library of Congress Catalog Card Number: 72-82221
Designed by Jim Mennick
Printed in the United States of America

Acknowledgements

For the loan of valuable stills I would very much like to thank, in particular, John Kobal, and also Michel Ciment, Bernard Cohn, Raymond Borde, Joel Finler, Robin Bean, editor of *Films and Filming,* Andi Engel, of Polit Kino Films, Contemporary Films Ltd., London, *L'Avant-Scène (Cinéma)* and the *Cinémathèque Royale de Belgique.* I must also thank Susan Bennett and, for help in the preparation of the manuscript, I should like to thank Clare Garrick, Judy Lawes, and Eleanor Caplan. I am also indebted to Mike Wallington for editorial consultation. This book is dedicated to J.A. Rowe.

R.E.D.

Contents

Illustrations

Since the text is arranged chronologically, film by film, the content of the illustrations is generally evident from the context, and captions are provided only when essential. The following list supplies character identifications for the stills, and in some cases comments on the action depicted.

Introduction

"No one has any doubt that Renoir is one of the four or five great *auteurs* in all the history of the cinema." So the French 'Dominican' critic Henri Agel. And Charles Chaplin: "The greatest film director in the world? In my opinion he's a Frenchman. He's called Jean Renoir."

Maybe "great" and "greatest" belong to an appreciative rhetoric rather than to the main business of criticism, but the drift of these remarks is borne out by the range of artists to whom Renoir has, with more or less justification, been compared: Beaumarchais, Balzac, Cervantes, Diderot, Flaubert, Montaigne, Renoir *père*, and inevitably, Shakespeare, the latter for the spread of subjects on which a diversity of styles confer a wise lyricism intellectually more densely textured than may at first appear.

All comparisons are eventually betrayed. There should be no need now to argue the parity of cinema with the older media. Renoir is a major artist of his century.

Critic, Tale and Teller

Renoir's courtesy, lucidity and frankness have made him a much-interviewed director. He is not one of those artists whose comments are best treated as charming curiosities. Yet many of his pronouncements have the rough-and-readiness of off-the-cuff replies. Nor would he claim papal infallibility about his work.

Comments made after a film's completion are subject to obvious distortions. Memory is fallible. An artist may have repudiated an earlier stage of development, and now see meanings other than those intended at the time. Renoir made *Nana,* under Stroheim's influence, as a realistic film, as it was, given the standards of its time. Thirty years later, what strikes its creator—a "mere" spectator like us—is its romanticism. We may feel that the two descriptions are by no means contradictory, or even that they are merely relative to changed conventions. Today it is difficult to see how one description can seem complete without the other. A critic who, at either period, made a pointblank contradiction of Renoir's description might be an anachronistic emissary from the *other* Renoir.

Observations made before or during the creative process are no more immune from distortion. As Renoir has remarked, he perceives the real theme of his films only in the making, earlier themes often acting as working hypotheses which he is quite prepared to revamp. Thus his description of *La Règle du Jeu* as a study in sexual relationships might be just such a hypothesis, subsequently abandoned or transcended. Comments made on the spur of the moment in interviews may have been influenced by a certain line of questioning, or by Renoir's desire to present a commercially attractive image of his film, or by recourse to a quick safe answer under the stress of crowded schedules and preoccupation with finer artistic problems. Very personal factors may intervene. Thus Pierre Leprohon suggests that Renoir's remark to the effect that the only value of his early films was that they enshrined their leading lady, Catherine Hessling, might be connected with her claim that at this time he was trying to mend a broken relationship with her. Yet at about the same time he dismissed all his previous films except *Nana* and *La Chienne* as "either sport or commerce". And ever since the Cold War began Renoir has consistently underplayed the extent of his involvement with leftwing films and film organisations in the context of the Popular Front.

A man who, in over forty years of film-making, never changed his mind would be a monster. Major contradictions by Renoir abound. In his Popular Front period, he made his much-quoted remark about his earlier attempts to emulate an American style. "I had not yet understood that the individual man, even more than his race, is a tributary of the soul that nourishes him, of the conditions of life which fashion his body and his brain, of the scenery which, throughout the day, passes before his eyes. I hadn't yet realised that a Frenchman, living in France, drinking red wine and eating the cheese of Brie, before the grey Parisian landscape, can produce work of real quality only by leaning on the traditions of people who have shared his way of life". More recently, asked whether he preferred working in France or in America, he replied, "It's all the same to me. Give me a shed with four lamps and I'll make a film". Yet neither remark accounts for the responsiveness to unfamiliar environments evidenced in *The Southerner* and in *The River*. Above all, interviews are conversations and as such subject to all the omissions, the exaggerations (some rhetorical, some involuntary, some the product of the obliteration of vocal inflexion or gesture by cold print), and to all the banalities and platitudes, of table talk. Some of Renoir's interviews are boring successions of half truths indicating only a general drift of thought. Others are extremely stimulating.

In interviews Renoir has, however, consistently made a distinction between *inner* realism (the truth one wishes to reveal) and *outer* realism (e.g. location photography, amateurs acting themselves, and all the trappings of neo-documentary). Particularly in the early '30s, he attempted to reach the first through the second. Yet, throughout most of his career, the second has been only one of the ways of reaching the first.

He has returned to the example of Chaplin, who *becomes* a sailor (when not even dressed as a sailor) whereas a bad actor remains simply a bad actor (even if dressed in authentic seaman's garb). He has observed that a "realist" like Zola or Maupassant "digests and composes" reality no less than Marivaux.

He relegates conscious purpose to a secondary role. "Ingenuousness is absolutely necessary to creation. A painter who says, 'I'm going to produce a work of genius by doing this or that' has an excellent chance of producing a flop. On the other hand, a Cézanne plants himself before a rock and says, 'I'm going to paint that rock' and no more, with no conscious afterthoughts. He paints a great picture."

"I came to the cinema in the most natural way possible. I was making pottery (painting has never tempted me); and pottery, of all the arts, is the nearest to the cinema. . . . You laugh? Well, listen. The ceramicist conceives a vase, makes it, glazes it, bakes it. . . . And after a few hours he takes from the oven something. . . . altogether different from what he expected. Just like the cinema. . . . I didn't have the feeling that I was trying to be an artist in making vases. I renounced ceramics for a very simple reason. I realised that either I'd have to be an artist, that is to try to be pretentious enough to create individual works of art and sell them as works of Art—and that, I was absolutely unwilling to do; or else I'd have to go into industry, and I knew nothing of it. I'd have to contribute to the fabrication of a million teacups annually. And . . . I couldn't . . . and I took up the cinema."

These remarks suggest that Renoir respects the word "art" as in the phrase "the art of medicine" but regards with suspicion art with a capital A. The conscientiousness which is *de rigueur* for the artist should attend any practice in any craft. The only difference is that art has the rôle of a communicative interplay with the hearts and souls of one's fellow men. Though this communication has its own techniques and its own requirements, its ends rank among the humbler activities from which Renoir's metaphors for art are always, pointedly, drawn. That which in Renoir seems spontaneous, to have sprung from an unreflective responsiveness, can turn out to have another source. "I made a study of French gestures through the paintings of my father and the painters of his generation". Renoir's conversation refers simply and naturally to life and art as aspects of each other. The latter's artifices are the procedures which nature—human nature—contrives, evolves or adopts for this particular sphere of activity.

His career shows a preference for the informal and the evanescent. Art is also an extension of conversation. This attitude helps to explain the apologetic or didactic purpose behind several Renoir films, notably *La Vie est à Nous, La Marseillaise* and *This Land is Mine*. Renoir, too, is an expert practitioner of the folk art of the anecdote; like this, concerning certain vicissitudes during the production of *La Chienne:* "I had a good friend at the time who was an exhibitor. He was a very interesting man, a Russian who had been a sailor in the Turkish Navy. I loved the man for a very important reason. He was the only man I knew who could put a coin on an anvil, swing a big smith's hammer and stop it exactly one half-inch from the coin. In such a man one can have confidence. . . . " Or concerning his arrival in America: ". . . it was Robert Flaherty, who's now dead, the maker of *Moana* and *Louisiana Story,* who met me. He was like a brother, a marvellous man. There was only one thing which annoyed him; it was my hat. I had the kind of hat that was being worn in France at that time, a hat with a very narrow brim. He thought it was ridiculous. He had an American kind of hat, with a very wide brim. From time to time, he'd say, 'Jean, Jean, you can't keep that!' And then, at last, he took my hat and stamped on it. And then he gave me his."

Renoir's fondness for the anecdote links intriguingly with the suggestion mooted in *Films and Feelings* that the novel is not so much the successor of the tale as a special form within it. In many respects the filmscript (as distinct from the film) shares with the tale an emphasis less on subtlety of articulation than on bold clear patterns involving paradoxes of behaviour (the near-contradiction in the last two lines of his Flaherty tale). The telling of tales has its roots in an oral, informal culture. Yet the characteristic mood in which tales are told or yarns are spun—over coffee, brandy and cigars, or ghost stories by the fire—parallels the characteristic artistic situation. Emotion is recollected in tranquillity, but mixed with awe and apprehension over its relevance, together with a certain enjoyment-in-appreciation of the tale as a tale. When art detaches itself from these social, evanescent forms, and takes on the elaboration, permanence and mystique with which our culture invests it, it discovers new opportunities, certainly, but at the expense of new perils. To say that art cannot take itself more seriously than life is not to say that sacrifice should not be made for it. For radical sacrifice is an inevitable and indispensible concomitant to many human activities. But insofar as art proposes itself as a substitute for religion, it puts itself in spiritual peril of deracination from that human experience which nourishes it and which it exists to transform. Art, or rather culture as a whole, is the baking of the bread of life, not its transubstantiation. It is an everyday reality, altered, no doubt, in the ovens of the medium, but still bread—*only* bread, offering sustenance not salvation. Human activities already possess the richness art reveals but does not always create. For both the strength and weakness of his art, Renoir must be ranked with, for example, Freud, Huxley and Tolstoi as a highly cultured man for whom art is consequential rather than absolute. It is spilled thought—like honest conversation—not spilled religion.

A desire to communicate with the general public played an important part in Renoir's career. For him Stroheim's *Foolish Wives* demonstrated the possibility of touching the public by "subjects in the tradition of French realism", and his lifelong purpose generates the wistful soliloquy which he puts in the mouth of Octave in *La Règle du Jeu*. His constant search for independence and autonomy within the industry seems to have sprung from a conviction that industry shibboleths were barriers to this communication, rather than from art for art's sake hermetism. Nonetheless his readiness to disrupt a preordained framework to allow a film to go the way it wants to go underwrites Claude Beylie's remark that "the essential mark of Renoir's art . . . is . . . his amateurism, which long kept him apart from the film industry and ensures his lastingness, where so many pseudo-professionals have gone under."

Beylie's point survives the objection that Renoir could remain apart from the industry because of his unusual private means, unstintingly risked and sacrificed. But Renoir is also a professional. "I always think the film I'm going to make will be a very commercial one, which will delight all the showmen and be considered pretty banal. I bend all my efforts to be as commercial as I can, and when failures . . . happen to me, they happen despite me."

Hence Renoir's integrity is not that virginal variety often wished, unrealistically, by academics on those artists whose pitch is in the public marketplace. It is an integrity of opportunism. It stalks its game under cover, accepts compromise and may forego artistic for other ends. One must perhaps extend Beylie's remark. Renoir's amateurism is sufficiently self-effacing and flexible to respond, with neither snobbery nor weariness, to professional purposes; and more often than not absorb them into itself rather than become absorbed.

" . . . if you want to persuade the public to accept a new point of view, to share in a discovery, you have to play the part of a prostitute, to put on a bit of make-up in order to attract . . . She may be wonderful inside, but if she doesn't put on a bit of make-up no one will follow her . . . You have to be a little bit dishonest, you have to give something the public can follow, and the easiest thing is the action. You must take a popular plot. For instance I am sure that initially *La Grande Illusion* was so successful because it was an escape story. The escape story has nothing to do with my film. But it's a mask, a disguise, and this disguise made *La Grande Illusion* a big moneymaker."

That one may be an artist one day and a hack the next is proved by poets who are also copywriters, by leftwing directors who also direct TV commercials. A temperament like Renoir's can keep the two functions less separate. One may suspect that Shakespeare would have had less challenge, less self-distension, less multiplicity had he refused to compromise with the Elizabethan theatre. The balance between integrity and self-renewal by honest response to outside pressure is a fine one.

3

The Teller of Tales

It is sometimes thought proper to ignore an artist's private life and personal affairs. No doubt the matching of work and man is often degraded by simple-mindednesses. But when W. B. Yeats, to discourage the crudities of Instant Biography, distinguished the man and the *persona,* he was reminding us that the artist creates out of a sector of himself which may give a very misleading image, either of the remaining, silent, sectors or of the whole. Doubtless one can profoundly appreciate the works of Renoir *père* without having read Jean Renoir's *Renoir My Father.* But who with a real love for the work of Renoir *père* would not be interested in his son's biography of him?

What is true of artists who work alone is even more clearly true of a film director who, be he as hermetic as Robert Bresson, must work with and through other people. It is truer still of directors like Renoir, who strive to accept the artistic contributions of their collaborators, and to become their accomplices.

The young Renoir, with his blond-reddish hair, appears in his father's paintings from 1895 to 1899. He didn't like keeping still. Later, the teller moves through his own tales. His notable roles include that of the wolf in *Le Petit Chaperon Rouge,* a malabar in *La Petite Lili,* the innkeeper who prepares omelettes with relish and finesse in *Partie de Campagne,* the poacher Cabuche in *La Bête Humaine,* and the musician Octave in *La Règle du Jeu.* He appears as himself in several short films, as Jean Renoir, director of the film-within-the-film, in *Le Téstament du Dr. Cordelier,* and he introduces the various episodes in *Le Petit Theatre de Jean Renoir.*

Renoir the businessman is described in 1925 by Jean Tedesco, moving amidst the opportunists and sharks of the celluloid jungle. "Chewing a toothpick with a dreamy air, Renoir, in conversation with potential purchasers or exhibitors, let his blue gaze wander and thought about his next film."

Some years later, L. Scholsberg, subsequently a producer, draws a very different picture of Renoir, with whom he collaborated in various capacities during the '30s (notably on *La Chienne, Chotard et Cie,* and *Le Crime de*

Renoir as the innkeeper in *Partie de Campagne*

Monsieur Lange). "His coarse side pleased cinema people. You must remember I've seen people like Baroncelli and L'Herbier shoot with their gloves on. . . . He was a brawler: He was a snob in beggar's clothing. . . . It was fashionably leftwing. . . . His friends soaked him. He picked up the bills. He was sociable, but not kind; Pierre Renoir, now, he was kind. But Jean was slovenly, truculent, he worked with his guts and his heart. . . . To please him, you had to be bohemian, amusing, a mocker . . . he was scoffing all the time. . . . "

According to André G. Brunelin, Renoir had a peculiar effect on his closer associates. Even Jacques Becker "had been affected by a strange imitativeness, which produced in him the same confused way of speaking, the same abrupt laugh, and even that astonishing gesture of stroking his nose to mark his embarrassment. . . . "

So often has Renoir engendered an unstinted affection that it is a relief to quote remarks which, falling something short of idolatry, portray him as being, in his own words, "as wicked as the next man, and in the same need of a smiling indulgence." Nadia Sibirskaia confirms the existence, at least in the '30s, of a boisterous Renoir. She tells how she, Pierre Lestringuez and Renoir were thrown out of a theatre because of the latter's loud and drunken heckling. To the Renoir of "universal sympathies" one may well prefer the creature rehumanised by the frailties so caustically evoked by his first wife, or by Sylvia Bataille's account of the dismal atmosphere reigning during the shooting of *Partie de Campagne*.

In an obituary tribute to Jacques Becker, so often his assistant, Renoir recalled the filming of *La Nuit du Carrefour,* and "our night rides in impossible old jalopies at mad speeds. We were chasing a reel of film. . . . When the rain had penetrated so deeply into us as to paralyse our movements, and fatigue had piled on too much weight for our clodhoppers, we returned to that house at the crossroads. . . . All crowded around the stove as it glowed a cosy red, we passed hours of delicious intimacy.

A girl was preparing mulled wine. Sometimes we lay sweating like horses after a race. But then we'd get up and rush out. We had to get that shot before sunrise! . . . Everytime I pass that crossroads, I'm plunged anew into that clammy warm fog; damp, because the rain never let up, but hot with our passion for our job, which we dreamed of wresting from the grip of commerce. . . . "

Alexandre Arnoux sketched him thus. "A little like a bear, a little slow, slightly lost in the clouds, Jean Renoir doesn't throw himself at people; nor do his films; one must merit their confidence . . . when he practises his craft, he's unleashed, he spares nothing, he delivers himself over to his demon, he pours himself without reservations. He confesses himself with an astonishing simplicity and candour which is neither rhetoric nor ornament, as a man substantial and ardent, a conscience which respects no lies, an almost puritanical lucidity and austerity, and the honesty of an ox at the plough."

Jacques Doniol-Valcroze, who visited Renoir with Bazin in 1952, wrote: "How to describe him? He really is the man in the bearskin in *La Règle du Jeu;* debonair, decisive, healthy, concealing his force and his finesse with a mask of slow deliberation and of patience, speaking in measured terms. For a moment one wonders just where the weak point of this cuirasse of bonhomie can be, through just what aperture escapes the special radiance which emanates from him and holds his interlocutor under the spell. And one finds the chink: it's in that gaze, extraordinarily clear, periwinkle blue, faded, an indiscreet window on an interior universe which one imagines seraphic, and opening outwards into an external world which masquerades as ours and onto which he focuses, through whoever faces him."

Brunelin commented on the production imbroglios of *La Règle du Jeu:* "Renoir, who is seduction itself, lets himself be caught by its effects . . . a certain walk, a way of wearing a scarf, or riding boots, a style of smoking a cigarette, of apologising, of blowing one's nose, or a certain manner of saying, "Madam is served. . . . " Then Renoir cries, "That fellow's incredible." Or, of course, "That girl's amazing!" Renoir loves, and it's the most amiable of vices, but it often plays him nasty tricks. Renoir is a continuous infatuation, from which he sometimes emerges bruised, but in which others are often completely lost." Indeed the film behind *La Règle du Jeu* is another film, remarkably like *La Règle du Jeu,* set in a film studio instead of a chateau, but involving several of the same personalities, and leaving little doubt that the tale is as it is because of the interventions continually made by the teller . . . and the recalcitrance of his characters.

Describing Jean Renoir's production of *Carola* at the University of California, Ernest Callenbach and Roberta Schuldenfrei observe, "He often rubs his thumb against his other fingers, as if trying to feel the real substance of what he is saying, thinking or feeling." One may see not only a vestigial potter's gesture but a certain sensuousness, that reflex wholeness of intelligence, affect and tactile imagery more common in visual artists (since seeing is a preliminary to touching) than in verbal ones, who are quicker to blot out the world around so as to follow the verbal thread of a purely mental thought.

Through his friendships and collaborations Renoir's life and art intertwine. The guests at Jean's christening included the caricaturist Lestringuez, whose son Pierre later became Renoir's regular script collaborator and, under the pseudonym of Pierre Philippe, a leading actor in several films. The idea for *Toni* came from an old school friend, Jacques Mortier. While *Toni* was shooting, Renoir was plagued by the noise from planes stationed at a nearby air force base. Its commandant turned out to be the pilot who during the war had several times fought off German fighters making for Renoir's slow, ill-armed reconnaissance plane. His reminiscences gave Renoir the direction he sought for *La Grande Illusion*.

Renoir's creative procedures, particularly during his early years, cannot properly be understood without bearing in mind his collaborators. On one hand, as a matter of principle, "When I make a film, I am asking others to influence me." This in itself might theoretically lead to a variety of collaborations, but in practice he is relatively faithful to certain collaborators; after all, artists whose ideas are at once compatible and stimulating, are rare and precious. André G. Brunelin explains: "What is less well known . . . is the special spirit which then animated all those who, like Renoir (one might say the same of Vigo or the Prévert brothers, or of Buñuel or Cavalcanti) were trying to make a way through the tough undergrowth of film production. They were guided by something of a family spirit, or rather, more like a phalanstery. There were then several phalansteries, all first cousins and consequently interlocked, and in each of them there was a guiding spirit, who was quite naturally designated by his peers. Without the group of friends which Renoir had constantly about him, it is hardly probable that he could have made half the films he did, and I would even more emphatically add that these films would assuredly not have had the character which they had. People practically lived together, they shared everything, the bread and wine as well as the ideas. It was a team without any definite hierarchy, where nonetheless one man, Jean Renoir, was rather more dominant . . . " Among the "essential elements of the phalanstery" Brunelin lists "Jean Castanier, . . . Jean Gheret, André Cerf, Marcel Lucien, Pierre Lestringuez, Pierre Champagne . . . Maurice Blondeau and of course Catherine Hessling" (Renoir's first wife). Jacques Becker was the closest to Renoir. Other long-

Renoir's *equipe* at work in the streets: *Le Petit Chaperon Rouge*

time collaborators included Marguerite Mathieu (also known as Marguerite Houlle, but usually as Marguerite Renoir), Eugene Lourie, Max Douy and Karl Koch. There was less demarcation of jobs than nowadays—Becker directed some of the scenes in *La Grande Illusion* between Gabin and Dita Parlo, and between Gabin and Dalio on their flight; while Karl Koch was a historical adviser of *La Marseillaise* and shot most of *La Tosca* from Renoir's instructions.

Renoir at Work

Creative work begins on a film long before a camera is touched. The following mosaic of accounts gives an idea of Renoir's creative gestation.

He described Vivaldi as a "collaborator" on *Le Carosse d'Or* and "turned for help to" Goethe for *Le Testament du Dr. Cordelier.* " . . . To help myself think out *La Règle du Jeu,* I carefully re-read Marivaux and Musset, with no intention of observing even their spirit. I think these studies helped me to establish a style. . . . "

A musée, imaginaire or otherwise, is also a telephone exchange; the conversation goes both ways. Adaptation is collaboration. Conversely, collaboration involves a more or less concealed repudiation, just as much as seduction and fraternity. Renoir's threefold response to Zola's *La Bête Humaine* is characteristic. First: "To hell with old Zola! I wanted to play trains!" Second: "I thought of certain works, such as the story of the stained glass window in *La Cathédrale,* of *La Faute de L'Abbé Moret* and of *La Joie de Vivre.* . . . I thought of Zola's poetic side." Third: a positive curiosity which is also a creative fidelity: "I had long conversations with Madame Le Blond-Zola. . . . "

"I have a tendency to be theoretical in my beginnings." But the script is only a framework for further development. For the actors also are admitted into the conspiracy.

During rehearsals or pre-rehearsal readings, Renoir follows what he describes as the Italian method, also used by Louis Jouvet, which "consists of reading the text as if one were reading the telephone directory, forbidding oneself all expression. You wait until the intonation you give a word arises almost despite you. . . . When an actor reads a text and puts meaning into it immediately, you can be sure it's the wrong meaning. . . . It's bound to be a cliché, bound to be a banality, because you can't insert anything original right off, so you turn to your filing system, to something you have done already. . . . "

Instead, Renoir advises his actors to "speak the words without acting"—to not think until after several readings of the text, "Because you don't understand a line until after you've re-read it several times. I don't think that even the style of playing should be adopted by the actors at this early stage. And when they have fixed upon it, I ask them to check themselves, to not act fully at first, to feel their way, to move carefully, and above all not to introduce the gestures until the very end, to be in complete possession of the meaning of a scene before allowing themselves to move an ashtray, pick up a pencil or light a cigarette. I ask them not to be falsely natural, but so to proceed that the discovery of the external elements comes after the internal, and not vice versa."

This insistence on dismantling the "filing system" of actions and intonations which seem spontaneous but are only preconceived, or borrowed from previous roles, also affects Renoir's choice of actors. He tends to reject those who fit their parts too well, who lack a certain discrepancy with them, as Bazin noticed in discussing the "miscasting" of Valentine Tessier as Madame Bovary. He has never hesitated to cast friends, or non-actors, or stars better known for their personality than their acting ability. Much of the good actor's technique is either wasted by the camera or revealed by it. The non-actor, less fluent, less quick with preconceptions, may not have to be held back. A certain tentative quality may give the air of a person discovering himself as he lives. He may not have learned to block off a certain "irrelevant" sensitivity which then enhances the beauty of a given role. This off-centre casting amplifies the character. Coincidence with his role is reserved for climaxes, for moments of emotional convulsion, or of truth. It cannot be taken for granted, it is *attained*. Thus stock notions of personality and character may be revised without denying the existence of such things with that counter-traditional rigidity of avant-gardes.

With his Hollywood films Renoir introduced where possible the French system of rehearsing before lunch and shooting after lunch, rather than shooting each scene directly after its rehearsals. "In the morning, arriving on the set, I study the script, if possible, with a few actors . . . (or) with two or three assistants, the script girl and the cameraman. I visualise the scenes and I half shape them. I don't pick out camera-angles. In my opinion, angles have to be decided once the actors have rehearsed. Nonetheless it's at this moment and not before that I acquire the general idea of a scene, which becomes a sort of line to be followed, and rigorously held, so as to leave all liberty to the actors."

Brunelin describes the shooting of a scene in *French Can-Can*. "He works without his manuscript, like an acrobat without a net. Very calmly, without preoccupation, he explains the ensemble effect of a scene without worrying over the shot breakdown which his technical collaborators will perfect with him afterwards. Rarely with Renoir does technique, that is to say the camera, move ahead of the players. He is always ready to modify a frame or a phrase of dialogue if that will give his actors more elbow room . . . Little by little the scene is built and Renoir approaches Kelber, the cameraman, and Tiquet, who will line it up. "Is that possible for you?" Renoir enquires. "If Yes, we're ready to go." If it isn't, Renoir always arranges matters so that the actors will suffer the least possible inconvenience from technical exigencies. When all seems ready, Renoir announces to the company, "All right, ladies and gentlemen, are we ready to go? We'll take the plunge. Let's go, maybe we'll change something afterwards. . . . " The scene's a flop, the actors haven't grasped their text, but Renoir is jubilant. "Bravo, that's splendid, that's fine!" And then without a pause, he continues, "We'll have a little retake. Just to be sure. It was fine as it was. . . . " And Renoir patiently, calmly, deploying all his resources of seduction, will shoot a scene, which at the first take he had judged perfect, six or eight times or sometimes more."

Gaston Modot: "Gently, without seeming to, he dismantles everything and begins all over again. Seduced, the actors purr, stretch, arch their backs under the velvet glove. They recommence the scene, quite confident, docile, attentive. Their smiling trainer flatters them, leads them on his invisible leash."

The method is not just a tactful formula, and Brunelin catches its spirit when he compares him to an acrobat without a net. Some directors demonstrate a scene and ask all the actors to copy their own performance of all the film's parts, allowing the human inability to reproduce anything exactly to restore a certain individuality. Hitchcock rehearses his actors in his mind's eyes as he writes a scene, and reduces them, if not to ciphers, at least to technicians of personality. Renoir's method does away with selfconsciousness and a glib spontaneity, yet it allows an unselfconscious spontaneity independent of the actor, and of Renoir, to develop beneath. He is insistent that an actor is one of a film's *auteurs*. He directs, as it were, *a recibiendo*—a beckoning-on combined with a forethoughtful opportunitism. The scene he finally sees is, one suspects, not the scene which at any previous stage he foresaw, but its functional equivalent: a *tertium quid* from the dialectic of collaboration.

Modot's phrase, *dressage en douceur*, a gentle breaking-in, stresses the aspect of grooming, of reining, of control. He describes Renoir on the set. "The scene to be shot is there, in the air, hovering impalpable. In the thick of his nebula, like a medium, Renoir springs to life. He agitates it, turns it this way and that, kneads it, places it, fixes it. He could say, with Picasso, 'I do not seek, I find', and the scene appears, sudden as doves flying from the conjurer's sleeve."

Renoir puts it more modestly. "What happens with me is a sort of inability to understand the sense of a scene until I've seen it enacted. I find the real meaning of a scene only once the words have been, let us say materialised, once they have existence, as Sartre would say . . . I need to see something before me which exists . . . at heart I'm a sort of opportunist. I ask others to give me all the ingredients. For my part I attempt to contribute nothing. I would like everything to come to me from outside." A film director is a chef, mixing the ingredients which his collaborators bring him.

The more a director accepts from outside, the more agile his reflexes must be. One would not expect this paradoxical mixture of passivity and virtuosity to be without rough edges, or to have put itself together instantly overnight.

André Thurifays described Renoir at the time of *On Purge Bébé* as "a hesitant nature. Whether in matter of form or of context, Renoir not only interrogates himself at length, but asks the advice of others, and submits those essays which he attempts to the criticism of various publics. He seems swayed by all those different factors, and in the end, accepts last-minute inspiration."

Such hesitation, with its awareness of alternatives, betokens a master-to-be in a period of artistic and professional crisis. Even more surprising, and rich in insights, is Scholsberg's description of Renoir in difficulties. "If you look at Renoir's films, you'll see that there is a unity at the level of the characters, but there's no camera style of Renoir's own. . . . You can't say he was a technician. He took everybody's good ideas, even the technicians'. . . . He only understood the job when his friends were around him. . . . His big thing was actors, he had great communication with them. . . . He never chose the camera-angles. He had people like Hubert, Périnal, beside him to do it for him. . . . He had an eye, an extraordinary visual acuity. . . . Renoir, you see, was adaptable, he didn't begin thinking about the direction until he got on the set. . . . "

Scholsberg describes an argument during the shooting of *Chotard et Cie*. "He'd made a whole series of close-ups of Pomiès. When the rushes were being shown I said to him, "This comes at the end of the first reel. There'll be no dramatic progression; nothing in the style . . . " He was furious. . . . Later, he wrote to me, he said, "Let's not stay on bad terms . . . Your reproaches were justified. There *is* a syntax in cinematographic style. . . . " He was a man of great intellectual honesty." It may seem strange that Renoir, as veteran of thirteen films, should be without an inkling of the then normal professional procedure for the construction of a film's climax. Yet there have been many Hollywood directors who directed actors and never attempted to understand the visual syntax from which their cameraman and editor together would create a dramatically coherent whole. Such is the complexity and the collaborative interaction of this strange medium called film that one can understand any "acrobat without a net" making, for one reason or another, mistakes from which it takes humbler functionaries to rescue him. The more responsive, the more *uncertain*, his style, the more profound and "elementary" his mistakes may be.

Scholsberg's observations are borne out by Brunelin's comments on the fascinating stylistic symbiosis between Renoir and Becker. "Obviously, it was Renoir himself who made the decisions and settled matters. His collaborators contributed their arguments, or their suggestions and Renoir adopted them or not. Of all of them, it was Jacques to whom he listened . . . most attentively, for Jacques rarely made a mistake. He had a sense, a vision of the scene or the shot which astonished his comrades. . . . Jacques was in the habit of carefully preparing a scene before Renoir's arrival. So he performed a kind of pre-direction. Some call it a "placement" *(mise-en-place)*, or use the expression "articulating a scene" *(désosser une scène)*. Jacques did it fairly freely because, as everyone knew, Renoir's scripts were thin, lacking detailed indications, Renoir being above all an improviser on a given theme. . . . Renoir, as he drove into the scene, modified, demolished patiently, obstinately, everything Becker had conceived . . . to substitute his own vision . . . but it's improbable, according to the opinion of witnesses, that Renoir would ever have reached the same result, or conceived the scene in the way he did, if he hadn't started from the "sketch" worked out by Becker. . . . Jacques worked particular wonders at these times when Renoir, having enthusiastically hurled himself into the execution of an idea, lost the track of it—which was quite frequent with him. "Well, lads, where are we?" asked Renoir. "It's like this," Jacques would say. . . . "

Jean Castanier relates that it was Jacques Becker who suggested to Renoir "the long lateral tracking shot following Michel Simon along the quays of the Seine. Confronted with shooting difficulties—shooting in the actual street, with "real passers-by"—Renoir decided to renounce the idea . . . Jacques asked to be given a free hand. . . . And so the long, crabbing shot at the beginning of *Boudu* . . . was shot by Jacques, without Renoir's participation. . . . " Ironically, it's just such a scene which a critic might choose as the essence of Renoir. Similarly, the "massacre of the rabbits" was shot while Renoir was miles away working in the studio. Yet, as Scholsberg insists, "the film is his, and that sequence as much as the rest"—in the sense, presumably, that he had indicated the kind of shot to the "second unit," and the kind of editing to Marguerite Renoir.

Scholsberg's comments on camera-style are particularly interesting. For it would be easy to pick on certain visual strokes which recur from film to film, and so, in a sense, are Renoir's traits. Yet an itemization of these traits is insufficient to account for every detail of style. It is impossible for the critic to determine how far, for example, the relatively static, framed images of *La Bête Humaine,* and the racing camera of *La Règle du Jeu,* arise from the staging of the action which Renoir asks his cameraman to photograph, or from Renoir's predetermination of a certain visual style, or from the suggestions or responses of a cameraman, and the limitations of his equipment. Visual differences between one film and another are due not to Renoir *in vacuo* nor to any one cameraman in himself, but to certain "vibrations" passing between the two. The creativity implicit in the disposition of protagonists in space—i.e. mise-en-scène as the structure of an action sub-

Renoir directing *Elena et les Hommes*

sequently translated into images—is, at root, a derivation from theatrical aspects of the cinema art. With some directors, certainly, the action is arranged to fill images which dominate its conception. But with Renoir the nature of the action often determines the character of the images. Renoir tells a gruelling tale of his attempts to persuade a studio art department that he wanted a country cottage without a beam under the ceiling, precisely because beams under the ceiling had become a formalized trait, while the art department refused, on grounds of conscientious professionalism, to construct a country cottage without this picturesque and therefore artistic feature.

5

A Creative Process

There is a general distinction between conventional creative procedures (where script and dialogue are more or less finalised before shooting begins), and improvisation (where substantial revamping takes place on the studio floor). Renoir: " . . . the ideas which come to you, when you're improvising, strike you with great force. It's very sharp, they're like needles which pierce your skin. I don't know if they're better than the ideas which you have in the silence of the study. At any rate, they're different, and give a different kind of film." Certainly there is something to be said for the generalisation that spatial, gestural and sensuous directors tend to revamp or improvise their films more extensively during shooting than those whose emphasis lies more exclusively at the literary end of the dramatic spectrum.

Even so, as intensely visual a director as Georges Franju remarked, "It's at the typewriter that you have to be inspired". René Clair makes only minor modifications after going on the floor. And one has to add another category of director, like Eisenstein, who would shoot a mass of material and only decide what to use—in effect, write the script—at the editing stage.

The variety of different procedures is worth insisting upon, because the contrast between preplanners and improvisers has been presented as a contrast between literary and cinematic values. Yet we know that the script of *Le Crime de Monsieur Lange* was largely rewritten by Renoir and Prévert together on the set. Charles Spaak's and Renoir's script for *La Grande Illusion* was the subject of continuous nocturnal revision kept secret from Stroheim, who nonetheless invented one very important character detail. Dudley Nichols' script for *Swamp Water* was chosen by Renoir from the Fox library and subjected to relatively little alteration. Yet all these completed films are every bit as well constructed, as literary, and as concerned with narrative, as the scripts which Prévert contributed to Carné, Spaak to Duvivier, and Nichols to John Ford. Ironically, it is in the most substantially improvised of the three scripts that the general pattern of a three-act play is clearly discernible. In *Le Crime de Monsieur Lange*, Act One would end

Batala's return as priest-imposter: *Le Crime de M. Lange*

with Batala taking flight, Act Two would relate the rise of the Co-operative, and Act Three would climax with Batala's return. Thus the script would very readily translate into a stageplay, particularly if given the multiple set. Armand Cauliez's structural analyses of several Renoir films shows that many of the discontinuities which might seem "anti-constructional" correspond to narrative jumps traditional to stageplays, that is to say, the temporal discontinuities between scenes and acts.

The origin of this rather misleading contrast between literary and cinematic qualities is clear enough. It originates not in "pure" literature at all but in the work of the playwright, who composes on paper what an actor speaks during performance. If the actor departs from them he is said to be "improvising." By analogy, departures from the film-script during shooting are commonly referred to as "improvising". Yet there is a great difference between revision on the stage during performance, and revision in the film studio, where a retake is invariably possible. Alterations during shooting correspond more to alterations during rehearsal. Take the case of an author present during rehearsals who, on his own account or in response to suggestions from director and actors, alters the lines then and there, which he then hands to the actors to speak. Is he improvising or revising? The latter is surely the more appropriate term, with "improvising" reserved for alterations during actual performance. "Improvisation" is often simply the final stage in a long process of "revision"—a less glamorous word, but often a truer one—particularly with a director like Renoir, who normally sees a film from the beginning of the script through several takes to the final cut.

Balzac rewrote many of his novels at top speed on the galleys: was he improvising or revising? All creation is, at the moment that the work is done, spontaneous and improvised. When one revises, one improvises it again. That there's no necessary connection between improvisation and inventiveness is confirmed by many jazz soloists whose reliance on a filing system of readymade phrases is only too apparent. The process by which Renoir attempts to restrain his actors from jumping to conclusions about the meaning of their lines is a negation of improvising, and what Renoir is insisting on is, precisely, repression, repetition and reflection, albeit of a subconscious nature. It's particularly striking that two of the screen's most complicated structures, Griffith's *Intolerance* and Renoir's *La Règle du Jeu*, never existed on paper but only in their directors' heads, and, in Renoir's case, arguably not even in his head. Just as it's possible to edit a film at script stage (like Hitchcock), so it's possible to script at the editing stage (like Renoir's *The River*). There, Renoir, uncertain whether audiences would accept the flash-back-and-commentary structure which he preferred, shot so as to accommodate either his preferred form or a chronologically straightforward one. He opted for the former only after watching a preview audience react to a rough cut. This might be described as improvisation, i.e. a very late choice (after the shooting stage!) or as it might be described as double premeditation, both possibilities being catered for from the beginning. *La Règle du Jeu* offers an even more extraordinary example, since the film underwent several re-editings during its first week in the cinemas.

The assumption that improvisation is somehow superior to revision (rather than a form of it) is really based on (a) the idea that improvising is somehow more like real life; (b) the tendency of big studios to hold the script sacred, to submit it to committees, and to shoot in a way whose expenses discourage change at the shooting stage; and (c) the association of script-centred films with the cause-and-effect sequences which the cinema had inherited from the 19th-century-novel and for which younger film-makers have quite legitimately wished to substitute a 20th-century sense of rupture, discontinuity of tone, and absurdity. This last is probably the real reason why Truffaut and his generation at *Cahiers* lambasted the Aurenche-Bost team yet adulated the very tightly pre-planned films of Hitchcock. While Renoir's improvisatory style was a valuable precedent for the nouvelle vague, it should be recalled that the Hollywood system never succeeded in dispensing with improvisation altogether, despite its attempts to exclude expensive unpredictables from its assembly-lines. George Cukor collaborated in a Renoir-like spirit with such actors as Spencer Tracy and Judy Holliday, while David O. Selznick was celebrated for increasing the scope of his films as he went along.

6

Only Begettors

The notions of artist as solitary, and art as the self-expression of a unique personality, do not apply to Renoir. Peter Ustinov has denied that the film is an art form, on the grounds that the director has to make do with available cameramen and actors, rather than the *alter egos* who alone could have created a film which was entirely his. Thus every film is only a hopelessly inferior paraphrase of an ideal film existing in the conscious mind of an eternally frustrated film-maker. There are several objections to this argument. In the first place, to restrict art to self-expression is a scarcely satisfactory definition since architecture, for example, is usually considered in relation to a style, age or collective spirit. In the second place, the restriction rules out Ustinov's own medium, the theatre. There too the playwright is condemned to see his work interpreted by a producer and actors whose style and interpretation may be diametrically opposed to the "ideal production" which he visualised. Even the most self-reliant of artists, the writer, has to collaborate with language as he finds it. Every medium exerts a certain resistance to a creator's intentions, forcing him to purely formal shifts which may in the long run benefit his work, but are certainly not what he "intends" or what he "originally" saw in his mind.

We frequently debate whether artistic inspiration arises from a conflict within the individual (either neurosis or perplexity), or whether it is a prophetic statement, a witness for his "age". We should perhaps be more conscious of artistic activity as wholly or partly a reflection of a conflict between the individual and the *mores* of his group, or between disparate cultures whose conflict the artist feels within himself (hence so many artists are Jews among gentiles, or have foreign surnames, or are otherwise déclassé). It is the similarity of the conflict within the artist and the conflict within others which gives him his most enthusiastic audience, those who feel that he expresses *them*. When a work of art expresses *both* aspects of general cultural conflict *and* aspects of a private conflict, audiences will regularly ignore the latter or distort them to fit the former (the cult of *auteur* self-expression exists only at certain cultural levels, and itself derives from socially agreed assumptions about individualism). Of artists who, like Zola, are extremely concerned with the condition of the society in which they live, it is probably true to say that their responsiveness is primarily extroverted. They are attuned to their internal psychodrama only involuntarily, or accidentally, or indirectly, through the problems of others. The critical conversion of their social testimony into interesting psychodramatic terms requires relatively elaborate and devious procedures which are far removed from the usual reasons for studying them. In other words, such authors are extremely *bad* at self-expression, compared with illiterate and semi-inarticulate oral culture which may be far more vivid, precise and rich in insights.

In the last analysis, no doubt, the man who expresses something of others also expresses something of himself, and vice versa. But the individualistic reason has no primacy over the other. The man who truly understands himself also understands his fellows, and in that way also loses the uniqueness of his identity. To that oceanic feeling Renoir's films are uniquely open.

We admit as much when we group artists into "schools". An artist's similarities with his contemporaries or his *amis inconnus* of other times and places may be attributed to mutual influence (which appeals to scholars, for obvious reasons), or to similarities of experience, or both. As Renoir commented on remakes of his films: "If the story is good remakes are perfectly justified. . . . I even think that to encourage good stories and good films, there ought to be medals, prizes of some kind, for people who plagiarise. We want to encourage plagiarism." Where creation is a collaborative matter, as it is in the theatrical arts and the cinema, "plagiarism" is the order of the day. Perhaps we are too readily preoccupied with the differences between, for example, the various Jacobean playwrights and too little concerned with their similarities. We think of them as islands, rather than as overlapping areas on a map; each at once himself, and the others also.

Excellence of expression is more than a matter of technique in the manipulation of a medium and the public. In the more vivid or thorough response to a spiritual reality which the rest of us have felt only as a dull confusion, here lies the "individuality" or "prophecy" of the artist. In a sense, the artist as midwife of his art is less conventionalised. He refuses to invent what he sees, or to hide it first from himself, then from others.

Jean Renoir: "There are no pioneers. Things do themselves." Everybody flows through everybody, and others are our alternative lives.

The collaborative nature of film-making makes interinfluences even more direct. At one extreme, this diversity can cancel out, can sterilise (thus Hollywood's concentration on the world market relied on the formularisation of a few common denominators, often to the exclusion of originality). The French cinema of the '30s was less organised, more artisanal, more parochial, and ballasted rather than burdened by its wider public. A director like Renoir could make of the movies an artform which transcended the limitations of the lonely *auteur* without obliterating his own traits within the work to which he contributed.

Renoir does not see himself as "onlie begettor". "When a film is being made . . . there is a kind of general fusion which often appears vulgar, but which is perhaps the real source of the 'true greatness' of our profession." Only the moderate forms of *auteur* theory can claim Renoir's adhesion. Certainly, "there is obviously one person who influences the team, and who practically animates it, leads the game, becomes 'the boss', as we used to say in the artisan crafts." But the more extreme and extensive forms of *auteur* theory, whereby every film belongs to its director as uniquely as a novel to its author, finds no support from Renoir. "In the early days of the American cinema the animator, 'the boss', was quite often the star. It's right to speak of a Douglas Fairbanks film or a Mary Pickford film, because they influenced the work of their teams more than anyone else . . . nowadays in Europe a film is primarily the work of its director; in America it is habitually the creation of its producer." Again: I have to admit that in all the films that I have made my influence has been sufficient for me to have to accept the greater part of the responsibility for the finished product. But it would also be useless to deny that my collaborators' influence on me has been enormous . . . how can one know life if not through other human beings?"

It was, indeed, on the grounds of Renoir's acceptance of collaborators that George Charensol almost refused to consider him as an *auteur* at all, but rather as a kind of ringmaster, which would have been an equal and opposite absurdity to the extremes of *auteur* theory à la *Cahiers du Cinéma* second (New Wave) generation.

Films in Review, startled by Renoir's "curious ruminations", observed with some asperity, "Jean Renoir thinks he's a collective." But if these good ladies of the Middle West discern, in such modest absence of egoism, the tips of the horns of the demon Socialism, Renoir cheerfully combines collectivism with something like a "Cleopatra's nose" theory of artistic creation. "A good film is an accident . . . a miracle."

As some good films no doubt are. Even extreme *auteur* theorists, despite a general tendency to deny that any film of their idols can be bad, sometimes ascribe a deviant film to an unfortunate concatenation of circumstances, or an unsuitable script, or a poor actor. That admitted, no principle remains on which to deny that factors other than a director's talent influence a film's quality and invade its content. No one has supposed that the films of the Marx Brothers were good or bad according to the talent of the director. Certain directors, like Dreyer and Bresson, will impose their own style on every film. More usually, the director contributes only traits. One need only return to our *cinémathèque imaginaire* and see the differences flowing from an interchange of casting within Renoir's own films. Let us project *La Chienne,* starring Catherine Hessling and Werner Krauss; and *Nana,* with Janie Marèze and Michel Simon. We notice that the substitution of one actor for another has forced Renoir to alter the dialogue; all the small-part actors have had to alter their styles to accommodate those of the principals; the cameraman has had to find new angles; even the tempo of the cutting has had to change, because of the different speed of gesture and reaction from the leading actor and actresses. Or to return to reality, let us compare Renoir's *La Grande Illusion* with Carné's *Le Jour Se Lève*. Is an almost indefinable yet pervasive affinity of mood merely the result of the fact that they so often figure side by side in the history books? Haven't they both registered something of (a) the cinematographic techniques of the time; (b) the feeling of France just before 1940; and (c) Jean Gabin, leading man in both? *La Grande Illusion* is both a Renoir film and a Gabin film. *Le Jour Se Lève* is simultaneously a Carné film, a Gabin film and a Prévert film, even though Prévert wrote only the dialogue, not the script.

The paradox of art as control versus art as acceptance of the uncontrollable finds another test case in the butterfly which enters, leaves and re-enters the frame of *Partie de Campagne*, with a rhythm and an *à propos* which no director, not even Renoir, could have bettered. Who is the *auteur:* Renoir or the butterfly? The most obvious answer is Renoir because he chose not to cut the shot out. But it's impossible to rule out the possibility that neither Renoir nor his cameraman noticed the butterfly at all until they saw the rushes, by which time it might have been impracticable to reshoot (after all, bad weather made it impossible to finish the film). The point at issue is not the presence of the butterfly, which Renoir might just possibly have prearranged, but the timing and direction of its movement, which no human agency could have contrived. It's an accident, a little miracle, and all the more extraordinary in that the heroine of the film has a pointed conversation about insects and caterpillars, to remind us that she, like nature, is teeming with summer fertility. And had the reference to that theme been anything less obviously accidental than a butterfly, few critics worth reading would have hesitated to consider it other than premeditated (perhaps even subconsciously, along lines vindicated by Cocteau's remark about just such an interreference in his novel *Les Enfants Terribles:* "I did not know that the book began with a white ball, ended with a black ball, and Dargelos sent both of them. The premeditated look of instinctive equilibrium."). That unpredictable butterfly seems to confirm the film's spiritual authenticity, to bestow upon it nature's blessing. Now even if it's true that Renoir is the *auteur* of that touch, in the sense that he didn't reshoot or remove the shot although he might have, it's still true that Renoir is not the *auteur* of that touch, in the sense that at no stage in the making of the film was he in the position to control the butterfly's arabesque. Ever since Marcel Duchamp we have become progressively habituated to the idea that passive acquiescence in accident is the same as the elaborations of positive creation. To accept the obviously accidental as some functional equivalent of intention is to "play the game" of assuming that every detail means something. If we play the game without reserving certain rights, in the way of requiring evidence of sophistication, we are, of course, condeming ourselves to treating as art phenomena which might have a very real value as a Rorschach test, or in various ways which do not involve close attention to formal detail. There may even have been another take of the butterfly scene in which the butterfly did not appear, but Renoir preferred the take in which it did; or Renoir's editor preferred the take in which it did. The only aesthetic response that covers all these possibilities is echoed in Renoir's remark that "only results count". The spectator has sufficient love of the film to play the game of accepting the butterfly as both within the illusion and a "beautiful accident" outside the illusion.

A film's meaning is like an avalanche: once under way, with sufficient momentum, it adds to itself all those points which, with less momentum, would arrest its impetus. The butterfly reminds us of the actuality but our participation is strong enough to sustain the illusion. Once we fully yield to a film then we succumb to a joyously circular argument. We assume that each detail is meant; we hypothesise a meaning; and then find, to our amazement, that that precise meaning would not survive expression in any other form.

Often we go further. We say that a close study of a poet's rough drafts, or certain autobiographical details, or other works by the same artist, or psychoanalytical or other interpretations, "throw additional light" on the final text. In other words we begin to find meanings which aren't quite in the text (since we had to resort to secondary sources). Nonetheless we transfer to the final text the credit for somehow "possessing" these meanings. Perhaps what we mean is that we are grateful to it for stimulating us to go deeper or further and begin to understand undercurrents and overtones between the lines. Every artist really has one particular complex of crucial experience to which he keeps returning, to explore in different aspects or permutations each time. One may say that any two drafts of a poem are different poems. But this is a matter of degree; for we often, quite spontaneously, become aware of two different poems as having areas of overlap. Hence Renoir's remark that one tells the same story all one's life, in different guises. And hence our surprise when an artist like Renoir turns out to have relatively little obvious overlap between his various works. Less puzzlingly put, an artist's every work of art has something in common with his other works, and something particular to itself. The common element tends to be emphasised. We might see fewer connections between an artist's work if he was known only under diverse pseudonyms. The practice of ascription leads us, regrettably, to underestimate the connections between works by different *auteurs*, to overlook often obvious and rewarding differences between their works (and, ironically, the connections behind the disconnections).

The fact seems to be that an artwork can absorb prodigious quantities of accident, of extraneous matter, of non-*auteur* content, yet be recognisable as one *auteur's* work, so long as certain conspicuous traits of his style subsist. Our concern in this volume is with the *films* of Jean Renoir, not exclusively with what Renoir contributed to his own films. Accordingly, we deal with *Le Crime de Monsieur Lange* as both a Renoir and a Prévert film, and we deal with Renoir's American films as both Renoir's films and as American films. If we have less to say about his actors as *auteurs,* it is for purely arbitrary, conventional reasons which we would not dream of attempting to justify, and which only shortage of space can excuse. We regard with the highest approval the gradual return in French film criticism of monographs devoted to such actor-*auteurs* as Louis Jouvet, Jean Gabin and Renoir's frequent associate, Michel Simon. There seems to us no difference in principle between a film director's reliance on his collaborators and a poet's dependence on the accidents of language. In a sense, organising *is* understanding, albeit of a synthetic rather than an analytic kind. If an artist's organising limits, like Renoir's, are wide, it is not misleading to say that the less he remains himself the more he becomes himself. A wide extroversion is more personal than a limited introversion. A film director, however elaborate his collaborative apanage, may be more fully himself, and ourselves, than many justly celebrated poets.

Prelude: Early Days

Jean Renoir was born in Paris, Château des Brouillards, near the Butte Mont-martre on the 15 September 1894, son of the painter Auguste Renoir, then 53, and his wife Aline, née Charigot. They had come to Paris while young from rural France. His father, a tailor's son, came from Limousin, his mother from Bourgogne. Jean's elder brother, the actor Pierre Renoir, was born in 1885, and his younger brother Claude ("Coco" in Auguste's paint-ings) in 1901. Claude became a film producer and should not be confused with the younger Claude Renoir, born in 1913, who is Pierre's son, and the director's nephew.

Jean's cousin Gabrielle was brought to the Renoir household as his nurse and, later, his father's model. Jean himself appears in such paintings as *La Famille de l'Artiste* (1895), *Le Déjeuner* (1896) and others named after him. On Saturdays his mother kept open house for his father's artistic and intellec-tual friends. Gabrielle took him on an early tour of the café-concerts. These first remembered introductions to show business perhaps inspired a sequence in *French Can Can,* which catches also the still rather countrified and proletarian character of Montmartre at the time.

Young Jean was sent to the Collège Saint-Croix at Neuilly, described as "a sort of elegant prison" from which he played truant at frequent intervals.

At the turn of the century the family began their regular visits to the South of France, staying from 1903 at the Maison de la Poste at Cagnes-Sur-Mer. The villa is featured in *Le Déjeuner Sur L'Herbe*. While his parents were at Cagnes, Renoir attended the lycée at Nice, obtaining his *baccalauréat* with distinction in 1910.

"I began to realise that my father was an important artist, and it rather frightened me, and I tried to set my mind to everything that was contrary to art. So I dreamed of being a businessman, a grocer, an agriculturalist in Algeria. I was very fond of horses, and so I wanted to be a cavalry officer." In 1913 he enlisted in the cavalry, not, as his social background would have indicated, as an officer, but as an ordinary soldier. The first World War found him an N.C.O. in the Dragoons stationed at Vincennes.

After a fairly serious injury occasioned by a kick from his horse, Jean was sent to the front early in 1915 as a sub-lieutenant in the *Chasseurs Alpins* (light infantry). In April a bullet fractured the neck of his femur. Gangrene set in and his leg would have been amputated but for his Mother's intervention. After months of convalescence Jean was left with a marked limp for life.

His mother died at 56 in June 1915, and Jean was sent home from hospital on crutches to find his father painting in his wheelchair. He discovered the cinema, and was immediately enthusiastic. "Rare were the weeks in which I didn't see 25 films, all American, of course. It was almost an enchantment." There was still no thought of making films.

By early 1916 Renoir was accepted as an observer in the photographic branch of the flying corps. He survived further injuries sustained during a crash landing and eventually flew Voisins and twin-engined Brequets. He returned home in 1918. Some critics have implied that Renoir was taken prisoner but no detailed biography mentions any such event.

Unclear as to which direction in life to take, and following his father's advice not to make up his mind too quickly, he collaborated as a ceramicist with his father and his brother. A few weeks after his father's death in December 1919, he married Andrée Heuschling who was his father's model and who became, for his films, Catherine Hessling. His son Alain was born in 1922 and is now Professor of English at the University of California, Berkeley. By this time Jean had set up a ceramic workshop with an associate of his father's in the Midi. His works earned him some esteem and many were immediately acquired by galleries and museums. Financial viability was of little importance since Auguste had left each of his sons a number of canvases and a very substantial fortune.

In an article entitled *Souvenirs,* written in 1938, Jean Renoir has recounted his own discovery of the cinema. His first memory is of a showing of some views of Paris and a comic film, *The Adventures of Auto-Maboul* ("Auto-Maniac"), one Sunday morning in 1902 at school on a strange apparatus, the cinematograph. He was eight years old.

"The postwar period was something of a golden age for film enthusiasts. It was the great moment of the American cinema. The major theatres despised it and preferred pretentious idiocies clumsily played by antiquated actors, or else absolutely ridiculous Italian features. The American movies came out in the very cheap little theatres. The programme changed twice a week. For months at a time I saw two or three shows a day.

"One day, at the Colisée, I saw *Le Brasier Ardent,* directed by and starring Mosjoukine. The theatre booed and whistled. I was overwelmed. At last I had before my eyes a good film made in France. Naturally, it had taken a Russian to make it, but it had been made at Montreuil, in a French atmosphere, under our own skies; and it was being shown in a major theatre. Without success, but it was being shown. After four years, I decided to put aside my craft, which was ceramics, and attempt to make films."

Une Vie Sans Joie/Catherine

Pierre Renoir and his wife, Vere Sorgine, were already leading lights in the Paris theatre, and had starred in movies. They introduced Jean to Alberto Cavalcanti, and to their theatrical colleagues. According to Pierre Leprohon, the actor Albert Dieudonné (later Abel Gance's Napoleon) took the initiative and found in Renoir a financier-producer more congenial to artistic independence than the magnates for whom he had hitherto worked.

Renoir provided the finance and a story outline for *Une Vie Sans Joie*, with Dieudonné directing and playing a leading role opposite Catherine Hessling (she later asserted that Renoir had threatened to "assert his marital authority" to force his reluctant starlet before the cameras). The film was shot during 1924 in the Gaumont Studios with exteriors at Cagnes-Sur-Mer and Saint-Paul-de-Vence, ran about 80 minutes and was released in the same year.

All critical accounts of the film are scant and summary. The fullest synopsis is provided by André Bazin. "A little maidservant who lives in Nice has fallen in love with the son of the house, a consumptive (Georges Terof). Her employers are thoroughly decent people. The father (Albert Dieudonné) is the Deputy for Saint-Paul-de-Vence. His political rivals exploit the idyll between his son and the maid, and set up an odious blackmail. The girl flees and hides in a wagon on the railroad line. The wagon is on the way to the depot, but, after a points error, begins to roll towards a precipice. The son manages to stop the wagon in time and brings the girl back home. A second political campaign from the opposite camp obliges the heroine to flee once more. She leaves for Nice where she falls into the hands of a squalid procurer (Pierre Philippe). After many different adventures she again runs into the son and they live happily ever after."

Both Bazin and Cauliez suggest that Renoir's principal aim was to construct a vehicle for his wife. It's tempting to see in the outline a simple and direct transposition of reality. The cripple became a consumptive, and the model a maidservant, the transposition being all the simpler in that Renoir

père's models often also helped with domestic work, Gabrielle having, in fact, been engaged to care for the baby Jean. Cauliez proposes an affinity with *Diary of a Chambermaid* (maidservants and socio-political feuds). Popular melodramatics, à la Griffith, appear to have taken over from such points of departure.

Some publicity material attributed the title of co-director to Renoir. There seem to have been some tensions since Dieudonné went to the trouble of declaring (in *Cinéa-Ciné*, 5 January 1926) that he was the sole director of a screen play which he composed from Renoir's outline, and "furthermore M. Jean Renoir was both my sleeping partner and my pupil."

The film did not prove a success, and was no doubt hampered by its drab and depressing title. The following year Dieudonné re-edited it, and added some additional material. It was released under a more prepossessing title, *Catherine*, in April 1927.

La Fille de l'Eau
(The Whirlpool of Fate)

Despite the insuccess of *Une Vie Sans Joie*, Renoir was convinced that the cinema was to be his vocation. This time Lestringuez provided a scenario, in which he was to play a leading role. Renoir again financed the film and this time directed and "conceived the decor".

La Fille de l'Eau was filmed during the summer of 1924. The exteriors were shot over two months, largely on Cézanne's property, La Nicotière, at Marlotte, chosen because its four buildings could conveniently give the impression of a village. Three weeks' filming followed in the G.M. Studios and the film was premièred in December 1924. According to *Cahiers du Cinéma*, the full footage, more than 6,000 feet, remains in only one copy of the film, in the Moscow archive. French ciné-clubs know only an English edition, apparently incomplete and presumably related to London's National Film Archive copy (5,349 feet).

Virginia is a lonely child (Catherine Hessling) who lives aboard a canal barge. "Virginia knew the secret of concocting an Irish Stew out of vague vegetables." Her father is drowned during a storm and she is delivered over to her Uncle Jeff's untender mercies. This brute (Pierre Philippe) dissipates their little inheritance in drink and soon the bailiff's men nail a notice to the barge. Virginia runs away and meets up with a poacher nicknamed· "The Ferret" (Maurice Touzé). He brings her to live with his gipsy mother, Crazy Kate, "who spent her life cooking stolen potatoes and smoking a pipe. And, when occasion demands she reads palms. The Ferret introduces Virginia as their servant." He undertakes to educate her in poaching.

Earlier in the film we were introduced to a happier family headed by M. Raynal, landlord, botanist and proud car owner ("Even Mr. Ford might have been jealous of the wonderful car M. Raynal owned"). Georges, their handsome son just home from college, falls in love with Virginia. The Ferret takes her poaching in Justin Crepoix's preserves, and the wealthy farmer gets revenge by breaking the Ferret's nets and bragging of his feat in the village bistro. In retaliation, the Ferret sets fire to Justin's haystack. M. Raynal offers his car to the fire service, "a suggestion which they naturally rejected." The villagers become a mob. The Ferret and Crazy Kate abandon Virginia, who is caught and terrorised by drunken louts. She falls dazed into a quarry and is so terrified that Georges has to leave food for her in the rushes.

A torrential downpour and a touch of fever clear her mind. At length Uncle Jeff returns and waylays her on her way to the village to run an errand. Georges believes she has stolen the money, and prepares to go to Algeria with his parents. But when Jeff accosts Virginia once more, George rescues her and gives Jeff a good hiding. Next day they all leave for Algeria together.

In a certain poeticism capped by a dream sequence, Renoir's first film flowed with an avant-garde current, in which as *Premier Plan* commented, "the story counted for little, or was only a pretext. Epstein, Delluc or L'Herbier chose unbelievable melodramas which they illustrated lovingly, to please elite spectators." Possibly it was hoped that a banal story would delight the larger public, while the finer effects would commend it to connoisseurs and posterity. The strategy can succeed but it more often fails, for different finesses, lacking the co-ordinating effect of a subtle story, may remain isolated and ineffective. A profounder objection is that style and content so interact that artists in whom this calculation is conscious tend to neglect, rather than transcend, the story and so irritate as well as dissatisfy both audiences. This is part of the difference between *La Fille de L'Eau* and *L'Atalante* ten years later.

Cauliez sees the film's lyricism as a reaction against the realism brought to the French theatre by Antoine. We may add more cinematographic influences. From Griffithian melodrama comes Jeff brutalising the golden-curled child-woman and demonstrating his strength by biting through a metal spoon. Yet Renoir's tone is cooler. A pal soon disuades Jeff from beating the girl, and when bested by Georges he swims off down the river, shamefaced but not quite cowed, and we don't want him to be. Again, Renoir relishes on un-Griffithian reserve. Thus the camera watches while the movement of a hand or a pair of feet implies the actions of a body hidden in shadow or behind a doorway. Georges is characterised at first mainly by his white horse, but, like Jeff's, his character gradually develops away from a melodramatic extreme. It transpires that he's painfully timid (the revelation is made very suddenly perhaps owing to missing scenes which also involve Mme. Raynal's puritanism—announced in a subtitle but never shown). There are many scenes, typical of bourgeois dramas of the time, in which nice sensitive people sit grieving on summery lawns, or walk in tears off the lower right hand corner of the screen, or sit alone, fragile and sad, in neat white attic rooms, by luminous dormer windows. There is also a faery impulse: Virginia

as watersprite, half-animal during her madness, and living in liberty among the reeds by the river.

The film abounds in those optical effects which used to be called "impressionist". The movie term, very different from its painterly context, suggests only that visual impressions are given a dramatic pretext. Georges, knocked out, sees things in triplicate. Rapid cutting suggests delirium. A handheld track recurs for juddering effect. But mood and effect relate perfectly as the

camera tracks after the departing pony trap, but more slowly, so that although we move, like the characters, through the landscape, we are also left behind by them—an interesting "double image" of involvement and detachment, presaging the screen-within-a-screen departure of *Les Bas-Fonds*. The girl's nightmare is enriched by fascinating ruptures of visual texture and of dramatic tone. Bleached double exposures are juxtaposed with hard contrast shots. Her dream drapery flows in soft motions as she drifts aloofly. The ethereal effect contrasts with a subsequent shot of a dragon; i.e. a lizard garnished with tiny artificial wings and magnified by the camera. Jeff hangs from a tree strangled by a rope, but he abruptly comes alive and the noose quickens into a snake. The dreamer perches on a branch, haughtily. The rivals on each side of her swing under the branch with an abrupt movement which is half-animal, half-demoniac, more insidiously phallic than any stock symbol. Later they pursue her, jumping over pillars laid eerily on their sides to make an uneven floor. We may think ahead to Brunius' long-legged satyr facetiously leaping after Jane Marken in *Partie de Campagne*. The film's lyrical realism has dated least: the naturalness of some stone-throwing kids contrasts with the only too conspicuous make-up in all the studio interiors. Several shots, already, are authentic Renoir; a wall creates a largely flat, frontal image, but over its top we see layer upon layer of roofs and hills. Evening doorways are lit with a deep and friendly reverence for cosy domesticity.

Fleeing shadows on a moonlit highway recall Dovzhenko, and not merely as a reference, but in a fugitive beauty. Gnarled peasant physiognomies isolated in a succession of close-ups may suggest Pudovkin. Such sequences in fact pre-date the films they resemble, and one's respect for Renoir's range is not mitigated by the reflection that a characteristic of the French avant-garde was its unselective eclecticism.. It is possible that there was a Scandinavian influence upon Renoir, at least in the sunlit solidity of the countryside and certain peasant characters dwelt on for their own sakes. More probably the quality is Renoir's own. Justin is characterised like an Eisenstein character (again before Eisenstein) in terms of his own physicality. With his long neck, long nose, and quick sullen eyes, the crow is perhaps his animal. But he is not a stereotyped peasant's son. He is uneasy, constricted, lashing out in fits of foolish malice which can never assuage his profound misery (he anticipates several Chabrol characters). The Raynals and the miller's family are relatively uninteresting, possibly because of lost footage, possibly because Renoir had settled for the period's less authentic conventions.

Catherine Hessling, with her orchid face and squirrel-like gestures, intermittently liberates herself from her role's Dickensian (via Griffith) *parti pris* to become the watersprite winnable by those who seek neither to cage her nor judge her. She is always that nervous, imperious, childlike exotic called La Hessling. The heroine's life on the fringes of society, her need for protection, and the film's preference for the poacher rather than the farmer, suggest a sensibly delicate balance between a bourgeois romanticism and a bourgeois commonsense. As in Dickens, the lower orders are the source of both pathos and brutality, suggesting that Renoir has yet to leave a general framework of middleclass assumptions. The nomad, whom the bourgeoisie easily romanticise, or despise, are seen with a similar mixture of sympathy and asperity. The poacher and the gipsy both adopt the girl, but as their servant, and both leave her in the lurch. That realism, rather than prejudice or incomprehension, underwrites this approach is suggested by the combination of appreciation and bleakness in Renoir's view of the solid middleclass peasantry whose cottages and crafts are genuinely beautiful but who rapidly deteriorate into a drunken mob. Upper-middleclass Georges and "lumpen" Virginia (by plight rather than origin) share, or rather achieve, a relative freedom from social pressures. Here again Renoir's thought is moving outwards from his own background, through the false freedom of sentimentality and an essentially whimsical "poetry". Though denounced, they are not altogether evaded. Georges sets out to save Virginia from the elements but fails even to find her. It is a metaphysical affinity with nature which enables her to survive. The film shows certain patterns of transportation (barge, automobile, horse, bicycle, ponytrap) although the camera remains too static to create the sense of unsettledness, of restless movement, which they might suggest. The prominence given to water (canals, rain) and to the preparation of food inaugurates other Renoir themes.

Renoir sees it as an apprentice effort. "I was able to learn some lessons from it. I seemed to notice that the least bad parts were exactly those in which I had least escaped from the direct imitation of nature."—from nature "as digested, as composed", as by Zola or Maupassant, but nature still.

Perhaps, now, the most apparent difference between *La Fille de l'Eau* and Renoir's next film, *Nana,* is the former's sentimentality and the latter's toughness, the former's indulgence of effects and the latter's sharpened plastic sensitivity, the former's eclecticism and the latter's consistency of style. In the former, the picture often controls the actions. In the latter, the action more often decides the picture.

Nana

Between *La Fille de l'Eau* and *Nana*, Renoir saw Stroheim's *Foolish Wives*. "I glimpsed the possibility of touching the public by authentic subjects in the tradition of French realism." At the same time came the realisation that "the gesture of a washerwoman, of a woman combing her hair before her glass, of a costermonger . . . possess an unsurpassable plastic value." This plasticity is more than implicit in *La Fille de l'Eau*, and Renoir stressed the lessons of the earlier film as much as the discovery of Stroheim.

The moment Renoir encountered Pierre Braunberger, then Paramount's director of publicity in France, he recognised a kindred spirit. According to Leprohon, "They met towards the end of the afternoon. At four in the morning they were still talking cinema, and at the end of the meeting Braunberger was to take charge of the organisation of Les Films Jean Renoir." (An influential collaborator, Braunberger subsequently produced many of the artistically more adventurous shorts heralding the Nouvelle Vague.)

Shooting on their first production began in February 1926. Braunberger had fixed up a co-production deal with a German company, and five months shooting was split between the Gaumont Studios in Paris and the Grunewald Studios in Berlin. *Nana* ran to well over 8,000 feet and much of its million-franc budget came from Renoir's personal fortune. Renoir discussed the adaptation with Mme Leblond-Zola (whom he again consulted for *la Bête Humaine*). The rights to the novel, the services of Werner Krauss, and the lavish and extensive sets made it a very expensive film for its time. It necessarily simplified the original, eliminating the relationship between Countess Muffat and Fauchery, selecting cardinal traits from Nana's innumerable admirers and redistributing them among her principal suitors. Muffat (Werner Krauss) is Nana's humiliated sugar daddy and father figure. Emphasis on his money and his inhibited personal style puts him among the haute bourgeoisie. The Comte de Vandeuvres (Jean Angelo) is the mirror of Nana's insolence. Georges Hugon (R. Catelain), in relationship, not age,

is a son-figure, and seems to incarnate the lover whose sensitivity she might have appreciated as integrity had the times been a little less brutal.

Renoir's film respects Zola's social theme and chief incidents, alongside his own, more personalist interpretation. His Nana, offended by her insufficient success as an actress in the role of *une honnête femme,* flatters her worldly vanity by becoming a courtesan. Each of her victims is also a victim of his own lies; the advantages of social superiority are the principal lie. Her conquest becomes a function of an instinctive egalitarianism. The privileges of beauty avenge those of status—but cannot redress them. Forced by her femininity to become merely men, her lovers, and their loved ones, become the victims of their privileges. Muffat drags his wife through the mud while Nana, making him crawl on all fours and beg for candy like a dog, reduces him to a level below that of the servants who smirkingly spy on his humiliation. He turns his back on Nana when she reveals her shock at Hugon's suicide—perhaps through jealousy of her *concern;* perhaps because, a true masochist, he rewards Nana's sadism but punishes her human pity. The Count Vandeuvres ruins himself by "debts of honour" and with characteristic aplomb ruins his bookies as well. Just as Muffat's eminence becomes degradation, so the Count's irresponsibility reveals itself as cryptic sadomasochism. Before committing suicide for reasons which, being financial, are bourgeois, and degrading to an aristocratic like himself (but the nitty-gritty nonetheless!), he sets fire to the stables and burns to death a horse named after his inamorata. Taken from Zola, the episode also inaugurates Renoir's recurrent emphasis on an animal's brute pain. The "inoffensive" youth lays one of Nana's dresses in a sitting position over a chair and repeatedly stabs and slashes it with scissors.

Nana's fate, however, is not quite the agonised death which her victims wish upon her. She, too, becomes the victim of the self-leveling of privilege and of nature. Yielding to nostalgia, she craves to lose herself amidst the mob from which she rose, and joins the Bal Mabille, dancing the can-can, kicking the gentlemen's hats from their hands, and befriending the lavatory attendant who is what she might have been and might still become. There she catches smallpox, and her disfigurement is not a "punishment" for, but an abolition of, her false face. Her loss matches Muffat's loss of his fortune, the Count's of his honour, Hugon's of his kindness—all their "false selves". Renoir is kinder than Zola. The masks are dropped, and as the long comedy of courtesan and client ends, the reality of mutual dependence and affection is achieved. It is arguable that Renoir allows Nana and Muffat an "end" which, in the profoundest sense only, is a "happy" one.

The servants incarnate the malicious servility to which Nana's ruthless egoism is a violently anarchic, a Sorelian, and a relatively proud reaction. If Nana ruins Muffat, it is also because she is a feminine Boudu, an agent of Dionysus, come to chasten a materialism which denies his kingship. When she herself takes social status too seriously, she must, like La Princesse in *Orphée,* be punished. Her aspiration to be "une honnête femme"—like Muffat's wife—was *hubris,* and largely social, an aspiration to the bourgeoisie. It was also an unnatural one, for, wherever her true happiness was to be found, it was in relationship to a man she loved and not to a social category. Another courtesan of Renoir's is less desperate, and meets her mate. But as Truffaut remarked, "Nana rime avec Eléna". It rhymes also with Nini (Francoise Arnoul) in *French Can-Can,* which film's moral is the rightness, the profundity, of coquetry between men and women. Thus Zola leads back to Degas, and to life as an "impressionist" sequence.

By posture and gesture, by their whole bodily rhythm, Werner Krauss and La Hessling create a disjuncture as haunting as Charleston steps danced to a hymn tune. The discrepancy is profound, for each is the other's nostalgia for another mode of existence. Muffat's slow sad movements betray the kind, humble, fatherly diligence which is the modest best in middleclass aspiration, but on which an alien pretension has had to be imposed, engendering the sado-masochism which brings him and Nana low, but cannot break their profounder love. All Nana's victims are victims, not merely of the pretentions, but also of their unconscious egalitarianism or gregariousness. As victims of their virtues, they are tragic heroes, and infinitely more human and complex than moralised exemplars of decadence.

The film has its bestiary. Visually, Muffat is half baited bear, half toofaithful dog. Nana, with her sinuous, spiky movements, is the cat. Young Hugon's nervous movements have a curious docility, even servility. The servants are snaky, particularly Valeska Gert as Zoe, Nana's maid.

La Hessling, Lady of Misrule, transcends Zola's blonde Amazon to become a pocket Venus of sulk, cajolery and command. With her prettily Napoleonic postures, her limbs light as petals, her air of *fin-de-siècle* Lillian Gish, Hessling's expressionistic pantomine of gestures becomes, precisely through its air of arbitrary, irrational selection, vitalist, and false. They are

the gestures of a goddess. Hurrying down a long corridor, her bustled gown is like a lizard's or a fish's fin. The scene where she confronts death reveals why Dreyer came so near choosing her for his St. Joan. Her tulip-shaped pout of a mouth, her fauve relentlessness (free from malice yet redolent of a childish egoism), her orthochrome-paled face eerily juxtaposing the catlike and the doll-like, her eyes blazing forth in close-ups like sunflowers, make her less the succubus on, than the catalyst of, society's internal aberance.

The film can be related to the German silent cinema, but to its "decorative" rather than its expressionist aspect. In place of the oppressively ornate plushness one might have expected in a portrait of the Second Empire, Claude Autant-Lara's sets memorably convert palatial interiors into broad fields of whiteness, and demonstrate the harmonious restraint of opulence by space. Yet they are empty and cold. They abound in wide corridors at whose intersections—with their variety of exits and entrances—the action is so often situated. The fixed-focus camera of the cinema's early days is used to almost agoraphobic effect. Hessling's frills and flounces create a titillating intricacy carefully maintained by Renoir at the expense of historical accuracy. Renoir trusted he would "be pardoned a small historical error which I deliberately perpetrated by costuming my artists in the more curious fashion of 1871."

Refraining from the interminable long shots with which a more commercial director might have converted lavishness into weariness, Renoir concentrates on small groups, on small areas, intermittently pulling back to reveal a spatial and spiritual framework. There are four long tracking shots, achieved by means of an old Ford chassis with deflated tyres.

The seedy bleakness of spirit backstage at the theatre renders Nana's desperate greed quite understandable, not just as a selfish guttersnipe's only hope, but as a Symbolist nostalgia. Paradoxically, the spaciousness of the Muffat palatial home remains potential space, that is, freedom. The characters are lost in it, as in the theatre wings. Or they use it minimally, and therefore with a perverse derisiveness (in the highceilinged room, Nana makes Muffat kneel, then stretch up and beg).

Renoir places his characters in groups whose compositions are always visually dynamic. The sophisticated forms of this "painterly" ability are surprisingly rare among film directors. In its dressing room scenes, or with its pit orchestras and dancers, Renoir's film almost quits Zola for Degas; yet, as in Maupassant, impressionist pleasures are linked with a sense of corruption.*

---

* Leo Braudy develops, briefly but valuably, conjoined themes: the interchange of theatre and reality, and voyeurism. Nana's stage make-up is equally conspicuous off-stage; she "is the consummate stage actress in her basic nature . . . Muffat is fascinated by Nana's stylization and lack of emotion." The theme of peeping and spying acquire "epistemological implication," underlined when Renoir frequently ends scenes that emphasize observation with the familiar closing iris, while other scenes merely dissolve to black. Braudy, with others, sees voyeurism as a conspicuous motif in Zola's own work.

The film bears traces of the stylistic uncertainties afflicting the French cinema of its time, torn as it was between the American example, the German example, the French bourgeois culture, and the mass audience. At times certain plot mechanics, such as the placing of the bets, seem laboured, mere suspense. Yet their relative "emptiness" adds to the effect of the film's editing, which, like many German films of the time, is essentially "pre-Griffithian". In the staging of the action tempo is a secondary, or tertiary, consideration. The film seems to hang in white space. That emptiness is not negative, a lack, but part of a sense of isolation in space, a precariousness of the residual implications of social frameworks and pressures. (A similar sense of space recurs, with the same paradoxical effect, in *Madame Bovary* and *Partie de Campagne*.)

In sometimes awkward blend with a moralising as respectful, suave and tragic as Ophuls's, the characterisation can resort to Stroheim's emphases, emphases so heavy that today's spectator may see not so much realism (as Renoir intended at the time) or romanticism (as he felt later) but a grotesquerie which is intermittently puppet-like; thus bringing the film towards the stylistic ambit of *Charleston* and *La Petite Marchande d'Allumettes.* † Closeups of Nana's dirty comb and washbasin water recall Stroheim's penchant for noxious sensuousness. Braudy remarks, "Renoir's cinematic naturalism. . . . concentrates on the relevant detail rather than on incessant accumulation."

According to Pierre Leprohon the film was ignored by French intellectuals because Renoir's concern was with dramatic content rather than with the avant-garde's interest in extending the new language of film. Despite critical support in Germany, it was a resounding commercial failure, as was a second attempt with a shortened version in December 1926. Sadoul speaks of a public and critical success betrayed by its distributors. According to *Cahiers,* Renoir was financially ruined by it, although Leprohon maintains that later in the same year he was still able to finance the delightful opuscule, *Charleston*.

† This creates an intriguing intersection between Renoir's responsiveness to the human and the toys iconography established later.

Charleston / Sur un
Air de Charleston

Cauliez suggests that *Charleston* was an amateur relaxation, a letting down of back hair amongst ciné-club accomplices, after the elaborate public tone of *Nana*. Leprohon suggests that producer and director hoped to recoup some of the losses on *Nana* by this ingeniously cheap yet engaging little jest.

Involving only one set and a handful of actors, the 1200 metres of *Charleston* were filmed in three days in the autumn of 1926 in the courtyard of the Epinay Studios. Extant versions include a section only of the original footage (the B.F.I. version runs to 1595 ft.), although the truncation appears to be the producer's own. It was premiered in Paris on 19 March 1927 and distributed together with a piano accompaniment by Jacques Doucet, pianist at *Le Boeuf Sur Le Toit,* a bar which owed its success to the jazz and Negro entertainers whom it presented to the fashionable Parisian intelligensia.

"In 2028 A.D.—years after the next war—an explorer sets forth from Central Africa into the Terra Incognita of Europa Deserta." A Negro (Johnny Huggins) in tailcoat and minstrel make-up steers his flying machine over Paris. Near the Eiffel Tower (whose upper half droops sideways), a savage maiden (Catherine Hessling) with flowers in her hair and somewhat soiled elbow-length kid gloves lassoos a friendly gorilla in papier-maché mask. The explorer's globular machine lands plumb on top of the publicity bollard which is her lair, and he begins his explorations. Taking a Road Up sign for a cross, he respectfully drops the flower in his buttonhole at its foot. Soon however the white savage has him trussed up, and begins performing a dance of courtship rather than triumph. "Why, it's the Charleston!" He manages to persuade his captress to chalk a telephone on the hoarding. It magically turns into the real thing, and he reports to distant colleagues, whose (literal) wing collars recall angels or aviators, that "I have discovered the Charleston, the original dance of the white people, and am going to learn it." He takes to it like a duck to water (not surprisingly, since Huggins was

principal dancer in a Paris black revue), and persuades her to climb up after him into his flying machine. "And thus was imported into Africa a new fashion—the culture of the aboriginal whites."

Some French synopses speak of a new ice age although there is no sign of it in the wild girl's South Sea Island get-up and companionable gorilla.

For another '20s view of syncopation and modern dancing as reversion to the barbaric, one need look no further than Aldous Huxley's *Antic Hay*. Renoir's response to jungle rhythms was rather more cheerful and the film compares—complementarily, rather than similarly —with another good-humouredly apocalyptic fantasy, René Clair's *Paris Qui Dort*. Clair's dry, methodical, oddly melancholy little mechanisms take us back, via Mack

Sennett, to 19th century rationalism and the moral and metaphysical geometry
of Descartes and Condillac. Renoir harks back via Georges Méliès to
Rousseau and Rabelais. It's a neatly paradoxical litle squib on the theme
of the Noble Savage, which was just about to take Hollywood also to
primitive lands *(Tabu, White Shadows In the South Seas, Trader Horn)*.
The film's frolickings with notions of Western civilization, the missionary
spirit and Uncle Tomism hardly need spelling out. Hessling draws on that
French tradition of quick, intelligent physicality to which one may relate
pantomimes as diverse as Debureau, Max Linder, Jean-Louis Barrault,
Ronald Petit, Marcel Marceau and Maurice Béjart.

About this film, objectivity is impossible. One is infatuated, enchanted,
ravished, or not. *Premier Plan* compares Hessling at once to "a Griffith
heroine" and on the mind-boggling notion of Brigitte Gish or Lillian Bardot
one must superimpose a pocket female Tarzan, or a Neanderthal Lolita à
la *Flying Elephants*.

Renoir attends to her performance with slow and fast-motion, and, most
effective of all, abrupt switches between the two, in mid-take, often precisely
cut to her changes of elevation, e.g. the speed changes just as her choreography brings her from profile to full-face. She moves fast enough for her
face and limbs to briefly blur before the camera, anticipating, a little less
arbitrarily, certain freeze-frame effects of the '60s. Higgins, pretending to
be learning the dance which she performs, produces some startling novelty
steps, including a distinctly Uncle Sambo-type shuffle.

Renoir's frivolous little movie gives, like Méliès, vastly more pleasure
than it "ought", which is perhaps a way of saying that its "illusion" is only
a pretence, that it belongs to an aesthetic line which is neither that of Lumière
(the documentary impulse) nor that of fantasy (e.g. the Powell-Berger-
Whelan *The Thief of Baghdad*), but that of fantasy-as-a-pretence-for-
spectacle (e.g. Méliès' *La Conquête du Pole*). However unfamiliar in aesthetic theory, it is a characteristic mode of contemplating art—especially
when one substitutes admiration at artistic achievements for admiration at
mere spectacle. Here, Paris in 2028 A.D. exists only as the Magnetic Needle
of the Pole exists for Méliès—as part of a play of ideas, of the Symbolism
unselfconsciously implicit in the parephenalia of show-business. *Charleston*
agreeably juxtaposes its shows-within-a-show (the street as informal theatre,
the publicity column as home). The sketched telephone which turns into a real
one (in a silent film!) is another little flourish of Renoir's on his abiding theme
of showbusiness and life as heads and tails of the same coin.

To relish a silent version of a dance-and-sound film is one of those absurdities which film critics have learned to take in their stride. The film depends
on dance rather than rhythm, and one can understand that many critics of the
time complained about its eroticism. However much one relishes it now, in
its time, it enjoyed success with few, and Les Films Jean Renoir ceased its
activities.

Marquitta

At this juncture Renoir received a commission from his brother Pierre, who had also founded a film company, to direct a film "vehicle" for Pierre's second wife, Marie-Louise Iribe. Pierre Lestringuez wrote the scenario and Jean Angelo played the Prince. But for all the old friends involved, the film's directive was unequivocal: to find the widest possible public for its leading lady.

Shooting began towards the end of 1926, in the Gaumont Studios, Butte-Chaumont, with exteriors in Nice. Its production was interrupted by an automobile accident which killed Renoir's friend, Pierre Champagne, and in which Renoir sustained serious injuries. He was found by poachers, who took him to hospital. Eventually shooting resumed and the film had its public première in Paris on 13 August 1927.

According to contemporary criticism, *Marquitta* was a sweet, sometimes sweetly sad, tale somewhere between Lubitsch in his less robust and roguish moods, *Champagne,* and the moralism of "big sentimental dramas, spiced with adventures, exoticism and slavonic passion, which opened to the public the doors of the elite." Its theme and title were those of an already popular song.

The various synopses extant are so diverse that they might refer to completely different films. The essential seems to be that the Prince of Decarlia, cursed with an exasperating mistress, falls in love with Marquitta, a Parisian streetsinger, and vows to make a star of her within a year. Despite the objections of his chamberlain, he takes her to the Riviera, where she disgraces him by eating her pear with her fingers, and by a variety of other caprices, such that when a sapphire tiara disappears he leaps to the conclusion that she has stolen it. Dismissing her with a cheque, he returns to his former love. But the streetsinger becomes a star while his dynasty falls on evil days. He degenerates to being a famished Caucasian dancer in a cabaret. When she gives him a leg of chicken he wolfs it down. Meanwhile she delicately and correctly peels a pear. He attempts suicide in the taxi owned by his ex-

chamberlain turned cabbie. After a breakneck automobile chase Marquitta is
in time to foil him and save him. The thief turns out to have been Marquitta's
father.

Télé-Ciné speaks of "very mediocre direction". Several critics of the
time appreciated various touches, and an amiable tone brought success to a
film which made no attempt to be anything other than a highlife daydream
fairytale for shopgirls. Claude Beylie describes the film as "almost a pastiche
of *Nana* . . . in the rocambolic conventions of the Slavonic operetta".

Renoir relishes the memory of his own "Schufftan" process. "I had the
idea . . . of showing the corner of a boulevard complete with Metro. It
was done with mirrors whose reverse sides were scraped to leave just enough
place for the characters; and then the decor which was in minature was
reflected in the mirror. I've always had enormous fun out of things like this."

La Petite Marchande
d'Allumettes
(The Little Match Girl)

After the première of *Marquitta* Renoir was approached by Jean Tedesco, about a new project. In 1924 Tedesco had founded the Vieux-Colombier cinema to show the art and experimental films which attracted only exasperated scorn from the functionaries of the commercial cinema. His success quickened the whole arthouse and ciné-club movement in France. Hopes of the gradual emergence of a new circuit prompted Tedesco to a venture even closer to his heart. This was a film workshop in which the creator would enjoy full liberty of expression, together with control over the marketing and presentation of his work.

"I was lucky enough to find in Jean Renoir an experienced director, perfectly adept in the most modern and elaborate techniques, and who brought to the organisation of the Vieux-Colombier Studio-laboratory the most rigorous principles. . . . We generated our own current, thanks to an electrical apparatus which Renoir rigged up, our negatives were developed on the spot." Renoir: "We constructed equipment which only subsequently came into studio use. The basic principle was the use of slightly overpowered electric bulbs. These bulbs were placed, either in boxes of polished metal, or in front of white, less reflective surfaces, or in front of spotlight reflectors, either isolated or in banks. . . . We kept a few arcs intended to throw strong shadows on faces and decor. . . . The filmstock used in studios was still orthochrome. Panchromatic film was used only in exteriors and that seemed to me absurd. The only reason was that the studios were equipped with mercury lamps and arcs which were unsuitable for panchromatic, because it uses colours nearer the yellows and reds . . . we shot in panchromatic and . . . we fitted up some wooden tanks and made the first print with an old Pathé camera."

Some material was shot in the Forest of Fontainebleau, and on the sands near Marly in January 1928. The story by Hans Christian Andersen may well have been suggested, initially, by the toyshop quality of the studio. Tedesco: "To imitate the snow, a distinctly apocalyptic machine hung from the ceiling, raining down cataracts of white paper. I can still see Jean Renoir in the theatre proscenium, directing the film like a ballet, while working mechanical toys jigged around in a *trompe-l'oeil* practical set before a camera placed in one of the audience boxes. Certain scenes were shot from different angles by five cameras simultaneously. The supernatural cavalry pursuit was shot using handheld cameras mounted on horseback. Certain special procedures were innovated by Renoir and perfected by the first cameraman, Bachelet, for superimpositions in certain particularly delicate scenes."

Karen, a ragged matchseller (Catherine Hessling) vainly offers her wares to passers-by. A policeman keeps a suspicious eye on her, while boys throw snowballs and scatter her matches. Afraid to return home, she shelters under a plank and dreams. She enters the toyshop opposite. A rich young passer-by whom, in reality, she narrowly missed, reappears as a handsome toy soldier. The policeman reappears also, as a jack-in-the-box, a Hussar with a skull and crossbones on his cap. Death pursues them on horseback across the sky; and Karen is found dead in the snow, the plank under which she crawled having been removed while she lay dreaming.

According to trade journals of the time, the film concludes with Andersen's happy end. But its loss is never mentioned by Renoir, and one might prefer to believe that its absence from both the copies shown in Britain since

the war represents Renoir's own revision. It would concur with his insistence that Andersen, properly understood, is a quite unsentimental writer. ". . . . above all, don't think of Andersen's poetry as mawkish. It's strong. Andersen is misunderstood in France, badly misunderstood. He is a great writer."

One might equally say that Andersen and "fairy" stories altogether are badly misunderstood almost everywhere. Sam Goldwyn cast Danny Kaye as Hans Christian Andersen, while the schematised whimsy of Walt Disney's seven dwarfs is only bearable if, in defiance of *auteur* theory, one rigidly segregates them from the surburban garden rusticism, the Samuel Smiles industriousness, which comparison with Disney's other work only too clearly underlines, that other approaches have always been possible is recalled by Jean Cocteau's *La Belle et La Bête*, with its inner affinities to *Orphée*.

All in all the film represents the antithesis of the realism with which Renoir is usually associated. André Bazin remarks: "Despite its avant-garde technique, it scarely relates to the oneiric expressionism of a certain cinema of the time. If the technique is expressionist, the style is impressionist. More exactly, what amuses Renoir is to graft impressionism onto expressionism." At the same time, for Bazin the film is, of Renoir's silent films, "the most interesting and the most instructive. The special effects exist not for their fairylike illusion, but for their mechanical execution or their optical substance. They are toys in the second degree." The comment accords well with Renoir's own remarks about his pleasure in the concoction of technical effects, but less than well with his remarks about Andersen. By and large, critics have tended to divide into those who prize his film for capturing a magic spirit (its meaning in the first degree), and those who esteem it as a technical *tour de force* or an intriguing *exercice de style* (in the second degree). More recently, perhaps, other attitudes to the faery and the fantastic have asserted themselves, notably the "camp" (with its infinite variety of equally boring subspecies), and a feeling that professional competence may produce authentic "magic". The older supposition that some special "spirit" is required for fantasy to ring true presupposes that fantasy is spiritually at a disadvantage, either on account of the vigorous factuality of contemporary thought, or because the unrealistic is somehow anticinematic or antiphotographic. Neither proposition has ever had a convincing demonstration, and the contrary is asserted by the number of adults who are more than a little scared by the witch in *Snow White* or saddened when Bambi's mother dies. Nor is any light thrown on the matter by the curious and only too familiar contrast between Lumière realism and Méliès magic. Lumière was interested in the photographic reproduction of reality, Méliès in the cinematographic creation of illusion. But Lumière was no more interested in revealing anything spiritually interesting about reality than Méliès was interested in the possibility of exploring other worlds, or the existence of spirits, or the fantastic itself. One was a technician, the other was a conjurer. Both were equally exponents of the spectacle, and the latter's genius, which is probably not too strong a word, involves his play with illusion recognised as such throughout. Both, in their concern with the spectator's pleasurable wonderment and amusement at the actual spectacle paraded before them, anticipate Godard, Warhol and others whom we may call actualists, in that they emphasise the spectator's consciousness of the film as film. (The consciousness of film as film is no innovation. The star system depends upon the fan's awareness and admiration of the star as star, an awareness so acute that no overt reference need be made to it. Usually, the agreed conventions between film-maker and spectator are such that overt reference is not appreciated; but the overt references made in, for example, *Pierrot le Fou*, or in certain private jokes, may shatter the illusion for a second or two only. Equally, the shift of interest from a combination of illusory realism and aesthetic admiration— (i.e. the awareness of the actual specactle)—to a continuing actualist awareness may constitute a revision of agreed convention. But it is in no sense the "revolution of consciousness" as which it is often touted: it's traditional in academic high culture). Certainly it would be absurd to call Georges Méliès' *La Conquête du Pole* science-fiction in the sense in which Jules Verne is science-fiction.

But Renoir's interest in Andersen's work incorporates a component of another order. Even if we assert the primacy among Renoir's interests of technicalities as sport, the result of our partial suspension of disbelief is a *magic* film, in the class of Feuillade's *Les Vampires,* of Josef von Baky's *The Adventures of Baron Munchausen,* of the Powell-Berger-Whelan *The Thief of Baghdad,* and of Albert Zugsmith's *Evils of Chinatown (Confessions of an Opium Eater).* Nor are we far from the territory of the cartoon, although the spiritual affinities are with Bartosch's *L'Idée,* Alexandreieff's *Une Nuit Sur La Mont Chauve* and in particular, Grimault's *Le Petit Soldat,* where fairytale imagery is *"revue et corrigé"* by a Prévert allegory. Renoir, castigating the French film industry's perennial assumption that dream films always flop at the French box-office, appeals to the example of Chaplin's *The Bank.* Few commentators have failed to see the affinities between Chaplin's tramp and Hessling's beggar-girl. One might propose a second comparison: with *A Dog's Life,* one of Chaplin's most bitter films. "The death of the bear and the rabbit prefigures *La Règle du Jeu,"* observes Cauliez, catching the film's serious spirit. Other touches twist sentimentality into irony. As Death, a little sadly, hangs a lock of Karen's hair on the cross by which she dies, it becomes a rose. Its petals fall. But those petals become the snowflakes which have killed her. The passers-by understand nothing: "How absurd, to try and keep warm with matches", much as adult rationality understands nothing of childhood dreams. Freudians will hardly overlook the pessimistic paraphrase of the theory of entropy in the visual equation soldiers=matches. The story's equal and opposite morals ("dreams kill," and "poverty renders delirious") are transcended by the cruel precariousness of existence. Renoir's 'fairy' girl anticipates the many animal victims in Renoir.

Within Renoir's "fairytale" spirit reality continually obtrudes in a way far more scathing than obvious contrasts between reality and dread could ever have been. As Cauliez puts it, "Renoir alleges no pretext for Karen's dreams; she moves her dark silhouette against a luminous background; she crosses a 'wall' of white sheets; she stretches her arms towards her dreams." Renoir insists on the permanence of his protagonist, whether in reality or dream; she remains fixed while the background changes. Karen awakes in the interior of her own dream; and she dances in the blackness. The "real" Christmas tree becomes stylised, geometric. Realistic are the meals which the restaurant's patrons enjoy, and the faces peering down at the match-girl's pantomime body. Reality is peripheral, posterior, merely the seal guaranteeing the objective truth of all we have "only" felt; or, it resembles the freeze-frame at the end of *Les 400 Coups.* Our childlike pantomime has become a tragic delirium and we have emerged, not at "the end", but into a reminder of the unperturbed, and therefore fictitious, consensus in whose margin this news-item occurred.

One hesitates to speak of a Dickensian or Griffithian pathos only *superficially* deprived of reality by (to reverse Bazin's proposition) a resort to an impressionism which is secretly an expressionism. The physical solidity of the world around the child-woman is sucked away by her febrility, as in the substantiality of her own body-image, and replaced by a fluttering hysteria whose climax is not so much a dream as a dying delirium. In contrast to the emotionless, enigmatic, glacial schizophrenies of affluence, à la *Marienbad,* we have a Victorian mixture of hunger, frailty and longing; *passé,* indeed, but important to remember as having been a human reality, and therefore remaining a human potentiality. The film belongs to Wagenknecht's age of innocence, even though its style is a virtuoso deployment of optical ruse. Carl Vincent contends that the film belongs to a Swedish tradition exemplified by Sjöström's *Thy Soul Shall Bear Witness*, (1920), Sjöberg's *The Road To Heaven* (1942), and Bergman's *The Seventh Seal*, even though the film's "impressionism" seems un-Scandinavian. Yet the writers of *Premier Plan*, who rarely give Renoir the benefit of much doubt, concede that the toys are imbued, by light, with so much "militant or avenging humour", or are transformed by the intricacies of shadow, and grant the film "a way of seeing the world through an infantile logic in which many verbal expressions are given a literal visualisation." There is more than mere aestheticism in the flouncing and swinging of Karen's hair, of Death's plume and his horse's mane and tail, as he draws alongside her; for their rhythms take up the galloping motion with a paroxystic energy and sadness. The rigidity of the toys contrasts with the fleeting shadows of the real humans. Catherine Hessling's fantastic style, sacrificing nothing of its provocativeness to achieve poignancy, is impeccably acclimatised to the story of automata and delirium. At once fairytale and *film noir*, the film seems, now, not so much a pretext for a technical experiment, as a minor masterpiece, Renoir's one all but perfect silent film.

It proved to be one of Renoir's financially ill-fated ventures. The playwright Maurice Rostand had adapted Andersen's story for the Opéra-Comique, and had placed, like Renoir, a barrel-organ in the street. Soon after the film's premiere, his relatives took legal action. The print was impounded and although the film-makers eventually won the case, the two year delay saw the introduction of sound. The film had been destined for a musical score to be played in the Théâtre du Vieux-Colombier. In 1930 another distributor hastily substituted a pot-pourri of musical hits, and added subtitles which are altogether superfluous and compound the music's disruption of the visual flow.

Le Tournoi/Le Tournoi Dans la Cité

After the failure of *La Petite Marchande d'Allumettes* Renoir the amateur had to accept commercial constraints. "I found work and I made anodine films to order. They met with little success, but my producers were satisfied. In cinema jargon, a commercial film doesn't mean a film which makes money. It means a film conceived and executed according to the canons of the businessmen."

Le Tournoi was the first of Renoir's commissions from the Société des Grands Films Historiques. The company disposed of massive resources and its policy would appear to have been to blend patriotic elements (thus procuring both official support and middleclass approval) and popular ones. It was filmed at the Studio St. Maurice. Again panchromatic film was used. Several filmographies quote *Le Tournoi* as following rather than preceding *Tire Au Flanc*, reasonably, since its Parisian première was delayed until February 1929. It was, however, shot first (in summer 1928) and enjoyed a Royal Gala première at Brussels towards the end of 1928, going on to enjoy a considerable public success.

Those copies of *Le Tournoi* still to be seen are brief (40 minutes) and incomplete, being conspicuously short on human interest. During the visit to Carcassone of Charles and Catherine de Médicis (Blanche Bernis), the cruel and debauched leader of the Protestant party, François de Baynes (Aldo Nadi) provokes his noble Catholic adversary, Henri de Rogier (Enrique de Rivero) to trial by combat before the fair Isabella (Jackie Monnier). Baynes, having brutally killed Isabella's father in the duel, is arrested in the course of the tourney and makes his savagely courageous last stand against all the knights of the Court.

Boldly and deliberately composed, the images might strike one as the work of an intelligent if uninspired admirer of the men-at-arms scenes from Dreyer's *La Passion de Jeanne D'Arc;* notably the silhouettes of the watch, plodding stolidly past the flashing duellists. Such a style might seem implicit in the very forms of such panoply as horse, rider, lance, battlements and towers. Nonetheless Dreyer's and Renoir's *clarté* contrasts with the romantico-rhapsodic tendencies of Gance, or the conventional Hollywood congestion of massed extras. Here individual items are selected, isolated and cherished in geometrically apportioned, clear space. Like Dreyer's film, *Le Tournoi* endows period ironmongery with a curiously modern, functionalist air. Swords, goblets and helmets possess a roundness, a weight, a lived life quite without antiquarianism. As the lovers ride out of the courtyard, a blacksmith seems to be watching over them, and his burly figure locates their idyll in an everyday society with its trades, heirarchies and divisions. The knight on horseback is so cumbersome that he needs his attendant squires to pull his visor down. The duelling with rapier and dagger has a nimble ferocity quite distinct from Fairbanksian swashbuckling, and a briefly first-person camera enables us to be dazzled by Aldo Nadi, an ex-world fencing champion. The acting establishes the appropriate emotions with an informal grace quite different from the stiffness too often offered as period dignity. Although its mythology is now less pleasing, the film has, in terms of its own myths, qualities matching those of the best silent westerns.

15

Tire au Flanc

Tire Au Flanc, made on a low budget, at top speed, directly after *Le Tournoi*, offered Renoir a startling change of style, from academic swashbuckling to something like intermittently poetic farce.

Asked in 1957 whether *Tire Au Flanc* had been a pet project or merely an assignment, Renoir replied, "I don't really remember. I know we were a group of friends who had resolved to work together. Braunberger was in the group. We chose *Tire Au Flanc* because it gave us a chance to do something amusing and which on the other hand would be easy to sell, thanks to the title, which was very well known. I think it's a mistake to allow oneself to embark on any enterprise toward which one is not attracted. But it's also a mistake to want to make a film against all commercial advice. Another very important point in favour of *Tire Au Flanc* was my admiration for a dancer called Pomiès." It was shot at Billancourt Studios with exteriors at the Caserne des Cent Gardes and in the woods nearby.

Like so many of Renoir's films, *Tire Au Flanc* is a master-and-servant story in which a basic friendliness contributes to a thoroughly democratic confusion. When Jean-François d'Ombelles (Pomiès) is obliged to report for military service, his valet Joseph (Michel Simon) is signed up also, to provide him with some shelter from the worst servitudes of military existence. d'Ombelles is gentle, dreamy, absent-minded, a poet (prefiguring characters in *Chotard et Cie, Lange,* and *Le Caporal Epinglé*). He scrapes from one peril to another. While he languishes in the guardroom his fiancée Solange (Jeanne Helbling) falls for the dashing Lieutenant Daumel (Jean Storm). But art and poetry triumph, during the amateur theatricals when the poet, dressed as a satyr, pulverises the company bully (Zellas). All ends happily with Joseph interrupting his own wedding to serve at his master's wedding to his ex-fiancée's sister. Thus Joseph achieves a servility which is unmistakably a triumph not of abjection, but of *métier*—of craft, of art.

The story is little more than pretext for the string of gags and episodes hung on it. The poet, for instance, throws down a banana skin and a few moments later slips on it himself. A critic in *Cinémagazine* for 27 July 1928 objected that the film garbed its comedians in World War I blue rather than the brighter, more picturesque and pacific panoply of *la belle époque*. In skipping through its farcical rhythms, the film constantly stubs its toe on poetry, or on realism, and for a few moments we lurch to a dizzier rhythm. The comic becomes a predicament of grotesque and derisory effort which grips the heart with a pang like beauty. The scene of a patrol stumbling about by broad daylight in open fields completely blinded by their gasmasks has, in its more convulsive, choreographic way, the quality of these philosophical moments of truth to be found in the films of Laurel and Hardy. Often cruelty presides. Languishing in his cell, then frightened by a mouse, Pomiès leaps up the wall, sticking to its stone through fear, but just in time to see, through the high barred window, his own fiancée kissing the lieutenant. The vulgarity of the play's farce is allied with a light melancholy more frequent in France than in Anglo-Saxon countries, where the *Carry On* mode and real feeling tend to sheer off from each other. As Cauliez remarks, the film "represents the watershed between more or less improvised burlesque (Mack Sennett) and the more or less elaborated lyrical caricature (Vigo)."

American achievements have unjustly overshadowed the French slapstick tradition. It can be traced directly from the *Commedia dell'Arte* through Debureau and the French music hall to the early film *cascadeurs* and Max Linder, Chaplin's mentor. The line continues through René Clair, Fernandel,

Jacques Tati, and the current freaky quirks of Louis de Funes. Possibly because we contrast its humanity with all that is deadpan, or slickly or poetically mechanical, in its American counterpart, we tend to relate it a little too closely to dramatic comedy à la Pagnol. Yet it is equally indebted to comedy and farce. Renoir's physical sensitivity owes a good deal to mime, being the link between acting and dance, and his mode of sensitized knockabout and intricate comic plotting (à la Feydeau) facilitates a flexible interaction between genres.

The *temps-mort* appears, to celebrate the eloquence of idleness. Michel Simon, in his first film, relieves the boredom of guard duty with gymnastic exercises, contriving abrupt little twirls on one leg. On fatigues in the square, the poet listlessly picks up the brush and the pan, alternately but never together. Unobtrusively, the garment of reality is coming apart at the seams, and the film takes on an absurdist cast, yet not in quite the same way as the American comics, because, if less classic in its format, it is a warmer, suaver, film.

Truffaut describes its camera movements as "hallucinatingly heroic", but, as in *Nana,* the camera's unleashing is restricted to climaxes and the film's sense of pace owes more to rapid plotting and physical knockabout creating slapstick associations. One can imagine Harry Langdon as the poet. Cauliez sees in Michel Simon's role a parody of (or homage to?) Chaplin, and the film as a faintly documentary satire on army life as well as an accusation of the bourgeoisie. Truffaut pretends to believe that Vigo must have learned *Tire Au Flanc* off by heart before making *Zéro de Conduite,* and implies that the former is to army life as the latter is to college life. For ideological reasons not strictly relevant here, he alleges that it's more antimilitaristic than *Hôtel des Invalides,* although in fact it's no more antimilitaristic than *Carry on Sergeant.*

Leprohon, who finds the film's comedy often laborious and lacking in ease, cites a contemporary *Cinémonde:* "A gaiety you can cut with a knife, and little charm." Yet I would be inclined to paraphrase these very points as descriptions of the film's qualities. The "absence of ease" becomes a grotesquerie interweaving with the tenderness, and the lack of charm is appropriate to that gently, or bracingly, masochistic nostalgic about army ways which afflicts almost all who have been through the mill. It has its fair share of clichés, but also its bursts of inspiration, and comes within an ace of continuously transcending its genre. At any rate it offers an unruly counterpart to Clair's chrono-metro-gnomic silent hilarities. Less perfect, it currently seems far more resistant to the sabotage of time.

Le Bled

Le Bled, a second commission from the *Société des Grands Films Historiques,* was intended to coincide with the centennial commemoration of the "pacification" of Algeria by France. The French government contributed towards its finance. The film was shot during February-March 1929, partly at Joinville Studio, but with extensive location work in Algeria (including the marine station at Algiers, the Bardo gardens, the Plain of Mitidja, and a model farm at Staoveli).

Young Pierre Hoffer (Enrique de Rivero) comes to Algeria from metropolitan France to dun his uncle, Christian, a prosperous settler and farmer. On the voyage over he encounters a young Parisienne, Claudie Duvernet (Jackie Monnier), who is also making the voyage to collect an inheritance. Pierre's uncle shrewdly promises him a substantial sum provided he works with him for six months. Claudie's perfidious cousin Manuel wants to marry her for her fortune. Eventually he takes advantage of a gazelle hunt (on camelback and with greyhounds) to abduct her. By dint of such tactics as leaping from one auto to another at full tilt, Pierre rescues the girl, while the villain is hounded by trained falcons and has his eyes pecked out by them. Pierre and his cousin marry and will no doubt establish their union of the best in Parisian and peasant stock on Algerian soil, thus maintaining the pioneer spirit of the first colonists of 1830.

Le Bled celebrates a colonialism which, after the FLN and the OAS, must appear less uncontroversially modest and agreeable than in its day. All the same it seems less slanted than such British counterparts as *Sanders of the River* or *The Four Feathers.* Here, at least, the villain, as well as the hero, is French. Over and above edifying propaganda (to encourage immigrants from metropolitan France), it proposes a moral parallel to King Vidor's theme of depressed or dessicated city folk finding new vitality in hard work on the land *(Our Daily Bread, Wedding Night).* The film indulges documentary interest, with glimpses of picturesque native customs and settlers' daily routine. The uncle's memoirs also furnish an evocation for such historical episodes as the landing of French troops in the Bay of Sidi Ferruch in 1830.

A parade of nineteenth-century soldiers metamorphoses into ranks of tractors, shot from striking angles reminiscent of Eisenstein's *General Line* (which had not yet been shown in France). In all these respects the film's documentary aspects belong to the older documentary school, of military and civic pageant, rather than the social avant-garde inaugurated in the previous year by Georges Lacombe with *La Zone*.

On its first release the film aroused controversy as to whether its comedy melodramatics à la Douglas Fairbanks rendered it unworthy of its patriotic purpose, or whether they were necessary, to attract a vulgar herd lamentably suspicious of serious and noble sentiment. Jean-Claude Allais sees it as a sad fall from the subjacent anarchism of *Tire Au Flanc*. It is "a colonialist hymn, made to order, which Renoir ingeniously transforms into a Western." Jacques Rivette contrives to see it as altogether non-political, and simply "a joyous allegretto with some graver notes (the love scene, the villain's bloody punishment) in the style of the American cinema of Renoir's youth." *Premier Plan* castigates Renoir for his "frivolous complicity" in French self-satisfaction. Their comparison between this pot-boiler and Vidor's *Hallelujah*, a labour of love, made in the same year, isn't altogether relevant. It may also be that Renoir's much-celebrated anarchism co-exists with a respect for any human enterprise, such that he has been able, quite without violence to his convictions, to appreciate the individualism of the right, albeit only in its more generous aspects, as well as the subversive egalitarianism of the left. Possibly the transmogrification of soldiers into tractors, or swords into ploughshares, was intended as a conciliatory gesture, rather than a mystificatory one.

There are divergent accounts of the film's success, the general French impression seeming to be that that its success was only moderate.

17

Le Petit Chaperon Rouge

Renoir's "private" films are usually bracketed with the French "avant-garde" cinema, of Delluc, Dulac, Epstein and others. And this is fair enough, if "avant-garde" is taken as implying simply a film made outside the usual commercial constraint. But one shouldn't associate Renoir with the avant-garde in the sense of a serious dedication to the advancement of the cinema's frontiers, whether in style, spirituality or subject-matter.

Ironically, his films have dated rather less than most of the efforts by his more narrowly intense contemparies. The freeze frames of *Charleston* are unselfconsciously adventurous. They result from an intimate understanding of visual movement, not from theoretical ideas about what might be cinematographically expressive. The transitions, in *La Petite Marchande d'Allumettes*, between the various modes of stylisation, are perfectly natural, while many of the comparable effects in contemporary avant-garde movies are so stilted and appliqué that they jar on the spectator, smashing a weak illusion before he can laboriously rationalise them back into a kind of second-degree expressiveness.

But now sound tolled the knell of the private sector. Costs rocketed and language fragmented the European market. Along with many other talents, Renoir's professional career was called into question. Of those films intended for the larger public, only *Tire Au Flanc* had been a marked success, while *Nana* and *Le Bled* had more or less disappointed. Renoir's private ventures, capped by the late release of *La Petite Marchande d'Allumettes*, contributed to producers' distrust of him as an erratic, untrustworthy semi-amateur. His visual flair offered no guarantee of his ability to handle the still static microphone, with all its apparently awesome requirements of new professional techniques. It is difficult to tell therefore, whether Renoir's next two private, essays are an amateur's sport, or the product of an unwished-for idleness, or a combination of the two. At any rate, his accomplice was Alberto Cavalcanti, who had already been Catherine Hessling's director. Now Cavalcanti directed husband and wife together, in two short films shot in and around Billancourt Studios in 1929.

Jacques Rivette describes it as "a Sunday *divertissement*, in the line of *Charleston*; that is to say Renoir's Sunday would probably scare any painter who planted his easel in his domaine. The aesthetic is less that of the fairy tale than that of the orgy, the Mack Sennett pursuit regains its association with fauns. Renoir or Cavalcanti? The question is an idle one, and merely to pose it is to settle the matter. Let's say that the one held the camera while the other ran about in the open after Catherine Hessling. He's a bold first cousin to the handsome hussar in *La Petite Marchande,* and finally carries her off in a ballon, by the seat of her pantaloons." The film was fleetingly shown with sound-on-disc.

La P'tite Lili

Although its date is sometimes given as 1927, *La P'tite Lili* (300 metres) would seem to be *Le Petit Chaperon's* late twin. Again produced by Pierre Braunberger, and directed by Cavalcanti, it described itself as "a tragedy on packing paper." Renoir played a Malabar sailor, and Cavalcanti a pimp. The film was probably more of a visual accompaniment to a long popular song than a film accompanied by a song. (Renoir's love of popular songs, street-music and mechanical instruments recurs in *La Chienne*, in *La Règle du Jeu*, in *French Can-Can*). Noted for its "let's pretend" sets and conspicuously gauzed-over photography, it seems to have been at once a parody and an affectionate reminiscence of soft-focus movie romance, whether (as Bardèche and Brasillach suggest) Hollywood-style, or (as Pierre Philippe suggests) Renoir's own *Une Vie Sans Joie* and *La Fille de L'Eau*. Brunius describes it rather differently: "the use of cloth with a very coarse weave gave the photography the texture of a painting on canvas". The London Film Society Programme notes feel the effect evokes an embroidered sampler.

According to *Cahiers*, it was meant to be shown at the Ursulines Ciné-Club, with the audience joining in the song, as they were often invited to do in popular halls, where the words were flashed on the screen as they still are in children's matinées. One might describe it as affectionate satire, rather like Eisenstein's *Romance Sentimentale*.

19

Die Jagd Nach Dem Gluck
(A la Chasse à la Fortune)
(Running After Luck)

1929 saw a third acting role by Renoir, playing a businessman in a now somewhat shadowy enterprise with Catherine Hessling and Berthold Bartosch. Its theme was the life of a travelling salesman. It was directed, successively, or (who knows?) simultaneously, by Lotte Reiniger, Karl Koch and Rochus Gliese. If it was ever finished, it was either never shown or shown once only in Berlin early in 1930. So far as Renoir knows, it no longer exists. The London Film Society showed a five-minute silhouette "interlude" from it in 1930.

On Purge Bébé

At this time, Renoir's career seemed to many critics in a sad decline from poetic promise to inexpert commercialism. He was already anxious to shoot *La Chienne*, based on a novel by Jean de la Fouchardière. But nearly two years passed (during which time, in 1930, he and Catherine Hessling were separated) before a film was offered him, and then it was very much of a hack job, obtained thanks to his old friend Pierre Braunberger. Braunberger had formed a company with Roger Richebé, bought the studios at Billancourt, and re-equipped them for sound. Richebé had to be convinced that Renoir could work rapidly enough to justify *La Chienne*, and: "My first sound film was in the nature of an examination. I managed to get the assignment of shooting *On Purge Bébé*, adapted from Feydeau."

The scenario of *On Purge Bébé* was written inside one week. Shooting took either four or six days in July 1931 (Renoir giving different figures in different interviews) at the rate of 30 or 40 shots a day. In six days the film was edited down from over 2,000 metres to 1,700, and its Paris premiere took place in August, 14 days after shooting ended. The film cost 200,000 francs, recovered its cost during the first week's showing, and rapidly earned its producer well over a million francs.

Possibly the aptest British title would be *Carry on Potting*. A M. Follavoine (Louvigny), a porcelain manufacturer, tries to clinch a deal for supplying 200,000 chamber pots to the French Army. On the domestic front, or rather flank, his wife (Marguerite Pierry) tries to purge their obstinately constipated son. The contract depends on their luncheon guest (Michel Simon), whom the wife cajoles into taking the purge to show her son how easy and pleasant it is.

For obvious reasons, *On Purge Bébé* is not the most admired of Feydeau's farces. Nonetheless the obsessive purpose which is the mainspring of its comic inventiveness evokes a Ben Jonson comedy with an amusing scatological and satiric edge. The exchanges between the fussy, humourless manufacturer and his beautiful, slatternly wife, who trails about the house

in curlers and negligée and petulantly sits on a pail of dirty water while steering the conversation round to matters sanitary, are really a contrast between the norms of socio-economic order (husband/breadwinner/pater-familias) and the loopy lurchings of human nature (the wife). One might expect to sympathise with the husband, so put upon by his disorderly, anally obsessive spouse. Yet in the event his correctness is far less fetching than the disorder with which his wife disorganises bourgeois routines. If she discusses the matter at length, publicly and in such a manner as to disrupt the function-ings of the entire household, thus turning the drawing room and the dining room into spiritual antechambers of the lavatory, it is by way of a feminine and poetically appropriate retaliation against the masculine *hubris* implicit in the military side of the plot. After all, the notion of 20,000 chamberpots being supplied for use in military barracks has an apocalyptic dottiness all of a piece with the husband's flair for expensive rhetorical flourishes, the specimen pot waved aloft at the end of an eloquent arm. An apparent order is undermined by the son's obstinacy, the wife's drunkenness, the servants (representing a sub-bourgeois style) and the guests' common-sense hedonism. The last scene confirms the secret complicity between mother and son against an imposed order.

It may well be that Feydeau was attuned to a scurrilous popular in-sight into the connection described by Freud between anal eroticism and such character traits as orderliness, punctuality, thrift, humourlessness and rigidity. Just these qualities loom large in the Puritan traits which R.H. Tawney describes in *Religion and the Rise of Capitalism*. Gordon Rattray-Taylor also indicates some such connections in the course of his intriguing attempt to attribute conspicuous aspects of the changing English character to changing methods of child-rearing between the 18th and 19th centuries. With an even closer relevance, J. A. C. Brown suggests that it was not until the 20th century that typically modern strictness about toilet training became the norm in the home, and that most Victorian families were far more easy-going in this respect than we. One should add that the 20th-century French bourgeoisie has been more addicted than the easier-going English middle-classes to the use of enemas, colonic lavage, vaginal douches, and so on.

French intellectuals were for a long time noticeably less influenced by Freud than their Anglo-Saxon equivalents (possibly because *either* they disposed of a less conspicuously inadequate rationalism, *or* because attention was monopolised by the Surrealists' romantic version of Freudian theory). The Anglo-Saxon critic and the post-Lacanian Marxist may now feel free to enjoy the film aware of the spiritual overtones of its pediatric anomalies. The film pleases in the same way as various anatomical jests of Tashlin's. If it's by no means a classic, it happily and hilariously demonstrates the curious veracity-in-absurdity of entertainment genres when permeated by a lively style. The microphone dominates its solitary set and anchors the characters in space, although Renoir's penchant for long shots does add a visual dimension to the verbal. Speed of shooting doubtless explains the small number of close-ups (less than ten). Renoir, against resistance, gave Fernandel his first screen role, as the cousin.

La Chienne

Though *On Purge Bébé* was hardly of Renoir's choosing, it seems to bridge the motifs dominating his first and second creative periods. Like the silent subjects (even the assignments), it immerses itself within a private, local world—whether village *(La Fille de L'Eau)*, the fairytale *(La Petite Marchande d'Allumettes)*, the myth of chivalry *(Le Tournoi)* or agricultural diligence *(Le Bled)*. *Nana* is further from Marx than Zola, and criticizes the social temptations to inauthenticity rather than social structure *per se*. *Charleston* indicates how far his films work on a level of a *truquage*, a virtually Symbolist figuring-forth of subjective passion and vission. All these films offer their creator a chance to experiment with a multiplicity of lyrical worlds-within-the-world, and to accept each on its own terms. The star who dominates this period, Catherine Hessling, incarnates its demiurge or muse, with her split second changes of mood, her devastating whimsicality, her artifice and spontaneity conjoined as poetic "sport", as exuberance of life-force.

On Purge Bébé inaugurates Renoir's dominant theme throughout the early 30's. This is the relationship between the bourgeois order and a disorder which is sometimes freedom, sometimes chaos.

Produced by the Braunberger-Richebé team, *La Chienne* was shot partly at Billancourt Studios but also extensively on location. "I made the film with no concern whatever for the producers' desiderata. I never showed a single portion of my rough cut or the least scrap of dialogue, and I made arrangements for the rushes to be all but invisible until the end of shooting. And that was when the scandal burst. The producer expected a comedy and found himself watching a sombre, desperate drama whose only attraction was a murder which was by no means agreeable according to the taste of the time.

"I was chased out of the studio, and in particular the cutting rooms, and as every day I tried to get in, the police were sent for. Once the producer had pieced together the version he wanted, he realised that it wouldn't work and that, having lost either way, he might as well let me manage my way. I got back into my cutting room and could more or less repair the damage." The film was premièred at Nancy early in November 1931 and in Paris on the 19th.

The story which might have been a comedy but became a drama centres on a dull, loose-mouthed cashier, Legrand (Michel Simon). He is the butt of his fellow clerks and his hectoring wife (Magdeleine Bérubet) never allows him to forget how mean a figure he cuts beside her first husband, regularly referred to as "the Adjutant". Legrand experiences some sort of moral awakening when this mythical character actually turns up, not dead after all, groping around the flat to filch the nestegg which their wife has hidden away. When Legrand comes across a shady character knocking a girl about in the street he impulsively, and successfully, intervenes, for which he is rewarded by a sound scolding from Lulu, the damsel in distress (Janie Maréze). Falling in love with her, he follows his predecessor's example and begins to embezzle sums from the bank, so as to set her up in an apartment. He decorates it with the paintings to which she has inspired him. He never suspects her continuing relationship with her ponce, Dédé (George Flament). When Legrand's canvases begin to enjoy a certain vogue in artistic circles, Dédé

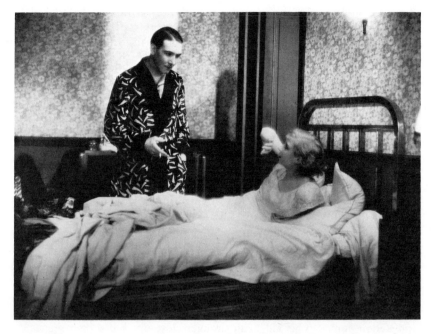

persuades her to pose as the artist, "Clara Wood". Eventually Legrand, realising her infidelities, murders her. Dédé is condemned to the guillotine for the crime. Legrand keeps his silence, and becomes a tramp. A self-portrait of "Clara Wood" is taken from an art gallery and carefully placed in the back of a shining limousine. Legrand is more interested in grabbing for a stray cigarette end in the gutter.

The character of Legrand is composed in layers. He is: (a) a crushed, nagged, browbeaten innocent; (b) a quiet, gifted, secretive Sunday painter, à la *Moon and Sixpence;* (c) a slyly resourceful crimnal; (d) a passionate murderer; (e) a callous cheat; (f) a masochist. Michel Simon imbues a character, who, on script level, remains somewhat theoretical, with a barbed life: reedy, quavering, suppressed, his cravenness is the apotheosis of what Orwell calls the "shabby genteel". Dutiful, fearful, a pilot light of malice burns dully behind his lowered and evasive eyes.

A similar counterpoint rules the character of Lulu, who is far from being merely the "bitch" of the film's title. She loves her ponce maternally, sending him off to the café to brag to his cronies with a wistful "Don't drink too much, it makes you ill." If she wheedles Legrand's money out of him, it is in a curious tentative way, as if she would like him to bully her just a little. She pretends to believe he would no more mind her having a more exciting lover than a father would mind his favourite daughter having a virile young sweetheart, and that her deceit is merely shyness. Such "bad faith", congenial to a certain feminine style, is neither altogether unkind, nor illogical. Leprohon points to her affinites with Séverine in *La Bête*

Humaine, whose deceitfulness is not the product of perfidy only but of its conjunction with a wistful desire to soften, to protect. Lulu is a vamp by virtue of Legrand's weakness; she is a gold digger by virtue of her ponce's urgings. She is still in many ways a "little woman": she shows off her fine new bath and geyser to a friend, in which respect she's much like any semi-detached suburban Mrs. Jones. Lying in bed with her *mec*, she discusses their *"petites economies"* like any young housewife. If there is crime behind the shabby genteel, there is a modest gentility behind crime. Brunius: "Her accent, her intonations were for a Parisian those of a half-refined suburban cockney, as spoken by a restaurant waitress. It must have been natural; I have never heard any actress do it so perfectly. Perhaps I should add that French actors are generally far from being so good at accents as English actors are. These are details, perhaps. But at a time when every word uttered in a French talking film sounded like a false note, it was no mean achievement."

As the young pimp-cum-ponce-cum-gigolo, Georges Flamart catches the bullying and vulnerabilities of the type with a rare authenticity. Renoir clearly cherishes his realism, often, it seems, for its own sake, and watches him from afar, passively, like a television cameraman who isn't altogether sure what will happen next, or which gesture he should emphasis. Often, the dramatic stress is weakened, a little, until, at last, Dédé is fully dramatically involved, and Renoir comes to his aid, with stronger close-ups and shorter scenes.

But Renoir's game is given away by the cutaways of a café waiter, who serves customers blankly. He seems neither to play his role, nor to be elsewhere. He is simply nowhere, a craftsman *in vacuo*. He is a bleak counterpart of the mechanical figurines and puppets which recur in Renoir's work (including this film's credits). During several studies in *La Chienne* of men talking in cafés, the long takes concentrate on the talker, to the neglect of the listener. Despite the cumbersome sound equipment of the epoque, the cinéma-vérité effect often recalls Léaud's confession to the unseen psychologist in the TV-influenced sequence of *Les 400 Coups*. The characters talk into space, into a non-responsiveness, perhaps scepticism, perhaps misunderstanding. Attempts at communication are left to hang in social space, echoing the deep deceptions from which the storyline is woven. In *La Chienne* Renoir develops his interest, initiated in *Tire Au Flanc*, in the *temps-mort*. The waiter is bored. A girl practises the piano in a room over the way. A military band conductor puts his heart and soul into his art. A crowd listens to a sentimental song while, in a squalid room, a dreadful sexual reckoning proceeds. The syntax is that of ironic counterpoint, a traditional dramatic device. Yet the effect is just a little more disruptive. Periodically the film floats off at oblique angles to itself, seems to slip through one's fingers. It can no more be summarised than Michel Simon's fantastic assemblage of features, which make his every expression a multitude of expressions. In the middle of a conversation a man turns, distracted by the sound of a mechanical piano. Consciousness, mind, life is a network of just such ruptures.

As Legrand takes a step towards his moral emancipation, the camera shows him shaving by a window opening out onto a courtyard. Beyond the court-yard a little girl practises her piano pieces (*moderato cantabile*, no doubt). Thus his confined space opens. His "corruption" is an integrity like her innocence. They are two artists together (yet unknowing). This doubleness, not to say duplicity, of composition might tempt one to comparisons with certain canvasses of Masaccio, or even with Renaissance painting, insofar as a struggle with the technicalities of perspective corresponds to a struggle with the technicalities of focus. Film is still, after all, in its primitive era. At any rate, the film constantly plays the cramped, subdivided space of apartment and office interiors against scenes where space is loose (the café, the street) and can flow freely.

In the shot of Legrand and the girl beyond the courtyard, the spatial contrast is underlined by a change of focus, from Legrand to the girl, within the shot. Brunius explains: "Renoir was trying to achieve what the technical equipment of the time made most difficult; he was trying to reintroduce the use of depth. In the days of the silent film, arclights were used in the studios and strong lighting allowed cameramen to use the full depth of focus for their lenses, allowing different actions to be seen at varied distances. But arcs were very noisy and could not be used with sound. Hence two technical innova-tions which are closely related: incandescent lamps for lighting, and the generalised use of panchromatic emulsions. With a much smaller amount of light, new lenses came into fashion, with wider apertures and different chromatic correction. In 1931 the lenses used in French studios were mostly the German-made Tascher, very wide aperture, but giving very poor defini-tion. Even the objects which were supposed to be in focus appeared soft. The foreground and the background were hardly visible at all. This gave birth to an extensive use of tracking shots, necessitated not by the action but by the infirmity of the lenses. Actors could not move without going out of focus, so the camera had to follow. These circumstances did not at all suit Renoir's style of direction. In spite of the technical limitations, Renoir managed to show us the little girl. The depth of focus was poor, compared with that enjoyed previously by directors of silent films, or with that achieved since, but the attempt was there, and one can recognise it in most subsequent Renoir films, in *Toni,* in *Partie de Campagne* (slightly shaded foreground on sunlit backgrounds), in *La Règle du Jeu.* When I read after Citizen Kane that the invention of depth of focus was credited to Orson Welles and Gregg Toland, I could only laugh at the ignorance of my fellow critics. There are now better lenses, that is all." Renoir's shift of focus in the course of a shot is not unique for its time, but the audacity of Renoir's effect lies in its being so conspicuous, at a time when the entire ethics of movie craftmanship were dedicated to preserving an uninterrupted immediacy of illusion and when audiences were less accustomed to acknowledging that the illusion was also a picture.

Brunius' account of the technical genesis of a style explains the flossiness of early '30s French movies, as well as the remarkable camera mobility of the epoch, a mobility curiously unnoticed by historians and theoreticians. It also demonstrates how conspicuously opposite aesthetic forms—(a) static composition in depth, and (b) very fluid camera—may also be functional equivalents, and that shifts of style must be related to technical epoch as well as to individual styles. Renoir's interest is clearly in preserving the maximal freedom for his actors, and actions, continuous in relationship in time and in space. Just as the vast depths of field in *Nana* are penetrated at particular moments by sensational trackings, so the "tunnel effect" of tracking and panning is here counterpointed by "open fields".

Like *Boudu* later, *La Chienne* features a short prologue. A fairground barker announces: "Ladies and gentlemen, you are about to see a great social drama—a comedy with moral tendencies!" Fairground barkers are not renowned for their truthfulness, or their puritanism, and no doubt Renoir reckoned that the audience would at least suspect the prologue of irony. If the film is not to be taken tragically, is it because Legrand, although ruined, is also freed? Or is it because life is intrinsically a cruel nothing-very-much, as Céline at about the same time was insisting? The *temps-morts* maintain the same ambivalence: the girl at the piano for innocence, or freedom, or a victim of lessons; the waiter for another kind of self-effacing dexterity, or tyranny; the bar's mechanical piano for caprice and fate. Legrand's preoccupation with cigarette ends concludes a tragi-comedy of myopias, of temperaments which are absurd if are closed to one another and tragic if opened to one another.

The subject was well timed. In Germany, from *The Street* (1921) to *The Blue Angel* (1933), the difficulties of the lower middle class had favoured the theme of the respectable little man ruined by a vamp (voluptuous wish fulfilment surrogate for economic forces). This may explain why Bardeche and Brasillach postulate an influence on Renoir from German expressionism. It certainly climaxes the blackness which Renoir indulges more often than recent writing about him suggests: in *La Chienne, La Petite Marchande d'Allumettes, La Nuit du Carrefour, La Bête Humaine, Woman on the Beach* and in certain motifs (the death of animals) in other films. From, or through, *La Chienne,* one can indeed trace the evolution of the *film noir* (if that genre is given a narrow definition as a realistic thriller with overtones of visionary pessimism). Its success initiated the 20-year French cycle which involves such names as Carné-Prévert, Duvivier, Clouzot, René Clement and Yves Allegret. An American cycle begins about ten years later and includes such remakes of French productions as *Scarlet Street* (of *La Chienne*), *The 13th Letter* (of Le Corbeau), *The Long Night* (of *Le Jour Se Lève*) and *Human Desire* (of *La Bête Humaine*). Fritz Lang's remake of *La Chienne, Scarlet Street,* is a study in conscious guilt: Renoir's suggests an implacable punishment for a socially instilled weakness of character. In the French film Legrand is caught both ways (by a strident harpy, by a soft-voiced siren; by

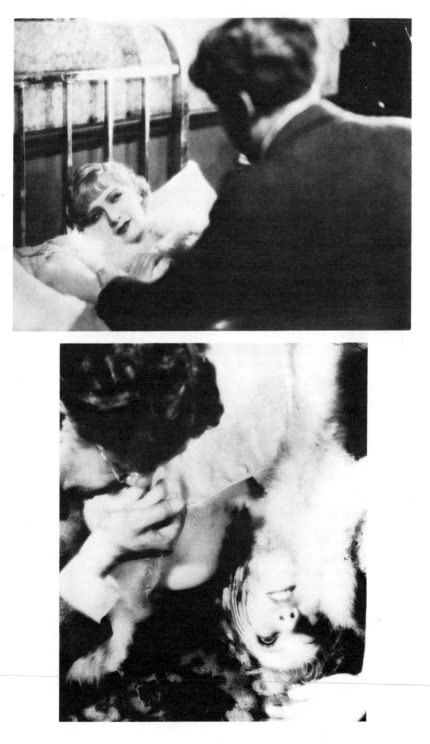

matrimony, by attempted escape; by respectability, by degradation). Lang's metallic, almost architectural fatalism contrasts with the "process of dis-aggregation" (Leprohon) which Renoir's softer style imputes to the tragedy.

The film may evoke the literary lowlife melancholies of an earlier avant-garde—notably Delluc's *Fièvres*. Relevant as they are, the livelier affinity seems to be with of its own period's film populism. Certainly a line can be traced from *Fièvres* to *Quai des Brumes*. But Renoir's film, like Carné-Prévert's, belongs alongside such films as *Lonesome* and *Street Scene* from America, *L'Atalante* and *Le Quatorze Juillet* (with its senseless shootings; and its mechanical piano), from France, and *Asphalte* and *Berlin-Alexander-platz* from Germany. (It is also extremely unkind to the dealers, middlemen and fashionables of the fine art racket, a theme of Renoir's which will recur. Crooks abound at every social, intellectual and artistic level).

In its parti-pris of realism, *La Chienne* has often been considered as a pre-cursor of neo-realism. And so perhaps it is. Nonetheless Renoir is following a current of his time. A French avant-garde had already moved into a "docu-mentary" phase, with such films as Georges Lacombe's *La Zone* (1928), Jean Epstein's *Finis Terrae* (1929) (in which he used no professional actors and no sets), Marcel Carné's *Nogent Eldorado du Dimanche* (1929) and Jean Vigo's *A Propos de Nice*. Renoir's originality lay in the conscious linking of location realism with a plot whose springs were psychological and internal. It looks forward not to the "semi-documentary", like *Man of Aran*, but to *A Bout de Souffle*.

In the long run, the advent of sound had its compensations. The talkies had given the French film industry a language barrier against American dumping, and the spoken word enabled it to thrust deep new roots into France's rich literary and dramatic culture. The war had enfeebled the French industry (which until 1914 had dominated the world market and even the American scene) and bled it of most of its potential talent. Hollywood, seizing its economic advantage, had developed a flair for pleasing the mass audience which, from 1918, Europe's more class-bound producers found hard to match. That early resonance with popular taste possessed by Méliès, Zecca and Feuillade, was not retrieved till young talents like Renoir, greatly influenced by the American cinema, had been forced away from the avant-garde (with all its temptations to preciousness), into the entertainment industry, where many galling concessions became necessary, but where it also became possible to hit upon an important confluence of high- and low-brow tastes.

Before World War I, the Surrealistists-to-be had admired the pulp poetry of Fantomas; soon Apollinaire and Cocteau praised the poetry of Westerns. Intellectuals and popular audiences alike relished a certain mixture of anarchism, populism, and scandal, and detested middle-class, middle-brow uplift. From the Russians, and especially the Americans, the French at last learned efficient, organic cutting, yet without making of speed and action a Procrustean bed for their own humanism.

With *La Chienne* Renoir had hit on just this mixture of ingredients which was to prove the passkey for the French film-maker. In a sense it was an aesthetic reaction, a move backwards to the 19th-century novel, with its concern for psychological consistency-in-depth, its sense of social context. But it was also a move towards the cultural mainstream. Whether this particular subject, at this time, put out "cold," would have attracted a public capable of recognising its coalescence of attractions, and cultures, remains doubtful. But the producer was able to exploit the public's appetite for scandal, and its immense commercial success was a potent influence on the French cinema.

Encouraged by the success of *La Chienne,* Renoir and Michel Simon hoped to find backing for a film of *Hamlet,* to be played, by Michel Simon, as a man plagued by indecision. But *La Chienne* didn't end Renoir's difficulties with the industry. Most of the critics of the era found *La Chienne* distressingly vulgar, and André Brunelin summarises Renoir's "brand image" at the time.

On the one hand, he was the *"auteur mal aimé,"* regarded with suspicion by the trade; on the other hand, he was the facile professional on whom—until *La Chienne*—one could rely to shoot a sellable quickie in a few days. Renoir's backers were rarely philanthropists, and more often than not Renoir productions proved to be a case of the backer backing out, after Renoir had first seduced him and then led him to advance his capital. "Then Renoir finished his film somehow, with any means to hand, borrowing wherever he could. We know how this type of artisanship characterised the French cinema of this period, giving it some beautiful works, sometimes ill-assembled, but which distilled that double perfume now vanished—simplicity and liberty." Of which atmosphere, Renoir's next film distils the quintessence.

Later, Renoir attributed the renaissance of the French cinema to the advent of sound. ". . . there was a sudden and magical transformation. It was as if someone had opened a secret door communicating between the film-maker and the audience. It was a great feeling. Everything we did the audience understood. The French cinema would not have made those enormous strides towards maturity without this wonderfully receptive audience."

La Nuit du Carrefour

Shot between January-March 1932 and premiered in April, *La Nuit du Carrefour* was the first film from a Simenon novel—narrowly, for Duvivier and Jean Taride both set to later in the year. The novelist signed Renoir's scenario, and Leprohon cites publicity material of the period, according to which Simenon had intended to direct the film himself but in the event assigned the direction, "par amitié", to Jean Renoir, while continuing to supervise the film closely himself.

The unit—or team—spent three weeks on location at a crossroads near Bouffémont, 25 kilometres north of Paris. After a run of bad weather, they beat a retreat to the studios at Billancourt. "As always with Renoir", wrote André Brunelin, "it was a business of make do and mend. Decor had to be made out of anything at hand, it was all painting and knock-up."

One Sunday morning an insurance agent, M. Michonnet (Jean Gehret), goes to his garage—and finds, not his bright new six-cylinder, but the little 5 h.p. car belonging to the mysterious pair (Carl Andersen and his sister Else) who live in seclusion in a nearby mansion. He complains to the police, and on his return he finds his own car once more, with a corpse slumped at its steeringwheel. A few hours later, the police arrest Carl Andersen (Georges Koudria) in Paris. Commissioner Maigret (Pierre Renoir) interrogates him but to no avail.

The dead man turns out to be one Goldberg, an Amsterdam dealer in precious stones. Maigret prowls about the garage, the bistro, and the two or three houses shivering in the misty fields around the dank crossroads. He suspects everyone in turn: Andersen, even Michonnet, and Else Anderson (Winna Winfried), of whom her brother seems strangely fearful. When Madame Goldberg is brought by the police to try and identify any suspects, she too is shot and killed by a hidden assassin. After the discovery of a hoard of drugs, and the intervention of the Parisian underworld, the mysteries are finally cleared up; at least to the satisfaction of the characters, although not necessarily to that of the spectators. Jean Mitry was rumoured to have lost three reels of the film after shooting. Renoir, when asked to confirm the rumour, replied, "It's possible, but even at the time, you know, it wasn't very clear. I don't think anyone of us understood anything. Least of all me."

Comprehensibility is no *sine qua non* of the detective story. In theory, certainly, a final explanation is mandatory. But in the cinema the "classic" detective story hardly exists, being replaced by the thriller, which depends much less on any intellectual puzzle than on suspense (melodrama), psychology (drama), and/or atmosphere (poetry). The cinema spectator, overwhelmed with audiovisual information and unable to check back for clues and discrepancies, is quite content to give up the intellectual ghost and turn from deduction to narrative for his satisfaction. Hence Hitchcock, so expert in and emphatic about the need for clarification of the mystery, treats it as an abstraction: the McGuffin.

Renoir's film certainly breaks Hitchcock's categorical imperative as to clarity. But other satisfactions are available. Godard suggests that Renoir "validates the otherwise somewhat theoretical equation, Simenon = Dostoievski + Balzac, and makes of Simenon another Balzac." Yet this film is quite void of Dostoievskian theology, and seems to immerse itself in atmosphere. Along with its contemporary, Dreyer's *Vampyr,* another purely perfunctory "mystery", its *Stimmung* is inspired by location. Where Dreyer's is a film of mists, moonlight and flour (photographic whites), Renoir's is a film of fog, night and rain (photographic blacks). In both films even suspense is soft-pedalled. A hand slips two bottles of poisoned beer through a window, but this echo of Fantômas is neither melodramatic nor Surrealist. It is, rather, an abrupt modulation of the confusion. Boldly composed shots seem veiled, clogged, muffled by the obscure osmosis of mist and night, of headlamps blurrily staring through rain, of strained-for sounds beyond a wall. This road is the Renoir river of uncertainty, but in its spiritually sinister guise. Though this was the epoch of shallow focus, there is little reverse-angling; Renoir works over the limit of focus, and the resultant softness and the black foreground silhouettes recall coagulations of tenebrous air.

The film smells of wet earth, of oiled metal, of woodsmoke and manure, of the sulky stove which Maigret has to coax. In the penultimate automobile pursuit, the camera watches an almost choreographed landscape slide past, not in crabbing shot only, but slewing, as the roadsters take the curves, from crabbing through panning to tracking shot, in which cuts quietly detonate. We recall the elaborate studio "rides" of Murnau, but with the warmth and diversity of real rural France.

"Atmosphere" is sometimes assumed to be a merely superficial quality, but it arises from an amalgam of sensuous experience and poetic reminiscence; a balance of feelings, not an absence of them. And balance implies structure. The film is impregnated with air, light, liquid, stone, fabric and flesh. A limousine interior is illuminated in night space; its city plushness contrasts with our sense of the fields. The mist and the rain conjoin the themes of liquid and air. Each element has its poisons (an inflated inner tube reveals cocaine, which Maigret sniffs; beer is laced with veronal). Else lies between bleak walls, on a bearskin, her elegant dress concealing underwear whose grubbiness reminds us of Nana's. The contrast matches, in a voluptuous key, the more frugal one of clear water and gutters. Air, as the wind of speed, is conspicuous in the automobile pursuit. The film rewards a structuralism of sensuousness as surely as Pasolini's *Teorema*. Its internal, psychic elements are the eerie continuity between sleep, drugs, delirium and dying; and the contrast between a diffuse yet pervasive ignorance, and the passive, roving acuity of Maigret. The events seem not so much committed by the characters as exuded by them, like sweat, or by the atmosphere like rain.

Of all its director's films, *La Nuit du Carrefour* is the clearest visual transposition of Agel's intuition: that at the centre of Renoir's generous vision loom the "swirlings of a fundamental nothingness, a state of *becomings,* a no-man's-land as unreassuring as the universe of dreams." For all its "location realism", it comes near to a vision of man condemned to confront the enigmas of man, of society as a melancholy, suspicious and always only provisional assemblage of shades in some strange purgatory or limbo.

Its poetry distilled from the everyday enlivens, fulfills, and complicates that of an earlier mood-piece, Delluc's *Fièvres*. It observes man, weather and idleness in those sombre moods with which impressionism, apart from

Courbet and Degas, is relatively sparing. One might almost say that it took the "poetic realism" of the French cinema of the '30s to fill the gap between impressionism in painting and realism in literature (Zola, Maupassant). Renoir comments: "After all, reality is always magic. In order to render reality non-fantastic, certain authors have to take a great deal of trouble to present it as really bizarre. But if you leave it as it is, it's magic." One remembers the comments of Franju, another "meteorological realist", on car headlights fanning through trees, and his remark that "film-makers always leave too soon." One remembers also the two cars in the same garage in *Les Yeux Sans Visage*. The similar theme arises less, one suspects, from any special affinity of temperament, than from the way in which two directors have tapped a vein of that poetry which exists before, and sometimes without, the poets who enshrine it.

The film's mysterious, almost hypnagogic, atmosphere may lull one into drowsy acquiescence, at least until Else's bizarre combination of Danish nationality, English accent and Russian eroticism reminds one just how many of these characters aren't essentially inhabitants of the hamlet at all. A Danish couple, a Dutch Jewish couple, two Parisian detectives, a gang from Pigalle: so many people are merely passing through, like the automobiles swishing through the rain.

There is more to this Maigret than his neat moustache, his smooth contented expression, his ample overcoat, his intermittent air of a salesman who has suddenly become Managing Director. Just a little less of Pierre Renoir and he would be the perfect Citroën owner of pre-war advertisements, the epitome of "middle France", of bourgeois selfsatisfaction. This social projction into his facial expression is not just a trick of the light, for his assistant is a humbler image of the same general ethos, class and system. And he, too, is the hero of a shot in which he plods precisely along the dead centre of the low apex of the gentle camber of an endless road, umbrella raised against the pouring rain, his rectitude and diligence as modest and as touching as a dog's. There is a third member of the same social class: Michonnet, whose characteristic rhythm is a kind of shifty darting, his greasy little bulk oddly permeated with all the alacrity of a rodent opportunism as he concocts and bungles all his sneaky devilments; his concealed firearm, his poisoned beerbottles, the clumsily mistimed strangulation attempt glimpsed through a balustrade. He is mainly kept scuttling about in the middle distance or beyond, secretly responsible for much of the action. The victims of the murders for which, with rancid xenophobia, he strives to throw suspicion on "those foreigners", are two Dutch Jews. His intended third victim is Else, the film's social "chameleon"; a foreign demi-mondaine, she is of all nations, classes, characters, and none.

He also tries to frame Carl, the Dane with a black monocle and Germanic-language accent, clipped and yet wavering, dismissing with aristocratic *hauteur* the first murder victim as "that little Jew". He is reminiscent of a Prussian. He is a Dane like the Vietnamese are Red Indians.

Another *haute bourgeois*, the stately surgeon, descends from his limousine in top hat and tails with an imposing solemnity which springs from the fact that his professional dignity, and dutifulness, are exerting themselves against the physical instability of inebriation. Two characters in overalls come from lower in the social scale. M. Oscar is apparently the garage's senior mechanic, a self-made, skilled manual worker. His sensitive hands are rendered conspicuous by his concertina playing. The upward flourish of both of his hands is strangely ambiguous, as between a café-conc' elegance and a veiled insolence. Is it copied from the music hall? Has he a performer's heart under his oily overalls? This strange hieroglyph is enough to make him other than what he seems. A little edge of faery makes him somewhat unreal, and frightening, particularly when he follows his wistful playing with a bitter tirade against society. Young Jojo is a lazy, feckless rascal whose cheek is at first engaging but who is more crooked than he seems and, when cornered, parades a second-skin insolence which never earns our respect.

Eventually also a clutch of crooks, some in cloth caps, some in evening dress, come rushing from Pigalle to attend this bizarre congress. They think they're Chicago gansters, or at least they've just seen *Scarface*, for they shoot up the garage from a passing car à la Capone. The gendarmes who take the call are grouped between two posters which appear to be recruiting for the militia and exude a patriotic confidence in the law.

Nonetheless, the forces of human order are put in their place against forces far greater. Instead of making much of the exhilarations of Bugattis and revolvers, Renoir stresses the difficulties of aiming from a jolting automobile, the smack of the slipstream in the faces. Even the revolver shots take on a derisory popping sound. The wind of speed strangely becomes a matter of nature's latent energies braved by man, rather than a by-product of speed. Mechanisms, conquering nature, only provoke from her infinite resources an equal and opposite reaction. The play of headlights on stones, trees, ditches, ploughed and furrowed earth, renders the intercity highway passive to the contour and lie of the land.

George Altmann stresses that Maigret solves the crime by his human, and humane, sensitivity, his quiet inquisitiveness, and not by the third degree, nor by impersonal or scientific techniques, nor by some such stereotype as the convenient meanness of "the" criminal mind, or the mills of God, or fate or poetic justice.

Premeditatedly or otherwise, this crossroads is that of many classes. The little garage is itself a cross between industrial and agricultural France. Thus it is, so to speak, the heartland of France. And here a variety of middle-and-lower-class characters confront one another, as well as that world of international high finance of which the French "little man" had long been so resolutely suspicious. The massacre of the Goldbergs is curiously prophetic of the field day which, between 1940 and 1945, was to be enjoyed by that covert but extraordinarily resilient French anti-semitism. And Maigret nearly

loses out to the most sneakily persistent of all the suspects, Michonnet, that is, the *other* "middle France".

One criminal enjoys, and that's the word, a special position. The deceptive Else enfolds several worlds within herself. During her first interview with a still unsuspecting Maigret, the camera dwells on a gramophone horn over a heavy stone fireplace, with a washing ewer nearby. Three emphatic emptinesses visually surround Maigret who is spatially isolated from his attractive interlocuter. This loneliness symbol contrasts with three highly decorative, equally isolated objects. The first is Else herself. The second is a giant tortoise with a decorated shell, which must recall des Esseintes, the exhausted dandy of Huysmans' Symbolist *A Rebours* (usually, in English, *Against Nature*, or *Against the Grain*). The third is a music box. Music boxes echo the infantry automata of *La Petite Marchande d'Allumettes*. They have the innocence of infancy. Like childhood stories, they repeat exactly, faithfully, their poignant stereotypes. Like children they are helpless. Their naive vivacity is all the more beautiful for being at once as nostalgic as the past which they evoke, for being at once dainty and dispassionate. In Renoir's films they recur, and at climaxes, particularly *crimes passionels*. That music box is Else's cover story; a *ritournelle* of innocence. But it tells Maigret more: of her nostalgia.

The lazy, ornamental, useless tortoise, a familiar childhood pet in exotic form, preludes Maigret's entry into her second world. Else, sensitized by a craving like nymphomania, has appreciated in Maigret something firm, kind, fatherly and approving, and now she receives him, lying on a bearskin rug

close to the floor. The long line of buttons on her dress catch the light, like gems, and diffusely recall another reptile, the crocodile, in piquant contrast with her soft mammalian warmth and docile ways. Her manner betrays a depressed indecision, a kind of abandonment, so that we hardly know whether she hopes to tease or placate or deceive or make some more meaningful contact with this man. Maigret recognises the would-be vamp as only a woman so nervous that to have the self-respect which she craves and which, despite herself, she deserves, she needs a man who will gently but firmly go through the motions of being her master. The theme of "damaged goods" continues with her revelation of the bullet-hole in her body, and Maigret's exposé of her unsavoury past, an exposé which, politely brutal in style, reveals its extenuating undercurrents. She is its victim, as of her own love for her first husband.

Else is the axis of two of Renoir's most quietly atrocious anecdotes. Her pretended brother is actually her second husband, and though bravely surviving the policemen's third degree, is terrified of her. When confronted with Maigret, she makes it quite plain that she finds him attractive. With a humiliatingly soft sharp curtness she sends her "brother" out of the room to offer their visitor, perhaps her prospective lover, tea. He obeys, trembling with anxiety, and through all the less erotic possibilities suggested by the detective story situation, something agonisingly sexual already appears. When, in retrospect, it is confirmed, we remember his trembling, and it becomes more appalling than Muffat's fear of Nana. With the tersely efficient aesthetic structure of the tale at its best, the scene which confirms our suspicions does so by compounding them. Carl survives the demoralizing effect of lack of sleep in the police station. Routinely his beloved, from her little hoard of veronal, spikes his drink to lull him to a little afternoon bye-byes while she entertains one lover, or another. The situation's nasty little screw is given a further twist. Unknown to her second husband, her first husband is still alive, using her favours as one of his means of rewarding, of assuring the complicity of, various members of his gang*. The film ends with her first husband (whose victim she has long been), now raging handcuffed. He loved her too in his way. After some hesitation, she abandons him, and turns her attention

---

* As a paraphrase on the Oedipus complex (with first husband as father, second husband as son, and gang as siblings), this has a pattern significantly similar to the Oenothea flashback of *Fellini Satyricon*, a subplot whose radical psycho-sociological importance I attempted to indicate in *Sexual Alienation in the Cinema*.

to the groans of her husband, shot by her first, and calling her name as he dies.

Maigret waits and watches to see whether her pity will prove stronger than her infatuation (i.e., her generosity than her craving; her motherliness than her childishness). It does. And so there is no doubt who her next lover is to be. On her way to the dying man she comes face to face with Maigret; they exchange glances; Maigret smirks happily. The woman whom they married will now become, gratefully, lovingly, and one presumes, without unfair obligation to him, his mistress. Surely, too, for his own pleasure as well as hers, he will bend the law a very long way on her behalf. There are occasions when a certain bourgeois trenchancy and kindness can get the best of both worlds. It's a very cruel situation, and a very cruel moral. We are aware of all three men's feelings; no one is *dismissed*. And the film is by no means complacent (except insofar as happiness may require a "minimum cruelty": but that's not a complacent, or amoral, moral, when sensitivity goes with it—as it does in Renoir, and not in, say, Hawks).

Other premonitions, still tentative, intuitive, float over the film. The surgeon, aloof, dreamy, declassé, intensifies the oneirism. We may think forward to Jouvet's dreamy Baron in *Les Bas-Fonds*. But whence, or rather whither, those silk gloves he wears, as white as butterflies?—are they not premonitions of those of Boieldieu, the aristocratic officer of *La Grande Illusion*, required by the misfortunes of war to muck in with fellow officers whose social origin and style are distinctly lower than his own? Once on this track one senses the long, lean Andersen, harassed, in the bleak police-station, by the scuttling functionary who retires to a hastily made-up bed, as a paraphrase of the long, lean Jouvet, resigned among the doss-house bums. The themes of internationalism, class unity, and the victimisation of Jews with foreign roots, recur in *La Grande Illusion*. But where the later film proposes, in Gabin, an image for France which is that of mechanic-turned-officer-turned peasant, the earlier film portrays good order and civic discipline in terms of its conspicuously middleclass sleuth. Its view of the working classes is an employer's or an officer's view. And yet it is in an unpatronising way that not only this film's detective, but also its director, seems fascinated and baffled by Monsieur Oscar, by his concertina, and by the curious way in which the feeling, finesse and flair of his playing is followed by a tirade as sudden and cruelly gratuitous as the jack-in-the-box which is Death in *La Petite Marchande d'Allumettes*.

For the moment, it would seem, Renoir can only record the mystery. Perhaps he is playing with a feeling that some mysterious poison afflicts many working-class people's relationship with the larger society. This poison is not their innate inferiority; and it doesn't lead to the theoretically possible right-wing option, for Renoir's every instinct is egalitarian. Nor would it be in character for Renoir to blame Communism. For to do so would be to suppose that an ideology in itself can form the whole man in its image. The grain of Renoir's thought runs the other way. He usually implies that a man is formed by every aspect of an entire life-style, in which various partial and local patterns must appear, of which ideology is only one. A French working-class Communist could not but be a human being, a Frenchman, a worker, and a Communist, in that order. The category Frenchman appears, not out of patriotism (still less chauvinism), but simply because the label France is a (misleadingly simple) umbrella word for a multiplicity of factors: geographic, historical, social, personal, pediatric and, yes, gastronomic. Renoir's sensitive awareness of "class" borrows from Marxism principally its sense of continuous class struggle. Though he, later, seeks conciliatory solutions, he never quite forgets it.

Given the prevalent identification of Renoir in the '30s with the Popular Front, it is worth noticing here how gradually and indirectly he comes to that position. *La Chienne* is a tragi-comedy of middle-class passivity, guilt and self-pity. Lulu and Dédé are the touchstones of Legrand's cowed passivity; their vulgarity also destroys his brittle shell of social viability. The film is the negative of *La Fille de l'Eau*. In Céline black instead of gossamer white it has a semi-prostitute for a waif, a pimp for a poacher, and Montmartre for a village. The middle class meets the underworld (the *lumpen* proletariat), and Renoir's eye briefly alights on the bistro waiter and his odd blankness; artisan or robot, craftsman or alienated worker? In *La Nuit du Carrefour* that waiter becomes two men in overalls. For the moment Renoir seems to leave the enigma which their sullenness and insolence represent to slowly mature in his mind. Later, with *Lange*, Jacques Prévert can expand and justify that insolent artistry and give Renoir his reverse-angle into the industrial world.

More central, for the moment, are two more socially more elevated antitheses. First Maigret versus Michonnet, or, the middle class as Jekyll and Hyde. The second has two factors. On the one hand are the virtues society derives from the aristocracy. Their incarnation is Andersen, whose death wish is composed equally of an unfunctional social arrogance and a sexual masochism. On the other are the qualities represented by the surgeon, at once a pillar of the *haute bourgeoisie*, a professional, and a manual worker. His white gloves (the functional concealed) rhyme with the garagist's accordion-hands (the off-duty delicacy of the mechanical). We notice Maigret's hands deft as he gently manipulates the recalcitrant stove (and we may remember how, in King Vidor's *Wedding Night*, the citified writer's ability to build a log fire reveals that his roots are sound).

Of all the worlds which meet, the most perfunctorily presented is the underworld, being much given to snarling in Griffithian style. One suspects that Georges Flament, in *La Chienne*, had given Renoir a Dédé whom he could recognise, but not engender without help—or, at least, not within the shimble-shamble circumstances of the later production whose weakest shots, whose melodramatic elements, whose disorganised air, should not tempt one to pass it swiftly by. Its qualities are not accidental. Its emblem is not at all the hypothetical loss of three reels, but its creators, "hot with our passion for our job, which we dreamed of wresting from the grip of commerce." *La Nuit du Carrefour* is, perhaps, Renoir's most strangely beautiful film.

Boudu Sauvé des Eaux

Renoir's next film was financed jointly by two of his leading men, Jean Gehret and Michel Simon. Renoir and Simon had first planned a story called *Emile*, with Simon to play a provincial seller of bicycle accessories. In the event they turn to a play in which Simon had already played the title part (at the Théâtre des Mathurins in 1925). The film was shot mainly on location, around the Marne near Joinville, and at the Eclair Studios at Epinay, in the summer of 1932, and given its first Paris showing on November 11th.

Because he can't find a dog which isn't his and which he chased away, but which he nostalgically decided had been his only friend, a shambling feeble-minded tramp named Priap Boudu (Michel Simon) decides to conclude his miserable existence by hurling himself into the Seine. He is fished out by an antiquarian bookseller of humanitarian principles, one M. Lestingois (Charles Grandval), who resolves to reconcile this maladjusted fugitive with society. His wife (Marcelle Haina) is far from pleased at so disorderly, and smelly, an accession to the family. Boudu also endures the mocking disdain of the maid (Sévérine Lerczinska), with whom M. Lestingois finds furtive nocturnal consolation for the responsibilities of matrimony.

Boudu's reclamation proceeds none too smoothly. He spits in first editions and when eventually prevailed upon to clean his shoes polishes them with the wife's silk stockings, plush knickers and satin sheets. He pursues the maid and eventually imposes himself upon Madame at precisely the moment that a fanfare proclaims the award of a humanitarian medal to his benefactor. Boudu's affections however remain fixed on Anne-Marie, the maid, who shows him rather more indulgence once his lottery ticket has won a substantial fortune. Boudu, however, abruptly renounces "embourgeoisement", upsets one of the rowing boats in which the wedding party are amusing themselves, and swims away. Flinging his formal attire into the weeds, he shares his wedding breakfast with a goat, and resumes his ignoble freedoms. Renoir remarked, "Since 1932 I've spend my life searching for a similar subject— and never found it."

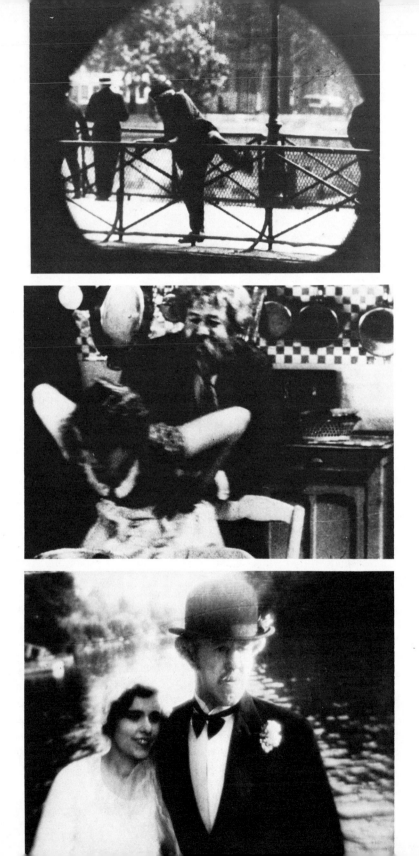

The original play centred on Lestingois (interpreted by the playwright Fauchois), affirmed his values, and Boudu's reformation. Michel Simon remained in friendly disagreement with Renoir's ending, preferring to have Boudu keep his money, and do amusing things with it, such as give a beggars' banquet. At any rate, the film avoids any shallow anarchism, of the "Hey for the open road" variety, even if it has no such crisis-points as *La Chienne*. Its tone is that of barbed comedy and Boudu's blend of idiocy and cunning sometimes give it an air of farce. Given the current prevalence of debunkings of the bourgeoisie, it's easy, in retrospect, to overlook the real virulence of a play which equates freedom with whimsicality taken to the point of nihilism. If Boudu, climactically, justifies his "Christian" name, his sexuality remains intermittent, opportunistic and not in the least Lawrentian. He is equally ready to die for the lack of a dog, or try a wash and brushup to ingratiate himself with the maid he fancies, and then to share his wedding breakfast with a goat—emblem for Pan, no doubt, but of a Pan further from the Bacchic overtones with which he is often associated and nearer the polymorphous caprice of a child of three. Shambling, snivelling, dishonest, this obnoxious autistic adult, is touchstone and Trojan Horse of disorder. In the park a child, coached by her mother, gives him five francs "to buy bread." Boudu rushes off to open a rich man's car door; as the latter fumbles for a suitable coin Boudu gives him the five francs "to buy bread." It's "let them eat cake", turned upside down. The beggar, being free, is the real aristocrat.

The film is an orgy of outraged etiquette. Wedging himself in the door-frame, Boudu swings both his legs up and around the maid's waist. Just as one remembers from *The Private Life of Henry VIII* not the tragic beheading with which it opens but Charles Laughton at table tossing gnawed chicken bones over his shoulder, so, according to Michel Simon, what most shocked audiences was Boudu eating sardines with his fingers. The dialogue hits the same dotty rightness: "Il a craché dans *La Physiologie du Marriage* de Balzac!". Or Lestingois's comment on Boudu's most repulsive aspects: "Je n'ai jamais vu un clochard si bien réussi!", meaning, to him, "a more perfect specimen", but meaning, for us something else: a tramp so pure in heart that he is essence of tramp, can surmount all instinctual temptations to consistency and cry, not without irony, "Hallelujah, I'm a bum."

Through the chastening of Lestingois, the film criticises the moral paternalism and optimism of the bourgeois. At first he remarks, "I gave him life, in a sense I'm responsible for him," and finally observes bitterly, "One should only rescue those of one's own class." Yet, in many respects, Lestingois is humane, sensitive, and not altogether devoid of the Old Adam, even if his philanthropy, because it stems from unexamined assumptions rather than alert awareness, is his *hubris*. The question "Would you rather be Socrates dissatisfied or Boudu satisfied?" admits of no easy answer, and it arises even though Renoir has substituted "Would you rather be Lestingois satisfied or Boudu dissatisfied?" For Lestingois is a philanthropist, and a rationalist intellectual humanist whose nearest English equivalent would be a literary liberal. If Lestingois had gone to the cinema to see *Boudu Sauvé des Eaux* he would undoubtedly have taken Boudu's side and laughed heartily at the "other" Lestingois.

But because Boudu is sleeping on the floor in the corridor, Lestingois can't tiptoe to his maid's room, i.e. can't be *prudently* immoral. Lestingois is sufficiently superior to the next man to jump into the river and save Boudu's life. It is his privilege, therefore, to be chastised by Pan, even if he then refuses the possible enfranchisement and sinks more deeply into his bourgeois logic. Finally, however, wife and maid rest their tearful heads on his shoulders, hinting at the possibility of a consolation prize, and, if he's very good, a sudden cessation within the household of monogamy and symmetry. Three, here, is not a crowd but a democratic, disorderly and delicious number.

The maid's flouncing insolence recalls the half-liberated creature of *On Purge Bébé*, although the other half of her mind is as bourgeois as her mistress's. It's precisely that combination of qualities that nearly entraps the outsider. She promises to give him a kiss if he shaves, then rats on her promise, and that's opportunist rather than bourgeois. In a curious way, though, her hypocrisy is transparent, in a sense perfunctory, and natural to the eternal feminine.

Such optimism as Boudu contains is also so ignominious as to be pessimistic, or rather, beyond optimism, pessimism or any form of foresight, and, for that more sombre reason, invulnerable. Bouduism goes beyond the hippie philosophy to become something acephalic, a state of being which is at once witless and divine. Boudu is not quite human, something of a satyr or a faun. Not that either of a film's heroes need be exemplary. A viable compromise between Boudu and Lestingois is so easily deducible from their polarity as to be far less illuminating than the utterly indefensible position which Boudu so astonishingly succeeds in opposing to the more plausible bourgeois "excess of moderation". More exemplary if more privileged, is the rich young lady who's looking for her dog while Boudu, jilted by his, totters off to suicide. She accepts the help of a gallant young gentleman in a high-powered roadster, and drives off with him "to look for it". In bed, we have no doubt.

We all accept that Boudu is in some weird sense happier than Lestingois. Lestingois doubtless has lucid, cultured and humane notions of the good life. He is an intelligent Epicurean. But he is the prisoner of his strategies, and he would be their prisoner however radical his notions. Boudu is the prisoner of his absence of strategies, and one might well see a subtle nihilism in this equilibrium. Boudu's life is state without enterprise, as Lestingois's is enterprise without state. Not that he never has his moments of happiness, for he surely has, but because his hypocrisies, his notions of reform, all bespeak his separation from what is profoundly and truly living: immediate sensation and relationship. No doubt humanity entails a substantial denial of the human—whence masks, whence *le jeu,* and much that Renoir will celebrate in subsequent films. Lestingois is unaware of them, because identified with them, and never quite himself. Boudu responds to details of the here and now as the impressionists to immediacies of hue. Or rather he is a *fauve,* with a will to disorder and whimsy, not a passive eye. His mind is pulled this way and that, irresponsibly, not, as in a crude associationism, by the most proximate stimuli, but by odd pulsations whose effect none can foresee; by, perhaps, an instinct to freedom whose mischievous function it is to disrupt the consistencies of the other instincts; a kind of instinctual pataphysics.

Boudu incarnates, in an appropriate rhetorical form, the challenges posed to our decorous educated hedonism by an egoistic utilarian atomic hedonism, a doctrine less well represented in philosophy than in practical life. Claude Baylis describes it as the doctrine according to which "there are no differences of quality among pleasures or among displeasures, or else such differences as exist do not affect the intrinsic values of the different hedonic states. These values vary only with the intensity and duration of the pleasure or displeasure." Renoir pixilates Bentham's felicific calculus and the utilitarian equivalence of pushpin and poetry, for he not only has no pretentions to poetry but could hardly remember the rules of pushpin long enough to play one game. Faithful if only through feeblemindedness to his unarticulated doctrine, Boudu constantly seeks immediate "pleasant consciousness", and is exasperated, sometimes to the point of suicide, if foiled. Boudu is happy whether begging food or conferring a tip, or sharing the companionship of a dog or of a Lestingois (but he must have companionship). "Ethical Hedonism may be combined with Ethical Egoism as in the view of Epicurus, or with Ethical Universalism, as in the views of J. Bentham, J. S. Mill and H. Sedgewick." If Boudu is clearly of the Unethical Egoist confession, his creed shows curious tendencies to personlessness—not *"Je est un autre"* but *"Ètes-vous je?"* One shares one's spoils with a dog, and if the dog runs off as ungratefully as one runs off from Lestingois then suicide is as sensible an answer as any other, for to abolish oneself is easier and therefore pleasanter than to abolish the world. Boudu's pleasures are undemanding and it's just as well, for were his exasperation a little more systematic he might become to Lestingois as Opale to Cordelier. One can almost see *Boudu* as a sequel to *La Chienne.* Legrand sinks beyond memory, beneath guilt, and emerges, like Lear at the last, into the new freedom of feeble-mindedness. Priap is self-evident: *'bouder'* means to brood, to sulk.

Michel Simon's Boudu is first cousin to Michel Simon's first mate in Vigo's *L'Atalante,* another film about river nomads. His astonishing actor-auteur creations link the lyrical seditiousness of Vigo with a style evoking Harpo Marx or Harry Langdon. Alien to the critical consensus it may be, but there are reasonable grounds for preferring certain comic actors, of whom

Simon is one, to the linear stylisation of the great slapstick clowns. It is precisely the compromises, i.e. certain reciprocal enrichments, between the real and the unreal which the clown lacks and which this great actor finds.

Renoir's split-focus long-shots and nimbly acrobatic trackings and pannings invest the interiors with the open space of exteriors. One has a sense of free pathways opening between the Lestingois' serried objects. From within a room in the house next door, the camera follows the maid from the dining room down a long corridor to the kitchen, glimpsing her intermittently at windows until she appears in the kitchen window hauling up a basket from the courtyard below—a fugue-like counterpoint of overt, covert and implied space.

Boudu continues Renoir's evolution towards the virtuoso camera movements of *La Règle du Jeu*. His evolution contrasts with that of most of his contemporaries, who were increasingly influenced by the Hollywood style, with its emphasis on the reverse-angle and tight compositions, and with its preference for the cut as the shortest distance between two points. Renoir declared in 1938, "the further I go in my profession, the more I'm led to direct in depth relative to the screen. The more I go the more I dispense with those confrontations between two actors placed neatly before the camera as if they were having their photograph taken. I prefer to place my characters more freely, at different distances to the camera, to set them on the move. For that I need a great depth of field."

Subsequently during the '50s and '60s, the impression grew that Renoir was almost alone in anticipating the rapid and expressive camera movements which are found in the films of Ophuls, Truffaut and others. In fact, rapid movements were particularly common in the later '20s and early '30s, whether one thinks of Lewis Milestone's *Rain* or the late Harry Langdon features.

As in *La Chienne,* a musical neighbour lives across the courtyard, here assiduously practising the flute; asserting the nostalgia for Pan and his pipes as each dusk falls over the city. The "panic" flute will reappear in *Partie de Campagne,* in *La Grande Illusion* and in *Le Déjeuner Sur L'Herbe.*

Boudu Sauvé des Eaux, La Chienne and *Les Bas-Fonds* comprise a triptych on the theme of tramp and freedom (it's interesting to imagine the last film with Michel Simon in Jouvet's part; both interpretations make sense; Jouvet's perhaps more precariously, and unexpected). *Boudu* forms with *Partie de Campagne* a diptych on the theme of self-abandonment to the river's flow, and on rash moments versus prudent lifetimes. There is one astonishing echo. *Boudu* features a cut-in shot of Darnaux, the seducer in *Partie de Campagne,* rowing alone, as, in the later film, he rows alone, in memory, to their island. Abruptly the films move into each other's orbit, the stories intertwine. The shot is so pointless that one would attribute it to a private reference, not joke, were it not that Boudu precedes by four years the film to which it refers. It's difficult also not to look forward to Godard, another

cinéaste of freedom, apathy and whim, of life as art and art as life, but Boudu Le Fou, lacking all idealism, is at ease in the world that anguishes Pierrot.

The poet on a parkbench is played by Jacques Becker. With his crazy freedom, Boudu's soubriquet might be: *Le Fils de L'Eau*, or *Le Chien*.

André Bazin comments on the strange behaviour of the people massed on the bridge, smiling and waving cheerfully as Boudu drowns. Clearly they are looking not at a suicide, but at a film being shot. Thus, even on location, what Bazin describes as a "private joke", a work of complicity between the director and any audience alert enough to look closely at the crowd, rather than merely assume its response is appropriate, is a sense of Méliès spectacle within Lumière realism.

The film was well received by critics, one of whom demanded a series: *Boudu in Society, Soldier Boudu,* and so on. Renoir and Michel Simon hoped to team up and produce two films a year, one a drama, the other a comedy, but the public response, though satisfactory, was not favourable enough to justify such a programme to producers.

Chotard et Cie

Renoir's next film continues the oscillation, between acceptance and sub-version of the bourgeois order, which is inaugurated with the contrast between *La Nuit du Carrefour* and *Boudu Sauvé des Eaux*. *Chotard et Cie* is all but a riposte to *Boudu*. It was commissioned by Roger Ferdinand, a playwright who, perhaps inspired by the example of Marcel Pagnol, set out to film his own regional comedies. Renoir made the screen adaptation, Ferdinand contributed the dialogue. The film was shot entirely in Joinville in 22 days during November-December 1932. Renoir's comment is terse: *"Chotard et Cie?* I don't remember it." In another interview: "It was an essay in light vaudeville. I'm not a rock. I'm made of pliable sand, and what surrounds me affects me." As *Premier Plan* reminds us, "Times were hard. Grémillon was emigrating to Spain and Feyder was still in the U.S.A. The American industry had a stranglehold on world production. England was dragged in its wake, and Germany expelled the artists of the left."

"At the time I much admired certain American light comedies and I had the idea that with a French subject in the style of *Chotard et Cie* I might do something comparable to an attractive American comedy." The English equivalent would be *Hobson's Choice*. Old Chotard (Charpin, a Pagnol reliable) is a robust, not to say brow-beating, self-made tradesman, and patriarch of a not too unhappy family. He dangles his lovely daughter before the eyes of the local gendarme, due for promotion to sergeant. But his daughter, in her softer way a chip off the old block, obstinately prefers the scatty and bohemian young poet Jean Collinet (Pomiès). Eventually Chotard gives in to his headstrong daughter, makes the best of a bad job, and reckons to make a businessman of the poet, despite his disastrously soft-hearted first day behind the counter. But when young Collinet wins the Prix Goncourt even Chotard is impressed. He calculates how many novels Collinet could write if he kept punctual hours in congenial seclusion, and signs contracts with every Paris publisher he can find. Collinet dutifully cudgels his brains, but finally reckons that there's more fun in real life, and joins his father-in-law

behind the counter. Thus the philistine preaches the claims of an artistic vocation and the artist renounces the ivory tower for life's hustle and bustle. Young Collinet is almost-a-Boudu who happily becomes Lestingois. The notion of an artistic career is philistinism and the tradesman's is the vocation. Chotard's enterprise is his *joie de vivre*, his fulfilment, and his son-in-law's conversion isn't a mere surrender to the system. What, in any case, is a literary career, but the bourgeois spirit of enterprise seeking to hammer profit and predictability out of inspiration?

Charpin, as old Chotard, holds the film together, with his acid warmth and his invariably inefficient reigns of terror amongst assistants and family alike. The studio backcloths, which reek of plaster and canvas, are not so much painted as daubed. A supple, simple technique enlivens the style which, overall, is that of filmed theatre. The decor was virtually a continuous set in a closed circle, the camera peeping in through doorways and peepholes concealed by strategically placed pictures and vases.

Summary and farcical, the film abounds in agreeable and even slightly touching moments. They recall Pagnol in their loving observation of meridional characteristics, but remain a little more flippant and fantastic. There is nothing here of Pagnol's occasional verging on a sort of neorealism. The poet who stands on the table in order to press his trousers with an ancient smoothing iron, and the obdurately prosaic couples at the Fancy Dress Ball, belong to warm and friendly farce. Renoir loves the rites and gestures of commensalism: Chotard's rhetorical gesture of moral intransigence modulating without interruption into a request for a slice of bread. Its caricature is a pretext for certain informal and disrespectful truths, the truths of derisive affection which, when comedy has a soul, is its soul and not its shallowness.

Madame Bovary

The producer rang Jean Renoir and said, "Will you make *Madame Bovary?*" and Renoir replied "Yes," over the telephone. He wrote the scenario, the adaptation and dialogues, shooting around Rouen and Lyons-la-Forêt before entering Billancourt Studios during September/October 1933. The first cut, unusually faithful to Flaubert's novel, ran three and a half hours, which was adjudged too long for the distributors, too disruptive to usual programming and a major impediment to marketing. The producers accordingly cut the film to just over two hours (3,200 metres).

"Valentine and my brother were essentially theatre people, with dialogue which seemed to me to need theatre people to speak it, the joy implicit in certain phrases which seem formulated by throats accustomed to deliver words. The further I went, the more I learnt to construct completely developed scenes. I don't think that the only method is to make films which are in effect one long scene. I prefer the method which consists of conceiving each scene as a little film on its own. That's what Chaplin does. I think it's very disorientating (for the public), and when it's not applied to a film whose action is very gripping, people resent it. To build a film out of complete little wholes, that's what most attracts me."

Madame Bovary depends on a certain dreamy passivity, on a faltering of drive, on a psychological negative, faithful to that lassitude Flaubert attributes to bourgeois culture. Flaubert's story concerns the domination of a life by (in default of anything better) romantic fantasy. The theme of spiritual emptiness exposing the soul to vampire fantasies has many modes—including Bunuel's. In Renoir's film, at least as shown, this aspect of alienation by daydream (in love and art alike) appears only obliquely; as when a worldly curé warns Emma against the dangers of art. It moves outwards from Flaubert's theme (inside a woman alone in an unsympathetic milieu) to concentrate on the predominantly negative interactions between the woman and her milieu. One is reminded of Franju's *Thérèse Desqueyroux*—though Renoir's film is in the key of daylight space rather than nocturnal compression.

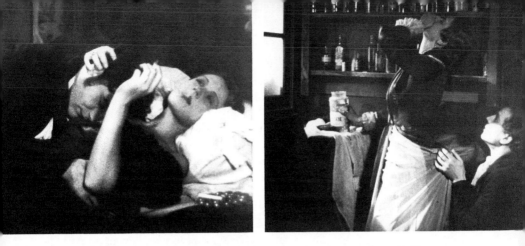

Alexandre Arnoux wonders whether the subject is not after all "impossible on the screen, its principal personage being, like Don Quixote, a secondhand one, fabricated by reading." But Renoir has spotted this trap and has resituated the drama, partly by transforming Emma herself. As Bazin points out: "Could one contrive any more sensational contrariety in casting then the choice of Valentine Tessier? Her age and silhouette rule out any possibility of our believing in her virginity, or, in any case, Emma's extreme youth. In Renoir, her character doesn't age physically throughout the film. Renoir doesn't choose his actors, as is done in the theatre, for their conformity to the role, but, like the painter, for what he knows he will force us to see." From another angle, we may say that Renoir "miscasts" so that a character refuses all our preconceptions, is given freedom to *achieve* moments of truth.

In another aspect Renoir profoundly transforms the book's texture. If the hothouse bourgeois interiors, foreground doors and furnishings often encircle the characters, it is far less oppressively than one might expect. Renoir clearly prefers the open air, the farmyard, the freshness of which Mme Bovary can make nothing because her bourgeois formation has made her pretentiously "urbanised". The film is built on the space around Emma, a reality which she cannot make hers. She is not closed to life; she craves it, and sensitively; but she is closed to the particular form in which it offers itself to her.

"Madame Bovary, c'est moi," said Flaubert. Albeit silly and romantic, she is also a mute inglorious poet at bay against a philistine practicality of which Renoir, almost too wisely for his own film's good, refuses easy condemnation. Like Chotard's grocery store, it is spiritually viable for some. In his ambiguity, Renoir is nearer Wyler's *The Heiress* (after Henry James) than Astruc's *Une Vie* (after Maupassant), even if his visual style resembles the claustrophobia of the former less than the openness of the later.

"Valentine Tessier," said Renoir, "has a way of walking, of moving her apron, of coming in, of going out, a kind of security." She is the least condemnable, the least pitiable of all possible Bovarys. The film is a tragedy, not of immature romanticism versus organised philistinism, but of two ways of life: middleclass woman versus the rural, in subtle and tragic alienation.

Cliché expressions are tragically transcended. Swooningly the men lay their heads on their beloved's body and say "I am your slave." She adopts Georges Sand poses, her lover reverently unbuttons her boots. Even the "saint" with her charitable works makes of her role a pose. It is just this fresh respect for other modes of behaviour, this fidelity to period style, this opposite to camp, which is the film's tenderness and wisdom. Pierre Renoir's Charles Bovary catches every nuance within incomprehension without that rigidity amounting to ill-will which characterizes the husband in *Thérèse Desqueyroux*. The philistines are no less vulnerable than the romantics.

Renoir spoke of a simple picture: "No big scenes, every day without exaggerated relief, a little on the grey side, a little monotonous like life." Apparent divagations do connect with the theme. A gruesome preanaesthetics amputation recalls the reality of the flesh, antithesis of Emma's dreams; her death (like Nana's smallpox) is another form of the same contrast. The film's texture establishes physicality—pigs rooting, Emma's softly swelling breasts under her parasol, delicately inflected by the flossy air. The agricultural fair is hardly more philistine, given its own sensivities, than the theatre which feeds Emma's fancies. One almost thinks of Hardy's *The Return of the Native*, of Sue in *Jude the Obscure*.

Champreaux states Renoir's dilemma sympathetically. "If he succeeds, Flaubert's name eclipses him. If he fails, the cry of sacrilege is raised." He compares Renoir's choppy, unemphatic style with the romantic close-ups of John M. Stahl (the Hollywood '30s romantic). He stresses the visual realism which makes Flaubert so filmic, cueing, as he so often does, long-shots, close-ups and all—Thomas Hardy's novels are often equally precise as shooting scripts. Champreaux repeatedly finds Renoir's dramatic tone too flat (the local official's speech, the Vaubyersand Ball). In consequence, Renoir "has painted neither the ardour of Mme Bovary, nor provincial boredom. Nevertheless, he has told us the story of a woman who commits suicide because she lacks 8,000 francs." If Emma Bovary and Flaubert are the spiritual antithesis to Jean Renoir, it is because the former reject so much of a world in which the latter finds so much richness.

The result is not that the film falls into two halves with the heroine's imagination a secondhand absurdity, which would be too cruel to Emma,* but that a certain lassitude strays from Renoir's identification with Emma into the languid rhythm with which most things are portrayed.

Jean-Claude Allais tries to save the day by appealing to a variety of Brechtian alienation. "The coldness, the distanciation, the theatricality of the whole are further exaggerated by the suppression of at least half of the original version: the elliptical quality of the story-telling, so remarkable in Renoir, is all but caricatured. To begin with, there's a first half hour which is a master-

---

* The theme of vicarious living through stereotype has since become obsessive—from *The Secret Life of Walter Mitty* through *Sunset Boulevard* to Warhol's drag queens.

piece of concise and precise exposition." Nonetheless, "finally it's difficult not to be submerged, like Emma, by boredom." In other words, there's insufficient alienation (in Brecht's sense) from Emma's alienation (in the social sense). But certainly one experiences the emptiness of fields and roads, a sort of wandering of attention as trees on the horizon cut into the screen, satisfying nothing. The openness becomes as oppressive as the claustrophobia of Franju's *Thérèse Desqueyroux*. But the intensity with which Flaubert uses external detail to communicate an intensity of internal pain is lost, as Ophuls might not have lost it.* François Poulle approaches the matter from a Lukacsian angle: "What's lacking is that kind of internal criticism of reality without which realism cannot be."

If Renoir's half-film dissatisfies, it is in a way which tantalizes to repeated viewings. It becomes a complement to the novel, rather than a rendition of it. One almost sees Emma elegiacally, as an intelligent, sensible farmer might have seen the meanings which she does not, might have understood her inadaptability and still loved her. Renoir stands on the brink of criticising Madame Bovary, and Flaubert, for their tragic, rather than their blameworthy, inability to feel the life of the countryside, which penetrates to them only in its morbid forms. The surgical operation, in domestic surroundings without anaesthetics, sharply intensifies the Renoirian theme of physical cruelty to animals. In this case, the animal is a human one. The deathbed scene, faintly reminiscent of *Nana,* contributes to what Henri Agel senses behind the film's freshness, its "funerary taint", its insidiously gentle emphasis on physical pain, where the spirit has absented itself, and the will to live has weakened.

At least as cut, the film flopped, almost as badly as *Nana,* though less catastrophically for Renoir, who had by now several commercial successes to his credit. The complete version was shown to Renoir's friends and acquaintances, among them Brecht. "They loved it. The film as it is now is, I find boring". Renoir believes that the original has disappeared, together with its negative, and that the out-takes were burned. The abbreviated version was re-released in 1968, in the wake of a preceding reissue, *La Marseillaise,* with very moderate success.

* The novel's reputation as a psychological masterpiece may lead us to expect a psychological explanation and analysis, which we never have. Its "psychology" lies in Flaubert's sense of detail as expression of an internal state.

26

Toni

Any danger of enforced inactivity was averted by an enterprise which also allowed Renoir to put into practice aesthetic ideas which in their time could seem extreme. He and a producer, Pierre Gaut, had agreed that it "would perhaps be interesting" to shoot a film out-of-doors, entirely on location with a few professional actors but a great many amateurs, with people speaking in their dialect and without makeup. They also succeeded in interesting Marcel Pagnol, who took a hand in the production of the film. It was made at his Marseilles Studio, although almost all the footage was shot at Martigues (Bouche du Rhône) during Summer 1934. The film was premiéred in Paris in February 1935.

For Pagnol the film medium was little more than a convenient method of packaging his warm, theatrical comedy-dramas. In 1934 Renoir's aesthetic involved the exploration of interior realism through exterior realism. "The cinema remains above all photography, and photography is the least subjective of all the arts.The good photographer sees the world as it is, selects from it, separates what is worthy of notice, and fixes it, as if by surprise, without transformations. And how can one think of alteration in respect of that principal element of our craft, the human face? At the time of *Toni*, I disapproved of make-up. My ambition was to bring the non-naturalistic elements, those which don't depend on the play of encounters, to a style as near as possible to that of everyday acquaintainship. Similarly with the decor; there is no studiowork; the landscapes and houses are as we found them. The human beings, whether played by actors or by the inhabitants of Martigues, strive to resemble the passersby whom they are supposed to represent. The professional actors, with a few exceptions, belong to the social class, the nation, the races, of their role. The scenario was a news item picked up by Jacques Mortier, the Martigues Commissioner of Police. The events actually occurred ten years earlier and were altered only so as to spare the susceptibilities of those involved, and their relatives. Everything was done to bring our work as near to documentary as was possible."

Toni is not, as is often supposed, a "first" in the sphere of neo-realism. Epstein had followed *Finis Terrae* in 1928 with *L'Or des Mers* in 1934. In 1934 also Marcel Pagnol shot *Angèle* in alfresco style, although, as Leprohon observes, "Epstein laid more emphasis on the elements than on the characters and Pagnol was still producing open-air theatre." *Toni* may, indeed, be seen as the point at which the whole documentary movement of the French cinema achieved its fullest coalescence with the fiction film, a coalescence of some importance in cinema history—especially as it occurred so many years before British documentary followed the French example.

Toni cleaves to '30s populism, rather than to the neo-realistic orthodoxy elaborated by Zavattini nearly 20 years later, in that its centrepiece is a *crime passionel,* rather than an everyday drama. Even so, the difference is less absolute than it may seem. The crime is deliberately demelodramatised, and the film hovers on the brink of being a study of the cultural problems of immigrants, directly analogous to Visconti's postwar *Rocco and His Brothers.*

In this case, the immigrants are French and Spanish workers settling around Marseilles and working the quarries. One such worker, Toni (Charles Blavette), a quiet, amiable man, moves in with his landlady Maria (Jenny Helia). But he falls in love with a spirited and flirtatious Spanish girl, Josepha (Celia Montalvan). Remaining true to the old peasant way of life, he asks her uncle for her hand in marriage. Meanwhile, Josepha flirts with Albert, the foreman (Dalban), and when he rapes her she marries him—also in conformity with custom. Toni's marriage to Maria is none too joyous, while Albert illtreats Josepha. When at last Toni summons the initiative to elope with her, she hangs back to steal her husband's money as he lies drunkenly asleep. Accidentally rousing him, she defends herself with a pistol and kills him. A gendarme catches Toni burying the body. Toni takes to the hills but is shot by the owner of a neighbouring estate and dies in the arms of his friend, Fernand (Delmont), near a railway bridge over which the same train brings its new loads of immigrants.

Toni is an ordinary labourer, straightforward, and contented. If he improves his lot by acquiring his own little niche (with Maria), it is on the strength of an unaffected amiability. He loses the woman he loves to a foreman who combines both the property sense and cynical brutality of a certain strain in the petty peasantry. The innocents are bound by traditional codes. Toni asks Josepha's uncle for her hand, Josepha feels that the man who raped her now possesses her. Their anarchism comes too late, and all is lost when Josepha yields to the middleclass prudence of her cousin Gaby (Andrex), who persuades her to steal Albert's money instead of simply fleeing.

The film touches on a variety of social and psychological, melodramatic and neo-realistic, points, without developing any one fully into a pattern. Its richness is that of a style in transition. The film's storyline is in Toni's image: almost prosaic in its simple and direct forward movement, although its tempo is relaxed, discursive, open to the moment. Many scenes (Toni sucking out Josepha's wasp-sting) amount to painterly subjects extended in time by the cinema's analytic and narrative structures. But they would be easily compressible into the painter's one moment, like the sequence of the girl on the swing in *Partie de Campagne*. The final shot of the opening master-scene (Toni's arrival) matches with the opening shot of the following master-scene (Toni's established domesticity). And although the clumsiness of the visual continuity is disguised by a rather odd subtitle—"Fin du prologue"— it would be plausible to suspect the still imperfect grasp of classical syntax described by Scholsberg. To say that Renoir could misjudge a sophisticated effect is not to say that he was still shakily literate, however.That the match-ing shots involve a jump in time and a change of state is unclear because the previous scene has not established time as a significant factor, nor a clear dramatic issue and its implied rate of change. Renoir's editor achieves a similar effect with very great beauty in *Partie de Campagne*, where the dramatic issues, the river's flow, and a change of weather, prepare us for the interval and give it an emotional sense.

The theme of *Toni* is incomprehension, bred of culture shock. Toni's preoccupations are simple: eating, drinking, singing, i.e. subsistence, com-radeship, and feeling. His "tragic" flaw is modest, ordinary and wholesome enough; manly enough, he is gentle, and slightly weak, with women. Yet, as an immigrant, he is exposed to the lures and jolts of a world which baffles him. He is all but a male equivalent of the lost and abused little nomad who was the heroine of Renoir's first feature. For very different reasons, he has something of Legrand's difficulty in understanding how the world really works. Toni relies on his shrewd, saddened, slightly cowed friend Fernand, as Josepha follows the—fatal—advice of Gaby. Both are spontaneously out-going, Josepha in her coquetry, Toni in his generosity. His last refuge is with the gypsies, and it is a property owner who, meanly virtuous, hunts him down.

Even Albert is infiltrated by fears of he knows not what, making him all the more violent. As he presses his attentions on Josepha, he dirties the sheets she is drying, not deliberately, but with an imperceptive clumsiness which arouses the furious contempt of the girl he is trying to seduce. Yet he feels no embarrassment, and, imperceptive to the scolding which might have

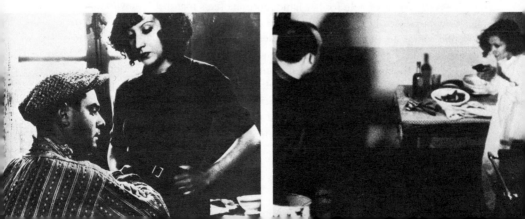

cowed a finer man, he continues his attack. Like Legrand, he is an ungainly, clumsy bear. But unlike Legrand, he has a bear's strength and steady aggressiveness. His accident-proneness has a sadistic, not a masochistic, bent, driving Josepha to hysteria, as his spoiling doubles the work she must do. The scene around the washing is a "black" equivalent of the satyr's dance in *Partie de Campagne*. Albert is saturated with race-prejudice (directed against Arabs). When Toni warns him, "Don't steal our women", he reveals a sense of a group ("our") which is ambiguous as between race, nation, culture, class and community (and, abruptly, patriarchal-proprietorial in its view of women). The very fluidity of the meaning indicates Toni's awkward and confused position as a man between two worlds—the old order, and the new internationalism. Both Toni and Albert are victims of a confusion which is malevolent in one case and benevolent in the other; they are almost two possibilities of the same person. Truffaut has seen Renoir's features in Albert, and one must see them in Toni also. Albert, as the bear-cum-satyr amongst the laundry, unites characteristic Renoir themes, and perhaps Renoir felt himself, at this point, a man between two worlds, as we shall see. Albert-Toni; Lestingois-Boudu; Cordelier-Opale. . . .

The story is melodramatic, in that it would make sense even if Albert and Toni were the stock types whom they superficially evoke. It is melodramatic because both Albert and Toni are forceful, simple, and rooted in the world of rustic feuds, to which violence is not alien. The story's relatively loose articulation of character and action accommodates that multiplicity of asides with which Renoir makes of his protagonists not characters so much as people who live from day to day and among whom a crime happens. Toni's easy kindness makes him a lady's man who breaks Maria's heart. The corollary of his freedom from society is his ignorance of its ways. What saves him destroys him. It never occurs to him that Josepha could plead self-defence. It hardly occurs to us. The law, to Toni, is part of a chaos as alien as Kafka's America. Neither bourgeois nor Boudu, he pays the penalty of his virtues as well as his weaknesses.

The flirt-victim, Josepha, is an exotic, softly vivacious little cat whose pedigree extends from Catherine Hessling through the quieter playing of Nadia Sibirskaia in *Le Crime de Monsieur Lange*, Simone Simon in *La Bête*

Humaine, Mila Parely in *La Règle du Jeu* and Françoise Arnoul in *French Can-Can*. In the foreman, Albert, Truffaut sees Renoir's covert autoportrait, and an equivalent, in weak villainy, of Boudu's inveterate anarchism.* Several of the actors came from the Marseilles *café-conc'*, their personality projection muted to the film's dull intimacy, the phrases fading sparsely against the walls and rocks.

The era's scruples deprived the film of much of the rape sequence as shot, as well as the long sequence of Toni's trundling Albert's corpse in a cart under Josepha's washing, followed by some merrily joking Corsicans.

Two scenes attain a timelessness, almost a placenessness. Josepha attempts suicide in dull grey seas whose skyline is erased by mist; Toni lies homeless with the gypsies by their fire under the sky. Instead of the sunsoaked landscapes of Provençal tourism, one is lost in a muddle of rocks and open spaces, of holes and corners of countryside. Small houses perch beside dusty roads along which gangs of labourers trudge. The viaduct lies like a huge steel cage erected at random, or perhaps dropped by some giant gamekeeper to catch men. The rolling meridional lilts are not at home here, any more than the men, who move in and out of houses, or form into groups and gangs, yet always seem nomadic in spaces which never allow them to settle, to nestle.

In Dreyer's *Vampyr* even the panning and tracking shots seem subordinated to a taut, locked grid of areas. In Welles's early films, the image is strongly locked in width and breadth alike. In his *Confidential Report* the sense of instability is induced, not by a sense of looseness or freedom, but by a low angle, wide angle, lens which turns so many architectural verticals into backward-toppling visual diagonals and gives an effect of empires falling. In contrast, Renoir's deep focus is straightforward, almost childish in its basic principles. A space rather like an informal stage exists in the mid-foreground. Characters often enter and exit from left and right, as on the stage, an effect whose naiveté is concealed only by its rapidity. Sometimes this space is framed by a none-too-oppressive, none-too-complex foregound (less complex by far than the foreground screens of Pabst and Ophuls). Sometimes the background is a functional equivalent to the stage limits. This background is rarely flat, rarely interrupting, rather, it enfolds the foreground area. "Entrances" and "exits" between the principal area and the enfolding area weaken the distinction between them, and have in themselves so little

---

* Given the affinities which many critics have noted between Renoir's style and the earliest, finest films of Truffaut, and since the latter's comments on Renoir are invested with a certain prestige, for obvious reasons, it's worth noticing their hidden bias: to establish the identity of passive conformity with mental reservations and these as the only radical form of revolt—both being forms of treachery. Perhaps indeed the mainspring of Truffaut's inspiration is a bittersweet honesty about treachery (rendered lovable by sensitivity and pathos) which in Renoir is controverted by a robust and resilient generosity. The energies which Renoir distributes with amiable equality between male and female characters, are, in Truffaut, attributed to the loved, formidable woman.

emphasis as static forms that they eschew the "labyrinthine" effect of Pabst, whose zigzag "seams" tunnel in and out of the image. In height and width, the cinema image is fixed (by the real frame); only its depth is apparent and variable. But Renoir's informal inner frames vary the actual frame and give the image a quality of layered depth, kept "open" by the variety of human movements (and later, colours) within it. People, landscapes and objects are related yet are still able to, as it were, slide past one another, to remain themselves with an informality impossible in more emphatic perspectives. Roads or corridors tend to cross the screen at a shallow angle, so as to accommodate simultaneous or rapidly successive actions at different points aong them. Rooms are arranged to allow bold, transverse movements, like a criss-cross of "ghost" corridors. Areas of the screen are marked, but not closed off against one another; actions are gently streamed, rather than narrowly channelled. Never inchoate, space is indulgent rather than measured. It is "fat" rather than lean, but is active. At any moment the characters may change their relationship to one another. The abundance of free space allows them to cross only the gentlest of boundaries as they do so. Nonetheless, they may alter the image invigoratingly, by revealing or closing perspectives or juggling configurations. It's rarely easy to tell whether a configuration expresses a momentary, or a decisive, relationship; and when immediate decisiveness appears, it often establishes an inturned loneliness. A main action easily involves, and as easily dismisses, a succession of encounters with colleagues, friends, passers-by and lookers-on. Fixtures (walls, rocks, tables) resemble a line of stones dividing the course of a river which flows round them and rejoins beyond them, rather than a steep bank within which the action must indivisibly run. Characters and the camera often run in parallel. As the camera quite straightforwardly follows a foreground movement, it may take in part of the background, in which Renoir is interested, and to which he allows just a litle more visual space than usual; thus the composition is pulled off-centre, momentarily, into something untidy or unstable. Thorold Dickinson once drew a distinction between the informal plasticity of Renoir, and the directedly dynamic or monumental forms of Eisenstein, and remarked that Visconti's *La Terra Trema* first blended the two streams. At any rate, Renoir space, like his dramatic emphases, is sufficiently unpredictable to evoke, at times, the saxophonist's remark about playing with Thelonius Monk, "It's like suddenly stepping down a liftshaft". His wide-angled deep-focus lens is spiritual before it is physical. The faces in the crowd are also worthy of attention, are part of the action.

Already, the space of *Nana* had balanced looseness and control. With *Toni*, a new, roaming looseness acquires the initiative, and one may be reminded of Focillon's contrast between "l'éspace-limite" and "l'éspace-milieu". Percy Lubbock, in *The Craft of Fiction*, emphasises Tolstoy's free atmosphere of natural living among wide spaces, and observes that he draws no horizon, no circumscription, around the world of *War and Peace*. *Toni* certainly lends itself to a Tolstoian interpretation, with its earthy, generous peasant cast adrift from his natural roots by a capitalist economy.

Toni met with a cool reception. "I think the public was unready for this kind of story. Even with *Angele.*" (Pagnol's more sentimental, more obviously warmhearted, version of peasant life). "The film was strange for its period, unexpected. . . . And it struck them as brutal, whereas . . . I saw it again the other day. It seems extremely soft . . . extremely kind. . . . " Nonetheless, Renoir's experiences with improvisation by screen amateurs "gave me the courage to try different things in different directions."

Interlude: In the Front Line

In *La Fille de l'Eau,* class barriers, and the possibilities of crossing them, were a subordinate theme, viewed with something between a liberal innocence and a liberal optimism. It comes close to the traditional American view, where the European class structure is seen as a caboodle of inhibiting but obsolescent shibboleths from which any sensible dynamic individual will rapidly extricate himself. Clearly, Renoir's work might stress "responsive" and "egalitarian" rather than all which "dynamic" can veil in the way of "savagely ambitious." At any rate, his first six sound films have as common theme the problem of the bourgeois order.

On Purge Bébé celebrates a triumph of sly sabotage. *La Chienne* concerns near-nihilist protest and despair. *La Nuit de Carrefour* leans a little to the petty bourgeois right, preferring police helmets to overalls: but it opts for Maigret, not for Michonnet. All those qualities for which, in fiction, the aristocratic principle so often stands—a suave awareness of enlightened self-interest, a courteous yet snobbish frivolity, concealing a stoic and responsible readiness for self-sacrifice—are enervated and rendered guilty by association with prejudice, masochism, and gutter gangsterdom. Privileged by hindsight, we know now that Maigret's kindly triumph was a pious hope. If *Boudu Sauvé des Eaux* reverts to the more cheerful mood of *On Purge Bébé*, it is also a reverse angle on *La Chienne*.

From the irruption into bourgeois respectability of the disreputable, absolutely everybody benefits. After his chastisement Lestingois seems all set for a *ménage à trois,* and though the serving-class girl with bourgeois aspirations is left, not so much "waiting at the church" as treading water, at least she isn't left strangled on a bed. In fact she'll undoubtedly be helped by Lestingois et Cie to claim the fortune which the husband who so wickedly deserted her has nonchalantly left behind him. *Chotard et Cie* is a tit for tat by a bourgeois household a lot more likeable than Lestingois's; to borrow a much later jargon, "I'm dropping out from dropping out."

In these five films, the nearest figures to Boudu are, in order, the man about town (Fernandel), Madame Legrand's first husband, "The Adjutant", Michonnet (the sinister side of Boudu, like, much later, Opale—but there is enough of Boudu in Maigret, we learn), and the young poet But in himself as old Chotard in *Madame Bovary*, the real polarity is *within* the bourgeoise. Emma, too sensitive to rest content with the cloistered abstraction of bourgeois culture, is illiterate in respect of all which is social, physical and manual, and can sustain only an etiolated relationship.

Toni is rightly celebrated as the first film of a new proletarian period. But if one sees the preceding period as forming a bourgeois series, *Toni* is not without fundamental affinities to them. Toni's affable, contented, relatively isolated existence, more lover to his landlady than involved with "mates", is proletarian enough. Yet he is very nearly in the position of Chotard's son-in-law, marrying into the middle class. Finally it is with the gypsies that he finds solidarity. It is not yet a Popular Front film; although it renders such a film increasingly likely.

This is not to say that Renoir's preceding films are the product of a conscious preoccupation with the bourgeois ethos. The French cinema was substantially dominated by bourgeois settings and subjects (as it still is), and Renoir's acceptance of assignments would be almost enough to explain the thematic unity we have observed. His more personal films *(La Chienne, Boudu Sauvé des Eaux)* seem headed for a nomadism which is largely an image for an *internal* freedom. Although Boudu's role is certainly like the angel-stranger's in *Teorema*, or a hippie's, the comparison has the disparities of its anachronism. Boudu hardly represents an alternative society (although Lestingois *needs* him). While few of us would follow Boudu to hobnob with the goats and the dogs, most of us might not mind being Lestingois, after his purgation, with two women, his books and, perhaps, a much less priggish variety of liberalism. In this preference we doubtless betray all that there really is in the way of a hard, a literal, edge in Renoir's last image, of a querulous, feeble-minded, indifferently celibate or promiscuous existence, more stray cur than super-tramp.

Renoir comes to proletarian themes via two detours, both common enough for the bourgeois artist. The first detour is via the underworld *(La Chienne, La Nuit du Carrefour)*. The second detour is via the poor peasant, subtenant or rural labourer. *Madame Bovary* leads to *Toni*, as if Renoir's mind had followed a long tracking shot, through space, class and time— beginning with an overshoulder as Emma stares languidly from her window. She sees the lace curtain but not the men in the fields. But the camera and the director see them, and move outwards, to lose themselves among the common people, who, like her, have their frustrated and complicated passions, their rules and myopias. Here the landowner is the intruder. Those who prefer to postulate contemporary influences rather than personal voyages will notice that the social class of Toni is some way nearer home than that of Epstein's *Mor Vran* and *Finis Terrae*.

Throughout the pre-Popular Front sextet, our principal identifications are with eccentrics, misfits and semi-loners. The star-emblem of the period is, if anyone, Michel Simon, and perhaps it's no accident that this more intense identification with square pegs follows a crisis in Renoir's professional life and perhaps his personal one. It coincides also with the massive onset of the economic Depression, moving in from America and coming last of all to the relatively self-sufficient France. The German realist school, destroyed by Hitler, has still to recover its rightful place in cinema history, and may yet reveal itself as the most sophisticated of all. A brief American flirtation with populist themes, through the mid-'20s and early '30s, yields to slicker or more sentimental themes. Comparable British films fell, perhaps more promptly than they deserved, into oblivion. In France, populism continued and with *Toni* Renoir moved in amongst it. Politically, it is an innocent film, affected by Renoir's anarchism, and by the internationalism which comes so easily, and valuably, to those with a wide culture and a broad spread of human sympathies. It stresses the split between the propertied and the propertyless which dominates Renoir's next, and politically enlightened, phase. And he sets that nomadic camera on the highway which leads him from the country mouse (Toni) to the town mouse (Lange), where he finds himself in the thick of the class struggle.

For would-be freelances like Renoir, the Depression proved a blessing in disguise. The consequent disorganisation of the big Gaumont combine forced the government to intervene on behalf of the native industry. Often enough in the cinema's history, bureaucracy has proved less oppressive than commerce. Now legislation provided openings for smaller, less hidebound, production groups.

The political crisis gave further encouragement to a shift of subjectmatter. The triumph of Nazism in Germany not only provided an external threat, but encouraged France's indigenous Fascists. In the face of this double threat, from inside and outside the country, a rough but fervent coalition, the Popular Front, formed itself, from Communists, Socialists, and all those men of the centre who recognised Fascism as the gravest and most immediate threat to France and to freedom. The Communist party, for its part, waved the Tricolor as often and as vigorously as the Red Flag.

Le Crime de Monsieur Lange

Under the title of *Sur la Cour* the first idea came from Jean Castanier, the Spanish painter who had designed the decour for *Boudu* and *Chotard*. Jacques Becker had hoped to make his directorial debut in features with it. He found a backer and producer in André Halley des Fontaines, but the latter wanted an experienced directorial hand, and offered the film to Renoir. For Becker this was a cruel disappointment, although the two men, at first estranged, soon resumed their partnership.

Even after elaborating the original screenplay with Castanier, Renoir felt it was "not very detailed and much too long" and "not quite right. We felt it needed something and I had the idea of asking Prévert if he liked it and if he'd give me a hand to finish it off, which he did." According to the producer, Prévert was so lazy that he had to be locked up in an office, and allowed out only at mealtimes, sliding the pages under the door as they were finished. Nonetheless Renoir was anxious to reconcile Prévert's mordant dialogue with his improvisational shifts. So "I asked him to come onto the set with me . . . and the film was improvised, like all my films, but with Prévert's constant co-operation . . ." The improvised quality was enhanced, not to say exacerbated, by Jules Berry. This brilliant and experienced stage actor suffered from a mental block as the result of which he could rarely remember his lines exactly; he substituted spur-of-the-moment paraphrases possessing their own unpredictable merits.

Through Castanier, Prévert and the anti-Fascist *ambiance* of the Popular Front at the time, Renoir and des Fontaines came into contact with the October Group, a left-wing, avant-garde theatre-cum-cabaret company which had been formed on a co-operative basis in 1929. The October Group provided the film with not only Castanier and Prévert, but Jacques's brother Pierre (as assistant director), Joseph Kosma (who wrote its theme-song), and, among the players, Florelle, Sylvia Bataille, Jacques Brunius, Maurice Baquet, Marcel Duhamel, Guy Decomble, Fabien Loris and Brémiaud. Gerard Guillot and *Premier Plan* agree in seeing the October Group influence as stronger than Renoir's own. In 1957, Renoir told *Cahiers* that the collaboration between Prévert and himself was so close that it was impossible to remember who wrote which line. In 1960, Renoir denied any didactic intention on his part, although it's hard to believe that the film hadn't, in Prévert's mind, a definite political moral, which Renoir must have understood and in which he must joyously have acquiesced.

"I didn't shoot in a real courtyard, because I was beginning to experiment with pretty continuous takes. I wanted whatever was happening in the courtyard, and in the rooms around it, to be filmed at the same time. I wanted to play backgrounds off against foregrounds. That's why we shot in the Studio at Billancourt; often under tenting and around the yard we constructed the decors. These decors were sufficiently manageable for us to position a camera inside the rooms. . . . "

The film was shot rapidly, in 28 days, for a million francs (a smallish budget for the time). Running 2,200 metres, it had its Paris premiere on 24 January 1936.

Amedée Lange (René Lefevre) is a humble employee at the publishing house owned by M. Batala (Jules Berry). Batala specializes in pulp fiction whose text he interlards with paid plugs for Ranimax Pills. His whole business is as shaky as it is vulgar and he has constantly to fob off creditors and others for whom he has promised to publish pamphlets of an uplifting nature. Lange spends his lonely evenings, and sometimes nights, writing little stories out of his fantasy life as "Arizona Jim". Batala cynically introduces him to a creditor (Brunius) as the genius whose work will make all their fortunes. But a telegram delayed by the absent-minded Lange hints at police enquiries and Batala abruptly decamps. Hearing of his death in a railway accident, the workers get together and, helped by an amiable young playboy, form a co-operative, which revives Batala's business. Later Batala returns, disguised as a priest, to reclaim his now thriving concern. Lange shoots him and makes for Belgium. The patrons of a frontier café recognise him as a murder suspect, but after his laundress, Valentine, has recounted their story (in a flashback which constitutes the body of the film) the locals guide them across the Belgian frontier to freedom.

In 1965 the wisely anonymous reviewer of *The Times* described *Le Crime de Monsieur Lange* as "entertainment and no more." But without some awareness of the political and ideological issues to which this overtly Popular Front movie refers it is absolutely impossible to understand what Prévert and his accomplice were about. Nor is it possible to understand important areas of meaning in a host of Renoir movies, in particular, *La Vie est à Nous, La Marseillaise, This Land is Mine, Diary of a Chambermaid, La Grande Illusion, La Règle du Jeu, Éléna et les Hommes, Le Déjeuner sur l'Herbe* and *Le Testament du Dr. Cordelier.**

Jacques Fauvet and Alexander Werth both describe the history of France since 1789 as one long civil war, generally a cold war, but erupting inter-mittently, into a "hot" war—as in 1848, 1870, 1940 and again with the OAS. The broad outlines of this war may be seen in terms of a three-cornered struggle, involving the bourgeoisie (the right wing), the working classes (the left wing) and the (split) peasantry. While certain sections of the peasantry sometimes erupt in right-wing activism, e.g. Poujadism, perenially depressed rural areas have registered a sizeable and longstanding Communist vote,

---

* In our account "right" and "left" are taken in their usual journalistic sense. "Right-wing" indicates a preference for unfettered capitalism or feudalism, the aristocratic principle, monarchy, authoritarianism, or Fascism, "left-wing" a concern with egalitarianism or Socialism, or the working and poorer classes, or Communism. But one must bear in mind that there are several rights and lefts, radically independent of each other, which may direct their hostilities against rival right- or left-wing groups, or even form temporary alliances with "opposing" groups against "rivals". French politics in particular are "molecular" as well as "polar".

owing much less to loyalty to Communism than to resistance to the system. For a variety of economic, demographic and cultural reasons, the chances of political consensus are small, and the chances of revolutionary extremism correspondingly more tempting. Disturbances from other European countries have made it easier for the extremes to pull the centre apart and for "revolutionary" strategies to seem viable. Hence Fauvet notes the rough alternation, in French politics, of shaky coalitions with weak dictatorships.

The continuity of violence in French politics provides the context for the murder which is the climax of *Lange*. The French Revolution was possible because the middle classes, the peasantry and the poor, combined to overthrow an aristocratic order. Subsequently, however, the victorious groups turned, logically enough, on one another.

Victory went, eventually, to the bourgeoisie (the upper-middle and middle classes). By 1848 too many of the new, industrial proletariat were starving to death. The "real nature of the Revolution lay in the conflict between the working people and the middle class. It was overalls against frock-coats; caps against hats." (André Maurois, *A History of France*.) In a four-day battle, the workers of Paris were defeated by the army and the (bourgeois) National Guard. When in 1871 France surrendered to Prussia the (largely working-class) Paris Commune rose in revolt against the surrender, and therefore the government. Again the conflict took on a left-right quality. The Dreyfus case (1894-1906) again pitted left-wing reformism against right-wing anti-Semitism. 1914-18 drowned the internal conflict in patriotic gore, although the extent of a 1917 mutiny by French troops, and the severity of subsequent reprisals, is still a matter of controversy. Two years

before *Lange,* in 1934, right-wing extremists, inspired by Hitler's success
in Germany, staged a Paris uprising, spearheaded by mercenary thugs paid
by M. Coty, the well-known perfume manufacturer. The centre was sufficiently alarmed to ally itself with the Communists, and give the Popular
Front its resounding electoral victory.

Its triumph was both shortlived and hollow. The alliance was, by the very
nature of the allies, an insecure one, and the Popular Front split wide over
the question of whether, and how far, France should intervene in the Spanish
Civil War, along with the Germans, the Italians and the Russians. Parallel
splits developed on the right. Some who sought a French Fascism for France,
found their patriotism stronger than their Fascism. A significant minority,
not restricted to Fascists, preferred a German victory over France to any
French victory which would strengthen French Communism and even any
potential allies, i.e. the French centre. When Stalin signed his non-aggression
pact with Hitler, the Communist Party suddenly discovered that Hitler was no
great danger after all and began to oppose preparations for war. Thus, in the
face of Hitler, France was paralysed by internal feuds and by a preference,
on right and left alike, for political ideas which were not French at all, but
which it was hoped to impose on France, without, or with, outside aid.

As Alexander Werth points out in his study of the French surrender and its
aftermath, the collaborationist government at Vichy enjoyed, initially, at
least, "the more or less wholehearted support of almost all the traditional
right, including the aristocracy, the army, the police and much of the
peasantry." The Vichy government campaigned energetically on behalf of
traditional moral values and against left-wing ideology. Until 1943 the
Resistance was overwhelmingly a working-class phenomenon (apart from a

few eccentrics like de Gaulle). A special branch of the Vichy police, inspired by the traditional anti-Semitism of the right, proved itself even more zealous than the Gestapo in hunting down Jews. Thus the battle between the Resistance and Vichy was also a real civil war on a right-left axis. As the Allies' fortunes improved, the Resistance broadened its social base, until by 1945. the hardcore Right was thoroughly discredited. Nonetheless, it gradually returned to respectability, until guerrilla warfare by another rightwing aggregation was marked by OAS terrorism.

This was another "Resistance", this time by right against the left and centre. It reached its climax when the French officers in Algeria, backed by the sons of the settlers in *Le Bled*, were ready to invade France. A full scale civil war was averted largely by the duplicity of General de Gaulle, a personality enigmatic precisely because he didn't fit the left-right divisions to which almost everyone else was at that moment geared.

Fauvet comments that the French are extremely patriotic, but that their patriotism is often to an idea of France rather than France itself. It may seem strange that so many Frenchmen should unfailingly vote for a party so obviously dominated from Moscow. Yet large sections of the French working class and depressed peasantry, accustomed to 150 years of violence and extremism, take extremism for granted, as a necessary balance, and vote in as sharp a protest as they can to the system in power, i.e. the capitalist one.

An equally foreign loyalty is maintained by the Roman Catholic Church, whose general political influence has been overwhelmingly right-wing. The Vatican itself has, of course, long been committed to right and right-centre politics in Italy, and, in the '30s, had come to terms with Mussolini. At the time of the French Revolution the Catholic Church, being part of the feudal

order, had tended to an ultra-right position, while the middle-class attack on feudalism invoked rationalism, liberalism, agnosticism and anticlericalism. In 1864 a Papal encyclical condemned socialism, liberalism, toleration and democracy, and those French governments which felt themselves attacked retorted with sweeping anti-clerical measures. Marcel Pagnol's *La Femme Du Boulanger* draws much of its humour from the rivalry between the village curé and the village schoolmaster. It's a good accurate stock joke, and religion in education and local government have remained a sore point. Thus, in Bresson's *Le Journal d'Un Curé de Campagne*, part of the priest's tragedy is that most of those who welcome him dwell at the local chateau.

Many French Catholics have other loyalties also, spinning more wheels-within-wheels. Thus small Catholic unions confusingly compete and/or collaborate with Socialist and Communist unions. Believing Catholics often take up anticlerical positions, i.e., seek to limit the *political* influence of the Church.

The variety of permutations, combinations and paradoxes helps explain the liveliness of French thought and art. French intellectuals have to define their cultural and political positions far more closely than their English counterparts. Questions of "commitment" are at once more complex and more pressing. The intricacies of problems tend to be crystallised rather than blurred over, while politics, culture and art move much more easily towards questions of general ideology than they do in England, or, until the recent radical challenges, in America.

Le Crime de Monsieur Lange is first and foremost a political comedy, no less partisan than *Our Daily Bread* and more openly so than *Mr. Deeds Goes To Town* or *My Man Godfrey*. It certainly possesses a plausible and off-the-cuff quality of realism, but it is also at once hortative and comic. Its theme is the spirit of initiative which the working class and its allies ought to adopt towards certain problems; notably, how to avoid being swindled out of the just rewards for one's labour.

The class issues could hardly be clearer. The co-operative is opposed to Batala, who cheats everybody, not only his fellow capitalists but, more important to us, the employees of his publishing house. He isn't the bloated capitalist beloved of vulgar Marxist cliché. He's a quick, slick, financially unstable middle-class operator, of a type intermittently prominent in French political scandals (some of which would have been fresh in the minds of audiences of the time) and always significant in the French economy (which was chronically under-capitalised). His return, disguised as a priest, and the irreverent atmosphere introduced by his disguise, is a simple and effective way of saying, "Priests are merely the bosses in disguise, in their Sunday best (i.e., priestcraft is just another way of bamboozling ordinary people)." The script takes care to show Batala, in his dying moment, crying out, "I want—a priest." His sincerity never prevented him from being a crook and a seducer. So what price sincerity? What matters in religion as a political force is not deathbed sincerity, but lifelong hypocrisy.

Since Batala has fled and the cooperative has made a success of the firm, his return outrages our sense of natural justice, as against the legal justice of capitalist ownership. It paraphrases Marx's notions of the capitalist as a parasite whose profit depends on the exploitation of his employees—and of the law as a part of a corrupt system, rather than above it. The scriptwriters want to associate Batala with the system of which the law is part. But at the same time, he has to flee for the cooperative to have its chance. The point is made without pedantry by coincidences and jokes. Batala is being hounded by his creditors and their agents, i.e., other, more powerful capitalists. Second, Lange has absentmindedly held up an important telegram, so that when Inspector Juliani appears, Batala assumes that he's about to be investigated and has no time to do anything but run. The Inspector turns out to be a shy, seedy, ingratiating man, and, he explains, only a retired Inspector, since turned croupier. All of which suggests that he was sacked for some scandal, sank lower and lower, and now, in despair, has called on Batala, his distant cousin, to ask for a job. So the law's avenging angel turns out to be disreputable and after a job; it's all an old-boy net. Batala's panicky misunderstanding typifies capitalism as a system full of haywire feedbacks and pointless panics (just like the 1929 Crash, notoriously a product of communications chaos and hurried scuttlings).

When order is chaos and tyranny, not all murders are moral crimes. Nonetheless the murderer has to face a "trial by his peers". The ordinary people in the frontier café discuss whether or not to hand him over to the police, or help him over the border. Their discussion of the crime frames the film's long flashback and ensures our alertness to its political morality. The man who, on principle, is in favour of calling "les flics" is a stunted, spiteful character. A robust patron jovially recounts his recurrent dream. "I dream I'm killing rats . . . and what if the man he killed was a rat?" The moral is, of course, a bloodthirsty one, and is another reason why, to understand the film,

it is necessary to bear in mind both the atmosphere induced by the Fascist threat and the way in which important sectors of the proletariat had been subjected to indiscriminate violence by the centre-right (in 1848 and 1870). But it's also softened by a certain humanity. Murderers aren't a race apart. Quite normal people are capable of dreaming brutal dreams, of recounting them with more relish than shame, and of finding that others understand. Given a good reason anyone, even the mild and dreamy Lange, can kill. Lange, having pulled the trigger, murmurs, "It's easy", in a strained way, yet evenly balanced between remorse and relief, so reminding us that it may be not only *terribly* easy to kill, but *liberatingly* easy to kill. The call is not to a bloodbath of minor capitalists, but to an (if necessary) violent reaction against the passivity and the docility which have become second nature to men like Lange.

As Clouzot explained in a prologue added to the English-language version of *La Vérité,* the French judicial system sets out not only to attribute guilt, but to understand the whole psychological context of the crime. This assumption helps towards an acceptance of the café trial, where Valentine immediately pleads guilty on her lover's behalf and then goes on to secure, as it were, a vote of confidence, in his motives. Obviously the trial also has its anarchistic overtones. Decency depends primarily not on the system's hard and fast laws nor on immediate recourse to the police, but on the extent to which people can spontaneously and unofficially manage to understand one another.

This unofficial jury and judge may seem uncomfortably close to the pat or sentimental. Yet a certain cautious sentimentality has a very real function, given that common middle-class combination of (a) a paranoia, far more freely expressed in the '30s than now, about the lower classes as idle, foul-mouthed oafs, incapable of judgement or sensitivity; and (b) a stupid trust in police and system. Nor does the film acquiesce, even briefly, in that endemic Marxist Manicheanism about rich and poor, middle- and working-class. The workers have their internal enemies. The nasty little dwarf-like character is one of Prévert's symbolic incarnations for the impotence, envy and spitefulness which skulk in the margin of all relationships (his other variations on the same theme include Zabel in *Quai des Brumes,* Old Jericho the old-clothes man in *Les Enfants du Paradis* and the machine-gun toting maniac in *Les Amants de Verone*). The caretaker nostalgically remembers his military service in Tonkin (Indo-China, later Vietnam), and he's upset and protests when the cooperative, with no authorisation other than its own, tears down the advertisement hoarding which bars the daylight from his own invalid son's stuffy little bedroom (the antithesis, sunlight and slums, is a '30s preoccupation, here deprived of all cliché). It's the caretaker's wife's lies which keep the young people apart, with the net result that Batala has his chance to seduce her, thus burdening her own son with another man's illegitimate child. The intricacies of these contrasts aren't accidental. Caretaker and wife take themselves as middle-class, they trick themselves into distinctions which don't exist, they are abused by those they trust and they abuse those with whom they have obvious affinities of interest.

The caretaker reluctantly goes with the cooperative, because there's no alternative, and he grudges any admission of what the cooperative has done for him. When he gets pleasantly drunk at the cooperative's celebratory banquet, the habits of a lifetime seize him again and tear him away from the general good humour. He starts singing a sentimental old tearjerker called *"C'est la nuit de Noël"* and, simultaneously, seized by a sense of duty, lurches out into the night to start emptying the garbage. Once he dreamed of Tonkin, and unblocked the drains. Now he dreams of Christmas, and clears out the trash. The tears, the duty and piety emerging in his drunkeness express the hidden counterpart of his identification with his superiors: it's his social masochism. The Freudian associations recall *On Purge Bébé*: clearing garbage—cleaning lavatories—what the English Other Ranks call brown-nosing, i.e., compulsive self-abasement to curry favour with one's idealised superiors. To the real, cheerful, communal feast, the old man prefers solitude (individualism), work, and the tinsel dream of religious goodwill: Christmas. Here in pointed comic metaphor is the whole syndrome of the working class Tory (traditionalist, sentimentalist, authoritarian, imperialist, militarist, Christian, and snobbish). He's not quite a Fascist, though he could easily be induced into an admiring acquiescence, and would surely have supported the Vichy government as enthusiastically as the gamekeeper in Buñuel's *Diary of a Chambermaid*. It would doubtless have been tempting to try and make Batala himself, or the system (perhaps some sort of industrial accident, or overwork), responsible for the young man being sick and laid up in his little cubbyhole. In the event, he just falls off his bike while showing off, a healthy exuberance.

If the workers have their internal enemies, they also have their external friends. The contrast to the flippant and irresponsible Batala is the equally flippant and irresponsible playboy, Batala's principal shareholder, who offers to finance the co-op and then buttonholes the foreman to ask, "By the way, what exactly is a co-op?" He's clearly been used to money and the immunity which it confers on his whims—for he just tears off the foreman's bowtie, which displeases him. But when, in riposte, his own handkerchief gets thrown out of the window, he takes it in good part. (Such rapid touches invariably carry more weight in films than is usual in novels because the film medium entails a more rigorous selection of incident). He's a silly ass type but he's okay because though he enjoys having money he doesn't clutch at it, he doesn't mind losing it in good company, he's capable of a man-to-man tit-for-tat. He's free from greed, fear, false dignity, and property-mania.

Adjacent to the printer's shop is the laundry, whose boss is Valentine. She does the deliveries herself (at least to Lange, probably because she fancies him); the film isn't attacking property rights *per se*, but the irresponsible exploitation of property and labour. Valentine's laundry already has the feeling of a cooperative (Valentine and girls rally round the pregnant Estelle, as the co-op rallies round the caretaker's son). Inspector Juliani's manner is that of a crushed, lower middle class functionary—a cousin of Legrand.

Lange is another white collar worker. More, perhaps, in the 30s than now, middle-class people prided themselves on being more refined than the working class, on being sensitive dreamers, like Amédée Lange, who eventually emerges from the prison of what George Orwell called the "shabby genteel". He is a secret writer, just as Legrand is a secret painter, and he shows an alternative route through which the shabby genteel may find liberation. He writes, he lives, in his imagination, Western comics, for children, and childlike adults. As Arthur Mayer and Richard Griffith point out, "It was . . . overcultivated old Europe which first saw the Western for what it was and what it meant. In 1919 the great French critic and film director Louis Delluc pointed out the part played in these films by their background and their physical material . . . bare grey plains, mountains as steep and luminous as the screen itself, horses and men in all their brute strength, the tremendous intensity of a life so simple that it has all the room in the world for beauty and harmony and contrast, and lends an incomparable spark of humanity to the simple sentiments like love and revenge which spring from it." So quick, indeed, were French audiences to adopt the Western that from 1909 on Jean Durand anticipated the spaghetti Western by shooting Westerns in the Camargue: one of his series' heroes, played by Joe Hamman, was Arizona Bill, whom Prévert evokes as Arizona Jim. Through Lange, Prévert is persuading the middle-class spectator to adopt a "vulgar" taste. Conversely, Lange has to stop using the West as a *beau pays du rêve,* and take its morality very seriously—i.e., shoot Batala, just as his Arizona Jim shoots the bandits who are "stealing the workers' payroll." One of Lange's stories is called *Arizona Jim Contre Cagoulard.* Les Cagoulards, ('the hooded ones') were the public's name for what René Rémond describes as "that small core of conspirators . . . which named itself the Secret Committee for Revolutionary Action. Founded . . . to root Communist conspirators out of the army, extreme methods did not frighten it, and it did not flinch from . . . attacks on the office of the General Confederation of French Workers." It was "even willing to do the dirty work of Italian Fascism by assassinating the two Rosselli brothers, militant antifascists."

The film's dialogue abounds in ironies whose gentle finesse carries a seditious virulence. When Valentine calls at Lange's room with his laundry, he tells her he's been writing all night. "Aren't you tired?" "No," he replies, "for me writing is like dreaming." (i.e., writing = dreamlife, a nicely Surrealist proposition). "Oh, I see, like a somnambulist," she says, and our intimation that dreamlife = voyaging = escape is confirmed when, sure enough, he replies, "Yes, it's a good way of travelling." The exchange of ideas, of humour and allusion, is as rapid and profound as Chaplin's comic ballets of gesture. The caretaker becomes Lange's inspiration for a counter-revolutionary general. Estelle inspires his Mexican heroine, and one of Arizona Jim's adventures involve him in hunting down three gangsters. Prévert wants to assert the childlike dynamism, the re-creativity, of the dream, as the Surrealists wished to use it, namely as a springboard for a revolt against the everyday; and Renoir's concern is with interior and exterior realism. The co-op members pose for a cover photograph for their comic. As they break up their absurd pose, Lange says sadly, "We weren't really natural." When they discuss whether to produce an Arizona Jim movie, he mutters, "Oh, I don't like the cinema, those painted backcloths are so unconvincing."

It's of the essence that Lange's Arizona Jim comics should be pop art with neither capital letters nor camp, and recalcitrant to even those canons of artistic quality which admit Rauschenberg and such. Again, Prévert and Renoir coincide, or intersect. In Renoir's *French Can-Can* the vocation which is vindicated is that of artist-entertainer, not that of fine artist. *The commedia dell'arte* of *Le Carosse d'Or* fits only uneasily into high culture notions of art. Renoir clearly isn't concerned whether Legrand is a great painter or just a fashionable cult. Similarly, the keynote of Prévert's view of art is sounded in a poem entitled *L'Orgue de Barbarie* (i.e., barrel organ, but by phonetic allusion "barbaric organ"). All the musicians are so busy discussing which instruments they play (harps, cellos, kazoos), that no music can be heard. When they turn to a silent fellow in the corner, and demand to know what instrument he plays, he replies "The barrel organ, and I'm quite a good performer with the knife," upon which he stabs them all to death and plays on his barrel organ music so simple and beautiful that a little girl who was fast asleep under the piano wakes up and marries him. They live happily ever after and have ever so many children who unfortunately learn to play all sorts of instruments and everything has to start all over again.

Lange learns, from art which is not art, to oppose his dreams to Batala's and society's wiles, and to pull the trigger. The film's very title is a pun on his name. He begins as "l'ange", an angel in the sense of being "well-behaved", and he concludes as the exterminating angel. In their political dimension, Lange and the caretaker are complementary characters. Lange incarnates that aspect of lower-middle-class culture which, amiable if timid, might be persuaded to throw in its lot with the Popular Front. The caretaker inclines towards that aspect of middle- and lower-middle-class culture which, in France, as in Germany, provided much of the support for Fascism, for fear that the working class would drag it down into its "cooperative". In *Lange* this is just what happens to him, and curmudgeonly as he is, he will hardly admit that it's not so bad; he's still ready to welcome Batala back. It is he, now, who is 'lost' in his sentimental dreams, and Lange is the 'militarist'. On a poetic level, Lange is clearly related to Baptiste, the victimised angel-clown of *Les Enfants du Paradis,* who only dreams of murder (in his mind).

Baptiste is befriended by an amiable irresponsible manipulator of art's illusions (the jovial ham actor Frédéric Lemaître) and is protected from a rightwing killer (the Count) by an anarchist one (Lacenaire). But he is unable to free himself from his idealism, and ends with a broken heart.

Batala, like Lange, moves in a cloud of illusions and confusions. But he ensures that the illusions and confusions are others', not his. He peddles anything literary, serials, plugs, edifying tracts, Lange's dreams, he lies to employees and creditors alike, he chats up all the girls and he concludes as a priest. His extraordinary gift of the gab fools everybody except the earthy Valentine, who sees through him, but only after having been his victim in the past, as Estelle is now. Jules Berry is another Prévert icon. In *Les Visiteurs du Soir* he plays the devil, in *Le Jour se Lève* he plays a conjurer who entraps everyone in his web of lies. In *Les Enfants du Paradis,* Lemaitre, the flirtatious and resourceful actor, typifies a successful and likeable compromise between Lange and Batala.

Where sexual morality is concerned the film is permissive. When Lange asks Valentine what she did before she ran the laundry, she asks, "Do you really want to know?" and he replies, "No", because he's already guessed (laundresses, like sempstresses and midinettes, were prone to augment their scanty earnings by casual prostitution). Batala's secretary is ready to try almost anything legal on his behalf. Estelle, an illegitimate child, all but becomes an unmarried mother. All of these women are very sympathetic, apart from the middle-aged prostitute who, physically, resembles the caretaker's puritanical wife, and who asks for American cigarettes. A pretty systematic repudiation of conventional morality is clearly going on. Clearly Prévert sees sexual jealousy as part of bourgeois property-mindedness, its opposite being the complete, liberating love of the free couple (in Surrealism, *"l'amour fou"*). Renoir is never so affirmative, romantic, or hopeful about the couple, and jealousy for him is part of a very human, but vain, attempt to arrest the dance of life. Both share an anarchistic view of human relationships.

The promiscuity of Estelle, Valentine and indeed of Lange, is very different from that prevailing among the bourgeois characters—Batala, his secretary, and the smirking man (Brunius again) who picks her up at the station. The working-class women are generous and in that sense "pure". Bourgeois men are exploiters, using the smirks, jargon and gestures of tired-out gallantry and threadbare pretence, the hypocritical, sterile world of Max Ophuls's *La Ronde*—a world which Anglo-Saxons tend to think of as worldly, sophisticated and "naughty", but which Prévert presents as a cynical, tedious fake.

At this time, and later (under Vichy and under de Gaulle), the right wing in France was very keen on a moral revival. Its evangelism tended to focus on three points which later made up a principal Vichy slogan: "Famille, Travail, Patrie", tagging a policy which Alexander Werth summarises as "back-to-the-land-and-let's-have-more-babies." Batala's publication of tracts like "Whither Are We Drifting?" coincided with a pro-Fascist swing in a large proportion of the French press. The contradictions between "famille" and "travail" are indicated when the caretaker protests at the removal of the hoarding from his son's bedroom, i.e., the father subordinates his own family to the dead letters of the law, not his job to his family. The conservative peasant cult of the extended family is guyed when Estelle's child dies at birth. Valentine appears in the doorway to say, seriously, "The mother's fine, but the child—no." Everyone is silent for a moment—clearly torn between respect and relief—until Juliani removes his hat, bows his head as if in grief and says, "It was a relative, all the same." At which everyone roars with laughter. Later, Lange, dictating his story about the Mexican girl, says "Write—she was very lucky, the baby died." Clearly the film is espousing the libertarian cause of abortion on demand, via a *reductio ad absurdum*, a device often adopted when an artist feels his audience may not too easily adopt the moral values towards which he hopes to influence them. The Inspector's obviously exaggerated response is taken as butt, so that the emotional balance tips against the conventional attitude. Again, respect for work is pilloried by Batala's desecration of Lange's text with Ranimax plugs. It's not work that's respected, it's money. Indeed the film anticipates several cultural issues of the '60s as much as the '30s—the new morality, commercials, job-satisfaction and workers' control.

As we shall see later, much which in Renoir seem prophetic is also retrospective. The concept of a cooperative owes less to communism than to revolutionary syndicalism which was an important sector in the French left until 1914 but could not survive World War One. It was less threatening to the petit bourgeois than communist theory. The Ranimax motif, and the workers' own concept of Batala's productions, recalls a remark of Sorel's: "To ensure future enfranchisement, people must be induced to see their work, to consider all they do as a work of art, which cannot be done too carefully, and to seek to understand everything which happens in the workshop. They must be rendered simultaneously conscientious, artistic and knowing in everything concerned with production." In Marxist terms, disalienated. When Renoir tackles the theme of the artist, as he often does, it is in no way to distinguish the artist from the artisan, or to romanticise him as the unacknowledged legislator of the world. It stands, rather, for any form of unalienated work—in contrast to the waiter in *La Chienne*.

So tightly integrated is *Lange* that many details near the beginning only make sense to the spectator who already knows the end. As the couple put their suitcase on a bed at the frontier hotel, Valentine remarks, "It's a nice room, the walls are all white, the sheets are white too." The remark associates her with candour, the optimism, but we don't yet know how it fits both her professions—laundress and, by implication, prostitute. For a laundress is one who makes dirty linen as white as snow, who can lose her virginity yet not her purity, that is to say, an honest, unsentimental, realistic freshness and hope. The association is confirmed by some lines in Prévert's poetry, as well as by the parallel motif of glass (virginity) in *Les Amants de Vérone*. Purity is a psychological, not a physical, condition.

It is worth exploring, in this respect, the contrast between the two characters in *Les. Enfants du Paradis*: Garance (Arletty) and "Old Jericho" (Pierre Renoir). Garance too had been a laundress and a prostitute. She loves Baptiste as Valentine loves Lange. We first see her in an art situation (a fairground booth) *unclothed,* as The Naked Truth in a well. (It's true that the sides of the well are so high that Garance is party to a show business swindle). In real life, she is the film's most naked, frank, and direct character. Old Jericho is an old-clothes dealer. When Baptiste, on stage, wears clothes like his, Old Jericho furiously accuses him of stealing, not his clothes, but his *character.* For his clothes are all he has in the way of character. They are other people's cast-off scraps, begged, borrowed and stolen. He is the negative of authentic being. He is a no-man-scarecrow concocted out of middle-class bibs and bobs, in particular, a crushed top hat. Like all the film's characters, his stock-in-trade is secondhand personalities. But all he has left in his lonely, penny-pinching nonexistence is his (misdirected) jealous rage. In his inauthenticity, he recalls a clumsy Batala. In his victimised solitude, he recalls a tragic Lange. In his spleen, he recalls the semi-dwarf. Clothes, as character, evoke also the artist's bequest to the deserter in *Quai des Brumes,* and the fancydress ball of *Lumière d'Eté*. The objects in Old Jericho's bag recall the Vichy collaborators' junkyard in *Les Portes de la Nuit* and the props which the Fascist aristocrat sells the film company in *Les Amants de Vèrone*. When Batala returns, he is garbed as a priest. His is a sort of second coming—for he is a dead thing, the ghost of a man, with all his trickeries and complications. It may be that his dying request for a priest is both sincere and insincere. It may be the last reflex ruse of a trickster to the reality of death. Maybe his falseness is by now his second nature, as incorrigible, as inexorcisable, by the last, or any other, sacrament, as the devil whom the same actor incarnates in *Les Visiteurs du Soir*.

Ingenious as it is, the story accommodates several mysteries. Scenes end with a soft abruptness and leave the spectator in a mist. Through uncertainties, the film amplifies its suspense, and creates a slightly confused atmosphere in which we can accept the big improbability, Batala dying and switching "old clothes" with the priest. We also hear the news during a story climax (Lange and Valentine in bed and settled at last), which helps to distract our attention. It is presented obliquely (from a wireless) while Valentine sings a song (the operetta touch being a further disrupter of workaday logic). Visually, too, the camera is on the move, from window to window. . . .

On three occasions the camera traverses the yard in this bold, sweeping, autonomous way. In the opening sequence it is so used, though less sweepingly, to introduce various characters as they come to work in the morning.

The second is during Batala's presumed death, a pivotal event in the story. The third is in the climactic confrontation preceding his assassination, and the movement is more energetic still. In Bazin's words, "the camera frames Lange in Batala's office, and follows him through the machine shop and down the stairway till he emerges on the outside landing. But then the camera quits him and instead of following in his tracks, it pivots off in the contrary direction, sweeping across the whole courtyard until it frames Lange again in the opposite corner, where he meets up with Batala once more, to kill him." As Bazin remarks, the feeling is one of vertigo, of madness, and of suspense.

In the climactic sequence, a song is again involved. For the co-op's good companions have amiably taken up the caretaker's drunken ballad, and cheerfully bawl, *"C'est la nuit de Noël"*, taking no notice of him as, suddenly sobered, he tries to tell them that Batala's dying.

As Batala's train speeds away into the night, railway lines skim under the camera. Later, the camera looks down on Batala's corpse and we dissolve, but very slowly, to the road, seen from the same angle as the railway lines, skimming along under the getaway car. The visual parallelism intensifies the effect of the dissolve, which means: The road to freedom is driving straight over Batala's dead body.

These formal "rhymes" are all the more surprising in view of the extent to which the film was improvised, and in view of its rough, off-the-cuff, free-flowing atmosphere. In fact, of course, Renoir's eye for the passing gesture had been sharpened by his studies of art, and Prévert's gift for idiomatic, informal and accidental-seeming phrases is one of the joys of his poetry.

The film has its roughnesses. The characters are jerkily introduced; an unpleasant, conspicuously Jewish-looking, girl is never seen again; and it's irritatingly uncertain whether Brunius on the platform is meant to be Daisy's master without Daisy or a similar but different character altogether. Intuition rather than accident may have determined the film's secret defeatism. The way ahead may be over Batala's dead body, but Lange and Valentine are in headlong flight (a flight impossible for subsequent Prévert heroes). Coincidentally the film achieves a minor prophecy. Batala's parting shot to a creditor's agent whom he has just bribed is: "Go and take a cure at Vichy!" France, alas, had no choice but to take his advice.

An understanding of the underlying structure of *Lange* renders it more breathtaking. Only if its ideological issues are sharply focused can one relish the speed, dash and magicianly insolence with which its authors present their points.

In his *La Femme Dans Le Cinéma Francais,* Jacques Siclier devotes a chapter to Florelle, a singer eclipsed by, but in the class of, Mistinguette. "Florelle alone, in this epoque, could render acceptable the romanticism of Hugo's vision of the prostitute. . . . " Maybe she was condemned, as

Siclier suggests, by her "very unfashionable feminine aesthetic". Yet this very spontaneity makes her a fertile collaborator of Renoir's. Siclier celebrates her "proletarian hips" and the subtle femininity with which she throws her head back to tell Batala "C'est que, mon cher, je suis amoureuse". In gesture after gesture, her very spontaneity re-endows that still unfashionable feminine style with its meanings, as a style of response, of self-discipline, of thought. It offers us an alternative sensibility whose interest may too easily be confused with a more superficial kind of nostalgia. If some excellent films have aged very fast, it is precisely because they catch the gestures of their epoque infinitely more accurately than either the clichéd approximations of less observant films or the necessarily imprecise approximations which is all the other media can offer. The critic who has to evoke, in words, just what is so touching about the way René Lefevre holds a teaspoon as Florelle smiles her freshly maternal way into his nervous little life, or wanders off a little punchdrunk, yet liberated, after renouncing jealousy of Florelle's past, has to reach for metaphors which he dismisses because they are not what he saw. The film touches us by as many such touches as brushstrokes may give a painter's "characters" a secret, radiant, rhythm and energy. Sylvia Bataille testified that "the characters changed, evolved. . . . Berry, for example, never played the Batala he was asked for. It was he who added all the cynical sauce, the smiles, the charm." His cool rascality, his shoestring resourcefulness are much to the taste of current student audiences, for many of whom the film thus has, not so much a hero and a villain, as a hero and an antihero. Indeed, if Boudu had the brains to be a capitalist, a Batala is just what he might be. Meanwhile, what matters is the antithesis l'ange-linge (fresh linen, laundered)—like Legrand-Lulu, but more happily.

Bazin asks us to "note a significant detail: the paving of the said courtyard is concentric. From this realization it is clear that if deep focus is, indeed, the logical mode of shot whenever the action occurs in one of the peripheric elements of the decor, the panning shot is the camera movement specifically imposed by this general disposition whenever the action is seen from the courtyard. Whence the direction's final masterstroke, the pedalpoint, the perfect harmony which comes to crystallise the entire spatial structure of the film: the "contrary" 360-degrees pan . . . it may have secondary justifications, psychological or dramatic (it gives an impression of vertigo, of madness, it creates suspense), but its raison-d'être is more radical; it is the pure spatial expression of the entire directorial effort." As so often, I would offer an alternative perspective to Bazin's, whereby the "secondary justifications" are primary, and the threefold repetition of the effect constitutes a climactic progression from routine through love to revolt. It also evokes an inner reality, a flowing, capsizing, giddy world—Lange catching for a moment at the ultra-reality of instability, of freedom. And after all a circular courtyard no more imposes 360° panning shots on a director than a square courtyard imposes crabbing shots set at right angles to one another. On at least one occasion Renoir's single deep-focus shots span the yard, establishing, between two peripheral actions, a relationship and a movement which is within the yard. From within the boy's room, we see the removal of the hoarding across its window. As he starts up eagerly the girls help Estelle over her window ledge opposite, and she hurries towards him. This is shot, in depth, despite difficulties with depth of focus, and despite the fact that the same action could have been shaped around a panning shot. For what matters is not the shape of the set so much as the disposition of action within it. Sometimes a set's perimeter may be such as to dominate the disposition of the action within it, but the shape of Renoir's set allows him considerable latitude as to disposition of the action, so that panoramic shots or deep focus would be just as useful were the yard square, or triangular, or rectangular. Curiously, Bazin had earlier ventured another, less formalistic interpretation, which vaunted that movement's *independence* from any physical configuration, and related it instead to what he calls the "personification" of the camera, its playing the role of an invisible spectator "which takes it on itself to turn its back on the action to take a short cut. Only in Murnau will one find examples of camera movement thus liberated from the dramatic personage and geometry." In a footnote, Bazin vindicates Renoir's abstraction as against the obvious alternatives in both of which "the editing process remains purely descriptive, directly determined by the process of the action and the position of the actors." Thus, in one sentence Bazin interprets the scene from a standpoint of a simple symmetry between camera and set, and in another, he approaches it from the angle of camera as independent spectator. Yet he never bears both considerations in mind simultaneously, which, of course, is what Renoir, like any other film director, had to do. For Bazin the real subject of film style is the spiritual relationship between film-maker (considered as a sort of personalized camera) and his physical world (décor), i.e., between artist as God (behind the camera) and the world which he creates outside himself for himself and through which he then moves like a demiurge and an invisible spectator alike. From Bazin's "spiritualised formalism" the plane of dramatic interest is frequently excluded, marking the limits of his (always interesting) film criticism. Hence one may well prefer, in the final analysis, to return to a more conventional approach whereby the director's philosophical beliefs may be included in the visual style, but are not fully stated in, and do not constitute the whole of, the visually implied (as arbitrarily distinct from the dramatically implied) content. We thus insist on correlating the two and arrive at the view of the camera spinning as a delirium, a view which our intepretation shares with Bazin's rather less unorthodox fellow-Catholic, Henry Agel. He writes of *Lange* in general: "It is less for its social realism that it must retain our attention, than for that quality of the authentically strange which emanates from its vision of things and from its gust-of-wind calligraphy." To this expressionist view of the style, exemplified by recognition of Renoir's chaotic depths, Agel adds: "With

La Règle this is perhaps Renoir's strangest film." For this strangeness he proposes an additional reason: "the choice and direction of the actors creates a curiously alienating climate: René Lefevre, who was still impregnated with vibrations from *Le Million* and *Jean De La Lune,* Jules Berry, Carné's future Prince of Darkness, Nadia Sibirskaia and Sylvia Bataille, who have always remained on the fringes of the cinema and haven't 'succeeded', Henri Guisol, Marcel Levesque (Cocantin in Feuillade's *Judex*), and Jacques Brunius."

The Fascist critics Bardèche and Brasillach are in a quandary, for they, too, detest capitalism, yet are well aware that the film is out on the left wing of the Popular Front. So they praise the film, cautiously, as curious and intriguing, while maintaining that although the milieu is poor, it is not squalid. In other words—shoot people, by all means, but poverty is rather idyllic and best left, poetically, as it is. *Premier Plan* suggest that the credits be revised to read: *"Le Crime de Monsieur Lange–An October Group Film– Technical Adviser, Jean Renoir."* Certainly *Lange* offers a fascinating demonstration of the extent to which a film can have two auteurs, for it expresses, not only Renoir and Prévert, with their distinct views of the world, but their common ground—as it were, Prénoir and Rêvert.

Renoir testifies that the film, without being a commercial triumph, was well received by the large public. There seems to have been some grounds for disappointment, though, since there were rumours that censorship trouble was followed by a covert, if erratic, boycott by distributors and exhibitors. Given analogies in France and England, it is by no means impossible that the film did good business despite the spontaneous aversion of all the Batalas of the film business.

La Vie Est à Nous

Since 1914 Europe had known the Great War, the troubled '20s, seven years of Depression, and three of Nazism. By 1936 a second great war was clearly in the offing. It was by no means absurd to see this descending spiral as the death-throes of European capitalism, and one might still argue that the outcome or aftermath of World War II would have been grim indeed without the involvement of two powers one of which was non-capitalist and the other non-European. In 1930 the democracies faltered while totalitarianism thrived. America was a long way away, and it seemed to many that only an international Communism could stop the panzers in their tracks.

Hence it is not in the least surprising that when the *Parti Communiste Français* planned a propaganda film the Communist poet Louis Aragon should have proposed Renoir as its director, and that Renoir should have enthusiastically agreed. "I played something like a producer's role, in the American sense of the word". The remark is more than a little equivocal: it sounds like a disclaimer, but Renoir had at other times pointed out that in the American system the producer was the auteur. The producer in the European sense of the word, and editor, was Jean-Paul Le Chanois (then known as Jean-Paul Dreyfus). "I was in charge of the film and we formed a team: Le Chanois, Zwoboda, Cartier-Bresson and myself. Each of us shot one sequence and supervised the whole". (Renoir's touch appears at points throughout the film and the style is nowhere conspicuously non-Renoirian: no doubt there was a profound confusion of tasks and diffusion of influences.)

"I was not a Communist, and neither was the majority of the crew," Renoir later observed. Nonetheless, Poulle reports that he appeared on the Communist Party congress platform beside its leader when the film's production was announced.* In 1936 the French Communist party had never been the great outsider which after 1945 it became and Renoir, like many

* Goffredo Fofi stresses Renoir's involvement with a radical, Popular Front ginger-group, *Ciné-Liberté*. And in at least one article, Renoir's perennial dissatisfaction with the film business, and restless search for other sources of finance and distribution, took a political turn: "Film

others, could mingle with it yet not be of it, be a travelling companion rather than a fellow traveller.

Renoir's co-writer was Paul Vaillant-Couturier, a leading figure in a party then less hostile towards intellectuals than subsequently. Substantial script contributions were made by Le Chanois, Jacques Becker (notably to the peasant sequence), Pierre Unik (notably to the mechanic's sequence) and Brunius (who selected the shots which illustrate the schoolmaster's lesson). The film was shot hastily in spring 1936, at the Francoeur Studios and with exteriors at Marlotte and Montreuil. Sadoul quotes the initial footage as 80 minutes; the 1969 release version runs 70 minutes.

Pierre Bost describes the overall conception: "at once a documentary, a montage, and an anthology, of persuasive sketches". The film opens on images, with a commentary, of the richnesses of France: agricultural, industrial, cultural. The speaker is a schoolmaster (Jean Dasté) whose pupils, on their way home, wonder why if France is so rich, their parents are so poor. And the film tells them, focusing its attack on the 200 families who control the country's economic policies. Capital, of course, has its answer to the crisis. A company chairman lectures his fellow directors on the need to fight inflation by decreasing consumption, cutting wages and increasing unemployment.* Simultaneously, the Fascist *Croix de Feu* movement amasses its demonstrators. (The movement was a veterans' association which turned sharply right, and, with a total membership of 2,000,000 contributed 7,000 able-bodied demonstrators to the Paris riots of 6 February 1934). By mischievous editing, Renoir makes their leader, Colonel de la Rocque, perform a ludicrous little dance, while Hitler emits barks (effects borrowed by the British documentarists when they made Hitler dance a jig). Fascist thugs begin to beat up a streetseller of *L'Humanité*, the Communist newspaper, but are routed by passers-by. This simple, spontaneous action leads us to the more centralised set-up needed for effective political action. In the

---

directors are the sons of the bourgeoisie and they bring with them to this career the problems of their decadent class. The audience in first-release cinemas, which very often decides the initial success of a film, is also bourgeois. And only after this audience has confirmed the success of a film do the local cinemas rush to get it. The result of this is that the cinema, an essentially popular art, is manufactured and directed by people who are gradually moving further and further away from the people. The gulf between the upper-class districts of Paris and working-class Paris, between L'Etoile and the Bastille, becomes deeper every day. Soon it will be impassible and the capital of France will be divided into two enemy camps. The French cinema must without further delay be given back to the French people. It must be taken away from the merchants of the industry, the crooked business men, the artificial stars." Which words lend a political turn to the consistent attitudes underlying his personal initiatives, his gift for compromise, and his, much later, comment on the need for dishonesty if a film is to appeal to the public. Taken together, all these aspects seem to me to provide the basis for an adequately complex understanding of artist-industry-spectator relationships.

* This was indeed the financial orthodoxy of the time, overruled, notably, by Roosevelt with the New Deal and Hitler with the New Order.

newspaper's offices, its editor, Marcel Cachin, reads three letters demonstrating the vitality and ubiquity of the Communist response. (1) A worker, unjustly sacked, is reinstated by the solidarity of his mates. A woman (Madeleine Sologne) plays her part in this hitherto "all-male" sphere. Although united against a crudely hostile manager, the men might have been tricked by his ostensibly friendlier superior had it not been for the cynical wisdom of a hard-core Party member. (2) In rural France, a gracious lady decides to economise at the expense of her tenant-farmers. A bailiff (Emile Derain) seizes the livestock and implements of a hard-pressed farmer. His neighbours sympathise, and a Communist (Gaston Modot) devises a scheme whereby they pack out the sale, lean on the auctioneer, buy the farmer's goods for a ridiculous sum, and return them to him. (3) A young mechanic (Julien Bertheau), unemployed and despondent, walks out on his fiancée (Nadia Sibirskaia). The only job he can find is in a garage, and he loses it thanks to a tetchy client. A sympathetic right-wing customer presses into his palm, not a coin, but a political button. However, the Communist party offers him friendship, a job, hope. Finally, Maurice Thorez, Jacques Duclos and other party leaders speak to the camera, and images of a fervent Communist Party rally offer a human, hopeful, and virile alternative to Fascism: in fact "liberté, égalité, fraternité".

The film doesn't offer a classic Marxist analysis, but it makes no bones about its didactic intentions. It was criticized for its directness by many left-wing critics, but Renoir would seem to have scorned that "sugar-and-the-pill" approach which smacks more of contempt for one's spectator than of fraternity with him, and more of an insidious manipulation than of that democratic openness which, if the film preaches it as a practical possibility, it ought ideally to practise. In any event, subtlety often becomes ambiguity and ineffectiveness. Clearly Renoir believed in his film's arguments as convincing, as answering an urgent need, and reckoned the very avowal of the need would imply a self-confidence which was itself persuasion. The arguments are not sugared but imbued with a warmth and hopefulness which, Renoir knew, would take didacticism in its stride. A choir speaks a commentary, rhyming a-b-a-b. Both the medium and the irony recall Brecht—except that the irony is less biting, less misanthropic and less easy to reject or misunderstand as cynical resignation. Those who have read only the long script extracts printed in *Premier Plan* may be puzzled as to how, not only the dogmatically antididactic Truffaut, but even Bardèche and Brasillach (aptly described by Thorold Dickinson as "Dr. Goebbels on the cinema") can praise this film. Those who have seen it will understand its charm. A minor film in the Renoir canon, clearer, easier, and in that sense more facile than any of his others, it is by no means marginal in the way one might expect.

The idea of offering hope through political action may strike some these days as naive. Subsequent revelations as to the discrepancy between Communist ideals and Stalinist reality may lead one to expect naive arguments which, from respect for Renoir, one agrees to overlook. Yet from the perspective of France 1936, the arguments were neither naive nor irrelevant. The 200 families correspond, in a French way, to the military-industrial complex against whose growing power the Republican President Eisenhower was later to warn the U.S.A. The peasant auction did have a parallel in interwar Britain. Ronald Rickett describes a group of Kentish farmers who began the National Tithe-Payers' Association to protest against a tax which in the depression years was causing real distress. "Members went to the special sales held after the bailiffs had seized stock, bought it back at very low prices, then returned it to the original owners." The mechanic episode works out the theme of demoralisation. Politics and personal matters aren't distinct: for unemployment shatters home and friendships. The rightwing offers the (valueless) medal of adhesion. The Communist Party offers jobs, hope and mates (the Super-Family). Despite the almost unrelievedly sinister presentation of Communism in Anglo-Saxon films, many commentators on French and Italian society have underlined the Party's success in offering its supporters a warm, all-enveloping social milieu, performing much the same function as church affiliations and fraternities in American society. This underlies important scenes in such films as Robert Ménégoz's *Jeanette Et Ses Copains*, Visconti's *Rocco and His Brothers* and de Sica's *Bicycle Thieves*. That political rhetoric and rallies can be deeply moving should surprise no one, and the film is beautiful precisely because its structure brings into vivid relationship (1) the concealed structures of society, (2) the organisation needed to combat them, (3) mutual aid (rather than a vicious circle of alienations, e.g., from unemployment to shame to solitude to cynicism to apathy or Fascism), and (4) individuality (the masses are not faceless; it is the faces which compose the crowd). Its specific politics apart, *La Vie Est A Nous* has a moral beauty akin to that of such English documentaries as *London Can Take It*. Intenser, perhaps; for though its sentiment is on the broad side, its lyricism is a response to a situation which is more complex. more daunting, than the simplicity of war. Humphrey Jenning's failure with peacetime subjects is relevant; and it is *La Vie Est A Nous,* not the English documentary, which helps one clarify a film genre too often subsumed under the label "documentary", and currently proving very much richer than it: the "essay", or rather, non-fiction, film, built on an intellectual argument (e.g., *October, La Vie Commence Demain, Description d'Un Combat, Loin De Vietnam, One Plus One*). Jacques Brunius comments: "A few people began to realise that newsreel cameramen had sometimes recorded incomparable spectacles, all in the day's work, without troubling themselves about meaning or artistic values. Cutting could endow them with both art and meaning. . . . When I was editing the first two reels of news from *La Vie Est A Nous* . . . I found myself on almost virgin soil, the only lesson I could occasionally follow being Ruttman's *Melodie Du Monde*."

Renoir later tended to minimise his participation in the film, perhaps with American sensibilities in view, perhaps out of disgust with the secret Stalinism of the party on whose behalf he had unsuspectingly made it, perhaps because his thinking had taken a disengaged or anti-engagement turn, perhaps for a mixture of all three reasons. Nonetheless, critics seem agreed that Renoir's touch recurs, and that he was producer as completely as was David O. Selznick, who directed certain scenes in his Hollywood films himself and oversaw every detail. Notably, the mechanic's quiet departure in the background while Nadia Sibirskaia in close-up chats to him, recalls the across-the-courtyard deep focus with the same actress in *Le Crime de Monsieur Lange*. Truffaut remarks that "the political speeches are handled like the opening of *Les Bas-Fonds;* the tirade of the Minister sermonising Jouvet, the camera very slowly moving around Thorez on curved rails; the same operation is performed around Duclos and Cachin."*

In the event, the film's fate proved characteristically ironic. While political and Fascist critics could scarce forbear to cheer, the Popular Front government banned the film, presumably because by the time of its release the Communists had organised a series of sit-down strikes in factories in an effort to push that government further and faster along the leftwing road than it wished to go. The film pursued a diminished career at "private showings of a political character", preaching only to the converted, finally enjoying a small-scale release in 1969.

* François Poulle attributes the direction of this particular sequence to Jacques Becker, as also the *Croix de Feu* and the peasantry sequence, with Le Chanois shooting all the working-class sequences.

Partie de Campagne

In 1949 Renoir told Satyajit Ray that he had wanted to experiment with the short story film. For ease of commercial exploitation, two such short films would have to be made, and Renoir had started out on the Maupassant story hoping to follow it up with a second one. In 1957 Renoir mentions only "a short film which would be made with the same care as a long" and instead of a twin film, "we would have to find a way of making economies, given that a short film couldn't bring in much money." In 1965, the film's producer, Pierre Braunberger, described the initial project as "a full-length feature running 55 minutes."

At any rate, the scenario was written "with an eye to the eventual locations, being as I was very familiar with that part of the Loing, near Montigny. I reckoned that the Loing thereabouts could represent what the Seine had once been not far from Pairs . . . without buildings or factories . . . above all . . . I knew at just what hour of the day the light would be falling agreeable on such and such a clump of trees . . . I knew there was a risk of rain . . . but I didn't expect the rain to be as massive as it was. We had very few days of sun, and, in no time, we had exceeded Braunberger's anticipated budget. So, once again, I modified the scenario, adapting it to rainy weather. . . . " From July to September 1936 they worked and still it was unfinished. Sylvia Bataille recounts how, amongst all these frustrations, the unit's morale deteriorated, no one could bear the sight of anyone else, until finally "One day Renoir turned up and informed us that he was dropping everything, that he'd signed up to make *Les Bas-Fonds*." Braunberger's recollection is that he himself decided to recall the unit, but on seeing the assembled and edited material decided to add scenes to give the film a more imposing footage. Renoir's impression was that his subsequent commitments—his run of immediately celebrated masterpieces—were the principal factor in delaying the editing. Jacques Prévert was asked by Braunberger for a scenario which would accommodate what had been shot.

"So Prévert . . . added complementary characters and scenes which were a remarkable enrichment to the subject. The scenario was not shot, because by the time Renoir was free, the actors were physically changed. . . . " Prévert's scenario, since published, sharpens the attack on the small shop-keepers amongst whom the heroine is lost. In Leprohon's words, "The poem became a tragi-comedy. It becomes, in effect, another film."

In refuge in the Vichy zone, Braunberger had the idea of replacing the missing scenes. Marguerite Renoir's original version had been destroyed by the Germans, but the Cinémathèque hid the unedited footage. Jean Renoir gave his blessing to a new version, on which Becker and Pierre Lestringuez collaborated with Marguerite Renoir and her sister to produce the current version (1,100 metres), improved, in Braunberger's estimation, by a more rapid rhythm. Marguerite Renoir says that odd scenes were directed by Yves Allégret, Claude Haymann and Visconti, during brief absences by Renoir, and that Becker played no part in the re-editing. *Cahiers* state that the only scenes missing from Renoir's script are one exterior shot and studio scenes inside the shop: "a prologue and a pre-epilogue," and that early in 1937 Renoir co-edited the original version.

M. Dufour, an ironmonger in Paris, accompanied by his mother-in-law, his wife, his daughter and his assistant Anatole, who is also his son-in-law to be and his eventual successor, borrows the cart of his neighbour, the milkman, on this Sunday in the summer of 1860, and takes his family off to commune with nature face to face. A glimpse of the plump fish caught by two urchins entices him to stop at a restaurant nearby. Two young men, Henri (Georges Darnoux) and Rodolphe (Brunius) observe the family. The grandmother is either deaf or feeble-minded, or both. The mother is amiably affected, plump and frolicsome. The rotund paterfamilias airs his universal prowess at the expense of the cowed, round-shouldered assistant. There is also Henriette, young, pure, warm, smiling with pleasure on the swing under the sun. Rodolphe rubs his hands at the thought of relishing her fresh flesh and apportions the mother to Henri, who, more experienced and thoughtful, thinks of the girl's broken heart, perhaps even life. But Rodolphe leads the way. Soon the middle-class family is charmed by the dashing young men, who row the ladies down river while the men of the family snore through their postprandial nap. Henri expertly switches the daughter from Rodolphe, who gambols like a faun with the mother while Henri takes Henriette to his island. "Several years have passed, the Sundays sad as Mondays. Anatole has married Henriette, and on a certain Sunday morning. . . . " Henri, rowing sadly downriver, finds Henriette on their island. Henri: "I often come here. You know, these are my best memories." Henriette: "I think of it every night." Anatole's querulous voice recalls her to reality.

The choice of subject—a bitter-sweet romance set in summertime in the past—might seem a contrast to, even a retreat from, the political commitment of *La Vie Est A Nous*. And some element of spiritual counterpoise may well have been involved. Nonetheless, Maupassant was a vitriolic critic of the bourgeois ethos, and the storyline retains the author's ironies. The more experienced of the seducers is also the morally most sensitive, and it is he who, in the end, makes the girl his prey. He has given her the moment of revelation which, perhaps, renders the rest of her life more consciously derisory—yet more fully human. But Maupassant's subtle sharpness is bathed in the sensual radiance of the life-force tremulous in the girl's body (on the swing), in the caterpillar and the life forms pulsating in the grass, in the blade of grass with which the amorous mother tickles her snoring husband's nose, and in the rain stippling the epidermis of the leaves like goosepimples—like death-shiverings. An exegesis of atmospherical suggestion would sound farfetched, yet what Jacques Doniol-Valcroze calls an "amorous dialogue between Renoir and nature" evokes at once Auguste Renoir (*'La balancoire'*), Tennyson (the reeds, the weeping river), and a pantheism inflected away from Lawrence's phallic assertion to a cherishing of the evanescence of rivers, of weathers, of naivety as richness of life. If some earlier sequences are ravaged by too-broad caricature, the mixture of a jolly sensuality and a tender nostalgia gradually broadens, and deepens, and saddens, from

Brunius's capering faun to the helpless startle of Sylvia Bataille's head as she meets her lost seducer and the continuous pain of remembered fulfillment reaches a new climax. The rain-stabbed waters race under a camera which slowly lifts its gaze to the further bank while Germaine Montero sings Kosma's wordless song: "When Kosma placed over it his marvellous score, the film came together at one stroke, without loose ends." (Sylvia Bataille).

Partie de Campagne has the reputation of being a "soft" film, like all love stories, even Ophuls's *La Ronde,* of which it might almost be one episode. In fact its epilogue closes with the pang of steel teeth. The comparison with game is apt, for the girl's seducer is a 'poacher'—as so often in Renoir, no altruist, but more sensitive than the gamekeeper. The apparently simple opposition (the dull family, the immoralists) conceals a moral paradox. Family joviality is revealed progressively as imperceptiveness, as foolish complacency, and as living death. The girl's husband, round-shouldered, prematurely aged, whining, and thoroughly mean, in both the pitiable and contemptible sense, is a spiritual brother of Crépoix and of Legrand at his least redeemable. Initially, the seduction seems calculated in style and derisory in purpose. Later, the double seduction of merry mother and virgin daughter carries a Decameronesque cynicism. But when the escapade is revealed—too late—as serious, it is the complacency of the virtuous, not that of the frivolous, which is the more cruel. Ironically, the mother and Henri, set as the original pair, have, in common a secret complementarity. For Henri, after debauch, has become serious, and the mother, within dullness, has kept her joyous frivolity. It is the more experienced seducer's impulsive switch from mother to daughter, his reversion to apparent irresponsibility, which facilitates the tragic liberation. No doubt the beauty which overtaxed his moral scruples was a radiant seriousness which touched him. One can understand why Christian critics have deeply loved this profoundly immoral film.

The subject offers every temptation to imitate impressionistic effects in the graphically inferior medium of black-and-white photography. A critic in *Le Canard Enchaîné* made the admirable remark: "Fine, but I no more visit the cinema to see the Manets of Renoir or the Breughels of Feyder than I visit the museum to see the Renoirs of Manet or the Feyders of Breughel. A well composed image has its charm, but an album of reproductions has never made a film." Renoir honours the spirit of impressionism by forgetting all but its subject matter and paraphrasing its means in terms of the film sequence. The equivalent of *La Balancoire* is not one frame-still, but the sequence as a whole, with those specifically cinematic qualities of form in motion, of images colliding in time against one another.

Cauliez out-Bazins Bazin with his comments on the camera's unobtrusive transitions from objective to subjective angles and thence to a *deus ex machina*, or rather a *machina in machina*. "Curiously, the camera seems to play the role of the 'serpent'; it incites them to land on the island, it precedes them into the clearing where they will lie. . . . " Magically, too, the camera weaves a certain reverence and a sense of time out of physical movement through space: "Finally, we back away, we retire from this world which fades and belongs only to the past (track back)". The river of losing flows. . . .

The film's alfresco air is enhanced, for those in the know, by the casting. The innkeeper who puts such loving care—wasted?—into the preparation of a meal for his patrons—or public—is Jean Renoir. His servant is played by Marguerite Houllé or Mathieu, who had been his editor on all his films since 1935, and is still professionally known as Marguerite Renoir. A passing curé is played by Pierre Lestinguez.

Released after the war, *Partie de Campagne* coincided with a vogue for nostalgic bitter-sweet, akin to Autant-Lara's *Le Diable au Corps*. And ever since, *Partie de Campagne* and *La Règle du Jeu* have been felt to be the flower of Renoir by those who love, above all, a lyrical cinema.

Les Bas-Fonds
(Underworld)

Maxim Gorky's play *Na Dne* (1902, usually *The Lower Depths*), with its trenchant sympathies for the doss-house derelicts of pre-Revolutionary Russia, accorded well with the film populism, the economic miseries and the anxieties of '30s Europe. As so often, the proletarian ambivalence towards the social order is expressed via a criminal hero (Jean Gabin as the burglar Pépél). In France, as Leprohon reminds us, Slav emotionality still tinted realism with exoticism—helped by the plethora of émigré talents which had lent themselves to the French cinema.

Renoir: "The subject was one which was proposed to me by Kamenka, and which I liked straightaway." Dropping a previous adaptation, he began again with Charles Spaak, who seems to have been his principal collaborator. Also involved was a contribution by Alexandre Zamiatin, the author of *We,* who won Gorky's interested approval of his work a month before the latter's death. The film went on location beside the Seine between Epinay and Saint-Denis on August 20, 1936 and continued at the Eclair Studio, Epinay, where shooting finished in October. It was premiered in December 1936.

A baron (Louis Jouvet) is dismissed from his official post for embezzlement, embarked upon to settle his gambling debts. Returning home he finds a burglar, Pépél (Jean Gabin), who invites him to supper and presents him with a hippic statuette whose obvious value results in the burglar's arrest. The baron testifies as to his character and, evicted, drifts along with him to a doss-house on the outskirts of town. The inmates of its huge squalid dormitory are all outcasts. Prominent among them are a sentimental streetwalker (Jany Holt), an alcoholic philosopher (René Genin), and a strangely energetic little creature, described as The Actor (Robert Le Vigan), who leaps about with his accordion. Far less savoury are the mean and irascible doss-house keeper, Kostileff (Vladimir Sokoloff) and his blousy mistress Vasilissa (Suzy Prim). Pépél loses interest in her when she suggests he help their amours

along by murdering her husband. He further infuriates her by falling in love
with the younger sister, Natacha (Junie Astor), whom they treat as a drudge,
only to smarten her up when they realise the corpulent police commissioner
could be induced to marry her. Perhaps as a consequence of the baron's
scepticism, the actor decided to hang himself, and sets about his preparations
for suicide, Pépél rescues Natacha from one of Kostileff's brutal attacks, and
in his fury kills him. Vasilissa, a woman scorned, informs the police, but
the doss-house inmates are inspired to their moment of affirmation on behalf
of their avenger. Their insistence on joint guilt protects him from the law.
Natacha inspires him to start a new life. He and the baron split the hippic
trophy, the latter humping it on his shoulder as he goes. But they present it to
a working-class mother and child whom they meet on their way.

Gorky's play, first staged at the Moscow Arts Theatre in 1902, has been
filmed at least three times, notably by Kurosawa in 1957. Renoir saw the
play as "a realistic poem on the loss of human dignity," while lightening
the mood of Gorky's sombre piece. The film's innovations include the happy
ending, the greater prominence given the burglar and the baron, and a stress
on themes which might appeal to a Popular Front mood. The discovery, albeit
brief, of solidarity and the killing of the landlord, recall Lange's co-op and
the killing of Batala. The baron and the actor represent opposing dreams.
The former's are ironic, sceptical, civilized, and placidly democratic. The
latter's are romantic, rhapsodic, religious, masochistic (one senses Gorky's
love-hate repudiation of Russian "soul"). The baron has dreamed his life
away, but his dream is that of an affable detachment; his consequent realism
destroys the other's dream. The baron is freed from his class by his dreams
and crimes (a Lange-like combination), but only Pépél liberates himself from
futility. The hippic trophy is a well-meant but dangerous gift (again, the baron
is involuntarily destructive); its splitting and eventual disposal are examples
of creative vandalism. If the straw-chewing baron is Gorky's view of certain
characters of Chekhov or Goncharov, he is also a dreamer like Lange, a
born bum like Boudu, and an unusually lucid member of a doomed class like
the officer in *La Grande Illusion*. He anticipates the nonchalant sceptics of
Renoir's Mozartian epoque. The fierce, dancing, smiling accordionist recalls
the flute-playing, high-stepping faun of *Partie de Campagne,* the deranged
dancers of *Le Déjeuner Sur L'Herbe*. The antithesis of aristocrat and actor,
of reality and religion, the possibility of illusion as a valid expression of life-
force and of life as a game, recurs in *Le Carosse d'Or*.

The story postulates a variety of responses to the doss-house condition.
If the actor finds death, it is no less an assertion than the baron's comfortably
destructive impoverishment of life. As Henriette in *Partie de Campagne* is
entranced by a caterpillar, so the baron philosophises over a snail. Pépél's
criminal activities hardly mask his despair. His rage is at once a condition
of liberation, and a danger to it. After all, Pépél and Natacha might simply
have fled, without killing Kostileff. Nonetheless the killing of the latter is a

crime passionel, and no more expiation is required of Pépél than of Lange.

Local colour was a problem, and has remained a bone of critical contention. Renoir tried to cut the Gordian knot. ''I stipulated one modification only from the original project . . . that there be no attempt to create the authentic Russia . . . an enterprise doomed to the ridiculous. . . . We didn't claim to be showing Paris either. But we gave our actors a purely French language, and of the twentieth century. . . . '' Yet a thoroughgoing shift to a contemporary French setting would have created other problems. The baron would lose much of his meaning, the philosophising would lose its roots in Russian fatalism, and, shorn of its historical detachment, the film would have been hard put not to sacrifice a certain tenderness for a more polemical tone. As it is, the film becomes an improbable, yet fascinating hybrid. Gabin is a 1930 Parisian, all the more interesting for his moments of weakness (the baron 'magnetises' him, he begs the commissioner to release him). His importance in Renoir's film may be obscured by the subsequent development of the Gabin *persona*. (Cauliez postulates three stages in the formation of Gabin and suggests that Renoir's Gabin marks the transition between Duvivier's "rough sketch" and Carné's completion and is, psychologically, the richest of the three.) The *guingette* scene suggests France in the era of *Partie de Campagne*. Kostileff, the bleak barn of a doss-house, and the spirituality of most of its denizens, are Russian. If criticism has frequently complained of this "Russia on the banks of the Marne", it is equally possible to accept Renoir's ideas of "interior realism" and to accept the film's illogical, even uncertain, compromises between nationality and epoques as a stylisation accommodating Renoir's love for the always incongruous diversity of man. Neither Donskoi nor cinéma-vérité, rougher rather than smoother, the film remains Renoir.*

The creative interaction of role and personality that renders the cinema a dramatic rather than a literary art is even more noticeable in the incarnation of the baron by Louis Jouvet, one of the character actors who endowed the French cinema of the '30s with a warmth and complexity of dramatic presence which were among its glories, which the Nouvelle Vague lost, and which Hollywood as a whole has never possessed. The interplay between actor and role is altogether at variance with the current critical emphasis on (1) *covert* context (camera-movement, plot-structure) and (2) detail as an expression of one *auteur's* vision. (To hi-jack McLuhan's terms, film criticism has multiplied its linear, rationalist lines of the expense of an over-all, "mosaic," awareness).

Jouvet's lean, shrewd, saturnine air, his aquiline serenity, his sharp equilibrium of detachment and complicity, implicates so many possibilities that, like Michel Simon, he does not so much *express* his dramatic roles as *include* them. It's not simply that Jouvet is always Jouvet, a more complex personality than his roles require him to be. He gives his bizarre impression of having understood every aspect of the characters with whom Gorky-Renoir-

---

* Goffredo Fofi quotes Charles Spaak, Renoir's co-scenarist, to the effect that they had decided to set the film in Paris (whether contemporary Paris isn't clear), until Renoir implied that he had been asked to re-Russianise the setting by a Communist Party official, worried by the "audacity" of the French setting—and also concerned to pay homage to Maxim Gorki.

Spaak presented him, selected from within himself a trait of style which fulfills them perfectly, such as that smile at once so sharp and so dreamy, so affable and so cold. A wealth of "passing tones" complete his role more fully than any single dramatic action could require, and we are brought once more before the paradox already indicated by Jules Berry's contributions to Batala. Any film by Jean Renoir which includes Louis Jouvet must include much which is not Renoir, but Jouvet. Yet for Renoir himself, "the film's first spectator", just such traits may number among the film's most precious trouvailles. That stilted, slanting, backward-sloping, stiff-light walk, like a drunken church steeple, exists in no other Jouvet film. Was it Jouvet's idea, egged on by Renoir? Was it Jouvet's response to Renoir's dissatisfied pleas for more help? Was it an idea of Renoir's intepreted by Jouvet?

Where the remaining performances are concerned, any critical consensus disintegrates. The diversity of attitude reflects not only Renoir's relish of the heterogenous, but the added inconsistencies of this particular enterprise, as well as the director's streak of vacillation and unevenness. Particularly controversial is Vladimir Sokoloff's Kostileff. For Henri Langlois, the actor "at first sight, and by virtue of his physique, is of astonishing truthfulness, but his performance remains too calculated, too composed, not to be irritating." Certainly Sokoloff's playing is more fantasticated than the reserved grotesques he had contributed to Pabst. Was he over-stimulated by Renoir? Or did he draw on that 19th-century tradition whereby a floridity of gesture enlivened a narrowly grooved character? He reminds one of Dicken's Fagin or Uriah Heep, and in the context of its time, a certain uneasiness about anti-Semitism was quite comprehensible. But it is equally possible that Sokoloff's performance relates not simply to an Eastern European theatrical tradition but to a personality type, a social style which was already obsolescent in France in the '30s, but was by no means inconspicuous in Russia at the turn of the century: that of a "ghetto Jew" who has pennypicked or swindled his way into grasping more than a little poverty. Now his dream of prosperity and good bourgeois connections to shelter him from persecution is shattered as devastatingly as the actor's dream that life should possess a meaning. There are, after all, excellent grounds for arguing that styles of behaviour change as society and its pretentions change, that gesture (like costume and language, like thought itself), changes as culture changes, and that fidelity to the personal modes of one culture may correspond to no experiences in another culture, and seem "bad." Equally, Suzy Prim's vulgar, vindictive, lustful *femme fatale* is of a type now so démodé as to be unfamiliar. But that her playing has dated may not mean that it was not true (any film critic over thirty has seen the "stiff upper lip" style evolve from being the touchstone of reality to a point where the wartime documentaries have the younger generation rolling in the aisles). Junie Astor's waif-cum-drudge, a type surely as significant in the play's epoch as in Victorian England, now dissatisfies, yet intrigues, in the same way as Valentine Tessier's Madame Bovary. Having overcome his *Toni*-period puritanism about make-up, Renoir allows this doss-house drudge the pencil eyebrows of a '30s Parisienne. Langlois, who, like Leprohon, finds the film's acting generally execrable, nonetheless excepts the scenes between Gabin and Jouvet. For here Renoir hasn't had to involve himself with what for most of us are imponderables—1902 Russia, and the despair of the social dregs. The disparity of style is aggravated by Spaak's dialogue. It is often rather more bitter than the images (he became Duvivier's favourite collaborator), usually more literary than the character's social origins justify.

Like *Lange*, this is essentially the story of a group, and the principal locales are two open, collective areas (once again a courtyard, and a dormitory). The idea of a group here is often thought to be a British development, bred by the influence of documentary on the fiction film. *Les Bas-Fonds* is based less on interwoven story strands than on tracking, panning and deep-focus which see more sharply into a quickly glimpsed face or background figure than anything the Ealing mill could grind out of an entire plot. In a sequence which spins us back to the world of *Partie de Campagne*, the camera follows the maitre d'hotel of a Paris 1900 *guingette* as he traverses his little kingdom. All that café's parts (the band, the waiters) function with the satisfying precision of a clock, and only a certain deadness in his face betrays that his professional satisfactions are different in spiritual kind from those of Danglard in *French Can Can*.

In the big barn of a dormitory, Renoir's camera can move freely. The lines of beds, beams, stovepipe, pillars and banisters, far from being used, as

Dreyer might have done, to subdivide the image and to apportion space, are left to drift across screenspace in search of the actors and their brief, but significant, groupings. A sense of drift recurs in gentle disruption of time. Cauliez notes how "after the supper which the baron offers Pépél, the camera advances towards the nocturnal window, to the sound of melancholy music; the diurnal window appears and a track back to allegro music, reveals, so to speak, a new awareness." This is a characteristic Renoir effect in that it follows the techniques of a slick sharp cut, only to achieve instead an anti-thetical quality, of diffuseness, of floating. A *Fiche Filmographique de la Fédération Française des Ciné-Clubs* remarks: "Several very important passages in the film begin (in a style rather unusual for the French cinema at that time) with a camera movement which at first seems gratuitous but which rapidly justifies itself by the dialogue context. We then understand that we have seen things as if through one of the characters within the transition from his own subjectivity to the objective vision of the director. There are two or three very beautiful successes in this style in *Les Bas Fonds*. The first shot (a travelling shot moving right-left-right and then right-left) terminates with a circular movement which registers the count's change of position round the baron, who remains immobile and silent in the centre of the mirror, and we pass onto a shot framing him." A final audacious effect, whereby the camera draws back from Pépél and Natacha as they walk down a long road to freedom, or to nowhere, until the image itself shrinks to a pinpoint within a blackened-out frame, marks the apotheosis of these identifications and detachments; a sense of life as a film, as a dream. It is as if the camera has become the baron's mind's-eye's-view of his friend.

In the doss-house space, issues dissipate like smoke so that, as Alexandre Arnoux remarks, Renoir, "although he has staked so much on derussifying Gorky . . . (draws) from the drama a substance which is almost abstract, independent of place and time, so as to depict realistically the flotsam of an unreal society in the environs of a town without a name. Neither Russian nor European, the work floats, etched in acid, indecisive—all in Jouvet's dream." If the baron's story is a diminuendo, and Pépél's a crescendo, Renoir resorts to this aesthetic ultra-realism to restore, at the very last moment, the balance between neo-realism and unreality. The contracting and receding film is like, in their different ways, *Saga of Anatahan, Gertrud,* and *Pierrot Le Fou,* all meditations on life as the interimpregnation of daylight and ectoplasm. It is as if Renoir himself were part-observer like the baron, part-drastic interventionist like Pépél, and (as he sets his delicate machines in their ornate motion) part maître-d'hotel. Yet the underlying spirit is that of *apathia* in a double sense: both the modern apathy and "in Epicurean and Stoic ethics: the inner equilibrium and peace of mind, freedom from emotion, that result from contemplation, for its own sake, on the end of life." (Dagobert D. Runes, *Dictionary of Philosophy.*)

In itself the conclusion could seem somewhat ambivalent as between flight (like *Modern Times*), conformism and rebellion (Pépél, burglar and killer, doesn't go straight till he has what he really wants). In the '30s, at least, the anarchism of the flight (like Chaplin's) was felt to be nearer left than right—certainly after the gesture to the proletarian woman and baby. One might see not so much a rejoinder but a complementarity to *La Vie Est à Nous.*

The film was both a commercial and critical success, earning its director the Prix Delluc for 1936, and the Popular Front government made him a Knight of the Legion of Honour.

Terre d'Espagne
(Spanish Earth)

The Spanish Civil War provoked an irreparable breach between those supporters of the Popular Front who demanded French intervention, those whose political dispositions were all but pacifist, those who preferred appeasement to any risk of unleashing World War II, and those who felt less concerned about a Fascist Spain. But unity endured long enough for the Communist documentarist Joris Ivens to direct an anti-Franco short for which Ernest Hemingway wrote an American commentary. Jean Renoir wrote and spoke its French counterpart. 1500 metres long, the film was first shown in April 1937.

The *Premier Plan* writers condemn the film for a failure to distinguish Stalinists from anarchists and others, and accuse it of confusing Spanish patriotism with Stalinism, neither of which was Socialism. They condemn Renoir for connivance with a Stalinist substitution of a sentimental general appeal for truthful political analysis. Yet the extent of tensions within the anti-Fascist ranks were clear to few of the combatants themselves, let alone those at home. George Orwell only stumbled across them by an accident of posting, and there seems no need to disbelieve Christopher Caudwell: "our Labour Party group meets in the Communist Political Commissar's room in the offices of the local Anarchist Trade Unions." Even if the tensions had been clear, Renoir might perhaps have been as justified as, later, the American and English governments were, in overlooking between 1941 and 1945 some of the less liberal political habits of Comrade Stalin. Renoir had precisely the same moral and political reasons for mobilising support against the Fascist threat; that in a crisis situation one may be justified in descending to the level of propaganda—a level above which, it must be admitted, the English documentary movement rarely rose, with or without a crisis. But the criteria which condemn Renoir also condemn almost every wartime documentary from every country.

Now it seems evident that Renoir was never one of Socialism's inner core, iron ring or old guard, but rather a political *homme moyen sensuel*. His unwaveringly egalitarian instinct, and strong sympathy for anarchist attitudes are without any resentment for responsible authority as such, and he has a soft spot for a certain patriotism so long as it is absolutely devoid of chauvinism. The difference between *Le Bled* and *Le Crime de Monsieur Lange* is partly that of a political position, but also that of a deepening understanding of political affairs. *Spanish Earth* is simply an attempt to mobilise a broad sector of French opinion, rapidly and directly, towards an intervention which, had it occurred, might well have warned Hitler that the democracies wouldn't eternally back down, sapped his support in Germany, and averted World War II.

La Grande Illusion

Renoir began the script of *La Grande Illusion* before shooting *Le Crime de Monsieur Lange*. Asked if his film resulted from an exchange of scenarios between Duvivier and himself, Renoir replied, "No, what happened was this. I was working with Spaak. We were busy writing I can't remember what, *Les Bas-Fonds* probably, and we had had conversations about *La Belle Equipe*. It's even possible that we conceived the story of *La Belle Equipe* together. . . . I can't remember exactly. . . . Then Spaak and I thought we should give the story to Duvivier, because it would make a magnificent subject for him. . . . As for *La Grande Illusion,* the origin of the film was an anecdote which I got from a brother-in-arms . . . who had really been a war hero, a character who had escaped seven, eight times . . . I put . . . (his stories) on paper, which have nothing to do with the film you know, but they were an indispensible point of departure." Renoir went on to interview other former prisoners of war, and rewrote the scenario with Spaak. They took it to the producer who had made *Les Bas-Fonds,* and who thought it was no good. "Finally, we went all around Paris. Happily Gabin liked the subject . . . and that's how I made *La Grande Illusion*—thanks to Gabin. . . . The others all turned us down."

If the film's production is a fringe affair, it is the first of three films in which "I toed the line absolutely, and technically sought no innovation. The only innovations are in the style of the actors . . . in pushing further . . . a kind of semi-improvisation. . . . Certain parts with Stroheim or Gabin or Fresnay are improvisations—Fresnay less, because, as an actor extremely disciplined in the theatre, he had more need than the others of a text learned in advance. . . . "

The Fresnay and Gabin parts were first offered to Jouvet and Pierre-Richard Wilm. The director of production had the idea of casting Stroheim, whom he met at a press reception in Paris where he was appearing in a play. At that point the part of the commandant was a very minor one, amounting to less than five minutes' screen time. On the spur of the moment, however, he approached Stroheim who agreed to call on Renoir the next day. According to one account Stroheim said, "For you, M. Renoir, anything;" according to another he said, "Renoir? Who's he?" At any rate André-G. Brunelin reports that when Renoir heard what had been done, "It took Renoir's breath away, Stroheim was a sort of God for him." He immediately resolved to expand the part. Arranging to have him booked in at a hotel on the other side of town when they were in location, he began shooting plausible scenes which he had no intention of using, like Stroheim inspecting guards, etc. Stroheim had the idea of neckbrace and corset. Meanwhile, secretly, each evening, Renoir, Spaak and Jacques Becker got together to rewrite the script around the additional character. Filming spread over the winter of 1936-7. The "German" scenes were shot in Alsace, around Neuf-Brisach and the barracks at Colmar and the castle at Haut Koenigsburg. After studio-work at Billancourt and Epinay, the film (in its current, definitive version of 3,542 metres) was premiered in June 1937.

World War I. The Germans have concentrated their more elusive prisoners-of-war in a high-security fortress. There a gulf subsists not only between the various nationalities but between the aristocratic professional officer, Boieldieu (Pierre Fresnay), and the lower-class conscript officer, Maréchal (Jean Gabin). The Prussian commandant, Von Rauffenstein (Eric von Stroheim) recognises in Boieldieu a kindred spirit, singles him out for

special treatment, confides in him and trusts his word of honour. But Boieldieu cleaves unto his fellow-countrymen, and arranges to meet Maréchal at Maxim's, after their escape attempts. Eventually he sacrifices his own chances of escape by making a diversion so that Maréchal and Rosenthal, a nouveau-riche Jew (Marcel Dalio), will get away. Rauffenstein insists that he, not peasant conscripts of lower rank, shall confer on his French fellow-aristocrat and fellow-warrior the coup-de-grâce. Maréchal and Rosenthal are helped to escape by a German peasant woman (Dita Parlo) whose husband and brothers died in the trenches, and to whom Maréchal will return after the war. Hunger goads the fugitives to a futile quarrel, but they help one another along and cross the border into Switzerland.

The film divides into two parts, the first lighter-hearted, the second colder and grimmer. The tunnel at the first is compared to a theatre (verbally), and its covering blanket to a theatre curtain (visually), while Carette makes a step with his hands for a fellow-traveller to step down on, just like a music-hall acrobat. But "escapism" by theatre proves a false trail, and, later, the theatre becomes, instead, an arena of open defiance (the prisoners respond to the *truth* from the front by singing *La Marseillaise*). But the punishment for "exhibitionism" is solitary confinement, and Maréchal is reduced to a mumbling, furtive, precarious communication between man and man (prisoner and guard). Which forms the other pole to "theatre" in Renoir's vision of human relationships. Much of truth is subversive, and Marechal, confined in solitary, like Boudu (a nomadic solitary), must communicate in bizarre, secretive, abrasive ways, that is to say, hardly at all.

Thus camp gaieties, like the "good manners" with which Rauffenstein introduces Boieldieu to his high-security camp, are sloughed away, and replaced by an earnestness which ought, in turn, to be purified by a new realisation of comradeship, and, eventually, of the relativity of frontiers. The shift from one camp to the other makes a natural alteration of tone, and the inconvenience of having two sets of minor characters around the principals is modified by having a schoolmaster in each camp. The first is a dreamy but open character, and the second a docile, melancholy clerk, who has devoted himself to Pindar and missed much life of his own (only after the flute-playing does he glimpse reality: "At last I know why my lads enjoyed a rag"). The first schoolmaster is really an unblossomed Lange, and the second is what he might become, i.e. a white-collar soulmate of Batala's caretaker, a type not exactly unknown in the teaching profession. The themes of thestre-poetry-dream reappear, in a different permutation, and emotional emphasis, in *Le Caporal Epinglé*.

After *Le Crime de Monsieur Lange* and *Les Bas-Fonds*, the film's general ideological line might seem quite straightforward. It calls for the unity of all Frenchmen across class barriers, and depicts, approvingly, voluntary sacrifices by the aristocrat spirit on behalf of a more democratic France. Nationalism is transcended in an alliance which is also that of a French

mechanic, a German peasant, and Rosenthal. The last is not only Jewish but, pointedly, of mongrel foreign extraction. He vindicates a group long victimised by the right-wing tradition of anti-Semitism. Nonetheless, as a banker's son (and Rosenthal may suggest Rothschild) he asserts on behalf of the centre and the reasonable right a relish of good living. He is cheerfully ready to spread his luck around and to muck in with all those whose families can't, like his, send food parcels containing caviar and pâté de fois gras. Being both Jew and capitalist, he enables Renoir and Spaak to appeal on behalf of the Popular Front for unity with the reasonable right. They go to some trouble to turn against each other two stock anti-Semite arguments: (a) the Jews are taking France over, and (b), they're unpatriotic. Goaded, Rosenthal retorts: "But you, you full-blooded Frenchmen, you haven't a hundred square yards of French land to call your own. Well, in 35 years, the Rosenthals have presented themselves with three historical castles, including game, pools, arable land, orchards, rabbit-runs, pheasantry, breeding-studs . . . and three gallery-fulls of genuine ancestors. . . . If you don't think it's worth trying to escape for all that . . . ?" It is the Jew who has the idea of carving the Holy Family out of potatoes and the projected reunion at Maxim's is forgotten in favour of a simpler fraternity at the level of farmhouse fare. Most important, it is with Rosenthal that Maréchal makes his escape, rather than with the schoolteacher (Jean Dasté), or the actor (Carette)—even though the last is a particularly promising Renoir candidate.

The overcoming of division and prejudice is international. It takes prisoners of all nationalities to get together to play their penny whistles and create the general row under cover of which Maréchal and Rosenthal escape.

This happily inarticulate affirmation of community climaxes a compound theme: language. All nationalities speak their own language among themselves (with subtitles), although French is their common language, except that Boieldieu and Rauffenstein speak English together (for the French, still, then, a "snobbish" language). The English can't understand Maréchal. The German guard tries to speak to him in solitary, but leaves him with the

---

* Marechal's preference, in this sense, for Boieldieu over the engineer (Gaston Modot) doesn't, however, have any sense of preference for the ancient over the modern. Aviation and engineering are, after all, closely allied! The engineer is as suspicious of Boieldieu as Marechal, and, being as tough as Marechal (one can imagine Modot in the Gabin part), is too close to him for any "reconciliation" to be useful. His real function is to intensify the general feeling that Boieldieu is the odd man out, and under suspicion, is on trial, rather than Marechal.

gift of a mouth-organ, to match the "Scratch orchestra" of community and
escape. Maréchal and the widow understand each other with no common
language. He talks things over with her cow, in French. Truffaut: "the
common denominator between man exists; it's Woman, and without any
doubt at all the most powerful idea of the film comes after the announcement
of the retaking of Douaumont by the French. It's the singing of *La Marseillaise* by an English soldier who is dressed as a woman and who removes his
wig."

The script deploys a European complexity of symbolism with an American speed. Kerans draws our attention to the motif of gloves. Boieldieu,
continuously and snobbishly, washes his and remarks, "It's this little grey
smudge that worries me." The smudge, like Lady Macbeth's, is that of
conscience, which will grow until he dies, playing the flute (a satyr, but
stressing his gloves), for the sake of the oily-handed mechanic. Rauffenstein
calculates that his two pairs of good gloves will last out the war—with peace,
he remarks, his kind will become obsolete. He closes Boieldieu's eyes with
a hand gloved to hide its burns. Boieldieu, with his aristocratic ego, disdains
disguise. Stroheim's exoskeleton implies his interior discipline. His carefully
tended geranium is emblematic of his bleakly surviving tenderness. Stroheim's mime is smooth, taut and beautiful, in Chaplin's class, his character's
very stiffness proving the functional equivalent of the clown's mask. The
sterility of a human juggernaut, inspired by loyalty to a code which he knows
to be doomed, intermeshes with another aspect of chivalry. As Boieldieu
lies dying, the camera passes over three crosses: a crucifix, a red cross, an
Iron Cross ribbon. Two officers read regulations to the new prisoners. One is
stiff and correct, the other fat, officious, rasping. Between them sags the
dejected figure of an aged guard, sinking under the weight of his rifle and
overcoat. We know all we need to know about German losses at the Front.
Later, there is something at once sinister, loveable and absurd about the bright
toothy smile of the German N.C.O. beaming in between the flung-open
shutters of the room in which the fugitives are hiding.

A close look at the cutting belies any first impression of naive, uncritical
responsiveness. The camera picks up a prisoner whose female drag, donned
in a spirit of burlesque, suddenly goads his comrades to an unbearable
nostalgia. From the group surrounding him, we cut to a close-up of a man,
rapt, whom we assume to be just another man in the group. But as the
camera moves from him across face after face, we realise that he was at the

outer edge of the group, and that the whole room is held in the grip of pain. After Maréchal and Rosenthal quarrel in the snow, the camera holds the men in separate shots as if they were far apart. Rosenthal sits slumped alone, in mid-shot, as if isolated, until Maréchal's voice is heard, close by. In each case, spatial deceit allows us to experience, firstly, the sudden blossoming of a terrible longing among the men, and, in the second, the quiet cessation of a separation like death. In a very traditional way, Renoir's presentation of a reality which is respected is rhetorical. Something of what is happening is initially concealed only to plunge us more deeply into the spectator's experience.

It is misleading of Bazin to write as if Renoir refused to edit or interfere with reality, or restricted such intervention to a minimum. The approach led Bazin to his fascinating programmatic anticipation of cinéma-vérité. There, indeed, a moviemaker must observe that at which he points his camera, but his filming is a matter of acceptance rather than direction. In some respects, Bazin also anticipates Warhol, although one must remember that Bazin stresses what Bresson and Heyerdahl showed by not showing, whereas Warhol's indiscriminate showing stresses a spiritually *empty* reality. Renoir's, very traditional, concern is with realism (the action) and with actualism (the audience), the latter element involving rhetoric, and the transactions between the reality and the actuality remind us how flexible, intricate and functionally efficient conventional aesthetic techniques can be. Renoir enjoys the vision of landscape seen from train windows (crabbing forerunner of the tracking sequence in *La Bête Humaine*). A very quick cut from the French to the German officers' mess (intended to stress their similarity) puzzles some spectators for a while, like the night-to-day window in *Les Bas-Fonds*. Our brief uncertainty turns a sharp cut into something rather softer, more fluctuating.

At an earlier stage the film was to be called *Les Evasions du Capitaine Maréchal*. As a title, *La Grande Illusion* is certainly more impressive. But there is never any indication of exactly what it is which is being described as an illusion. The new title thus throws everything into question. The illusion might be something which the film criticizes; or something which it seems to confirm or advocate; or something which all the characters take for granted. More probably the title should be taken as the subject of the body of the film, and one would expect that certain indications of an illusion would be principal points of the plot, or the subject of discussions between the characters. From this point of view the film's pattern and tone would suggest (1) a denunciation of wars in general, and (2) an advocation of French unity in view of a renewed German aggression. If Maréchal and Rosenthal are escaping to Switzerland and a neutral internment, this would really be a continuation of the imprisonment from which they have just fled. But their spirit seems to be that implied by Maréchal's growl: "We've got to finish it off, this damned war . . . even though we hope it's the last!"

Despite the deluge of fire-eating American war films and their English imitations, and the implications which they cast into the more sombre stiff-upper-lip style, this last remark does catch the spirit in which the British and French both went into the Second World War. Renoir hopes that Frenchmen, once united amongst themselves and with their natural allies, will escape from supposedly escape-proof prison-camps, i.e., he hopes that French disunity and weakness are more apparent than real. At the moment of truth, Frenchmen will sink their differences. Even the insular English, and the Russian steamroller, will be there. Without lending itself to militarist enthusiasms, and deploring war, the film reserves the right to self-defence, and anti-Nazism, although not mentioned, is obviously implicit and understood (Rauffenstein's 'death' is that of all that is noble, albeit extreme, in German devotion to duty).

Internal evidence suggests that the scenarists bore in mind the film's meanings for foreign audiences, including those of Germany and Italy. Even as late as 1938, many people subscribed to the view that the Germans might be disembittered, or the winds of public opinion taken out of Nazi sails, by a show of friendly respect for the German people (not necessarily appeasement, Chamberlain-style) and by a reminder of the common humanity of ordinary people everywhere. About the rights and wrongs of the 1914-18 war the film is tactfully silent. It contains no boast which might provoke a German or Italian audience, or a censor. For Nazism, it substitutes an older chivalry, thus putting German militarism in the best possible light. But there are certain barbed reminders: Rauffenstein's role as an active oppressor; his injuries; the fatigued old soldiers; the widow reciting the names of the battles in which her family died; the endlessness of war.

The "classic right" (Boieldieu) must forget its traditional class allegiances and ally itself, even sacrificially, with those whom it disdains: the mechanic classes, and the Jews. We have seen how, by making Rosenthal the representative of capitalism, the film turns arguments about the selfishness of the race against the spirit of the class. Rosenthal and Boieldieu would appear all but traitors if they didn't muck in. So the film suggests, like *La Marseillaise,* a kind of voluntary liquidation by the privileged classes of some of their own exclusiveness—whether loyalty to "connections" or subsistence-luxury. But there is a form of loyalty to "connections" which is neither sterile nor selfish, and it is the peacetime alliance of French mechanic and German peasant. Internationalism, repudiated in its obsolete, divisive forms, is accepted in its lower-class forms. In the solidarity of the proletariat lies a long-term hope for the end of wars. These at least are the meanings and the emphases which the film suggests to me. Other meanings hit different kinds of spectator.

Renoir says he pleaded for better uses to which to put the spiritual qualities which war pointlessly squanders. He was also concerned with giving an accurate picture of the spirit in which he and "the class of 1914" had gone to war, and with paying a tribute to the chivalry of their German opponents.

In 1937 Renoir declared to the American public that he was a pacifist, but resolutely opposed to Hitler's aggression. Already a certain contradiction appears. The problem is that "pacifism", like "anti-war", can mean almost anything, ranging from unconditional pacifism, through a preference for trying all reasonable peaceful solutions before defending oneself reluctantly, but effectively, to the much more belligerent postures suggested by "We don't want to fight, but by jingo if we do" and "If you wish peace, prepare for war," both of which, in the face of Nazism, were arguably more "pacifistic" than appeasement. In the '50s Renoir saw his film as a premonition of "the Six", and this sounds rather like an afterthought, except insofar as any hope of closer European harmony could later seem an intimation of economic unification.

Renoir's two meanings, rather than having tripped one another up, might belong together if we suppose that he had intended to portray this spirit of the '14-'18 generation, with its expectation of patriotic chivalry, as "the great illusion", swamped in the mud and blood of the trenches. But to have shown the destruction of that spirit might have seemed to urge the preparation of "total war" (as per *The Life and Death of Colonel Blimp*), or to despair of human decency, or to enhance rather than mitigate the bitterness between the French and the Germans.

Renoir's war injuries as an aviator may have spared him (or deprived him of) the spectacle of the near (though not total) disappearance of this spirit in the trenches. In any case by the mid-'30s a movement to retrospectively "ennoble" World War I was already well-established. The reasons were often politically contradictory, include *both* militarism *and* the 'pacifistic' respect for the ordinary German mentioned above. These contradictory aspects gave the uncomplicated military chauvinists and the Fascists their chance to overlook, or to relegate to second place, the film's less congenial aspects. For the chauvinists, Jean Fayard: "Yesterday, M. Jean Renoir insulted France and preached Civil War. Today, he exalts what for us constitutes the essence of intelligent nationalism, the secret tie which unites all men of one country. What will he do tomorrow? What strange broken line does this director follow, and what motives or what masters does he obey? We do not know. It hardly matters, for today his great talent puts him in the service of a just cause."

For the extreme right, Jean Barreyre: "M. Jean Renoir passes (but I believe that is only a false reputation) for a political revolutionary. But whoever sees *La Grande Illusion,* that beautiful film, can only emerge exalted. . . . A Barrès might find in it topics with which to strengthen his most noble themes. . . . "

Barreyre continues, "He seems to believe that the elite is no longer useful, and that they might as well perish in the flames, while he turns his hopes towards a French democracy the purity of whose blood can, according to him, only gain by the heatedness of a somewhat oriental admixture . . ." Nonetheless, "these are only slight defects, a limp due to a leftwards bent. . . . " Similarly, Bardèche and Brasillach regret Renoir's judgement on the '14-'18 war and on its "fraternity-in-arms", but contrast his judgement with his description. "The film as a whole shows a very great beauty, and the sentiments evince a simple grandeur to which we are not yet accustomed. One can remember the reception of the captured flyers by their German captors and the very noble conversations between the French aristocrat and the German aristocrat, each drawn to the other by their common civilization." ("Civilization" would seem, by implication, to exclude the lower orders).

"The protagonists are magnificently characterised, and certainly the most original among them is the Jew Rosenthal; courageous, obliging, intelligent, ironical, and who fights, says he, to consecrate the worldly goods which his family has by its ingenuity acquired. Céline rightly sees 'the tips of the horns', and the first Jew whom the Popular Front has dared to show us as sympathetic, and in his very Jewishness. Which is extremely disturbing."

Twenty years later, Truffaut reads the morality of Renoir's post-war films back into his '30s commitment. Truffaut's Renoir, as usual, is at the service of no cause at all. But, as in *La Marseillaise* and *La Règle du Jeu,* he is animated by the "great idea that . . . the world is divided horizontally rather than vertically." And, apparently ought to be. For "Renoir clearly explains that the idea of class must subsist, even if certain classes disappear of their own accord. On the other hand, one must abolish the idea of frontier, which is responsible for all misunderstandings." Certainly Renoir, around the time of *The Golden Coach,* commented on the advantages of the internationalism obtaining among the upper classes in Europe before the nineteenth century. Nonetheless Truffaut's implicit reference to this remark rather summarily disposes of the Popular Front aspect of a film made nearly twenty years earlier. Indeed he goes on to echo Bardèche and Brasillach. "To condemn war is within anyone's powers; to describe it is more difficult . . . Renoir considers war a natural plague which has its own beauties, just like rain, or like fire. Style prevails over subject and what matters is, as Pierre Fresnay puts it, 'making war politely' . . . one great illusion is therefore that which consists in believing that this war will be the last." In other words, Truffaut's Renoir is warning us that another war is on its way, that it can't be helped, and that war can be redeemed by etiquette and aesthetic sensitivity. But Truffaut, the quietist, not Renoir, is preaching a pessimistic acquiescence in bureaucracy, fate and the beauties of slaughter.

Under its earlier title, the script had a very different conclusion. A rendezvous is arranged at Maxim's for after the war; and no one turns up. It's not clear whether this was because they had all been killed (we think of the widow's table), or because wartime solidarity gets shrugged off in peacetime. The latter implication, which carries the subtler irony, is paraphrased in Autant-Lara's *La Traversée de Paris;* and this pessimistic conclusion would have brought Renoir nearer the sad truth about French unity. The reason for altering the ending is sadly obvious:precisely because French unity did not exist it was necessary to urge it.

The film's respect for German decency fared less than well, after such "beauties" as the Gestapo and the S.S. The points made admiringly by the right before the war were taken up critically by the left just after it. In 1946, Georges Altmann, critic of the Communist *L'Ecran Français,* attacked the film's very discussion of Rosenthal's privileges as a future source of anti-Semitism, while Rauffenstein's chivalry would justify "all the vague collaborations, all the concessions, all the desertions." Nearly twenty years later, *Premier Plan:* "It's . . .war in periwigs. The anecdote is transfigured by the distancing effect of memory. That ocean of mud, boredom, sweat and death . . . becomes a sort of chivalry. . . . The hideous sides of war are occluded. Renoir is fabulating, like his generation . . . P.O.W. camps are presented as glowing with patriotism. . . . Demagogery, Tricolor-style, is associated with a merely amiable patriotism. Everybody chatters. Carette plays the fool, another chump fills his face with grub, a third reads Pindar. It's the little world of Jean Renoir." (A reference, abusive, to *Don Camillo*). We've seen that the film in fact depicts the purgation of such a world. But it is quite possible for its first half to remain the dominant impression of day-to-day life in captivity, particularly after its reinforcement by so many post-World-War-II escape films.

Armand Cauliez sees another set of illusions altogether. "The first of the illusions is the hope of rapid peace. . . . The second illusion is the friendship of Boieldieu and Maréchal, whereas the connivance of Boieldieu and Rauffenstein is affirmed." (Cauliez doesn't enlarge on this; presumably his argument is that Boieldieu died for France, not for Maréchal, i.e., he

chooses nationality against Rauffenstein, but never acknowledges Maréchal's equality. He dies for himself, i.e. the French aristocracy, not for France as a whole). "Third illusion: the idea of frontier" (at least for the lower classes and in nature).

The film was premiered at the 1937 Venice Biennale, and was less well received by the foreign Fascist press than by the French Fascist press. Goebbels pressured Mussolini to deprive it of a festival prize, so the jury created an International Jury Prize to award it instead. Although Goebbels described it as "Cinematographic Enemy No. 1", Goering liked it, and, after it had been deprived of all the scenes in which Rosenthal figured as sympathetic, it was widely shown in Nazi Germany. It was banned in Italy, although Mussolini kept the impounded copy for himself, and it was shown privately to Italian film-makers. It was also banned in Belgium for reasons not known, by edict of the minister responsible, who was also the brother of its co-scenarist. Roosevelt declared, "All Democrats should see this film", and it won a special place at the 1939 New York exhibition. In France and elsewhere, censorship deprived it of a scene where Gabin comes to Dita Parlo's bed at night.

Possibly helped as much as hindered by such controversy, the film proved an immediate commercial success. An abbreviated version was re-released in August 1946, and Altmann's objections were fairly widely raised. Eventually Renoir and Spaak purchased the rights to the film and produced a definitive version based on a negative which had been seized and stored by the Nazis and found by the American army in Munich. In a list of "the twelve best films of all time", produced by a joblot of film critics at Brussels in 1958, *La Grande Illusion* took fifth place, on the strength of which it enjoyed a successful third release in October 1958.

La Marseillaise

Even before shooting *La Grande Illusion* Renoir had begun work on a film whose production arrangements were, as Leprohon remarks, the spirit of the *Lange* cooperative made reality. Through trade unions and workers' organisations, notably the Communist-dominated *Confederation Générale du Travail*, "individuals and societies were offered shares of two francs each entitling the subscriber to a seat at the first run of 'the film celebrating the union of the French nation, the Rights of Man and of the Citizen'." The offer was launched at public meetings supported by such notable Communists as Vaillant-Couturier and Jacques Duclos, by less partisan film personalities like Germaine Dulac and Henri Jeanson, and with the full cooperation of the Popular Front government. But as sharpening political crises splintered the Front, the film could be completed only by recourse to a normal source of commercial finance. There are no reports of this having influenced its content in any way, for Renoir was already working in terms of an appeal to moderate, centre opinion.

"It's the only film in my career in which I applied myself to what's known as research, documentation. So I called on collaborators, notably my old friend Carl Koch, who helped me with *La Grande Illusion* and *La Règle du Jeu* and Madame Dreyfus, who was brilliant at foraging through archives . . . in the Journal of Grievances brought before the General Estates, I found almost everything said in the mountainside scenes (when the priest complains of the youth and debauchery of his bishop)." Renoir drew the political discussions from the newspapers of the time and the minutes of political clubs. " . . . for the doings at Court I had to consult history books. . . . I wrote very little dialogue . . . I found three-quarters of it amongst the documents."

Shooting took ten weeks. "I moved around accompanied by a crane, and I think that crane saved more than it added to the costs . . . The . . . departure from Marseilles under the plane-trees was shot in one single take. Obviously, we took five or six hours to line it up; then I shot it in just about the time the shot runs, which is around five minutes. If I'd broken it up into several shots, I would have had to keep that whole crowd for three days. And I think that actors, when interrupted during a scene, have difficulty in finding the same feeling in a scene which might be shot an hour later . . . there was among the extras a sort of ensemble spirit which I felt and I didn't want to cut it up. . . . '' Locations include Antibes, ''because the streets . . . seemed to . . . correspond pretty closely to what Marseilles was like in '92, and I constructed this little room with the tomatoes and the window, on a roof . . . ''. The schedule called for exteriors at Provence, Alsace and six weeks at Fontainebleau (for the Paris exteriors), concluded in the Paris-Studio-Cinéma.

The story is merely a guiding thread through a tapestry—the development of France's national anthem—and a subtitle marks its theme, ''A Chronicle of Certain Events Relative to the Fall of the Monarchy.'' It comprises a series of episodes in which our characters act as something between by-standers and participants, but linked almost as loosely as the sequences in Duvivier's *Carnet de Bal*.

In a brief prologue, the Duke of Rochefoucault-Liancourt begs to inform His Majesty Louis XVI (Pierre Renoir), supping after a hunting expedition, that a crowd of Parisians have taken the Bastille. ''Is this a revolt?'' ''No, Sire, a revolution.''

Provence, June 1970, Anatole Roux, a poor peasant (Edouard Delmont), is on trial for catching a pigeon, his Lord's game. A tenant farmer, he pleads defense of his own crops but the local judge condemns him to the galleys—for the sake not of the pigeon, but of the principle of Order. While the village mayor, a worthy bourgeois, windily pleads on his behalf, his friends cut the rope that binds his hands and he escapes into the mountains. There he meets two other outlaws, Arnaud (Andrex) and Bonnier (Ardisson), who live in hiding off the land with a poverty-stricken priest. Far off they see a chateau burning. Realising that the revolution has begun, they return to the town.

Marseilles, October 1970. The King has made certain concessions to revolutionary demands but is himself dominated by the aristocrats of his court. At a stormy meeting the revolutionaries, who include lower and middle classes combined, express their anger at the fact that the town forts are still

commanded by aristocratic officers. A winebarrel "Trojan Horse" is wheeled into the fort and its officer, the Marquis de Saint-Laurent, sensibly capitulates, with little loss of life.

Coblenz, 1792. Exiled aristocrats dream of returning to France in the wake of German troops of the Duke of Brunswick. Most expect him to win a quick victory over a revolutionary rabble. Meanwhile they lull their homesickness with a delicate song of Chateaubriand's. With some surprise they find they can no longer recall the finer points of their court dance.

April 1792. Two French soldiers (Carette, Gaston Modot), stationed near the border, watch refugees streaming by. Demoralised by poor supplies, they suspect their aristocratic officers of treasonable sympathies with the Austrians. Meanwhile, at the Jacobin Club in Marseilles, Citizen Louise Vauclair (Jenny Hélia) denounces the monarchy (especially Marie Antoinette) and provokes a walk-out by the bourgeois members. Volunteers are sought to march north via Paris to face the crack Prussian troops. Only respectable men without debts are accepted; Bonnier has debts and feels he can't leave his mother and fiancée. But his mother finds a shrewd solution to his financial problem and insists on sending him off.

The battalion marches north amidst rumours, dissensions and groans over swollen and bleeding feet. At Paris they join in revolutionary demonstrations and are taunted by a group of aristocrats. Sword-fencing breaks out, but is interrupted by a shower of rain. At court, Louis, against his better judgment, allows himself to be swayed by Marie-Antoinette (Lise Delamare) and accepts the bloodthirsty ultimatum issued by the Duke of Brunswick. Bonnier and a pretty Parisienne (Nadia Sibirskaia) who has won his heart go to the shadow theater and watch a political satire whose theme is the chasm now separating the people from their king.

August 1792. Revolutionary troops are massed in readiness for an attack on the Tuileries, defended by loyalist soldiers and Swiss mercenaries. Roederer (Louis Jouvet), representing Parisian civic authority, persuades the king to leave the palace, thus in some sense renouncing the aristocratic side. The Swiss and certain extremists welcome his departure and resolve to be the rock which will break the wave of revolution. Though many of the guards change allegiance when appealed to by the revolutionaries, the remainder are able to offer a savage and heroic resistance. Bonnier dies in the arms of his Louison. The reactionaries push their way into the streets until stopped by reinforcements which include a Parisian militia. Roederer stops their summary execution of prisoners. The reminder of the Marseillais, veterans now, march with the citizen army which, as we know, but they don't, will defeat the much-feared Prussian battalions in their immaculate formations.

Renoir's subtitle carefully disclaims any attempt to portray the revolution as a whole. The notion of France invested in the person of the king, and the feudal, aristocratic order, must give way to a democratic unity: the fraternal union of all Frenchmen. Hardly hidden behind the historical theme is the

contemporary one: "given the menace of Hitler and the diversity of the responses of the people of different backgrounds. . . . The goal of the film was to reinforce in myself, and in the spectators, the notion of French unity. . . . "

After *La Grande Illusion* there is little need to labour the historical parallels behind the alliance of unreconciled aristocrats, an Austrian queen, a German prince and a Prussian army, or an egalitarian fraternity as the soul of France. The insistence on the revolutionary role of the poor clergy may be Renoir's own but it also corresponds to an appeal by Maurice Thorez to French Catholics.

All the same, Renoir has to deal with historical events concerning which both prejudices and the most rigorous historians may acrimoniously differ. Probably the average cinemagoer is prepared to enjoy Renoir's film one day, and on the next, *A Tale of Two Cities*, in which pure and gentle aristocrats are rescued from ruthless fanatics and a bestial mob. A sense of contradiction there would undoubtedly be, but spectators are normally prepared to allow their admiration for personal qualities to override their ideological sympathies. (It's surprising how much film propaganda, from Eisenstein's to *Loin de Vietnam*, boils down to a matter of physiognomies and styles suggestive of decency and generosity vs. those suggestive of savagery and meanness). Nonetheless the prevailing identification in English, and perhaps, by now, American popular entertainment mythology, of the French revolution with the most ferocious phases of the Terror, has had in its time, and still has, a serious propaganda weight behind it. So far as a French audience is concerned, Renoir's film can buttress itself on a middle-of-the-road French attitude whereby the revolution is disfigured by its excesses, but by no means defined by them. In Maurois's summary, "it established social equality into the legal code, by 'disestablishing' the Catholic Church it introduced freedom of worship, and achieved finally, French unity" (e.g., French citizenship was conferred on hitherto stateless Jews).

Thus the English spectator is likely to admire the film as (merely) a film, a self-enclosed aesthetic affair, or a generalised assertion about democratic man. He will indulge, but will secretly shrug off, Renoir's view of revolutionaries as decent enough fellows managing a *moderate* revolution. And of course there is a sense in which Renoir is offering us historical *myth*, in which respect the film merits the same indulgence as, say, *The Young Mr. Pitt*, or *Henry V*, or *Alexander Nevski*, or *The Alamo*. Yet Renoir has taken such care to root his myth in historically significant reality that one should appreciate the careful intellectual game which he is playing, and the political maturity which puts his film in a class altogether different from the Manichean tendencies of all the films mentioned above.

André Maurois confirms Renoir on many points where one might suspect the filmmaker of sentimentality. Renoir is correct as to the unity, at this stage, of all classes against the aristocratic order; as to the relative readiness of many aristocratic elements to abdicate their powers without force; as to the anger of an impoverished lower clergy against its prelates; as to the conspicuous role of a force of men from Marseilles; and as to the political affiliations and influence of Marie-Antoinette.

It is certainly arguable that an only marginally firmer king might have acceded to certain demands and so arranged a smooth transition of power from the aristocratic order to the bourgeoisie and its aristocratic sympathisers. There would then have been no breakdown in the central power, which might thus have contained the interventions of a brutalised Parisian mob and a traditionally insurrectionist peasantry.

If Renoir reminds us of the *other* side of the revolution, of a scatter-brained yet real conviviality, of a kind of Rousseauism, it is partly because he has something to say about the Popular Front. On another level, he also wants to correct the too-mechanical assumption that any revolution must release the beast in man, can never be a moral "festival of the oppressed"— as Renoir's revolution was, and as, Eisenstein reminds us, the celebrations near the Odessa steps were too. What bred violence was not revolution, but an insensate resistance to it. On another level still, Renoir remembers that the past is as open-ended as the present, that the French revolution, like the American revolution, which did so much to inspire it, could have minimised rather than maximised its potential for senseless violence. And by his resort to many stylistic anticipations of neo-realism, Renoir frees the possibilities in the past from their fate. This is *cinéma-vérité* in the sense not of *Culloden* but of *The War Game*. Unless one is a thoroughgoing determinist, he makes it possible to see how the bloodletting, instead of escalating, might have remained larval. Arnaud evokes with religious fervour the names of Danton, Marat and Robespierre—as they might have remained before desperate situations forced their hand. And "Louison" remains the name of a rightly sharp-tongued girl, not, as it became, the nickname for the guillotine.

Not that Renoir, in 1938, is pacifist. The summary executions of the defenders of the Tuileries are presented with a chilling and curiously fearless

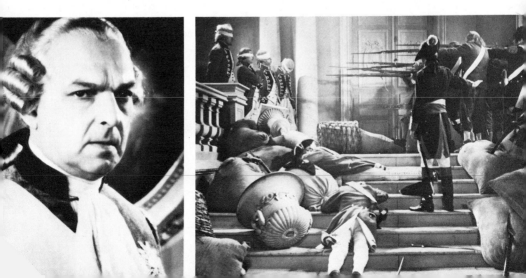

zest. Firing squad rifle bolts and salvoes clash with the rhythm of the repeated descent of a guillotine blade, and reverberate hideously around the palace grand staircase, until stopped by Roederer, who shows neither pity nor horror, merely a certain disgust. From a meta-historical viewpoint, what Renoir has done has been to purify the historical revolution against an old hierarchic order of what we might call its secondary complications: the irruption of the Paris mob, and the later stage when the bourgeoisie and the lower orders turned on one another.

It is from the defeated that we can learn an optimism which is altogether distinct from the hysteric need for a "happy end". One of the stranger beauties of *La Marseillaise* is that Stalinism is put aside. It shows us a crowd of lower- and middle-class people inventing their ideology as they go along, in rough scathing debates which are like a premonition of Paris in May 1968. In both historical and contemporary terms Renoir was right, surely, to make a little issue of an understandable (and undesirable) bourgeois exclusivism; only men with neither debts, dependents nor bad characters may rebel. He isn't frightened of hordes of Boudus on the march; he is countering, as precisely as in *Lange,* that pervasive fear, felt on every social level, that social upheavals unleash those barely civilized creatures in the classes below. But those below see themselves as respectable citizens, and that's the point of Bonnier's baffled expostulation: "What sort of a revolution is it, that only men of good character and no debts can join?" Whatever his social position in 1792 (and it's bourgeois), Bonnier corresponds to the respectable working classes of 1937, who *won't* be dismissed as rabble and cannon-fodder.

Though the Roman Catholic Church, in 1792 or in 1937, was thoroughly reactionary, one must look deeper than the cassock to the man. Reaction's lackeys (the palace guard) include some who are amenable to reason. The Swiss guard, immune to reason and pity, possess, even as mercenaries, their professional honour. No "purge" mentality is to be countenanced. Louis himself is, in no way implausibly, a decent, peaceloving Frenchman— complacent to a fault, just a little too fond of food and hunting, liberal enough when he allows his spontaneity to emerge, and by no means a fool. But like so many by no means foolish French prime ministers throughout the '30s, he was never quite able to make up his mind to push a matter through and to assert his intuition against pressure. He is (perhaps unconsciously) the middle class whom Renoir hoped to warn, just as Bonnier represents the working-class citizen who is a little too gentle, and who needs as his comrade-in-arms the relatively fanatic Arnaud. The gentle one dies—the balance is disturbed; but Arnaud is not evil either; and perhaps that's why Roederer doesn't stop to hate or to regret either. He understands how easy it is to kill, as do Prévert and Renoir. There is a sardonic pessimism in his face but his low expectations of man are matched, made into a paradoxical affirmation, by his *fiat* that the prisoners be spared, and by his negotiations with the forces of reaction, conducted with a nobly hypocritical tact.

La Marseillaise could carry as subtitle *The Birth of a Nation*. Renoir's film has a certain romanticism and like classicism it balances its hope with wry concessions to realism. "Of course, first and foremost, they were revolutionaries, but that did not stop them eating, drinking, feeling too cold. . . . " When Delahaye and Narboni expressed their surprise at finding something as serious as the revolution endowed with the conventionally comic accents of Marseilles, Renoir replied that he sought precisely that discrepancy, that he was bending all his powers "to avoid solemnity. . . . In a film like *Toni* the people seem so ordinary that one can permit oneself to make them speak a poetic language. But on the other hand, in a film where their appearance is . . . remote from reality, one must use one's dialogue to return to the everyday."

The film abounds in quite straightforward political and philosophical discussion whose issues are never prepared in terms of human interest merely. If the psychology is nearer *La Vie Est A Nous* than *La Grande Illusion,* it is to counterbalance this abstraction, and to accommodate a staggering quantity of allusions to (or rapid synopses of) off-screen events. Politics becomes interesting not by being glamourised or personalised or melodramatised but by being treated as a hope, a force which people express as they express other invisibles—love or hunger—by their face, body and words. For the most part, the film reduces historical action to conversations and to discussions, but imbued with an energy rendering them equivalent to action. Renoir's elegant unifying device (the song) becomes structurally supererogatory, and remains almost outside the film, like an emblem, goading the rightwing spectator to hear and to accept all that is ferocious and leftwing in the National Anthem, revivified by context.

Not that the least problem is finding concise visual symbols for dauntingly abstract or amorphous social or historical realities. The king's palace guard are toy soldiers, yet their booted march incorporates a dinky little goosestep. The mayor's intervention during the peasant's trial for poaching defines the captive liberalism of the moderate bourgeoisie. Renoir, surely too charitably, felt that the besetting sin of the reactionaries was their inability to distinguish minor issues from major, their confusion of seriousness and play. At Coblenz, a bewigged youth experiments with a yo-yo while a woman sings "Oh, mon pays". From discussing the superiorities of the disciplined Prussian army and debating whether they, as Catholics, should accept the aid of Protestant mercenaries, against, my dear, a mere rabble, they switch to recapitulating the steps of a court dance.

Louis, whose subsequent execution looms large in our minds, is a tragic centre of these contradictions. He can never quite escape the personal situations in which his wife and his courtiers entrap him and elevate himself to the level of the historical situation which he glimpses and to which he responds, too late, with a humility which is profoundly democratic. His sin is the opposite of *hubris*. His inadequacy is that of a man whose democratic humility is entrapped within an aristocracy. To Marie Antoinette's ardent wish that massacres conclude "this whole wretched comedy", he replies, "Unfortunately we are actors in this production—a position less convenient than that of spectator—if one could be *deux ex machina*. . . . " Yet, as king, he almost *could*. Conversely, we share his psychological shock when one of the guards whom he is gratefully inspecting turns and snarls a revolutionary slogan. His cerebral confusion, bravely restrained within his demeanour, is indicated by his fear that his already adjusted wig is still awry, and by his hesitations about when to doff his plumed hat.

The web of dependencies of which he is so easily the victim is mirrored at another social level, when Bonnier broods over his own ineligibility for the Marseilles battalion. The gentle paradox of Bonnier naturally requesting disobedience from his womenfolk, and the matriarch obstinately asserting her own subordination, is as absurd as the king's subservience to his own order, and to its gallantry to the "gentle" sex. But Bonnier's mother hits on the solution which enables him to leave her, first lonely, then bereaved. The theme of feminine emancipation appears covertly again in the separate groups of chambermaids and soldiers in the palace corridors, in the provocative roles played by Jenny Hélia and the women at the Club des Jacobins, balancing Marie Antoinette for the old order, and in the appearance of armed women among the Paris militia.

In his selection of contemporary prose for his dialogue, Renoir has borne the revolution's philosophical infrastructure in mind. The aristocratic magistrate announces that the severity of his sentences is intended to inculcate respect for "les forces naturelles et divines". All the while a peasant knife hacks roughly at the rope around the prisoner's wrists (direct action!). Escaped to the mountains, the poacher meets two men already in hiding and shares with them an outlaw life which suggests nothing so much as the natural state of man, according to the philosophy of Rousseau (it's difficult not to think, briefly, of Buñuel's *Robinson Crusoe*). The debates, tirades, verbal duels and songs continue the theme until the fraternity of the original Maquis is asserted in the notion of freedom as one and indivisible. It is arrested, here, at the "liberty, equality, fraternity" of the nation-state. But such is the tone that one doesn't need *La Grande Illusion* to confirm the hope of, eventually, an internationalist synthesis.

Insofar as the film identifies the interest of the nation with that of its lower-class majorities, it is more Marxist than it seems. Insofar as it sees some hope of class reconciliation, Marxists must consider Renoir a bourgeois liberal, maybe useful during a Popular Front tack, but to be repudiated at other times.

Nevertheless the film is permeated by its play of contradictions. That *La Marseillaise* should have remained France's national anthem at all is as mind-boggling as the adoption of Blake's *Jerusalem* for the hymnals of schools which are perfect examples of Blake's "Satanic mills". Renoir's use of the song catches just that curious fluidity, that slide of meaning, from which not

merely political songs but all art suffers. It is the Parisians who name it after
the Marseillais whom they first heard sing it, but the Marseillais got it from a
Jewish peddler from either Strasbourg or Montpellier, they're not sure which.
It belongs to nobody, it's borrowed by everybody, it unites everybody and it
never stops changing as it goes. The words in particular undergo incessant
revision, and so the ideals implied become the very opposite of a sacred text
or an inmutable order.

The morality of violence remains a crucial revolutionary problem. Renoir
dwells on the violence implicit in the old order just sufficiently to justify,
condone or understand, the revolutionary violence of the new. Renoir often
comes rather near classifying killing in rage as a natural act, maybe wrong or
foolish but neither unnatural nor essentially a matter of wickedness. At the
same time he carefully vindicates the path of minimum force. The alacrity
with which the fort's garrison decide to believe that the attacking force numbers 20,000 and ought to be surrendered to, is of a piece with the brisk
engagement in the Champs-Elysées whose flurry of fencing-master postures
and bubbling bravados are quashed by a sudden shower. Rain stopped history. The sequence is as hilarious as anything in *Tire Au Flanc*, even as a
couple of sharp deaths remind us that this is not at all, but not at all, a lunch
on the grass. No less serious, though, than violence, is food. If the border

sentries stare glumly at their thin stew it is not merely out of hearty appetite but as a symbol of their officers' betrayal (at another level, the scene is a converse of the omelette which Jean Renoir prepares for his doubtless unappreciative guests in *Partie de Campagne*). You are what you eat and with whom you eat. Louis is just a little too concerned with offering even the bringer of bad news a chicken for his pains; the unenlightened, merely personal, democratic gesture is curiously ominous. A mother refuses to abandon the priority at table to the head of the family, a priority which, one suspects, has, at some past epoch slid from the physical needs of the breadwinner to a hierarchical ritual. The Marseilles battalion baffles the Parisian waiter by ordering tomatoes, a fruit of which the Parisians have never heard. Thus nature follows culture. The inevitable transition from feeding to grooming (Renoir, we remember, was a cavalry officer) is indicated by Louis's interest in the toothbrush. Meanwhile the Marseillais discuss, with a curious mixture of regional and professional pride, the relative merits of straw, paper or tallow as stuffing for one's boots. Naturally the pedestrian becomes poetic: one method guarantees arrival "with feet as fresh as roses", another is sure to "make your feet take wing."

No less important is the poetry of poetry, for a democratic army marches on its voice. It's the intellectual who says, "It touched my heart" and the plain man who complains that it breaks the rules of harmony. The pronouncements of a rotund and jovial painter marching with the revolutionary army are pertinent. Under the old order he painted nymphs for aristocrats, but now he feels even happier and, he believes, all the more inspired, by painting heroes of antiquity for the revolution. He boasts genially, of the enormous number of people who appear on one of his canvases; and they're not just extras, each is individually delineated (one thinks of *La Grande Illusion*). Thus the artist and the man march in the democratic ranks, yet his art—all art?—remains historical-topical (like this film, which conflates 1792 and 1938), inspiration-fabulation, untrue to everything, relevant to everything, a product of continuity as well as of conversion.

Insofar as art is "spilled religion" its summit may seem to be high seriousness, tragedy its essence, and the comic always a contrivance. But insofar as art is a branch of the natural sciences, its major mode is psychological realism (not necessarily *individual*, analytical psychology) and the humane didacticism characterising this and a surprising number of Renoir films smacks of distortion and betrayal. But for Renoir the essence of art is the fertility comedy (the dying god reborn) and a certain sense of anyone's ego as permeable by everything one loves allows even tragic sacrifice to become comedy.

The paradox is at once terrible and liberating, and no less profound than "high tragedy". Bonnier dies in Louison's arms, and a very slow dissolve, analagous to that over Batala's corpse in *Lange*, introduces a long shot of the same scene, in the background of which the revolutionary militia press home their advantage. The free man dies, like a dragon's tooth. The camera moves from a two-shot (with its identifying involvement) to an objective view. Yet even the long shot has its subjective role; Bonnier dies, a part of the whole, and only accidentally conspicuous to us. For the free and generous man death is not a matter of *ending* but of *becoming*. Bonnier dies without having known liberty, as he dies without having known his Louison; yet he has possessed both. François Poulle comments on the relative rarity in Renoir of the sexual kiss; and one reason is, perhaps, that there is as much love and less apparent possession in a look.

As a conception, *La Marseillaise* represents a fusion of two currents: that of *Nana* (the elaborate costume-piece, in whitish tones) and of *La Vie Est A Nous* (the semi-documentary idealised in the interests of actual intervention). In comparison with contemporary British production, it represents a synthesis of most of the best in Grierson and Korda, and, with André Malraux's *Espoir,* it precedes "reconstructed documentaries" like *Target for Tonight*. It is slightly to one side of the development of the *fait-divers* subject of *Toni*; its intimacies are the refraction of a generalised social upheaval. Its other cousins include Thorold Dickinson's *Hill 24 Does Not Answer,* even Peter Watkins' *The War Game* and Pasolini's *The Gospel According to St. Matthew*. Its episodic form, the "fragment" story around an abstract theme, its urgent political concern, and its function as an *intervention* in a crisis, suggest the essay film as well as the story film. If we allow for the fact that the past poses a problem to which *cinéma-vérité* can never find an answer, it paraphrases the essays of Chris Marker on present history: *Cuba Si, Description d'Un Combat,* in its internal reflections on art and itself, *Lettre de Siberie,* and, of course, *Loin de Vietnam*. (Indeed a multi-director version of a topic as multifaceted as the French revolution offers fascinating possibilities; so, indeed, might an anthology of sequences from existing films). In its means of production most particularly, the film anticipates Godard's conception of the film as revolutionary act. The similarities are concealed by the traditional humanist style of Renoir's moral affirmations, in contrast to Godard's strange mixture of solipsism, nihilism and hope. But, if we allow for the differences imposed by technical and cultural change, Renoir's cloister-and-the-hearth oscillation between orthodox and unorthodox financing gives him an outsider's position not so far from Godard's.

The question of idealising semi-realism can be approached from another angle. Despite all its accuracies, the film must be misjudged if it is forgotten that its title is that of a song, of an ideal, coming to replace the monarchical ideal which figures in its subtitle. The film is a work of historical extrapolation. "What would have a revolution been like had it been truer to its ideals, more fully explained by its ideals, than it was?" Though Marxism, in one of its aspects, is drawn towards a determinism and *Realpolitik,* it remains, in others, as idealistic in its strategies as in its propaganda. To object to the film's idealistic urge is as irrelevant to the real subject of its interior realism

as to object to, say, the omission in *Fires Were Started* of the interesting fact
that officialdom, which there seems so benevolent and alert, also tried to pre-
vent London's cheery Cockneys from using the tube stations as air raid shelters. Fortunately London's cheery Cockneys smashed their way past gates,
padlocks and constables alike.

If anything, Renoir's propaganda films (*La Vie Est à Nous*, this) confuse
one less than Jennings'. By pretending to be purely and simply about "ordinary people", the Jennings film induces us to accept the best in a very good
bunch of men as the index of an entire organisation and an entire society.

Renoir appears twice in his own film: as Louis XVI, and as the painter.
The first, though temperamentally suited to the new order, cannot escape from
his milieu and his wife and adapt himself to it. Another painter, Legrand, in
La Chienne, attempts emancipation and adaptation, tragically. The painter
in *La Marseillaise* succeeds, with a supple ambiguity which tips us off as
to Renoir's own aesthetic intentions. One might define this film's spirit as a
kind of "Idealistic Realism". Edificatory purpose has so long been trotted
out in defence of so many lies that one may too easily forget that from the
dawn of art until nineteenth-century realism, it remained a dominant, if not
the dominant, aesthetic mode, and is still a popular expectation from the less
educated. Nor is it only the less educated and the idealistic who complain if
a work of art is not simultaneously realistic within certain accepted conventions and in some way a demonstration of the better examples of or attitudes

to its subject. In response to criticism from the alerted right and left alike, Renoir might reasonably have replied that he made his film to influence a range of spectators going from Bonnier towards the left to Louis within the right.

The film was a commercial failure, and Renoir attributed it to the French public's lack of interest in the subject—one wonders if that public wasn't too depressed by events. The film was shown in London in 1940, but very few copies remained in existence until an almost complete version was assembled by the French Cinémathèque, to which the Soviet Ministry of Culture donated missing portions of the soundtrack. Renoir retrieved commercial rights to the film in the mid-'60s and the film was re-released in late 1967, with only moderate success. A still missing scene shows Roederer finding Marie Antoinette sorting out her private correspondence and advising her to burn all the letters from the Duke of Brunswick. "Family mementos are not of great importance, it is best to be rid of them", he observes, suavely overlooking her high treason, reminding us of the curiously personal and parochial world of Europe's rulers. We remember, again, the "200 families" of *La Vie Est à Nous*.

35

La Bête Humaine

For many years Gabin had planned to realise a childhood dream. He wanted to be an engine driver, on the screen, and drive the locomotive himself. He had got as far as setting up a production entitled *Train d'Enfer*, to be directed by Jean Grémillon, but remained dissatisfied with its screenplay. Grémillon suggested *La Bête Humaine*. But after the success of *La Grande Illusion*, Gabin had a hankering to be directed again by Renoir, who was approached by Gabin's producer, Robert Hakim. Renoir wrote the screenplay at speed (specifying, variously, 8 and 15 days).

"Then I read it to Hakim, who asked me for some . . . trifling modifications . . . I'd read *La Bête Humaine* as a boy, but hadn't reread it for something like 25 years, so my work as a scenarist was rather superficial . . . So something began to develop which had also come about with *Les Bas-Fonds*. While I was shooting, I kept modifying the scenario, bringing it closer to Zola . . . the dialogue which I gave Simone Simon is almost entirely copied from Zola's text . . . Since I was working at top speed, I'd re-read a few pages of Zola every night, to make sure I wasn't overlooking anything." Shooting began on 12 August 1938, with exteriors at the Gare St. Lazare in Paris, at Le Havre, and on the line between, and interiors at Paris-Studio-Cinéma.

At steam-hauled express thunders on the Le Havre-Paris run. In the driver's cab, Jacques Lantier (Jean Gabin), and his fireman, Pecqueux (Carette), can communicate only by gesture. To indicate that the locomotive wants water, Lantier points at his own mouth. The overtone of brutal strength, rendered inarticulate by industrial society, is confirmed by Lantier's relationship with Flore (Branchette Brunoy), a healthy country lass who is also his mistress. As they embrace, he has to struggle against an impulse to tighten his fingers around the neck he is caressing. The victim of the laws of heredity, his incest and violence are the product of a brutalised and alcohol-ridden stock.

This ferocious society has many kinds of victim. In a compartment on the express which Lantier is to drive back to Paris, Roubaud (Fernand Ledoux),

station-master at Le Havre, confronts the obnoxious Grandmorin (Berlioz). Grandmorin, a man of wealth and influence, was god-father to Roubaud's wife, Sévérine (Simone Simon), whom he had seduced at the tender age of sixteen. Roubaud has learned of his wife's past, and torn by indignation and jealousy, threatens to expose her seducer. Grandmorin, confident in his connections, threatens to ruin him. Whereupon Roubaud kills him, making Sévérine his accomplice. Lantier, the only witness of the crime, keeps silence, partly through fascination with Sévérine, partly because he has no faith in the justice of the *flics*. A poacher, Cabuche (Jean Renoir) is accused of the crime. Guileless and inarticulate, his honest testimony implies that M. Grandmorin was a man of immoral habits. The examining magistrate indignantly repudiates the slander of so eminent a citizen by this "bad" character with his many previous convictions. Lantier's testimony could save Cabuche; but Roubaud, to ensure his silence, allows Sévérine to seduce him. Little by little, she is caught in her own, and Roubaud's, trap, and begins to return Lantier's love. By the time Grandmorin is exposed, and Cabuche freed, Sévérine has cajoled Lantier into attempting to murder Roubaud in a shunting yard. But he cannot do it; his hatred ricochets back to Sévérine, and he murders her. As the train careers back to Le Havre he jumps from his cab at speed. Pecqueux is able to stop the train. But it must resume its journey, subject to a timetable which symbolises not so much the tyranny of routine as the fatalities predestined by a social system.

Zola's setting, the Second Empire, is transformed to the 1930s. Running-time restrictions forced Renoir to omit several of the novel's celebrated peripetia.

Both novel and film are regularly misunderstood as a "Greek tragedy" of fatalistic overtones, or as a one-sidedly moralistic piece about weakness, temptation and retribution-remorse. But Renoir's plotline is broadly faithful to a plot mechanism whose accusation is aimed, as one would expect from Zola, at a social network. Lantier and Pecqueux are two aspects of the working class. Lantier is its strength, its initiative. Its degeneration into sadism is the product of heredity, that is, of generations of brutalising by grinding toil without culture but with alcohol. Pecqueux is its fidelity, which without Lantier can be docility. Roubaud and Grandmorin represent a parallel antithesis within the bourgeoisie. Roubaud typifies, like Legrand, the *petit bourgeois* ethos, apparently subservient and well-meaning, yet capable (like Michonnet) of real violence in what it conceives to be self-defence. Grandmorin represents another streak in the same class, somewhere between the *haute bourgeoisie,* sometimes vying with the aristocracy in bedecking its courtesans with jewellery, sometimes closer to the middling- well-off *rentier,* who isn't puritanical but prefers to be hypocritical (Other examples include the men-about-town of *Partie de Campagne* and the smirking man who raises his hat to Batala's tearful secretary at the station). Roubaud's rage at Gandmorin parallels the indignation of the puritanical lower-middle classes at the permissiveness of the upper-middle classes. He wants revenge because his wife when under-age was sexually initiated by a much older man. His rage at his wife's past contrasts with Lange's attitude to Valentine's and the care-taker's son to Estelle's. Given Séverine's quiet, catlike yet practical style, was she, one wonders, so difficult to seduce? Isn't Roubaud's retrospective indignation not merely misplaced but much more like a pathological jealousy, that is, a sadism as irrational as Lantier's? Except that it may well include a certain selfishness; Grandmorin can retaliate. When Roubaud later connives at Séverine's affair with Lantier to save his own skin, he reveals the in-authenticity of his "righteous indignation". By initiating Séverine into the advantages of murder he corrupts her even more profoundly than Grandmorin had done. And when Lantier initiates her into something else again— reciprocated love—she follows Roubaud's little homily to its logical con-clusion. After all, Roubaud might turn Grandmorin's methods against Lantier. Séverine has learned that idealism is all very fine, but one has to be practical, and being practical comes to the same thing as Lantier's path-ology. The legal system, coldblooded and calculating, is indicted by its way with Cabuche. It wants a scapegoat and quite without evidence it assumes that a poacher is more likely to be a murderer than an eminent citizen. The prejudice is so marked that political social convenience must lie behind it. The novel concludes with a driverless train, packed with drunkenly singing soldiery, thundering on its way to a smash-up suggestive of the débâcle of 1870. On the eve of another war, Renoir had to stop the train and not emphasise any soldiers on it. Had he not, he would have accurately predicted the débâcle of 1940, and maybe goaded the audience into wrecking the cinema.

One can imagine how Renoir, with Prévert, might have handled such a plot in the hopefully aggressive climate of earlier years. Just as we are glad that Lange murders Batala, just as we are glad that Pépél murders his landlord, so we would have been glad that Lantier murdered Roubaud, and fled with his Séverine. The suspense throughout would have been based on our fear that Lantier's confused violence would after all turn against Séverine instead of restraining his rage until its time has come. To allow a hero to murder a murderer is doubtless a step on the path to anarchy, and so on and so forth. One might have to make Roubaud a little more obnoxious, like his counterpart, Zabel (Michel Simon), who so deservedly gets it from Gabin in Prévert's *Quai des Brumes*. But there, at least, is the plot's other fork.

As it is, François Poulle is extremely astute when he diagnoses in Renoir's treatment something a little more regrettable than defeatism; a loss of direction. The naive goodness of Cabuche, Poulle argues, blunts the edge of the film's accusation of the police, and therefore of society, particularly since it has to assert itself against a murder plot in the foreground. Renoir's Cabuche acts on us like Melville's Billy Budd. He makes it easy for us to blame not "Captain Vere" but—fate, destiny, bad luck, everything, anything, nothing. Maybe Renoir sought a shaft of light to relieve, and yet to throw into contrast, so much black. Maybe he sought the Uncle Tom effect—the more saintly Tom is, the more indignant we feel about Legree. There is another danger in that if Cabuche had blamed the police he might have rendered us too indignant about his subplot or, by analogy, more indignant than we are at Lantier and Séverine for their silence. But even that isn't insuperable, and maybe the real reason for the passive bewilderment of Cabuche is the same as the inability of Lantier to kill Roubaud—the confusion of proletarian will.

Usually films identify the *crime passionel* with madness. But Lantier's madness links with his inability to commit a crime. Cabuche, also, is too confused to defend himself. Our feeling that Lantier's crime would be worse than Roubaud's, since it is premeditated, is certainly in the air, and it's in the same spirit that his slaughter of Séverine, since it isn't premeditated, but insane, leaves him more sympathetic morally than his victim, since she envisages murder with the coldest blood of all. So softly silent is the female of the species that we may even have to remind ourselves why the lovers don't just forget Roubaud and elope. The reason is that Roubaud, who is also homicidally jealous, can always persecute Lantier as Grandmorin could have persecuted him. Séverine has learned from Roubaud that passion, indignation and defence of one's livelihood all justify violence. Lantier, confused animal, has learned it from Séverine; as Lange learned something very like it. Zola's theme certainly isn't the rights and wrongs of murder, particularly given the strong streak of social predestination running through his work. It's an accusation of a social system and the confused ignorance of its victims. Renoir's real theme is the confusion of all those who should be

marching in the column of *La Marseillaise,* or helping Lange/Lantier to make
it over the Belgian frontier. Maybe Roubaud, like Batala, like the mercenaries, *ought* to die.

The pessimistic swing to this film isn't accidental. *La Marseillaise* was
commissioned on an upsurge of optimism from the left and centre-left. *La
Bête Humaine* reflects a pessimism conspicuous in the poetic realism of most
artistic films of the time *(Quai des Brumes, Carnet de Bal).* Renoir's apparent
despair with the Popular Front would fit a widespread mood. The structure
of *La Bête Humaine* is that of an *anti*-cooperative. Lantier's way with Flore
is a hideous parody of Maréchal's union with a German peasant woman. The
crimes of which Séverine is the centre involve even poor Cabuche, who, like
Boudu, asked only to be left alone by society and to fend for himself—even
in doing that he broke the law. Society is a trap, of whose network none of the
characters ever becomes aware. It allows no one to contract out, and it pits
everyone against everyone else. Two seem less confused than the others:
Pecqueux and Séverine. Pecqueux has his straightforward, warm, canine
fidelity to his "mate". But he's confused in the sense that he has less of an
idea than anyone else of what is going on. Séverine, perhaps corrupted by
Grandmorin and certainly corrupted by Roubaud, has a straightforward,
warm, feline passion for Lantier. But she's confused because she is so clear
and direct that she expects Lantier to be. Of all the characters, she is at once
the softest and the hardest, and very near indeed to some of the justified
murderers in the poetry of Prévert. We can understand why Renoir does not
dislike his vamps. They are no more selfish than a great many other people;

their methods bestow upon their victims some reward. Séverine's love inspires in her a controlled strategy, of which Lantier is incapable. She is betrayed, destroyed. She is one trap for men, but a corrupt social system is another, and *it* cannot love. Certainly, we appreciate the sensitivity which may exist within a "human beast"; and insofar as he incarnates the violence which the upper classes then were too ready to attribute to the subcivilised proletarian species, he reproaches society as a whole. His confusion paraphrases, but only in melodrama, the contradictions which tore the Popular Front. Consciously or otherwise, Lantier embodies Renoir's criticism of the Communist Party, as the expression of France's proletariat. Powerful it certainly is, but it is also so deeply contaminated with the in-bred violence of the industrial revolution that it destroys its natural soulmate, the healthy peasant girl, and refuses to help that which is freest and most anarchic. Renoir would be the last to reproach the French Communist Party for whoring after the middle classes; but its decision that Nazism wasn't the enemy was another matter. *La Marseillaise* portrays a revolution with little violence. *La Bête Humaine* describes a non-revolution with berserk violence.

Renoir is remarkably faithful to Zola's structure, but the question of texture is another matter. Renoir's attitude to Zola is as complex as his process of composition suggests. First, "To hell with old Zola! We wanted to play trains!" Yet, during shooting, the script shows a progressive return to much of "old Zola". And: "I had in my head an idea which, by the way, I've never abandoned, that the realistic, or naturalistic, side of Zola is not all that important, that Zola was, above all, a poet, a great poet. So it was consequently necessary to try to locate in his style the elements which would allow me to render that poetry on the screen."

In stressing Zola's non-realistic poetry, Renoir finds support in Franju's comments on his version of *La Faute de l'Abbé Mouret*. Yet one may feel, in contrast, that the bulk of Zola's poetic force is expressed through his relentless sense of causality. Zola's poetic ferocity explains also why the obsolescence of his science weakens his work as little as it does. To his emphasis on heredity the course of nature-versus-nurture controversies has been unkind. Nonetheless this aspect of his novels becomes a crude yet appropriately obsessive symbol for the pressure of social environment upon one generation after another. Cauliez puts it differently: "Naturalism is like a physiological romanticism: 'I am a force which moves . . . ' says Hernani." However monolithic and unsubtle it may appear today, Zola's vision exists at a crucial rendezvous of Marx and Freud, of Bergson and Céline. But his reaching for a psycho-bio-social totality, with its sense of culpability at once exteriorly imposed and interiorly incurred, gives his work a depth like that of Greek tragedy. There is no real contradiction between the notions of destiny as capricious or positively malicious (from the individual's point of view) and destiny as an inexorable system of cause and effect.

The game of attraction and repulsion between Zola and Renoir must be intricate. One cannot but suspect that Renoir, in *opposing* Zola's poetry to his naturalism, is really seeking out whatever in Zola lends itself to a sea-change into Renoir. "What helped me to make *La Bête Humaine* were the explanations which the hero gives of his atavism: I said to myself: "No, it's not particularly beautiful, but if a man as handsome as Gabin said it . . . in the open air, with a great deal of horizon behind him, and perhaps wind, it could take on a certain quality. That's the key which helped me to make the film." A key which, of course, brought it nearer *Toni*—and which one may well suspect is a way of gently prising open the bars of Zola's determinism, not intellectually but as a continuously felt force. Renoir's stopping of the train substitutes for Zola's berserk society an apathetic rather than optimistic mood. It is certainly less pessimistic. A man dies, an apocalypse is averted, a social life which is a living death goes on.

Zola's characters are plausible types invested with an obsession. His characterisation is simple, emphatic. Renoir's often exquisitely intricate and fluid individuals seem to possess a freedom which separates them not only from their environments but from the past which formed them and even from their present response. Certain characters are so delicately formed that their past would require the subjective ramifications of a Proust rather than the piston-like forces and iron-age girderwork of Zola. Renoir's characters seem to float; their lifelines are not rails but currents and winds. Not that *La Bête Humaine* allows more than a glimpse of freedom. It is subdued, depressed, each setting like a pool of oil in which its characters lie inertly or, if the pool is stirred by a bar, move stickily and lose their momentum almost immediately. The train n ves, but its movement is implacable, metallic, inorganic. As the landscape rushes by us, it seems not so much animated as violated.

The strange, viscous drift seems to owe less to Zola than to a mood of Renoir's; there are variations of it (lighter in *La Chienne*, with its streak of roguish cheer, freer in *La Nuit du Carrefour*, softer in *Woman on the Beach*). Renoir's film is a study in hesitant intimacy, for which he sacrifices Zola's epic drive. It seems itself to hesitate, to be caught in some fascinating doldrums between determinism and freedom, pessimism and openness. It is often described as poetic, but perhaps it would be truer to say that it is atmospheric, lyrical. If one expects the conventional '30s style to which Prévert and Carné were faithful, Renoir's film seemes to falter. Dialogue reminiscences about picking flowers remind us that Lantier's mental world has, at least, a high, barred, grubby window opening onto a *Partie de Campagne*. Renoir, in more fastidious mood, remarked in 1959: "Zola, as naturalist, is very often wrong. His idea that a worker is necessarily squalid and dirty and employs a coarse vocabulary is odious to me. To my mind, people who are coarse are coarse whatever their social class. I'll even maintain that to show a character like Coupeau is not a good thing. Coupeaux exist of course, but they are everywhere and I believe that in the extremely leisured classes drunkenness is more developed than elsewhere." Already, twenty years before, his *La Bête Humaine* refuses squalor and prefers texture (wood, steel, rain, oilskins, mists, flesh, rocky forms) and a certain tenderness. "I'll simply quote a phrase which is taken directly from Zola and put in the film. The first encounter between . . . Lantier . . . and Sévérine, happens in a square. . . . Lantier doesn't dare speak to Sévérine, so moved is he by her beauty. He looks at her, says nothing, and she says to him, 'Don't look at me like that, you'll wear your eyes out.' Well, I find that very pretty."

Black as the murders are, Renoir, rather than settle for an uncomplicatedly lyrical squalor, is always shifting his interest from murderer *qua* murderer to the diffuse anxiety of a man who can't remember his bouts of madness too well, who has had to live with those urges too long, and who outside those violent moments has the sensibility of a man. Grahame Greene vividly describes Lantier's questioning of Sévérine about Grandmorin's death. "The very gentle twitching of the eyebrows as the silent excitement begins to work, the uneasy movements of the mouth, the strained, too casual voice seeking details, 'And how many times did he strike?' . . . Watch him after the murder of the girl as he passes by the mirror on the bourgeois sideboard—the relaxed muscles, the unobtrusive weakening of the mouth, the appalling sense of melancholy satiety. . . . Mlle Simon acts with intensity the little, sensual, treacherous wife . . . helped . . . by a cameraman who knows how to deal with the close black electric hair, the snub nose, the rather African features." Pierre Leprohon speaks of "her clumsiness (becoming) . . . subtlety, her gentleness—we recall *La Chienne*—strangely cruel." Both gentle and cruel, neither facet of her character disqualifying the other. Appositely, she played a catwoman, a human animal, on her return to Hollywood. For Claude de Givray the film's suspense is vitalist, psychological and moral. "Gabin in *La Bête Humaine,* just like Humphrey Bogart in *In a Lonely Place,* carries his own drama within himself, his own suspense. His problem is established from the first moments of the action; will Lantier's undermined organism resist the trial? From then on each of his gestures strikes us like a blow: his way of eating, of working, of speaking, his way of making and unmaking love. Love is Simone Simon, the most charming provincial vamp that could exist."

"Provincial" suggests another approach to what Leprohon described as "clumsiness"; and Sévérine acquires, along with the other principal characters, a social background of which her murderousness, like that of her partners in crime, is an expression. Apart from being a kind of waif and dreamer, she is another Madame Bovary, of a lower class, perhaps, and against a grimmer landscape. "She expresses herself", Givray goes on, "by weighty banalities", and he cites, 'I have lived more in this minute than in my entire past existence.' " Yes, it's a banality, and yet it's also true. Most of the characters endure a kind of affective frustration, or ambivalence, or sly, poised hatred, which, in each, including Lantier, is concealed, oblique, diffuse. To such remarks, Givray continues, "a particular affectation of the

voice gives an unmatched preciosity. She is profoundly bad, she plays with her lover's nerves like a cat with a skein of wool. She is anyhow a cat herself, her first appearance shows her in sympathy with a white angora. But we don't know how the little cat died; the shot of Séverine's corpse was cut by the censor. In Renoir's mythology, Simone Simon finds a place just between Catherine Hessling and Leslie Caron, but never has one been more sensitive to the dangers of woman."

Renoir maintains Zola's iron pessimism, hydraulically, as it were, within his own vision of an open, neutral reality which is neither congenial nor squalid, but which is loved, whatever it is, with an admixture of paternal irony and childlike enthusiasm. Grahame Greene speaks of a director who knows how to get the most out of all the same incidents. "Renoir works a depot and a crowd into every scene—conversations on platforms, in washrooms and canteens; views from the stationmaster's window over the steaming metal waste; the short sharp lust worked out in a wooden platelayers' shed among shunted trucks under the steaming rain." Bazin notes the carnal gesture with which Lantier caresses the mechanical beast which is his own energy. The constriction of physical and emotional energy informs also the love scene in oilskin, and the journeys between Paris and Le Havre which open and conclude the film: the camera, mounted on the train, crashing through the countryside, long lunging trackings gulping the arrowhead of steel parallels, rocketing around curves, battering through such visual explosions as viaducts, stations, tunnels, bridges. The railroad runs alongside the Renoir river, but where the river sometimes races, sometimes meanders, always flows, the locomotive howls at inhuman speed along the inexorable trajectory of an industrial system, and the predestination it embodies.

The "travelling" contrasts with the characteristic approach to railroad speed typified by Abel Gance's *La Roue* and Jean Mitry's *Pacific 231*. Both make the equation that speed means speed of cutting, between various details of locomotive and track. The effect is of an *implied* fast forward movement; in fact a combination of *rearward* movement (the track) with stationary forms (locomotive details) or rotating ones (wheels) with the to-and-fro and up-and-down of pistons helping out. Renoir's long takes are in no sense the result of a passivity towards reality (as Bazin might have tried to persuade us). Their dynamism depends just as much on an implied forward movement against a backwards stream, with visual contrasts and shocks provided by the undulations and types of scenery, the sudden crossbars of bridges, tunnels and cuttings like funnels, the relative movements of fore-, mid- and background features, in fact, a *choreography* of scenery, which gives an impression of a continuous "scoop" but in which each contrast bursts in upon us with the shock of a cut. Nonetheless, the effect of long sustained, unstoppable momentum is quite different from the other films', and rather more like the experience of leaning forward out of the window of a train. The shunting-yard sequence catches another machine-age tempo—a kind of railway swamp, with grey smoke as soft as ferns or bracken. Certain scenes are framed in compartment windows and cut across by bars. Reticent, hard, they are Renoir's nearest approach to the Fritz Lang style, although softened by the kinds of body and their movements, and the softer contrast between greys. Certain deep-focus shots suggest that Renoir had better lenses at last. The use of "deceitful" camera movements in *La Grande Illusion* for dramatic emphasis is renewed, and two murders are "accidentally" hidden from us, one by a windowblind, the other by dance-hall jovialities, with a subtle calculation for which Renoir is too rarely given credit. Bazinian and post-Bazinian criticim, meaning well, would attribute it to Renoir's "commercial" side, or maybe to a sort of somnambulist's awareness of what he was doing for which he shouldn't be held responsible in case it finds a chink in his divinity. It is more sensible to assume that Renoir likes his audiences, that he believes in communication, that he cuts as often as he does because he doesn't believe that cuts disrupt any ontological flow, and that he cuts as rarely as he does because he thinks it helps his actors or is appropriate to certain kinds of scenery.

In fact the *ellipse* (the interruption, the evasion, the aversion of the eye from the fullness of reality) is crucial to Renoir's cinematographic syntax, and is as organically part of it as the track or pan. Poulle notices it in relation to kisses and to girls in beds, whose appearances are not only rare but glided over. The continuity of a track or a pan, Bazinians have never noticed, has as result the continuous appearance and disappearance of every object in the field. It no more respects the authenticity of the object than your eye does as it moves past it. Violence, in *La Chienne* is hidden, circumscribed, or paraphrased. We have seen how much certain scenes in *La Grande Illusion* owe to omission. In *La Bête Humaine*, the extremely dynamic railroad sequences exist to underline the heavy yet hesitant immobility. The lovers' kiss, in rain, in oilskins, is a kind of double negation of flesh by rain and by protection against rain. The murders are glimpsed and yet interminably brooded over. The dance and the murder, life and its negation, are one.

La Bête Humaine was a substantial financial success internationally and it was arguably a major stimulus to the American *film noir*. For if we pare the narrative down to its skeleton (the lovers who plan murder of an inconvenient spouse) we arrive at a paraphrase of *The Postman Always Rings Twice*, which Pierre Chenal filmed in France in the following year (as *Le Dernier Tournant*) and which Renoir showed to Visconti, who based *Ossessione* on it in Italy in 1942. Although it's an American novel, the Americans didn't get around to filming it until 1946. If we define the *film noir* as a crime thriller with a pessimistic, cynical, sardonic approach and mood, then Renoir pioneers the French *film noir* of the '30s with *La Chienne*, while *La Bête Humaine* teaches the Americans that such a film needn't be an all-action, all-swaggering picture as most of the '30s Bogarts, Cagneys and other crime movies are, but can be pitched in the key of dramatic intimacy and remorse. In Hollywood Fritz Lang remade both movies, and Lantier's fits of violence prelude another post-war American *film noir* motif—the sympathetic psychopath, or victim of amnesia, or shellshock, or some other trauma, who can't stop himself beating up his friends (e.g., Burt Lancaster in *Kiss The Blood Off My Hands* (English *Blood On My Hands*), Bogart in *In a Lonely Place*, William Bendix in *The Blue Dahlia*, and so on. Presumably Hollywood wouldn't have taken the genre (and worked it to death) if America hadn't been spiritually ready for it. Possibly both the French and the American cycles parallel a reflux of popular energies away from democratic reform (the Popular Front, the New Deal), and mark a regression to a confusion and cynicism which does in fact conclude in an identifiable historical upheaval (the 1940 débâcle, and the McCarthy/Cold War hysteria). At any rate, Renoir's film hits a queasy compromise between the heavy social insistence of Zola and the anomic atomism which with rare exceptions the American *film noir* assumed as the natural condition of man and which for so long held it off from really open and probing comments on the social realities connected with its crimes.

The film was re-released in France in 1945, when its moral blackness (all the more insidious for its gentleness, like Séverine herself) proved to have lost no virulence. Church organisations and right-wing local authorities cooperated on a nationwide campaign against it. It certainly challenges the common belief that great art possesses a quality such that it can purify but not harm. The American psychoanalyst Edmund Bergler describes how a "young man consulted a physician, stating that after seeing a motion picture he became impotent with his wife. The situation persisted for months, his depression and despondency were marked. The film was *The Human Beast*.

In it, the protagonist shrinks from having intercourse because he fears that in his sexual frenzy he might strangle the heroine. . . . The young man could not forget that central scene, applied the situation to himself and feared that he too, would commit such a crime. He became completely impotent, and felt close to a 'nervous breakdown' . . . "

Successful as it was, the film seems to have provoked Renoir to one of those social, aesthetic and thematic reactions so conspicuous between successive subjects. "Working on this scenario inspired me with the desire to change tack, and perhaps to escape from naturalism altogether, to try to approach a more classic and poetic genre; the result of these reflections was *La Règle du Jeu*." Even more extraordinary is the way in which all Renoir's efforts to escape naturalism brought him to a film whose social impact surpassed that of *La Bête Humaine*.

La Règle du Jeu

Both *La Grande Illusion* and *La Bête Humaine* enjoyed such success that by 1939 Renoir's old dream of productorial independence was now within his reach, and for the first time since the coming of sound. Renoir himself, his brother Claude (the producer, not the cameraman, who is his nephew), André Zwoboda (his assistant), Olivier Billioux (previously executive producer for the Hakim brothers), and Camille François (an old school-friend turned successful songwriter), each subscribed 10,000 francs to form a co-operative, "La Nouvelle Edition Francaise", to produce two films a year. They sounded out René Clair, Julien Duvivier, Jean Gabin, Simone Simon and others, and procured their agreement, in principle, to collaborate on the creation of a French equivalent of United Artists. The French government offered its co-operation and prepared to turn over to Renoir and his friends all the facilities of a large production-distribution combine which was in financial difficulties.*

Renoir's first project was an updated adaptation of Musset's *Les Caprices de Marianne*. As he developed it, with Zwoboda and Carl Koch, its title changed to *Fair Play* (in English) and the story evolved into an early version of *La Règle du Jeu*. The eventual script was completed in detail only as far as the guest's arrival at the chateau. From that scene onward only a brief synopsis had been worked out when Renoir, confident in his long experience of improvisation, felt that the subject was all but ripe for shooting. But the deciding argument for a precipitate start was that early advances for foreign rights were forthcoming. A budget was set at a substantial 2,500,000 francs. Special lenses were ground for deep-focus effects (in the event their extreme sharpness of definition seemed unsuitable to the mood of this particular subject and was softened with filters). The cast was to include Simone Simon (as Christine), Pierre Renoir (as Octave), Fernand Ledoux (Chesnaye) and Roland Toutain (Jurieu). In the Princess Stahrenberg Renoir felt he had found

---

* See André G. Brunelin's uniquely detailed account, *Histoire d'Une Malédiction*, in *Cinéma '60* No. 43, January 1961.

his Christine. Wife of the claimant to the Austrian throne, she had fled Austria as the Nazis moved in. Her lack of dramatic experience, her relative maturity, and her inadequate French struck Renoir (though not his collaborators) as minor matters and he engaged her on the spot. For the screen she took the name "Nora Grégor". Her warm, gracious and responsible personality wrought substantial changes in Christine's character, and complementary alterations in several other main parts. Alterations involved casting problems too. Renoir, at the last moment and possibly in haste, cast as Christine's husband, the Marquis de la Chesnaye, Dalio, a popular actor so clearly Jewish that he had to be given a line explaining that "his mother was one of the Frankfurt Rosenthals". Renoir himself replaced his brother Pierre as Octave, perhaps because Octave was taking an autobiographical turn and perhaps because Renoir liked the idea of being involved at one remove with his Princess.

Shooting began on 15 February 1939 around La Ferté-St. Aubin in the Sologne. Throughout the first fortnight it rained without stopping. Studio charges kept mounting in respect of the château interiors which sprawled expensively over the huge double soundstage at Joinville. It was obvious that the budget would be overspent. Gaumont was happy to provide additional finance to the tune of 2,000,000 francs, but from now on the moguls had a finger in the co-op pie. Renoir had to start studio work immediately, leaving the "massacre of the rabbits" to be shot by two assistants, Zwoboda and Corteggiani, on the basis of a very detailed shooting script. The sequence proved astonishingly expensive, since rabbits shot in mid-course and dying are not the most obliging of extras. An enormous number of rabbits, which had first to be collected and loosed, ran the wrong way, or were missed by the marksman, or died in a visually or dramatically unsuitable manner. If the marksman moved closer to the rabbit, it was blown to pieces, and if a cameraman was placed conveniently close to the rabbit he and his lens ran a great risk of ricochet effects. A modern zoom lens would have simplified matters. As it was, the sequence took several men two months to shoot, the final solution being to install camera and crew close to the rabbits, but in an armoured shed.

Renoir's improvisational methods proceeded at a snail's pace. In one scene the actors spoke different words in each take. This freedom gave full scope, according to Brunelin, to Renoir's realisation that his Princess was not quite as gifted or ideal an incarnation of Christine as he had supposed. Greater dramatic scope was accordingly given to Paulette Dubost as Lisette the maid, and to Mila Parély as Chesnaye's mistress, Geneviève. Jean Jay, the Gaumont representative, although he admired the film as a whole, thought that Renoir himself was over-acting disastrously, and Renoir obligingly began writing his character out of the picture as much as possible, (after first suggesting all the Octave scenes be re-filmed with Michel Simon in the part).

Since films can rarely be shot in narrative order, but only according to some-times complex patterns of set-striking and actor availability, the problems all these changes added to a virtually scriptless film almost defy imagination. Nonetheless Renoir kept matters more or less in hand, and simplified his task by adding certain "explanation" scenes, e.g. the conversation between Octave and Jurieu after the automobile accident. For safety's sake, he shot two last scenes; one being La Chesnaye's final address to his guests; the other a separation between Octave and Marceau. Eventually the first was preferred.

By June 1939 42,000 metres of film, which had cost over five million francs, were ready for editing. The enormity of the task left Renoir exhausted and confused and, according to Brunelin, he simply fled, occasionally offering his editor, Marguerite Renoir, advice from afar. By the end of July she had cut the film down to 1 hour 53 minutes. Jean Jay, for Gaumont, insisted on further cuts, particularly of his *bête noir*, Octave, and Renoir finally acquiesed in the excision of another 13 minutes. To explain the film's public reception it is first necessary to describe the plot.

A record-breaking aviator, André Jurieu (Roland Toutain) touches down after a sensational solo flight. To an admiring radio reporter he declares that, far from feeling pleased at his triumph, he is dejected by the "disloyal" absence from the airport of the woman for whose love he achieved it. The woman in question, Christine (Nora Grégor), is married to Robert de la Chesnaye (Dalio), a marquis whose principal hobby is collecting musical boxes of every description. He assures his wife that he has complete con-fidence in her discretion, and her warm reaction prompts him to decide to break with his imperious mistress Geneviève (Mila Parély). Robert loves all his lady friends dearly, and has great difficulty in ending his affairs with them. His attempt to dismiss Geneviève is flummoxed by her (disingenu-ously?) tragic reaction. Jurieu, still disconsolate, makes an attempt at suicide by driving his automobile off the road. His friend and passenger Octave (Jean Renoir) scolds him for being so inconsiderate and petulant and talks him into making another attempt to meet Christine. Octave fails in his attempt to persuade Christine to invite Jurieu to a country weekend, but he does per-suade Robert to do so.

The La Chesnayes, arriving on their estate to prepare for their guests' arrival, find their gamekeeper Schumacher (Gaston Modot) has at last caught his old enemy, the poacher Marceau (Carette), red-handed. But instead of sending the latter off to prison, La Chesnaye finds him amusing and decides to hire him as an extra servant. Schumacher's gamekeeper mentality is baffled by his master's leniency, but his young wife Lisette (Paulette Dubost), Christine's maid, finds the amiable rogue's saucy patter much more stimu-lating than her dull rustic husband. The guests arrive, commented upon by the servants, whose below-stairs snobbery echoes, sometimes exceeds, and satirises, their masters'.

During the rabbit-hunt, Christine, through a borrowed spy-glass, chances upon Robert kissing Geneviève. She does not realize that this is a kiss of parting. Disillusioned, she concludes that she might as well be like everybody else, and play the games of love lightly and without too much sincerity. After the hunt comes a fancy dress party. While the guests dress up, Schumacher gives Lisette a warm hard-wearing woollen cloak which she finds not at all flattering. The charade style amusements include: Octave, dressed as a bear, being led around by Jurieu dressed as a gypsy; a "dance macabre" in skeleton tights; and Chesnaye's presentation of the orchestrion which constitutes the *pièce de résistance* of his mechanical music collection. Christine, desperately rather than spontaneously, gets herself drunk and flirts with the pompous St.-Aubin, while Marceau gives La Chesnaye advice on how to handle women. "I always try to make them laugh," he explains, demon-

strating the excellence of his advice by pursuing Lisette, with every sign of eventual success. Meanwhile Jurieu discovers Christine with St.-Aubin. The two men engage in fisticuffs, each looking as ridiculous as the other, although Jurieu emerges victorious and declares his love afresh to Christine. By now she decides to forgo her loyalty to Robert altogether, and leave with Jurieu, regretfully breaking the heart of her young friend Jackie (Anne Mayen) who also loves him.

While Chesnaye and Octave look for Christine, Schumacher catches Lisette with Marceau. The latter barricades himself in a room with the lovers, until La Chesnaye appears to swap punches with Jurieu, before an affectionate reconciliation. Schumacher, now mad with jealousy, pursues Marceau among the guests, brandishing a firearm. The guests are deliciously startled by shots which they assume are blanks and applaud this little comedy as the best entertainment of all. La Chesnaye dismisses Schumacher brusquely and Marceau regretfully.

Lisette adds to Schumacher's misery by refusing to leave with him, asking instead if she may accompany Christine to Paris as her lady's maid. She persuades her mistress to borrow the warm coat Schumacher gave her before slipping off with Jurieu. Christine waits for him in the conservatory, where Octave keeps her company, confessing that he considers himself a failure. His dearest wish was to be an orchestral conductor, yet he has never found that real warm relationship with the public which he craved. Their mutual sympathy tips over into an impression, or perhaps a reality, of love, and on the spur of the moment they decide to elope together. Schumacher, misled by the coat, takes Christine for Lisette, and thinks his wife is allowing herself to be seduced by Octave, who earlier admitted to being strongly attracted to vivacious lower-class women. Schumacher strikes up a maudlin friendship with Marceau and consults him as to whether an outraged husband has the moral right to shoot his wife's lover. Marceau sympathetically assures him that he has, and Schumacher goes off for his gun. Octave returns to the house, intending to arrange their elopement, but runs into Jurieu, and repentantly sends Jurieu to Christine in his place—to be shot, and killed, by Schumacher, who thinks Christine is Lisette and Jurieu is Octave. La Chesnaye informs his guests that there has been a tragic accident. One of the guests, a general of markedly right-wing mould and morality, remains convinced that La Chesnaye has shot his wife's lover. So the bounder has some style after all!

Renoir looked on the film as an elegant comedy whose deeper meanings were well hidden from that audience which resents anything more than mere entertainment. Halfway through its première (at two Paris cinemas on 7 July 1939) the spectators in the smarter of the two halls were completely drowning its dialogue with boos and whistles. Others set about smashing their seats in protest, and at least one gentleman began throwing lighted newspapers around the auditorium. At the more popular hall, there was less violence, but there were derisive whistling, raspberries, and raucous laughter.

The film-makers were absolutely stunned by the audience reactions. Perhaps some spectators found the film's action too fast, complex, and sophisticated, and they became exasperated. But on what everyone knew was the eve of war, Renoir had offered the French public a film which in at least one important implication could seem defeatist. One doesn't need to know of the special prestige which throughout the '30s attached to aviation records to appreciate that the death of Jurieu suggested the death of French heroism. Renoir seemed to be attacking, and, worse, attacking frivolously, the country's "best circles", its upper classes and leaders. It was bad enough that the French flying ace should be shot by a patriotic, disciplinarian country-man. It was even worse that the most "moral" woman in the film spoke with an Austrian accent. Her husband was partly German (!). The Jewish marquis exacerbated the ever volatile anti-Semitism of the French right-wing. Far from taking the sting from the matter, the film's humorous tone would come to seem unforgivably callow or mocking. The Boulangist song could be wrongly interpreted by the right, and by the left. (Cartier-Bresson later testified that the Boulangist song was inserted as an afterthought and a joke.) And even the more level-headed middle-of-the-road spectator may have felt dazed by a deliberately giddy film. It was praised only by the extreme left, which assumed that it intended to denounce the decadence of high society. And the Communist party, which in view of the Stalin-Hitler pact was just then opposing the war, liked the film because it was vaguely depressing and could be written up as anti-war account of French unfitness to fight.

The press reviews were distinctly more balanced and even friendly, but the film was all too clearly set for commercial disaster. Renoir deputised Marguerite Renoir and André Zwoboda to study audience reaction and excise those scenes which provoked the most vociferous rage. As soon as those scenes were cut, the next audience simply selected other scenes for its special attention. Presumably annoyance was caused by major characters and issues recurring in many scenes, but maybe the film's reputation attracted people who felt like any pretext for rowdy behaviour, and maybe, as was suspected, the demonstrations were not spontaneous at all, but part of a nominally "patriotic", actually rightwing extremist, campaign against a director whose celebrity made him still a figurehead of the left. Presumably all factors were involved. Four recuts and five days later the film had lost a further ten minutes, including the whole climax between Christine and Octave. (Even the director's every appearance could have become a target for the crowd). Then another five minutes were cut to accommodate second-run cinemas which wanted to run two performances an evening. Either way, the film's receipts were everywhere so dismal that alarmed overseas dis-tributors were able to renounce their contracts, and La Nouvelle Edition Française was bankrupt even before the film had had a chance to reach its

"court of appeal", the international arthouse market (which might well have had trouble with a rapidly dialogued subtitled film).

War broke out on 3 September 1939 and in October the French government banned the film as "demoralising". A few months later, the ban was lifted, just in time to be reimposed by the German occupying forces. In 1942 an Allied air raid destroyed the film's only negative. Thenceforward, existing only in severely truncated and somewhat worn prints, the film seemed doomed. In 1946, however, a French exhibitor discovered in a cellar a virgin print of the 85-minute version from which another negative could be struck. Five minutes were excised as substandard. From 1946 on, *La Règle du Jeu* went the rounds in three different versions, of 90, 85 and 80 minutes respectively, on the bases of which it began to build its reputation as Renoir's masterpiece. In 1956 two enthusiasts approached Camille François (who was still in debt over the film), and began to collate all the prints and negatives with a view to re-establishing the 90 minute version. Their dedication led to the discovery of 200 tins of rushes, so it became possible after a great deal of ingenuity and labour to recreate the 100-minute version of 7 July 1939 and, finally, all but one short scene of the original cut. (In the still missing fragment, Octave attempts to persuade Jurieu of the pleasures of seducing maid-servants rather than their mistresses.)

One might expect the fullest version to be more virulent than the shorter ones, since the purpose of the cuts was to mitigate the film's real or apparent condemnation of high society. The effect is the reverse. The longer the film dwells on these characters, on their hesitations and sensibilities, the more indulgent and understanding of them we become. They soften from strangers, whom we somewhat peremptorily sum up and judge, into friends whose scruples and absurdities we tolerate or share. Maybe, too, our 30 years' distance from the crisis of 1939 makes it easier for us than for its embattled contemporaries to appreciate a film whose ambiguities spring not from equivocation but from the adroit and honest oscillations of a spirit at once fauve and classical, realistic and comic, farcical and tragic, moralistic and amoral, caustic and fraternal. The film is not so prominently *about* such dualities of tone, or about the poetico-philosophical issues which the conduct of its characters may suggest, as certain later films of Renoir's. Yet the innumerable switches of tone give it its own philosophical dimension, much as slightly divergent views, juxtaposed, give the effect of stereoscopic relief. In the "novel of the film", or a Godard film of the film, such effects might be obtained by *appliqué* comment (author's first person), or by abrupt switches in verbal or visual style. In movies of this time directors counted much more on disjunctions within the behaviour and attitudes of the characters. If such disjunctions are noticeable but too subtle to be understood then they may seem to the spectator to disrupt the character, to jar against mood without creating a new one, and merely to confuse the thematic issues. If they are so subtle as not to jar at all, then of course they will be altogether lost. Kind as the French critics were, this seemed to be their feeling. René Clair: "The film begins as a drama of sophisticated adultery then, about halfway through, turns into burlesque. There's a rupture of tone, which is a serious fault." Foreign critics ran for cover by assigning the film to a genre established by Stroheim and already familiar to them: moralistic realism about highlife decadence appropriate to the demoralisation of France. Renoir's subtitle described it as *une fantaisie dramatique*, which surely implies something lighter-hearted than Stroheim, but no one took any notice of so unfamiliar a category. *La Règle du Jeu* is far friendlier towards its protagonists than the crushing severity so often imputed to Stroheim—also wrongly, if we adopt that alternative view whereby morality is merely a convenient mask adopted by Stroheim's saturnine, perhaps Sadeian, *faible* for the derisively grotesque.

Already, though, Renoir's evolution during *La Bête Humaine* had inspired him to turn away from realism, to seek a "more classical, more poetic genre . . . The result of all these reflections was *La Règle du Jeu* . . . I reread Marivaux and Musset quite intensively though without a thought of following them even in spirit . . . " Beaumarchais' *Le Mariage de Figaro*, with its master-servant parallels and intersections— overtly revolutionary in their time—is relevant. Already, Renoir had touched on the counterpointings of reality and role (the play-within-the-film of *Nana*), of sincerity and detachment (in *Les Bas-Fonds*), of moral earnestness and play (the prologues to *Boudu* and *La Chienne*). In *La Règle du Jeu* all these themes are swept into an urgent, earnest interrogation of spontaneity, convention and self-deception, not at all on that intrapsychic level which made psychoanalysis so congenial to Anglo-Saxon Protestantism, but in the fast, full interaction of impulse, inhibition and action, within an intricate network of relationships at once personal and social, formal and informal.

Technically and stylistically, the film is a *tour-de-force*. The slowness of Renoir's shooting is in converse ratio to the rapidity of the action. A social subject not altogether unreminiscent of Galsworthy is conjugated with a Pirandellian theme and choreographed at Feydeau tempo. There are over four hundred shots, many in deep-focus multiplane, with no reverse angles. The unleashing of deep-focus precedes Toland's work in Hollywood with John Ford *(The Long Voyage Home*, 1940) and Orson Welles *(Citizen Kane*, 1941), even though the special lenses were never used as intended. (Certainly the American subjects can accept a hard-contrast, silhouette-and-spotlight mood altogether inappropriate to Renoir's theme and tone). If Renoir's film makes less conspicuous a break with '30s techniques than Toland's it is because he scarcely uses maximum depth of focus behind an item in close-up—which helped everyone to spot the deep focus in *Citizen Kane* which they'd missed in *The Long Voyage Home*. But the camera's swift agility is no longer, as in *Les Bas-Fonds*, imposed by those shallow focus lenses which had forced Renoir to choose between either the monotonous and inappropriate alternation of reverse angle close-ups or letting the actors roam while chasing them to keep them within a shallow focal zone. If Bazin's word "triangulation" admirably schematises an element of *Kane's* visual style, the model for Renoir's style is that of a camera tracking along a wide corridor, at such an angle that it need only pan slightly to stress, first, a foreground conversation, then an animated midgroup, and finally a background figure, each centre of interest appearing and disappearing laterally from tributary doors and corridors as the camera moves by at its "soft", slightly unstable angle. There are few close-ups, in the American sense, in this film, and Renoir is continuously involved in the interesting question of "dramatic perspective", whereby an actor in the background of a shot may have to overact (by film standards) if our attention is to be rapidly attracted to him; but as the camera moves towards him to place him in the foreground, so his style will have to modulate towards something quieter.

The great number of shots in this film reminds us that for Renoir camera-movements are not substitutes for cuts. A track or pan from A to B, rather than a cut from the first frame of A to the last frame of B, may be slower, less bold, and involve more background distraction, but it may also enhance our awareness not only of the relationship between A and B, but of the possibility of gradually shifting relationships between the two within an external environment. The very distraction of shifting background sets us in a more detached kind of involvement, it intensifies our sense of relations within groups and subgroups as against the alternation of individual identifications, and the antagonism of supplanting of one subjectivity by another, which is facilitated by successive separate shots. This film's rapid tempo is determined by the actors rather than by the camera, and in this sense its nearest stylistic relative is the Hollywood comedy of Leo McCarey, Gregory La Cava and George Cukor.

Bazin inaugurates a new critical awareness of camera movements, when he notes that Renoir's "editing doesn't proceed from the habitual anatomy which disassociates the space and duration of a scene on the basis of an *a priori* dramatic hierarchy. It is that of an informed and mobile eye. . . . During the whole final section . . . the camera behaves like the invisible guest, strolling through the salons and the corridors, looking about with curiosity but with no other privilege than its invisibility. Even its mobility is not noticeably greater than a man's (if one allows that a great deal of running goes on in this chateau)." Bazin's anthropomorphism about the camera shows a Christian phenomenalist awareness of the continuity between director, aesthetic set-up, illusion and spectator. Presumably this awareness is an aesthetic, not an objective ontological one, and it would be irrelevant to argue that if the camera is in the position of a person the characters ought to address him, that the lovers are only alone when they're off-screen, that there are, after all, about 400 cuts in the film, and that *La Règle du Jeu* is neither *The Lady in the Lake* nor *The Connection*.

Nonetheless Bazin can be carried away by just this sort of logic, as when he implies that one long-held shot respects the integrity of reality in a way in which it is not respected by a succession of close-ups. It's true that certain rhythms and relationships are best served by long-held long shots, but anyone can think of actions whose integrity and continuity are best served by at least one cut. Hence the advantage of discussing film technique in the non-transcendental terms of ordinary aesthetic psychology, and of the artistic situation as one which is variably ambiguous, from moment to moment, as between illusion and spectacle. Subsequent *Cahiers* writers, while supposing that they were responding to the current of inspiration which flowed through André Bazin, in practice departed from his phenomenological sense of relationships, for they considered camera-movements as "calligraphy", that is as an autonomous, abstracted, formalist element, related to the director. But they increasingly abstracted it from the psychological realism of the action in the vicinity of which the camera happened to perform its introverted gyrations. Of all the *Cahiers* subsection of the *Nouvelle Vague,* only Doniol-Valcroze and Truffaut (in his second and third films) made a boldly calligraphic use of the camera, in which respect they went no further than Max Ophuls had done already. The superimpositions in Truffaut's *Tirez Sur Le Pianiste* could certainly have been absorbed by Bazin into his emphasis on the camera's ontological fidelity to visual surfaces considered as an emanation of the essence of things. Bazin admires certain gaps when they occur in documentaries (e.g. Thor Heyerdahl's Kon Tiki film is all the more moving because in every crisis the photographer has to stop filming and start doing something else). What is curious is the twist in Bazin's arguments when he comes to consider semi-documentary and fiction. The cut which in documentary is doubly moving as a guarantee of authenticity becomes in semi-documentary and in fiction a caesura in the authenticity which would have been maintained by a continuously exposed camera! Logically one would have had to be equally annoyed each time a character of Renoir's strays in and out of frame, or, indeed, annoyed by the fact that the camera is restricted to one particular viewpoint and sees only w..at comes before its lens. The reason why Bazin doesn't notice the cuts is that he's so moved by, on one level, the action, and, on the other, his reverence for Renoir, that he experiences the interventions as part of a whole, just as the rapid action of *La Règle du Jeu* carries his mind across the cuts, making them as invisible for him as they are for 999 spectators out of a thousand. In effect, he doesn't mean what he says about the superior authenticity of continuous takes at all. What he is suggestively rather than logically trying to translate into terms of aesthetic argument is his liking for films which can be seen as suggesting a sort of compatibility between an overall visual gestalt and the essence of things. It's important for Bazin to believe that Welles's deep-focus in *Citizen Kane* is, like Wyler's in *The Best Years of Our Lives,* democratic and open to the freedom of the spectator's spirit. But probably most of us would see a contrast between the deep focus in Renoir, which is democratic (though not so open to option as Bazin implies), the deep focus in Welles, whose effects are egocentric and hierarchical, and the deep focus in Wyler (which is as carefully controlled and controlling as everything he does).

If, for Bazin, *Le Règle du Jeu* is Renoir's masterpiece, it is because "he has succeeded in totally dispensing with dramatic structures, the film is simply an interlacing of resemblances, allusions and correspondences, a carousel of themes." Here, too, Bazin anticipates critical attitudes which subsequent *Cahiers* writers will take to the point of caricature, notably Truffaut in his attacks on the "well-constructed script". The "interlacing of resemblances, allusions, and correspondences" has happy results, however, in the case of *Jules et Jim*, which is no less well-structured than the extremely classical plot of *A Bout de Souffle;* all that's lacking is a few transitional devices, and a certain tempo (of playing and acting, *not* of script). The manner in which Renoir has amplified his almost academic structure (parallel and interlacing plots) is the very traditional *ars celare artem.*

An intriguingly contrasted view of the film's plot structure is given by Armand Cauliez, whose recourse to topographical, geometrical and choreographic metaphor is doubtless inspired by the sprinting and pirouetting of camera and characters. "Starting with Octave, the dramatic spiral finishes with Schumacher, after having involved, on its way, all the participants of this *ronde*—of this farandole. Further, this spiral incessantly dislocates and re-establishes itself, traversed by the straight lines of trickery (the sighting aided by binoculars), or violence (the shootings). Thus, certain players (comedy) . . . become actors (drama). These spirals, overloaded with right angles, constitute the magnetic field of force of the work; the world is

neither linear nor circular, neither fixed nor sealed off, but—ajar. . . .
Renoir, as "calculator, develops his theme mathematically; but he is also a
dancer. . . . "

There are, perhaps, two lords of the dance: Renoir as camera (the
involved spectator) and Renoir as Octave (spectator as involvement), and
they circle about each other like a double star as they pursue their action. In
Partie de Campagne, Renoir runs the inn where the encounter occurs, and
"cooks up" the meal which lures the family towards their daughter's
seducers. Within *La Règle du Jeu*, Octave constantly plots and revises *before*
the camera as frantically as Renoir behind it. Octave, whose ambition it was
to be a creative musician, endeavours to conduct an orchestrated *élan*, a
harmonious tension between the energy of each motif, each cadence, and the
whole. But society is at once too chaotic and too rigid. All the movement
which throughout *La Bête Humaine* drifts uneasily, sometimes within
frames, sometimes unleashed along narrow tracks, here moves in rapid
arabesques. *La Règle du Jeu* would be rococo were it a comedy but
instead, with its suddenly dramatic and tragic volumes, it approaches the
baroque, the point of departure of Renoir's next project.

Alongside the generosity of *La Règle du Jeu* there is also an ironic
pessimism reminiscent of Julien Duvivier (who, we recall, earlier inter-
changed subjects with Renoir), and the wistfulness of René Clair (human
friendships as a wayward puppet show). We have seen how most Anglo-
Saxon critics, like the French left, chose to see the film as an indictment of
French high society, except that Anglo-Saxons, even more severely, saw it
as a cautionary tale about the decadence of, not only a permissive society,
but even a merely frivolous one. After a reference to Prévert's *Les Amants de
Vérone*, the *Spectator's* critique continues: "Both films show a silly and
decadent group stewing in its own juice, wildly out of touch with the world
outside, sinking lower and lower into pointless and selfwounding cruelty
because in each case there is nothing in their lives to keep them active." The
film may, of course, be using French high society as one particular case
through which it aims at the Western world's high societies in general. But
it is equally possible that if the riot of murders in *La Bête Humaine* isn't
ipso facto a condemnation of lower class people, one murder in *La Règle du
Jeu* isn't *ipso facto* a condemnation of upper-class people. And are film critics

altogether innocent of fiddling while the Vietnamese burn? *La Marseillaise* suggests that Renoir's didactic tactics would involve the fairly commonsense assumption that partly or largely sympathetic characterisation would prove more acceptable and plausible than knockdown evangelical denunciation.

One can't altogether accuse Jurieu of having "nothing in his life" to keep him active. He's only broken a world aviation record, that's all. One can't altogether accuse La Chesnaye either, since he collects mechanical musical instruments, not as an investment, but because he is profoundly moved by his latest acquisition, and moved to tears, as a lover of art should be, by beauty and by poetry. Surely Christine is a basically serious and moral person? And once we decide to respect her, would we really wish to chase Octave with bell, book and candle? Yet Octave is the idlest character of the lot. He failed to become an orchestral conductor and ever since then, he tells Christine, he has lived on the generosity of a few friends. The poacher at least *works* for a living. As for those critics who admire the anarchism incarnated by Boudu, and would then condemn Octave for not making a profit and living off friends, there's only one word, and it's a three-syllable one: Lestingois.

Almost all the principal characters are not only the most agreeable of companions, devoid of real malice, but also attractive on many of the deeper, more authentic levels of being. Gavin Lambert sees the protagonists as, on the whole, "a party of lively, easygoing, unprincipled people. They are not vindictive or pathological; if not rich, they are still elegant and charming. Their 'sin' is something much less obviously abnormal. It consists of having no values at all, of always evading the important issues." This is so near the mark, that my disagreement may look like cavilling. I wouldn't know what, by Lambert's standards, qualifies as "rich," but most of Renoir's characters certainly qualify as rich by mine, and in fact most critics seem to take the film as concerning high society rather than, say, impoverished gentry. I would hardly have thought that middle classes were likely to constitute the majority of the guests invited down for a weekend's hunting at a country chateau along with the aristocracy and the latest lion of high fashion. Again, a weakness of moral values and an evasion of important issues may be sins, but they are far from being abnormal. On the contrary they would seem to me at least as much the rule as having mistaken convictions. But just which issues, precisely, do they evade? What inkling does Renoir give us of the items which ought to be on their agenda? If Renoir does not pose them, how can they possibly face them? It's quite true that they hesitate, prevaricate, procrastinate, and dissimulate, not only to others but to themselves, all of which, in matters of love and in many personal mental processes are, surely, every-day "sins", a congenital hypocrisy being our natural condition. Most of the characters are generous, but are unsure which behavioural strategies to follow, or which aspect of which moral or social code is relevant to any given situation, or whether the other characters have the same morality as

themselves. It's not enough to have a moral code, as Christine begins to realise in the first reel. You also have to know whether or not other people share your code, and whether they know what your code is, both of which are surprisingly difficult to ascertain, since communication itself depends on the code, and "code" is meant in a sense much nearer the Biblical than the semiological one.

Renoir's own comments on the film show a baffling contrariety. Once, he flatly stated: "There is not one character in *La Règle du Jeu* who's worth the bother of saving!" Not even Octave? Christine? Jurieu? If we didn't care for the latter, his death would hardly seem the tragic waste it does, and the Renoir in the film, Octave, rings truer: "There's one thing, do you see, that's terrifying in this world, and that is that every man has his reasons!" Renoir's very ability to see all points of view renders his various remarks on the film disturbingly double-jointed. Jurieu's "sin" is that "he brings into one caste the ideas of another. . . . And the fact that he is honest and pure renders him much more dangerous. In reality, in killing him, one eliminates a microbe. A very sympathetic microbe, but a microbe which could kill a whole body." I find it difficult to know which caste Jurieu represents, as opposed to that which he invades. The killing of a patriotic aviator is approved by a patriotic general, so it's not a matter of a militarism appropriate to the times as against civilian irresponsibility, and the conflict would seem one of attitudes within a caste rather than caste against caste. Jurieu's code

overlaps with the general's, in its earnestness and its evocation of the age of chivalry. One might argue that although the shooting is accidental it represents an unconscious collective resolution by a society which fears Jurieu's vitality. Except that of the three characters who approve of the shooting, only one, the general, is a member of that society. Another is a poacher, and the closest he comes to being a member of high society is being a temporary servant. The murderer is a gamekeeper, something of a feudal retainer, with the essential earnestness of the general—and Jurieu himself. The earnest kill the earnest.

Renoir's remark might be understood another way. Despite Boudu, I don't think one can attribute to his creator the rather sentimental notion that rules are the root of all evil. The rules which run this social group are nothing to do with law and order, they're not particularly prohibitive (in fact accusations of decadence imply that they're too permissive); and apart from the master-servant parallelism one could very easily set a sufficiently similar story, including the collision of castes and codes, among a hippy commune. Another remark of Renoir's might seem to concur with a conformist view. "I want to demonstrate that every game has its rules, and that if you play otherwise, you lose the game." Which is hardly true of Boudu, who wins it for precisely that reason, and Renoir's remark is unobtrusively ambiguous. For it's not at all clear whether *la règle* means something like those strategies or tactics which are normative because they frequently get good results, or whether it has the sense of the injunctions and prohibitions which are imposed on the players and within whose frameworks they are free to vary their strategies as they please. There's the difference between "As a rule . . . " and "Obey this rule!" or between "rule-of-thumb" and "the rule of law." My suggestion is that Renoir's remarks indicate, with a conversational looseness, the film's real theme. It is a dance-collision involving two codes, or rather two categories of codes. On one hand, there are the earnest characters; on the other, there are the liars and hypocrites. There is no moral difference between them, and there is a gradual transition between the two. For instance, Christine is serious at heart but affects frivolity and so is misunderstood; Octave who pursues maid-servants like an unprincipled rake is an essentially serious character; and the general is certainly a dissimulator in that he keeps his moral convictions for his close companion. There are also lower-class codes (gamekeeper and poacher), but the most violent clash comes between adherents of a generally similar code and a similar earnestness (the aviator and the general). If one takes the over-all spirit of the château as a mixture of sincerity and affable hypocrisy, rather like civilized life anywhere, then one might see the title as a play on both senses of the word *règle*. Jurieu pursues a mistaken strategy, while Schumacher breaks the rules. But strong as this suggestion is, it isn't altogether borne out by the logic of the plot. For it is the blindest of accidents which results in Jurieu's death. Jurieu, with more than a little help from his friends, has won his Christine. Nobody wanted to murder him, certainly not his murderer, and the fire-eating general didn't feel strongly about it. Had the elopement occurred, he would merely have shrugged righteously and concurred with the left about the decadence of the times.

The logic of the plot seems to me to suggest something rather like this. As a rule of thumb (i.e. as a tentative procedure, as a first strategy), the nature of human society is such that every individual must exercise a certain caution and a certain discretion in showing his hand. If this is condemned as hypocrisy, then this film is a defence of hypocrisy—approaching what Renoir, nearly twenty years later, was to say about *Eléna et les Hommes* (whether that Renoir has reneged on the earlier Renoir, as left-wing critics have maintained, is another question, but it must at least be admitted that nearly twenty years is time enough for a man to change his mind and that only the logic of the earlier film's plot confirms the later remark as relevant to it). In general, the hypocrisy required of an individual by society is less dangerous than self-deception. It is important to be ruthlessly honest about oneself to oneself while still having cogent selfish, unselfish and ethical reasons for revealing the truth to very few people indeed. All consideration for others depends on a flexible denial of spontaneity, and on a deliberate dishonesty. Effective response to social situations depends on a certain balance between spontaneity, calculation and hypocrisy. Yet, however sane and clever we are, life is sufficiently ironical to take all our kindness, all our lucidity, all our zest, all our noble renunciations smoothly in its stride, to produce another fine mess. In *La Règle du Jeu* no one and everyone is to blame. The system is no more guilty than coincidence. The murder is a *crime passionel,* its counseller has half his mind on his own minor misery; everywhere there is the menace of death—the car-crash (in which, incidentally, Jurieu very nearly murders Octave, which would have put him in the Schumacher category), the massacre of the rabbits (of which Renoir is equally guilty, for the sake of his film), the skeleton dance (which is perhaps the right attitude in the face of inevitable death), and guns.

"With *La Règle du Jeu* I was beginning to get a clearer understanding . . . of relationships, to realise that the world was also divided into little groups, into little circles, within the bosom of which men pursue their activities linked by ideas, by conventions, by common interests. I began to be interested in the cinema of groups." Leprohon energetically protests: "This is to forget *Toni, M. Lange* and *La Nuit du Carrefour.*" Nonetheless, an intriguing aspect of the pattern is the fluid interpenetration of groups, climaxed by Schumacher pursuing Marceau through the festivities, and continuously asserted by the abundance of conversations between employers and servants, with La Chesnaye seeking instruction in amorous affairs from Marceau, with Lisette helping Octave to renounce Christine for the sake of Jurieu, with the cheerful miscasting of an Austrian and a Jew, as if Renoir were anticipating his later remarks about the internationalism of the eighteenth-century aristocracy as a useful model for a more democratic twentieth-century spirit. One might suggest that the pessimistic angularity of *La Bête Humaine* is dissolving, or disintegrating, into a reaction against the Marxist notion of social class, and that Renoir's remark about groups implies that this is moving to a secondary place in his mind as against a non-political interest in groups, cliques and sets. All the same, his later films show that he continues to regard social class as a major determinant of both history and the individual's intimate sensibility. It is arguable that the major defect of the usual Marxist notion of class is that it lacks this film's sense of the extent to which many members of most classes have intimate or influential personal contacts with one or more other class cultures and are in consequence formed by situations corresponding to no one class culture. Up to a point, the Marxist is in the same position as the Freudian; class, like sex, is, as they remind us, absolutely everywhere, but for that very reason it is rarely the sole constituent of a situation. Christine has moved through this frivolous society thinking with a kind of German Protestant moral seriousness, a Kantian kind of well-tempered affection, a strong sense of conjugal loyalty, and an ingenuous confidence in her husband. Indeed, she initially seems to be reacting very lightly as she discusses the rules of love and friendship with Lisette. And maybe she is deceiving herself, confusing her natural response with her moral rules. Her loyal dismissal of gossip about her husband's infidelities is as ingenuous as certain traits of Jurieu's—it is her *règle,* her falsity. When her hunting companion persuades her to look through his special lens at "the private life of the squirrel", and she sees Robert kissing Geneviève, she fails to distinguish between a passionate kiss and a kiss of fond farewell, reacting in a straightforwardly feminine way which also, perhaps, carries just a hint of the readiness with which moralists fail to distinguish sexual permissiveness as lustful attachment and its elements of friendliness and restraint. When she jettisons the false frivolity which is her impulsive and apparently superficial response to infidelity and disillusionment, and opts for elopement, she contemplates the moon with a romanticism which is like the other face of German Protestant transcendentalism. Like Octave, she has devoted her life to an illusion, and now she, herself, is misled by that very propensity for friendship which makes her Octave's double.

The persistent contradictions between appearance and revelation come close to inducing in us a kind of hilarious despair, or desparate hilarity, about the relevance of any gesture to any relational or emotional reality. The instrument which reveals the kiss, with its cruelly liberating mixture of truth and lie, might have been directly inspired by the special lenses which Renoir had ground for the film. "Its optical quality is so fine, and its structure such that by using it like a tele-microscope you can catch the animal unawares and observe all the details of its intimate life."

Octave is unstable because he confuses what I take to be his moment of authentic communication, of shared experience with Christine, with love. But he could love her only as he could love several other women like her (or unlike her, i.e. maidservants). Christine could love Octave or Jurieu; but Octave realises, probably rightly, that his friend Jurieu can love only Christine and that Christine will be happier with her slightly chivalrous hero than with himself. Despite which one can't altogether rule out the possibility that Octave was right to woo Christine, that he had loved her all along, that his preference for servants reveals weakness as well as egalitarianism, that his self-abnegatory turnabout in favour of Jurieu springs from a confusion of sympathy, a loss of confidence, and a preference for the path of least resistance. Maybe Octave does the right thing for the wrong reason, or the wrong thing for the right reason. His honest chameleonism gives him a special position within and without high society, part universal confidant, part procurer. Yet without his hesitations Jurieu would not have been kept waiting so long and so missed the gamekeeper's bullet. Some of his plots and plans have a genial irresponsibility. "Could we get Geneviève interested in the aviator?" he wonders (as, no doubt, Renoir the scenarist must have wondered). To which Chesnaye sensibly replies, "No, that's too simple, it only happens in stories." Octave imports his own confusions, even if they are at times an antidote to society's (perhaps he is the intruder from another, the bohemian, caste?). As artist, "I thought I had my little word to say! But I'm a failure!" Outside the castle he conducts an orchestra of shadows, shadows thrown by "the moon with its halo", in a scene which, given Octave as Jean Renoir, eerily foreshadows Ionescou's *The Chairs*. For the evening's entertainment, he dons a bearskin, and as crisis suceeds crisis he finds that although he can remove the animalhead, he can't shed the body. He dashes

about trying to find someone to help him, so that he can, as it were, plunge back into the intrigues of which he is co-author and rectify the manner in which their protagonists insist on being their own *auteurs* and improvising regrettable developments. But, as if in a Pirandello play, everyone is too preoccupied to bother with their *deus in fera*. Eventually Geneviève the vamp roughhouses him out of his disguise. Nonetheless, "All I know how to do is to spit into the water . . . " And stir up eddies.

Those who see the film as an accusation of degeneracy rarely go into much detail, since the criticism resides in a suggestive overall atmosphere rather than individual traits. Presumably they disapprove of Robert de la Chesnaye who, as marquis and as host, is "patron" of the goings-on. This disapproval might take a "noncomformist" line. Or one may censure an apparent effeminacy indicated in his initial scenes (though never subsequently) by his silk dressing-gown, langorous flowers and only too visible make-up; his adultery (with Geneviève); his weakness of will (his difficulty in breaking off with her); his frivolity (collecting musical boxes); and his weakness for the entertaining rascal (the poacher). Not only that, but to avoid scandal he disseminates a false account of Jurieu's death, sparing Schumacher an amply deserved sentence for murder (at least, if we suppose that he knows the truth, as I think we are intended to assume). Of most of these sins he's probably guilty; that they make him wicked by normal standards is less certain. The effeminate air never goes further than a kind of aestheticism, or the late '20s-early '30s style of lazy droop, analogous to various P. G. Wodehouse characters. If Chesnaye connives at Marceau's pursuit of Lisette it is because, with Geneviève clinging to him, he wants to learn the knack of

keeping his relationships with the ladies light and agreeable. Marceau assumes Chesnaye is complaining of a lack of success in seducing women and demonstrates his method: "I always make them laugh!" A deliciously circular irony.

It's easy to see why he was ready to waive the letter of the law where the poacher was concerned: to avoid scandal. Marceau was in fact helping Schumacher to exterminate the rabbits which were in danger of overrunning the estate, and Marceau belongs, if anywhere, on the estate staff.

Marceau, like Octave, is an adept of the light and flirtatious approach. Both are, in a sense, parasites on society. Marceau approves of Schumacher's right, as deceived husband, to kill his wife's lover, although he does protest when Schumacher speaks of killing his wife too. Marceau's extrasocial role as poacher may identify him as a Rousseauist innocent, like Cabuche, but he is, of course, a player of games and an actor too (pulling pathetic faces). No doubt blarney is involved when he confides to the marquis his alleged dream of being an indoor servant in a fine house. But there's no reason to disbelieve him altogether: the conditions can be rather more comfortable than a poacher's, especially with a variety of maidservants flitting to and fro.

Schumacher, agent of order, becomes the agent of anarchy in its revengeful, carnivorous aspect. There is nothing of the game about his earnestness. He arrests Marceau for killing the rabbits which he is himself attempting to exterminate. He might at least have tolerated the poacher's clandestine co-operation, as the "frivolous" Chesnaye has the practical sense to spot immediately. Schumacher's straight sincerity must compel our sympathy. But his devotion to the rules is alienation, since no relationships are entirely determinable by rules. There are poachers, of women, within the castle, and there the rule of the shotgun really doesn't apply. His gift of a heavy cloak to his wife illustrates his sense of a formalised situation and his unawareness of human realities. In hot pursuit of Marceau, who in point of fact isn't Lisette's lover yet, he's stopped dead in his tracks by a head valet who lectures him as to correctness of behaviour. But Schumacher when cut to the quick appeals to an unofficial code, which Marceau shares, that considers murder an appropriate penalty in cases of adultery. One may well prefer the Chesnayes' code, of adultery as socially permissible, but kept from one's wife so as not to hurt her, or even the head valet's code with its insistence on stoic impassivity. Neither is 'decadent'. Maybe Renoir thinks that the luxuries and snobberies of high society have corrupted Lisette, for her feather-brained vanity might seem like an imperceptive copy of upper-class frivolity, and yet her mistress is Christine, and Lisette's frivolity is no more modelled on Christine's than Schumacher's ideas of orderliness are modelled on Chesnaye's. Both spring from characteristic middle- and upper-working class attitudes. Lisette's style is so thoroughly urban that one wonders why she should have married Schumacher in the first place. This may have crossed Renoir's mind too, since in one or two shots he has her ostentatiously munching an apple, perhaps because he fitfully remembers that she's supposed to have a vaguely agricultural aura, perhaps to remind us of Eve, who was no more a lady than Adam was a gentleman.

Schumacher, like Roubaud, kills a man who in some way or another is associated with his employer. And Lange, of course, kills his employer, though for another reason. Schumacher's counterpart there is the caretaker. If one imagines Chesnaye as he might have been played by Jules Berry, then the morality of *La Règle du Jeu* begins to look rather different. Surely, however, Renoir intends us to like Chesnaye as much as we like the amiable playboy who mucks in with the Co-operative and helps Lange and Valentine to cross the frontier. He, too, connives at a *crime passionel,* and if we don't disapprove of him we can't be too hard on Chesnaye either.

Christine represents the "classicising" emphasis on balance and moderation, which does not become conspicuous in Renoir's films until later, and is there usually assigned to the men—women inclining to the life-force which disturbs men's neat little systems. At once motherly and even brotherly, Christine has spiritual cousins in some other films: the wife in *The Southerner,* the Anglo-Indian girl in *The River,* and Éléna, although more on the level of acting than of script. Here the Renoir vamp is Geneviève, whose glance mingles affectionate contempt with a detached sympathy, a mixture which might lend itself to that misogyny in which Renoir's other vamps never involve him; perhaps because what one easily calls a vamp is merely a woman seeking equality through her seductiveness rather than through her profession. Reverse the sexual viewpoint, and a surprising number of Renoir men are "vamps" in their irresponsible or purposeful seduction, while neither Séverine nor Geneviève are "vamps" in the sense of seeking economic advantage from their "victims". Geneviève, less feline than Simone Simon or La Hessling, looks forward, with her more statuesque postures, her Arab fancy dress, and her imperious hysterics, to La Belle Abbesse (Maria Felix) in *French CanCan* (who is also pulled, though rather less uneasily, between the poles of respect and caricature). Geneviève comes close to the near-farcical idiom in which Renoir sometimes couches his criticism of the bourgeois ethos: the police chief in *Les Bas-Fonds,* the bourgeois family in *Partie de Campagne*; even Grandmorin in *La Bête Humaine* is played by a specialist in farcical eccentrics. It's difficult to decide whether burlesque blunts the attack (the character is always inferior to and different from every spectator) or whether it furthers it (without some such intensification of characteristics the bourgeois spectator would sympathise with the character, and adopt his viewpoint) or whether the currently finer blend of observation and criticism would have been viable in the '30s (certainly few contemporary critics gave any sign of sensing the critical meaning of, say, Roubaud, or of Zabel in *Quai des Brumes*). In some scenes Geneviève is condemned to tiresome behaviour, pretentious fashions, drunkenness, a ridiculous slink and extremely tedious fits of temperament; she is last seen incapacitated by tipsy hysterics which might seem Renoir's unflattering judgement on her. In other scenes, she is frank and lucid, suggesting, perhaps, that her fancydress histrionics are merely the idiom in which she has learned to deal with men too pompous, or immature, or imperceptive of that intelligent directness which is her natural style and which she exasperatedly has to keep to herself. She is a very efficient rabbit-killer, and somehow there seems to her more than an instinctive rapacity and a good eye. Shooting is something to which she can openly apply a careful intelligence with no nonsense. She concedes defeat to Chesnaye with the observation, "I can fight hatred, but not boredom", and there's a worldly wisdom, an awareness of her own limitations, a capacity to summarise a situation, such that one feels inclined to place her alongside the other good losers in Renoir. Despite the attractions of the idea that the contradictions within her are deliberate, the switches of idiom do seem rather haphazard, albeit camouflaged by the film's swift changes of mood. But it is Lisette, not Geneviève, who gives Octave sensible advice over Christine and Jurieu. Indeed, it isn't at all difficult to conceive of a version in which Geneviève and Lisette are one and the same person; an actress or an artist's model would make a convenient starting-point, combining the ideas of lower social class and of images, one woman as all women and all women as one woman for the same man, and so on. One step further and it resembles *Diary of a Chambermaid*, in which a rapacious maidservant "poaches" her employers' son. The similarity is enhanced rather than diminished if our maidservant/model—more Geneviève than Lisette—is engaged to another murderous gamekeeper, the "hero" of Buñuel's version of Mirbeau's novel. Certainly, critics have likened the disruption of fashionable social function by lower order scandals here to the parallel scene in Buñuel's *L'Age d'Or*.

Jurieu, the dashing aviator, is as helpless, once landed, as Baudelaire's albatross. His manner of death is prefigured by the slaughter of the rabbits. He lacks not courage nor its occasional concomitant, the foolhardy petulance of a spoiled child thwarted (over the air he reproaches the woman he loves, thus complicating her life vindictively and humiliating her before all their friends). On terra firma, he takes off, nearly killing Octave as well as himself. Confronted with the practical problems of elopement, divorce and remarriage, he sheers away into the weird suggestion that Christine live with his mother for a month, an idea vaguely suggestive of an obsequious demonstration of respectability or of some Christian medieval chastity cult. He's a solo flyer, and if he fits so awkwardly into society with its rules, it's not simply because society is frivolous and its rules are conventionalised or pettifogging or not meant to be taken seriously; it's just as much, or even more, because he can be very inconsiderate, absurdly despondent, absurdly irate and generally impossible. At least his love is not a matter of selfishness, status, convenience or habit. But consider how straightforward his pursuit of Christine might be, if he weren't so inept. For though in their relationship Christine is the adult and he is the child, they have important affinities. She too is an idealist. Her elopement will spare her affable husband, whom she loves as a friend, the harrowing necessity of having to choose between her and Geneviève. A divorce had in 1939 manifold social inconveniences but no more. Yet it takes the failed artist to keep the man of action, against all social pressures, most of them imaginary, steady on course: love her, woo her, win her. Who's to blame if an eagle thinks like a rabbit? Not this chateau and its rules.

Nonetheless, the film possesses a moralistic angle, associated with a left-wing position, and it leans heavily on two unspoken factors. One is the '30s social background of slump and war, and the other is the assumption that what happens here isn't just a weekend away from it all, but typifies the way in which these idle people spend all their time. There is a "weak", or discreet, sense in which Renoir is dissenting from the values which Lubitsch, Chaplin and cinema audiences so often accept as the *summum bonum* of existence. (Chesnaye, pampered and irresponsible, selfindulgently prefers the poacher to the gamekeeper, and that apparently peripheral little whim is enough to trigger off the death of French vitality.) I say "weak" because he is no more guilty than anyone else. One wonders if Renoir himself was aware quite

how heavily the climate of the times would force itself upon a film in which the relationships between the classes (aristocrats and servants) are in a sense idyllic.

Surprisingly enough, the film lends itself to certain right-wing positions. If things go wrong it's because Chesnaye fails to observe the basic rule of the game, which requires him to back up Schumacher, right or wrong, against Marceau. If only he had behaved conventionally, Marceau would have enjoyed no opportunity to get near Lisette, the whole weekend would have gone according to plan, and Jurieu would never have been shot. Jurieu and Christine should have been much less uncompromising, and settled for a long, discreet, perhaps semi-official, adulterous affair, leaving the social order stable and secure. Galsworthy might have seen things this way: Chesnaye, the cosmopolitan Jewish *nouveau riche*, just jumped up from the middle classes, naturally hasn't the instincts of responsibility which our native gentry have had bred into them over countless generations (!) of the public school spirit. One could quite easily go on to construct a chauvinistic and anti-Semitic interpretation. Renoir has with involuntary intuition hit on just what a century and a half of liberal ideas have done to France! The rot sets in because Chesnaye is half a Rosenthal from Frankfurt, that is to say, from anywhere. No wonder he instinctively promotes the criminal, humilates the guardian of law and order, and indulges himself in effete activities. And while tormenting simple honest law-abiding folk like Schumacher, he brings in, not a French wife, but a woman whose loyalties must, like Marie-Antoinette's, remain half to France's hereditary enemy. She, and the typically parasitic and indecisive artist, lead Jurieu to his doom! It's *Jew Suss* all over again.

Renoir heads off the right-wing interpretations not only by the type of sympathy which his human tone suggests to the spectators but by the general, applauding a murder which he thinks was Chesnaye's, as a traditional moral affirmation. Through two unlikeable old traditionalists, Renoir castigates not the new, Fascist right so much as the old, traditional right. Their reaction is quite perverse since the man whose death the general induces St.-Aubin to approve is a flower of French heroism. Spiritually they are saboteurs. At the same time, their morality is not an exclusive to the aristocracy. Schumacher (for the peasantry/labour aristocracy/petty bourgeois) and Marceau (for the lumpenproletariat), suggesting between them the Populist classes, see things in the same way. Renoir further heads off any separation between Chesnaye and the aristocracy by a discussion in the kitchens among the servants, who are snobs to a man. When the matter of Chesnaye's low-born ancestors rears its ugly head, the chef settles the matter by insisting that where his cuisine is concerned Chesnaye's palate is impeccable and exacting and that this makes him as aristocratic as can be. That convinces everyone, and whatever alternative morals one might logically deduce (that Chesnaye ought to have the Spartan tastes inculcated by public school education, that the pleasures of the palate are sybaritic and degenerate, that being exacting is tyranny, and that the chef is displaying the characteristic masochism of the insufficiently revolutionary working classes), dramatic suggestiveness sees to it that we take what's good enough for these snobbish servants as good enough for us.

The style of most of the guests and the attitudes of the servants suggest that Renoir's film is set amongst a rightist milieu. The song sung by our friends at their little entertainment is a Boulangist song. But since our friends' performance guys the bushily bearded bourgeoisie, and identifies the movement with a danse macabre, there is also a suggestion of a strong streak of self-satire, and therefore an absence of extremism, a flexibility, a balance, a readiness to make concessions, however topsy-turvy, much like that with which Renoir credits the more level-headed elements on the right in *La Marseillaise*. But it's equally true that in several Prévert films, fancy-dress, and acting parts, symbolise a hidden identity which is a kind of spiritual declaration or premonition. If this sense is imputed here, then Renoir is indicating that the emergence of these people's political selves from their personal selves will unleash the chaos which kills Jurieu. The two overtones may be sounded together, i.e., These people are essentially likeable people who think they are coolly sceptical and beyond extremism, but the sum of their carelessness will turn them into what they mock. In sum, the film seems to me a criticism of the right, but not at all a criticism of its characters in the way in which it has too readily been assumed to be. Nor would it seem appropriate to suggest that Chesnaye, instead of collecting musical-boxes, should have used his connections and his resources to help finance Jurieu's next flight and so make the French public air-conscious and renovate France's sadly obsolescent *armée de l'air*. This might have made a very topical movie, but wouldn't have had much to do with Renoir, and would probably have been taken by the suddenly pacifist Communist left as marking Renoir's violent swing to the militarist right.

Beyond all question, it is by the destruction of Jurieu's and Christine's love that society, and the rules of its game, are found wanting. Doubtless the rule of the social game is hypocrisy, with its morally higher and its morally lower forms. But maybe hypocrisy is less dangerous than self-deception, so that the real agents of chaos are those who, infatuated with sincerity and spontaneity, surrender at the wrong moments, to sensibility (Chesnaye), friendship (Octave), duty (Christine), petulance (Jurieu), and so on. Just as there is the higher and the lower hypocrisy, so there is the higher and the lower childishness—the former knowing, and accepting, the cost of its gratification. To attain and to balance the higher hypocrisy and the higher childishness is the most exacting of spiritual arts. And is the social dance any more destructive than the dance of life? Is *La Régle du Jeu* any less an interrogation of life and love themselves, or rather *itself*, than Bergman's

Smiles of a Summer Night (with which Gilles Jacob establishes so many intriguing parallels)?

Unable to decide how the film should end, Renoir prepared another final shot in which Octave and Marceau stand side by side before going their separate ways. Perhaps it's these two free-wheelers who, in the end, are society's real antibody. Perhaps everybody in the film is society's antibody? If life is a dance, it has no tragedies: only casualties. The film quietly preludes *The River*: human purpose, social design, are *la grande illusion*.*

The *règle* is not a responsibility before God, or a categorical imperative, or conscience, or custom, or convention, or any purely negative shibboleth. It is instructions for a dance, producing at worst musical automatons, at best a quite indefinable creativity, a gift for improvisation within the group. The art, or dance, is not at all a set solo on a stage before a passive and separate audience, but an involvement in which one may want to observe others, and hope that a little of what we are and do will sometimes be glimpsed by our fellow-dancers and please them. But the dance is, first and foremost, a process of becoming.

The sense of dissolution apparent in Renoir's earlier films here reaches its climax. The film's visual and narrative styles, its improvisatory procedures, suggest a liberation from the prevalent European tradition which retains far deeper traces than it knows of the Christian notion of a private and inalienable soul which, by its relation to an abstract or internalised God, is both intrinsically guilt-inducing and mysteriously inviolable. Doubtless those traces have been even further incised by economic individualism, with guilt the internal aspect of a fear of falling into the class below. Doubtless both fears of God and fears of social failure draw on the unconscious pressures deep within the mind. Yet whichever view one adopts, one is presented with a vocabulary which all but implies that each life must complete its own meaning.

In another, very disturbing sense, it is true that our internal world is constructed out of our relationships and that it rapidly deteriorates without the appropriate relationships. We have only the immediate present, and that is too short to offer more than a few trivial satisfactions. Conversely, memory and fear, creating our sense of time, long ago threw us out of the Paradise of the eternal present. But if we can consider ourselves as being of no particular importance, and of no particular unimportance, we sense ourselves as something that *is* only insofar as it is constantly transforming itself, by its openness to impressions, and feel less as *one self* than as an intersection point of many

---

* Three minor echoes between *La Règle du Jeu* and other Renoir films:
(a) The name La Chesnaye resembles one La Chesnaie in *La Marseillaise*.
(b) Jurieu's record-breaking 'plane is a Caudron, an earlier type of which Maréchal is flying when shot down by Rauffenstein.
(c) Chesnaye's mother's maiden name was Rosenthal, which is the name of the same actor's character in *La Grande Illusion*. One might just devise a family tree linking the Rosenthals of France in Germany with the Rosenthals of Germany in France!

selves. Rimbaud: "Je est un autre." Renoir: "Je sommes n'importe qui." To be faithful to change and to oneself is not easy, is not a passive drifting, and it involves a certain detachment, just as it involves a multiple involvement in which the idea of sacrifice is replaced by that of generosity, and that of repression by that of exchange. Repression is a *hubristic* strategy which, in several Renoir films, leads to a violent eruption of its degraded forces. Not everything one can choose to do, or be, is right. Everything one is, or does, is partly wrong. The pattern of continuity in contradiction, of balancing imbalances, is evident not only within each Renoir film but in his switches of viewpoint, subject and tone between films. The dancer must learn that subtlest, hardest and least conspicuous of disciplines, whereby one makes a definite gesture which establishes a loss of equilibrium, then accepts and retrieves that loss by an impulse in a different, yet balanced, direction, only to lose it once again, and so on until *rigor mortis* sets in. We may, if we wish to pay the price of many falls and humiliations, thus learn to touch, to interlace ourselves with, and tenderly to quit, our partners. This is not to imply that they are merely yielding; the only true generosity is that which accepts the selfishness of others as inalienable, and treats it with courtesy, with neither weakness nor indifference. The model for human relationships is not the largely theoretical generosity of saints, nor the exclusivistic hoarding of economic man, but the potlatch of the tribe, a steady exchange maintained. As tragic as it is, something in the style of *La Règle du Jeu* approximates to that world, with its rush, its chaos, its energy. It is not so much a world of decadence, as an ideal world which keeps failing to construct itself, yet constantly repeats the attempt. Thus *La Règle du Jeu*, whose starting point was a certain *classicism*, seems visually, as well as in terms of its production, the giddiest of Renoir's movies. It seems giddy because it allows *so much* classicism into itself, and perhaps inaugurates Renoir's "classical" period.

Alain Resnais described his reactions on first seeing a version of *La Règle du Jeu*. " . . . it remains, I think, the single most overwhelming experience I have ever had in the cinema. When I first came out of the theatre, I remember, I just had to sit on the edge of the pavement; I sat there for a good five minutes, and then I walked the streets of Paris for a couple of hours. For me, everything had been turned upside down. All my ideas about the cinema had been changed. While I was actually watching the film, my impressions were so strong physically that I thought that if this or that sequence were to go on for one shot more, I would either burst into tears, or scream, or something. Since then, of course, I've seen it at least fifteen times—like most film-makers of my generation. I even recorded the whole sound track on my tape recorder, and it's amazing how well it stands up on its own."

La Tosca

Although Mussolini's censorship banned *La Grande Illusion,* the dictator's personal enthusiasm for the film exceeded even Goering's, and he not only kept a copy for himself, but indirectly suggested that Renoir come to Italy to direct a film. Perhaps he entertained ambitions of emulating the French success in the international film market; and certainly he was far less anxious for a European war than Hitler. When Renoir hesitated, the French government informed Renoir of its hope that his presence in Italian society would complement its intensive diplomatic efforts to influence Italy towards a continuation of her neutral policy. Presumably encouraged by the disastrous first runs of *La Règle du Jeu* and the collapse of a company whose promise had been so bright, Renoir left for Rome. With Karl Koch and Luchino Visconti (who had been his assistant on *Partie de Campagne*), he began work on a dramatic (not operatic) version of *La Tosca.* He also gave "some sort of lessons in film direction at the Experimental Centre in Rome." Subsequently he returned to Paris, where he was drafted into the army's cinematographic services with the rank of colonel, sitting on its committee for the resumption of film production.

According to *L'Avant Scène du Cinéma,* Renoir also helped Jacques Becker to prepare *L'Or du Cristobal,* a subject set to be his first feature. Renoir wrote the dialogue and exerted some sort of technical supervision. Becker quit the assignment after three weeks, although it was finished by Jean Stelli and premièred in Paris in April 1940. The Ministry of Foreign Affairs then requested Renoir to resume his work on *La Tosca.* The film's first six set-ups had been shot when, in the spring of 1940, the German blitzkrieg opened, and Renoir returned to Paris, leaving Karl Koch (helped by Visconti) to finish the film.

Renoir's aesthetic interests had already begun moving towards Italy. "You can't think of Marivaux without thinking of Italy; you mustn't forget that Marivaux began by writing for an Italian troupe, that his mistress was Italian, and that he's essentially a perpetuator of the Italian theatre—you can put him in the same basket as Goldoni. All this work on *La Règle du Jeu* had brought me closer to Italy, in a fantastic mode, and I wanted to see the baroque statues, the angels on bridges, their garments with too many folds, and their wings with too many feathers."

The film's opening sequence, with a rider galloping between Roman architecture by night, catches a kind of aghast turbulence, the start of an old order challenged and shocked into response. The effect is less obtrusive, yet far more pervasive, than the stone lion rearing at the base of Eisenstein's Odessa Steps.

The subject could seem to involve an intriguing spiritual equivocation. In the Romantic style, the scenario more or less identifies folk, freedom and the ideal nation (or the nation idealised), as against the despotism of foreign imperialism. It could move towards a mystic nationalism congenial to Fascist ideology—although certainly much less to Italian Fascism, faced as it was by the racial and cultural diversity of Italy, than to German Nazism, which could draw on such Romantic concepts as the German soul, blood and soil, and the *Wanderwogel*. That a fascist cinema should entrust so national and ideological a subject to a foreign director conspicuously associated with the Popular Front may startle, but one should beware of attributing too monolithic a policy to Mussolini's Italy, particularly given men with Visconti's background and influence.

Concealment in a chapel, a fan behind an altar, a fugitive in a well, a suicidal leap from a roof—the scenario is conceived around buildings, their internal spaces and stonescapes. What, on the stage, would create a dramatically intense foreshortening of space, lends itself equally to cinematographic movement and deep focus. Karl Koch's direction seems utterly faithful to Renoir's intentions, and to his aesthetic at this period.

The whole film is pervaded by traits characteristic of Renoir. The camera proceeds from one pair to find another, located along the same diagonal corridor or wall. The camera slowly tracks forward to the horizontal roof-edge over which La Tosca has just thrown herself, in a triumphant suicide, as if in reverence to the victim, who, absent and destroyed, is more magnetic than ever. The soft, flat, firm lighting varies but never contradicts the physical space. Exactly what characterises this style as merely intelligent imitation, is difficult to define. Maybe it is simply the absence in the action of that fullness and turbulence generated between Renoir and his accomplices. Given his description of his work as initially "rather theoretical", *La Tosca* remains in its beginnings—beginnings respected by intelligent talents, rather than revised, scrapped or replaced. And it's not completely impossible that for Renoir the subject was an assignment arising from a patriotic duty, or even a case of what Hitchcock described as "running for cover".

In its general plan, however, the film shows Renoir's mind moving in a way similar to other notable artists of the '40s. From *Alexander Nevski* on Eisenstein confounded expectations of fluidity and realism by moving to historical, monumental, stylised subjects. *Ivan the Terrible* has often been called an "opera", and *La Tosca* is a European counterpart of an anti-realist, in one sense baroque, movement paralleled in America by *Citizen Kane* (an anti-epic of a failed national hero) and in England by *Henry V*. It may well be that *La Tosca*, even in Renoir's hands, would have frustrated his best and remained a challenge become curosity. Yet it is in the nature of genius to seize possibilities of which others catch scarcely a glimpse. Premier Plan describes the style of *La Tosca* as "a cross between *La Marseillaise* and *Senso*". Visconti describes it as "a horrible film—it was all we could do."

At any rate, Renoir's presence at the birth of Italian neo-realism was more than spectatorial. His first project for a version of *The Postman Always Rings Twice*, with Sylvia Bataille, had been passed on to Julien Duvivier and eventually to Pierre Chenal who shot it as *Le Dernier Tournant* in 1938. Now Renoir passed his own manuscript translation of the novel on to Visconti, who in 1942 commenced his adaptation, *Ossessione*, generally acknowledged as the first Italian neo-realist film, with Giuseppe de Santis, subsequently director of *Bitter Rice*.

Visconti testified: "Renoir had an enormous influence on me. One always learns from someone. One invents nothing. Or yes, one does invent, but one is enormously influenced, especially when making one's first film. It's not the case that *Ossessione* was influenced, as has been said, by the French cinema in general, but it's Renoir who taught me how to work with actors, and this brief contact with him was enough, his whole personality fascinated me . . . " The other young Italian directors knew Renoir through his teaching, and through, in particular, *La Chienne, Les Bas-Fonds, La Grande Illusion* (privately shown), and, from 1942, *La Bête Humaine*.

Interlude: Aftermath

Renoir's work exerted a powerful influence towards realism, as it was again to do for a subsequent generation, that of the *nouvelle vague*. But there are degrees of realism. His drive for literal realism—the direct recording of sound, the use of locations, the choice of non-professional actors—reached its apogee between *La Chienne* and *Toni*; he fed many of the lessons learned back into his more conventionally set-up productions; he came nearer still to Zavattini's definition of neo-realist subject-matter with *La Vie Est à Nous* and with *La Marseillaise*, which certainly possess an alfresco air, but were scarcely known outside France and weren't the films which exerted the influence, re-emerging only in the wake of Renoir's celebrity in the '60s. Even Renoir's most realistic films represent, as we have seen, a middle way (rather than a compromise) between the "Epsteinesque" documentary and the studio fiction film. It is no doubt for this reason that they proved more influential.

Contemporary critics, wishing to distinguish between their notions of documentary realism, described the French compromise of the late '30s as "poetic realism". Exactly what "poetic" means is far from clear—perhaps it means "lyrical", an effect, which is, after all, quite possible within the means of prose. At any rate, Renoir seemed then one among a group of directors who were represented, pleasantly and uncontroversially, as typifying the humanity and artistry of the French spirit, compared to the brashness and glamour of Hollywood. Nor was Renoir accorded a unique place, or recognised for his individual charcteristics, among Carné and Clair (who were both reckoned to be more perfect), Duvivier, Vigo and Pagnol. When, in 1949, Gavin Lambert singled him out, following the long-delayed English release of *La Règle du Jeu*, it was to speak of "the most distinguished unsuccessful career in cinema. Curiosity, tolerance, understanding have sustained Renoir, lack of concentration seems too often to have dominated him. One can only remember two unflawed successes, *Partie de Campagne* and *La Règle du Jeu*." The choice of examples, while distinctly ironical, is probably inspired by the fact that it's just these two films which, of the Renoir films known in England, least resemble the pessimistic poetic realism or populism of his contemporaries.

The difficulty which Renoir posed for critics was the way in which his interest was constantly flickering from the narrative point to the *temps-mort*, from the obvious climax to some adjacent distraction or unemphatic theme. In consequence his most conspicuous purpose was accomplished always a little roughly, or flatly, or tentatively, or unconvincingly. "Lack of concentration" there is indeed (although hindsight reveals the Carné-Prévert symbiosis as a balance of cross-purposes, and not at all the harmony it was then supposed to be). But why did Renoir's camera linger on figures peripheral to the main action? Why did his photographic palette lack the perfect monotonality of Carné's? Was Renoir a wayward child, or only erratically gifted and always a little clumsy?

Apart from the pressure of Renoir's view of reality, his interest in realism never excluded his awareness of spectacle. Its most conspicuous reassertion is the screen-within-a-screen of *Les Bas-Fonds*. Even within the conventions of '30s realism, the effect is acceptable, since it merely exaggerates the silent screen's iris effect, or the later convention of a track-back to long-shot. Yet unless one apprehended some other significance one would have to wonder if Renoir hadn't proved childishly unable to resist a striking gimmick. For the effect is a bold defiance of a basic convention of illusionism, that the film must be as self-effacing as possible, must not acknowledge itself to be a film. The convention was accepted by film-makers, public and critics alike; filmgoers of the '40s can remember the impatience to be done with those seemingly endless credits and plunged into the dream, while even the dawning of flashbacks, beloved by producers for the sake of neat construction, would provoke audible resentment, as one dream-narrative was disrupted by another.

Yet these conventions, acceptable insofar as convention implies a tacit agreement to certain procedures, were never absolute. Comedies and musicals always enjoyed a degree of exemption; the star was not considered as an intrusion into the illusion; and the public never shared that grand delusion, which has stumbled from the primitive dogmas of the documentarists to its fascinatingly sophisticated development in Siegfried Kracauer's theories, whereby fantasy and photography are somehow incompatible. Renoir always distinguished interior and exterior realism, with the latter merely a means to the former. As we have seen *Charleston* allows the consciousness of spectacle to predominate over the illusion of realism, in the Méliès tradition. In *Les Bas-Fonds* the film comes to frame the vanishing reality. The reality disappears into and also with the film, as if to say, "Life is, after all, only a dream. A dream one must live seriously—yet, as it ends, it flies, as dreams must, into the night . . . " Later, of course, Renoir will allow a similar message to permeate by orthodox, "realistic" means, his Technicolor films of the '50s.

With "Socialist realism" his interests keep interweaving rather than coinciding. His sense of class groupings can bring him very near to it, and some such label is highly relevant in the case of *Lange* (if one allows it a comic spirit), in the case of *La Vie Est à Nous* (if one includes within it the more sensitive examples of propaganda) and *La Marseillaise* and *La Grande Illusion* (if one allows it a didactic optimism). Yet none of these films would qualify if one insisted, against the weight of Socialist critical opinion, that Socialist realism, should have led the artist to prophesy, correctly, the inefficacy of both Communist Party and Popular Front policies (in the context of which the individual might allow himself to take evasive action, to abandon an idealistic and not altogether natural identification with long-range historical inevitability, to adapt himself to short-range historical inevitability, leave political defeat to look after itself, and *cultiver son jardin*). From this viewpoint the evasive sense of Renoir's adaptation of Gorky's play is the most realistic. One is reminded how widely Renoir's realism is permeated by a desire not to propagandise, in the accepted sense, but to intervene; and that his films, far from being purely realistic, often contain a powerful didactic strain. All but the Gorky of his Popular Front films conclude by showing the French doing what they should have done, and didn't.

In practice Socialist realism can appeal to the precedent of Jack London's *The Iron Heel,* and accommodate, as *sufficiently* realistic, the didactic prophecy which turns out to be wrong—the self-negating prophecy. But it then becomes difficult to exclude Renoir for retaining many of the options of the best in liberal bourgeois individualism *(Chotard et Cie)* or anarchism (if this is the sense of *Les Bas-Fonds*).

It's arguable that Renoir comes nearest to Socialist realism in the fullest and most conscious sense in *Partie de Campagne*—despite its petit bourgeois setting and its lyricism which make it seem a "holiday" film after *La Vie Est à Nous*. It is also the clearest example of what Alexandre Arnoux describes as Renoir's "double allegiance", on the one hand to the tradition of Zola in literature, and on the other to a thoroughly cinematic transposition of impressionistic subject-matter, which so often celebrated the freest aspect of bourgeois society as it was, and so could seem to celebrate it even as it made the most of a discreet escape from it. In fact, the two traditions are not so completely distinct. Maupassant often brings a critical asperity to the holiday mood of impressionism (vide Ophuls's *Le Plaisir*), while Courbet, Degas and Toulouse-Lautrec often venture, like Renoir, into intermediate territory. François Poulle interestingly argues that Renoir's entire career evinces a failure to reproduce and develop the accusatory realism of Zola.

At any rate, the bitterness of *Partie de Campagne* is exceeded only by that of *La Bête Humaine,* which, whatever its relationship to "old Zola", terminates an era of Popular Front optimism, and leads to the exclusion of the "solid working class" from *La Règle du Jeu*. Which film restores us to the social pattern of *La Fille de l'Eau*, with the well-off bourgeois, the poacher with a sense of hierarchy, and the respectable "villager" who lets the worst violence loose. But no one can save *Le Fils de l'Air*.

We have commented on the shift from Michel Simon as star-emblem in Renoir's "bourgeois" period, to Jean Gabin as his proletarian hero, with his forceful and embittered masculinity. Something of Legrand's shyness remains in Toni, in Lange, in Bonnier, in Louis XVI, in Roubaud. The dreamlike air of *La Nuit du Carrefour* recurs in *Les Bas-Fonds*, and the reality of nightmare in *La Petite Marchande d'Allumettes*. In all three films, a hideous social structure intersects with an internal incoherence. Insofar as Legrand expresses a loss of confidence in bourgeois solutions, Lantier expresses a loss of confidence in proletarian alternatives. In that film, Lantier is matched by Cabuche, the innocent bewildered. And in *La Règle du Jeu* Octave represents precisely the mid-point of Maigret and of Boudu. The role, first meant for Pierre Renoir (Maigret), almost assigned to Michel Simon (Boudu), is played by Jean Renoir. It is as if the two alternative identities of an earlier period had coincided, and compromised.* Maigret is no longer a detective, but drawn into a giddy involvement; Louis XVI has been freed from his formality; conversely, Boudu has acquired a great many social graces. The coalescence is reflected in the film's classicism, implying a close, fine interaction of impulses. The clarity with which it emerges, and a possible development, through *La Tosca*, to the baroque, are obscured by Renoir's departure for Hollywood.

It is, after all, through peasant and artisan roots, and a social experience stretching from a household-full of domestic servants to the *haute bourgeoisie*, that Renoir derives his liberalism. It becomes easier to see how long and devious a journey his was, not to the Popular Front, which was his only natural allegiance, but to exclusively proletarian themes. Few of his films assert the virtues and values of the family. It is the interactions between individuals of different social classes that remain his theme. An understanding of this aspect of Renoir has been complicated by the prevalent confusion of *proletarian* themes with *Populist* themes (using Populism in the film, not the political, sense).

Normally, I take it, "Populism" emphasises a wide range of "little people", including, on the one hand, small peasants, small shopkeepers, white collar workers, "decayed gentlewomen" living on small investments in shabby gentility; and a *lumpenproletariat* of criminals, vagabonds, poachers and so on. The intermixing of all these classes, in the street, in fairgrounds, in cross-section sets enabling the camera to peep in through the

---

* There are lean Boudus, as well as plump ones—Pomies, Brunius—while the most miserable of the constrained characters is the lean and bony son-in-law-to-be of *Partie de Campagne*.

windows at separate little worlds hilariously unaware of or exasperated by their neighbours, is, of course, one of the delights of the Populist film. A proletarian film would have a narrower class as centre of focus, although it's reasonable to describe some Populist films as proletarian by implication. A notable example is *Les Bas-Fonds* which hasn't a single representative of the "solid working class" in it, but a variety of fringe personages—a burglar, a prostitute, a disgraced baron, a landlord and his family, and unemployed characters whose artistic, or philosophical traits loom large—almost, indeed, a "decayed bourgeoisie". Nonetheless the film has enough feeling of a middle/lower class helplessness to align this Populist joblot of bums with a proletariat; and spiritual self-respect is defined in terms of a proletarian, not a bourgeois, status. Much the same argument applies to *La Marseillaise*; and one might almost make out a case that *Chotard et Cie* is a Populist film, because, although old Chotard is on the fringes of the civic establishment, he maintains so many characteristics of the peasant-turned-petty bourgeois— which provides many of the quieter jokes. It is possible that the proletarian elements in Renoir's films derive from their director's responsiveness towards such collaborators as Prévert, Gabin and Carette, and less from Renoir's intimate observation than the Populist fringe (Legrand, Boudu, Cabuche), a little sentimental, often consciously so, but nonetheless honestly man-to-man and not patronising.

In *La Grande Illusion* the mechanic turns officer turns peasant. Renoir is always interested in those interstices in which a man can come to own his "two acres and a cow", to possess a modest independence, within which to be a Boudu with roots. Not surprisingly, throughout his long career he has consistently turned his back on safe success (Lestingoisism) and struck out for independence, for an *artisan* independence, in which there is no clear line between the working owner, the foreman, and the trusted workman who, far from being exploited, was expected to marry into the family. That image is insistent, for it paraphrases the psychological and social freedom of Renoir's childhood home. Indeed, it is just that idyllic image which Renoir, in *Partie de Campagne,* attacks, as if to remind us, and perhaps himself, of the prevalence of its abuse. In a sense, this is a tardy addition to his reflections on the bourgeois ethos. Throughout his Popular Front period, the emphasis is on intermingling, egalitarianism and a kind of collective anarchism which is not at all exclusive. Far from any dictatorship of the proletariat, there is a pointed admission of the poor priest, the rich Jew, the doomed aristocrat, the white-collar worker.

While Renoir has several working-class heroines, his proletarian heroes tend to be less typical. Lange is a clerk, Marechal is an officer, who turns peasant and it thus doubly déclassé. Lantier is hardly typical, although common-sense, and the presence of Carette (as Pecqueux) beside him, effectively dampens any anti-proletarian overtones. Generally, his heroes are "compendium" figures, who suggest the urban proletariat along with other lower-income groups. Valentine in *Lange* is a petit bourgeois capitalist, but what matters is the class from which she has arisen, and her "proletarian hips". Much the same is true of Bonnier in *La Marseillaise*; what matters is not the apparent status of his house, but his debts, and the overall air of "self-consciously respectable lower-class". This end of the lower-class range fits the Popular Front programme extremely well, and seems to give Renoir a more direct expression of his own experience and temperament. If a certain emptiness seems to make itself felt in certain images of *La Vie Est à Nous*, as of *La Marseillaise*, it is because of Renoir's temperamental aversion to the kind of hardened, cramping bitterness before which his camera hesitates in *La Nuit du Carrefour* and which Gabin's mouth and glance bring with them. But Renoir's is a genuine duality, not an equivocation. He finds similarly dual heroes in America, where they prove far more controversial, by their contrast with the lavish helpings of the optimism, opulence, heroism, or myths of tough and innocent frugality with which Hollywood, by 1945, almost universally edulcorated its Populist themes.

Interlude: Renoir Américain

Renoir quit Paris on the day the Germans marched in, and fled to Les Collettes, in the Unoccupied Zone. As with Fritz Lang, Goebbels was only too ready to forgive and forget: "The propositions of the German emissaries were at once attractive and fervent—they frightened me." *Cahiers du Cinéma* attributes Renoir's decision to leave for America to a long and persuasive letter from Robert J. Flaherty, while the U.S. government put a passport at his disposal. In Autumn 1940 he left for Lisbon, taking with him Dido Freire, Cavalcanti's niece, who had been his continuity girl on *La Règle du Jeu,* and whom, for visa purposes, he described as his wife, although they were not married until 1944. In the event, he tarried in Lisbon, apparently waiting to decide whether he should, or could, work with the Vichy régime. There are reports, possibly ill-founded, of Renoir having difficulties with Portugal's neutral, but Fascist, government, and being able to extricate himself only at the price of being quoted as having made anti-Semitic statements. At any rate he arrived in New York on 8th February 1941, where his first stay was with an old acquaintance, Antoine de Saint-Exupéry. "My first thought on leaving France was a film about the exodus of children to the South. . . . " One wonders if his long stay in Lisbon was connected with the possibilities of such a project.

Hollywood had always been ready to accommodate European talent, even if only to deprive Europe of it while keeping it in expensive idleness, and maintaining the American dominance of world film markets. Not only the Roosevelts but Hollywood executives had been impressed by the success of *La Grande Illusion* and *La Bête Humaine.*

Although the World War deprived Hollywood of its European markets, the war years were boom time. Even before Pearl Harbour, rearmament had begun pulling America out of the lingering Depression, and America's direct involvement resulted in a combination of full employment and a shortage of consumer goods. As Renoir was assured by a friend: "Jean, at this moment all films are making money—even good ones." Military service and similar contributions deprived Hollywood of much of its creative talent, and since there was obviously going to be a great box-office future for stories of Occupied Europe a European director was likely to prove more useful than ever.

Earlier European émigrés had had mixed receptions. Lubitsch had helped to make Hollywood what, through the '20s, it became. Stroheim and Pabst had not survived. Others, like Michael Curtiz, acclimatised themselves so colourlessly that their European experience left not a trace. Hitchcock and Fritz Lang had successful careers and remained individuals despite controversies about whether or not Hollywood had lowered their artistic sights (no one seemed alive to the possibility that a film director might have lost his inspiration anyway, whether he went to Hollywood or not, and this certainly happened to several near-contemporaries of Renoir). Such fears must have been in Renoir's mind, all the more in that the '40s were the heyday of Hollywood's conveyor-belt system. Location shooting was a relative rarity. Studio overheads were expensive, but sending stars and crew to location was even more so. An actor's contractual commitments might make it virtually impossible for a film to go more than very slightly over schedule. If improvisation was impossible to banish altogether from film-making, it could be, and was, systematically minimised. Would Renoir's realism, his moral sophistication, his warmth, survive Hollywood's wish-fulfillment, its formulae, its happy ends, its superficiality and slickness? Would he find the congenial *co-auteurs* whom he so prized? Hadn't he himself declared that his spirit was essentially French, that an artist is rooted in his cultural soil?

Renoir accepted an offer from 20th Century-Fox, and it is easy to see why he should have thrown in his lot with this particular studio. Its executive producer, Darryl F. Zanuck, followed a policy of relatively realistic subjects, far less alien to Renoir's approach than any other studio's at that time. Fox had after all produced, in the teeth of opposition from the banks, John Ford's *The Grapes of Wrath,* a proletarian story filmed on location, and which, in one way or another, it wouldn't be absurd to put in the same bracket as *La Grande Illusion.* Fox already accommodated the *March of Time* unit, and went on to pioneer both the American wartime documentary and the "semi-documentary" thriller, with *The House On 92nd Street.*

Fox offered Renoir his choice among their library of unassigned scenarios, and assumed that his interests would lie in French or European subjects. Yet Renoir's mind was moving away from Occupied France. His discoveries of the different sectors and levels in French society, his voyages to Berlin, Algeria and Italy, had already made him a cosmopolitan. His very responsiveness to his collaborators indicated an adaptability which would make him at home, if not in Hollywood, at least in America, the land of immigrants. Indeed he soon visited actual cousins, his maternal grandfather having left France in 1865 to set up the first white farm in North Dakota. And it's less surprising than it might otherwise seem that Renoir's first choice should lie within the category of American rural regionalism.

Swamp Water/
The Man Who Came Back
(L'Etang Tragique)

If Fox possessed Dudley Nichols' script for Swamp Water, it was presumably
as a possible follow-up to box-office successes like *The Grapes of Wrath,
Tobacco Road* and even Hal Roach's *Of Mice and Men*. All three had
evoked the agricultural depression which for a quarter of a century had
loomed large on the American scene, and *Swamp Water*, in terms of action,
is closest to a swamp Western instead of a plains, desert or forest one. The
Western genre had recently begun to move towards popularity in middle-
class halls. The faint overtones of the supernatural were a little less dissonant
than they may seem now, for the wartime popularity of fantasy subjects
produced a subcycle of rural-supernatural films, including Howard Hawks's
Sergeant York. Walter Huston who plays a backswoods Mephistopeles
who haunts Henry Fonda in William Dieterle's *All That Money Can Buy*
would not have been out of place in the Walter Brennan role in Renoir's film.
As it is, *Swamp Water* abounds in John Ford faces (Ward Bond, Walter
Brennan, Russell Simpson, John Carradine) and music *(Red River Valley)*,
while the Anne Baxter character evokes Gene Tierney's in *Tobacco Road*.
The barndance provides another point of intersection for the Ford and Renoir
thematic. Dudley Nichols, the author of the screenplay, was frequently
Ford's scenarist, and it's natural to wonder whether the screenplay hadn't
been written with Ford in mind, but languished in want of a director since his
mobilisation. An ironical implication, from the point of view of *auteur*
theory, is that much of the John Ford thematic can be introduced into the
script, which presumably the director had never seen, by a writer who knows
his work well and is sympathetic towards it. In this case, Dudley Nichols'
long personal friendship with both directors suggests certain affinities between
the three men. All three have shown themselves capable of taking, and

transcending, Hollywood formulae, and imbuing them with a kind of rustic humanism—for which Nichols has an intellectual's respect; whose heartier, more simple and sentimental affirmations are Ford's inspiration; and to which Renoir's peasant roots were spiritually a great deal nearer than all but a few American directors. It is interesting, though, to remember how much nearer Hollywood, throughout the '30s, was to American regionalism. Apart from the Ford films, one can quote King Vidor (for his *Our Daily Bread,* with its right-wing co-operative, and *Wedding Night,* with its European immigrants, a parallel of *Toni*), William Wellman (one can imagine Renoir's version of *Beggars of Life*), and Allan Dwan (like whom Renoir subordinates the action climaxes to a moral structure).

Fox was surprised by Renoir's choice of a profoundly American subject, by his selection of Dana Andrews and Anne Baxter (then hardly known) and by his intention of shooting on location, especially so distant and disagreeable a location as a Georgia swamp. Renoir proved both obstinate and persuasive; the production was slated for a 40-day shooting schedule and a low budget. When Renoir overran his allocation of both time and money, the project was threatened, but Renoir defended himself vigorously, was supported against the front office by Zanuck, and, on his return to the set, was applauded by the crew in a demonstration of affection which in Hollywood was far from being the rule. 8,088 feet long, the film was completed before the end of the year in which Renoir arrived in America.

The story is set in a community near the Okefenokee Swamp in Georgia. When his dog, Trouble, gets lost in the swamps, Ben Ragan (Dana Andrews) disregards the warnings of his father Thursday (Walter Huston) and goes in to look for him. There he finds not only Trouble, but—trouble, in the person of Keefer (Walter Brennan), an escaped murderer long believed to have been swallowed up in the snake-, alligator- and quicksand-infested swamp. But Keefer has come to terms with it, and survived. At first almost crazedly suspicious, he keeps Ben prisoner, but Ben persuades him that they could form a partnership. Keefer will secure racoon skins, and Ben will take them back to the village to trade them.

Ben's periodical disappearances deep into the much-dreaded swamp arouse the neighbours' suspicion, and his apparent prowess at trapping provokes their envy. His father sees his authority vanish as his son braves the swamp with impunity. After a family quarrel Ben moves out, and deepens his friendship with Keefer's semi-pariah daughter, Julie (Anne Baxter). This angers the two women who pursue him—the village belle Mabel (Virginia Gilmore) and his father's blonde wife Hannah (Mary Howard). The Dorson brothers (Ward Bond, Guinn Williams) begin to fear that Ben is on the scent of the murders which they committed but for which Keefer was convicted. Ben himself is framed, and virtually exiled, like Keefer, to the swamp. But a final confrontation, and an atrocious death in the quicksands, brings about an end which might be called happy, even though the unflattering examination of a grass-roots community leaves us with more disturbing matter for reflection.

So secret and ambivalent are the films of Luis Buñuel that comparisons with them can be too lightly drawn. Yet Renoir's contrast of a hard, benighted community, and the difficult, limited, camaraderie of criminal exiles, does

evoke *Death and the River*. Keefer's survival in solitude, and his emergence, slightly crazed, followed by a brisk battle for ascendancies whose solution is the interdependence of trade, takes us from *Robinson Crusoe* to *Islands of Shame*. Here, too, is the propinquity of man and disturbingly non-mammalian animals. A cottonmouth bites Keefer, and he dies. Ben is about to bury him when Keefer revives—bitten, as he cheerfully explains, so many times that now even the cottonmouths can't kill him. Whether or not such immunity is a medical possibility, his explanation "I just will myself to get well" is doubtless congenial to an American optimism which is antipodean to Buñuel's vision. Nonetheless Renoir's and Walter Brennan's Keefer is far from a reassuring or cosy figure, with his mixture of sly immortality and selfishness. In its view of human beings, the film is further from nobility à la Ford than from Buñuel. If they're not scorpions, people can be swamp animals. "You gotta know them bull-gaters and cottonmouths like you gotta know the folks outside . . . " All the film's friendly animals are associated with cruel deaths—the dog feared lost in the swamp, the kittens drowned in a sack, the raccoons hunted down.

A dour, unforgiving spirituality looms in the face of Ben's father Thursday. The Hobbesian (jungle) overtones of swamp life are echoed by the suspicions ricocheting around the community. If this is Renoir's nearest approach to a Buñuelian style, it is, doubtless, for fortuitous reasons. The actors with whom he is collaborating are Hollywood veterans whose already formed style is dryer and terser than the French. At the same time, Renoir is directing them, and the film around them, with less emphasis on the dramatic "point". The playing, refusing a French expansiveness, retains a certain muteness and reserve; a sense of solitude with uncertain potential.

Keefer's resurrection, the danger posed to man by animals and to animals by man, the variety of hatred and cruelties within the community, imbue the film with a sense of life suddenly slipping into death.

In its twists and turns the plot is intricate rather than emphatic and here again it recalls Dwan and Buñuel, whose only common ground is a moralising, philosophical use of melodrama. The photography is harsh, abrasive, apparently inelegant. It exists at the opposite pole to the heroic pathos and exuberance with which Ford dignified the denizens of *Tobacco Road*. Visually the film is nearer *Island of Shame,* and the use of *Red River Valley* registers like a weak studio attempt to soften Renoir's harsher tone. Earth, and the wood of cabins, are its predominant surfaces, and key its tactility. Renoir recurs to his variations on what the French call the *plan américain*—three or more people, head to knees, in a single line—which by 1940 only old-fashioned directors and B-features retained—for the same reason that Buñuel used it—it's the cheapest format for fast tempo comings and goings.

The film's lighting is unemphatic and flat, presenting characters and background as an "open field" and as a whole, without the heavy shadows then the Hollywood mode for a relatively sombre drama. Renoir's similarly motivated preference for the long to medium shot range, rather than medium to close shot, was beginning to be anomalous by those notions of good style which mid-'40s Hollywood shared with the then critical emphasis on sharp angling, bold cutting and close-ups. From this point of view the film could seem cheap, old-fashioned, and so unemphatic as to be uninspired. The quality extends, as we have seen, to the acting, and the tempo differs from, say, Hawks or Ford in its penny-plain absence of emphasis. Scenes end *after* their climax, rather than *on* it. Its dramatic graph has shallower peaks. Thirty years later, we can appreciate Renoir's refusal to allow the film to climax itself out of "ordinary" life and a sense of life's sequences.

So far as the relationship between camera and action is concerned, the film marks a striking transfiguration of style. One might plausibly attribute it to Renoir's versatility (adapting his style to his material) or his prudence (adapting his style to the Hollywood consensus), or his responsiveness to actors (allowing the Hollywood actors to key the film's tone and tempo), or even the influence of producer, photographer, editor and studio, or to all these factors together. Its individuality lies in its sense of people handing things to one another, rather than confronting one another.

Auteur theory as it stood in 1940 would have pronounced the film as stylistically uninspired compared with the noble lyricism of John Ford, and deplored Hollywood's neutralisation of yet another European talent. In terms of 1970 *auteur* theories, the film becomes a *tour de force* of self-effacement and adaptation. No doubt the truth lies somewhere between these two extremes, with the proviso that if it seems neutral, even anonymous, it is not so in a negative sense, but as a consequence of Renoir's wish to find a real America.

In certain aspects, *Swamp Water* compromises between a Western and *Toni*. It resembles the former in that violence is consistent and integral rather than spasmodic and, as it were, incidental. Yet the integration of violence and communal emotion is simpler than in the tortuous constructions of William Faulkner. The western genre itself is now readily acceptable as a valid aesthetic idiom, and the presence of melodrama would not now normally be seen as shattering a sense of everyday reality. Critics at the time felt the film false, apparently because it was unlike the middle-class life which the critics knew. C.A. Lejeune was straightforwardly supercilious. "Could you force yourself into the mood, no doubt, it would be an absorbing picture of life in the great Georgia swamps, where the most lively event is a barn-dance, where folks talk ve-ry slow and kinda corny, where the nicest girl would have to be a lot brighter to be a half-wit, and where even the sun prefers to shine in chiaroscuro." Dilys Powell thought the film might be a concoction, intended, no doubt, to honour Renoir, but a concoction nonetheless. " . . . did the producers perhaps base their offer on an examination of the director's native choice? *Toni* was a regional film, a story set in the South-

East fringes of France, that sunny, violent, brooding district, with its sandy wastes and its overlooking hills. What about setting Renoir to direct a piece about the seamier side of life in Georgia and an extensive bog called, believe it or not, Okefenokee? *La Grande Illusion* (which I might as well say here and now I find overpraised) dealt with the POWs shut in on themselves; what about a fugitive from justice (Walter Brennan in his old-timer's beard would do) living alone in Okefenokee with the snakes and the skeeters? *La Bête Humaine* presented us with murder, adultery, the infamies of the heart. Why not a couple of backswoods toughs who fill in the intervals of murder with pig-stealing from Mother's old shack down by the crick? Why not a village siren with two strings to her bow and her golden hair hanging down her back? Why not a bit of false evidence before the sheriff (doggone it, let's give Eugene Pallette a serious part) and a bit of gunnery in the swamp? Do I embroider? Very well then, I embroider. The instigator of *The Man Who Came Back* thought of none of these things, but merely of a job for Jean Renoir. The result is the same: a banal, confused, crime-and-rehabilitation piece to which Renoir's grave harsh talent contributes precisely nothing."

Certainly the film accepts several ingredients from the American regional drama, including its violence, and the Manicheanism which is a product of its Puritanism. But the modification of material by style, or rather of genre by detail of content, may, in practice, as in *Les Bas-Fonds*, have an opposite effect. Renoir moves us directly from Ben in the swamp calling Trouble, to Ben back by his home still calling Trouble. Yet it leaves us in the middle of two uncompleted notions; it takes time for the second milieu to assert itself in our mind after the conspicuous action; it has an effect of *hanging over*, of incompletion, of sad human discouragement, rather than of a hard conflict. It is *indefinite*. We live in a world of confusion, of constant worry, of everyday desertions.

Similarly, its characters are quiet not because they are tough beyond anxiety, but through worry and defeat. Their toughness has become ordinary, functional, as everyday and uninspired as pioneering; here, indeed, the pioneers have come up against something they fear: the swamp. Toughness is felt as fatigue and still less as an effortless indomitability in the face of everything Mother Nature can throw at man. If men turn guns and fists on each other, it's in meanness, without exhilaration. If they rise from the same wellsprings as their facial synonyms in the films of Ford, they flow down the other side of the watershed, Ford's towards myth, Renoir's towards the ambiguities of reality. In Ford's heroism there's a barnwide streak of blarney, of braggadocio, as if all who came to America are thereupon inspired. Renoir, a cosmopolitan who has never forgotten his roots in peasant Europe, notices how constricted, defensive and frightened these small, struggling backwoods rustics may be.

Instead of denaturing his heroes, he disintoxicates them. The fascination of *Swamp Water* is precisely the homely and realistic *perspective* which it brings to the pioneer myth. In a sense, it belongs, with Delmer Daves' *Cowboy*, or Sjöström's *The Wind*, and John Huston's *The Treasure of Sierra Madre*, in its refusal of pioneer mythology. Whether we expect the realism of *Toni*, the impeccably black brisk action of Hawks, or any other familiar key-signature, we will be disappointed, as we will be if we expect the swamp to be lyricised like the river in *Partie de Campagne*, or the swamp in *The Louisiana Story*, and for a very good reason: the characters are closed to its "atmosphere". In this swamp, Keefer manages to survive alone. Another hunts for skins, and that's just another mechanism of survival. A dead man returns to life—a miracle? Maybe, but this Lazarus still has to eat, and hunt to eat. These shrewd gnarled suspicious men may grasp their land but they don't love their land. By nature, they're the makers of dustbowls, and thus a good deal nearer the pioneers of fact than the pioneers of myth. Renoir devotes less screen time to Keefer's apparent resurrection than to Ben's search for his dog, and that matter-of-factness is the key to the film, as to many bizarre scenes in Buñuel. One would like to relate Renoir's film to the last, moving essays in American regionalism: Borzage's *Moonrise*, Laughton's *Night of the Hunter*. But it relates by contrast. It is not a poetic film, it is resolutely prosaic in the best sense, and moves us by an unrelentingly dull tone.

We have seen how many of the film's motifs are characteristic of an already firmly established American *genre*. Their relation to Renoir's previous work is not really so extraordinary. It has been plausibly suggested that there are only 36 basic dramatic situations, on which all the narrative arts' infinity of plots are permutations and variations. Hence *auteur* theorists have little or no difficulty in finding similarities between an *auteur's* various films. The problem is that one can find an equal number of similarities between films by different *auteurs*. For films relate not only to their *auteurs* but to their subject-matter and to their spectators. The number of motifs is limited also, and the study of thematic or associative themes must eventually lead us towards an impersonal "structuralism". If Renoir chose *Swamp Water* it was possibly because it already contained within it "his" characteristic iconography. One can also see Ford's characteristic iconography in it, by, one presumes, a kind of action-at-a-distance. There's no doubt that Walter Brennan is, in Renoir's as in our sense, an *auteur*. If he weren't he wouldn't be a recognisable and welcome character actor. At one and the same time he becomes, in Renoir's film, a village scapegoat, a loner, a sort of rustic Jurieu. And he also breaks the uttermost *règle du jeu*. He won't die. He's that slippery anarchist Boudu, and he's halfway to being the more saturnine spirits of Renoir's later films, Opale and the piper in *Le Déjeuner Sur L'Herbe*. And just as Jurieu is shot with the full approval of the poacher, for the poacher's own sin, so young Ben has to take Keefer's place in the Swamp as scapegoat and exile. His sojourn in the swamp is that great American test: self-reliance and survival in the Darwinian wild. But it relates also to that curious reconciliation-by-purgation, that rebirth-through-self-abandonment, between nature and oneself, as in *La Fille de l'Eau*. Or one can see Renoir as preoccupied, between *La Bête Humaine* and *Diary of a Chambermaid*, with one big question: how far can one trust others, society, fate?

The film is also, of course, a *film noir*. Anglo-Saxon critics customarily restrict the term to urban murder mysteries, but to do so is to miss the force of the phrase. For most of the profoundest *films noirs* are not murder mysteries at all: *Citizen Kane*, *The Little Foxes*, *The Set-Up*, *Ruby Gentry*, *Stalag 17*, *Carrie*, and so on. In *Swamp Water* the mystery is only a secondary theme, a kind of atmospheric abstraction. If much of *Swamp Water* recalls Buñuel, it recalls also that "air of being crushed. . . . A sort of vital malediction . . . a sort of funerary hue . . . that presence of the absurd and the derisory" of which Agel speaks. A swamp is a kind of flowing without issue, a too-swift growth decomposing while proliferating, a confusion of earth, water and vegetation, a seething with miasmas, suffocations, and quiet murders. In it, Keefer suffers the parallel condition, a kind of self-envelopment and self-poisoning. His strange blend of willed and acquired immunity is like a last-ditch form of the life-force, a counterfeit death which is an extreme form of withdrawal from others. In contrast, Ben and Trouble are linked not simply by a straightforward spontaneity but by an anxiety stronger than the swamp into which Ben plunges, just for the sake of a dog. Contact between Ben and Keefer is tortuous and perilous. Keefer won't trust Ben until Ben makes the sacrificial gesture of trust, standing up to be shot at.

Only then is even the beginning of a relationship possible; it is that of a mutual advantage, rather than of real fraternity; and before the story ends another innocent has had to flee. In a sense Keefer has become the snakes whom he survived, a principle of cunning and distrust. Ben represents the principle of the dog, whose naive and total fidelity is also inadequate to society and the swamp.

Nonetheless, as the two principles converge, so progress is made towards a solving of the crime representing the treachery and selfishness within the community. The crime is solved, and justice done, but the lightening of tone is not sufficient for us to feel that this particular crime was the fountain-head of the communal poisons. There will be other crimes. As Keefer is to the snake, and Ben to Trouble, so the community is to the swamp.

In terms of political philosophy, the swamp is a state of Nature, and Ben, Keefer and Trouble recall the mountain outcasts of *La Marseillaise*, but by contrast, for the swamp is a Hobbesian state of Nature (the jungle) whereas the mountains lend themselves to a Rousseauist "contract". The antithesis to swamp exile is not the community per se, but the barn-dance. Yet the venom of rivalry and suspicion seeps through here too, and perhaps the most lyrical sequence is that in which Julie dances alone. Incest hovers over Ben's family. Community treacheries drove Keefer into the swamp. Man, existentially, must shift unsteadily between the injustices of neighbourliness and the futile liberty of a poisonous solitude.

Psychoanalytically, the film is structured about Ben's efforts to come to terms with, and take his true place in, society against two equally disquieting father-figures. Ben's father, Thursday, rules him with a rod of iron, and won't admit his concern for his son in any form that doesn't involve sternness. Keefer, father of the girl Ben comes to love, is the *other* older man, dis-possessed, childlike, innocent yet deadly. The two-generation sexual conflicts richochet in a complex way through Thursday's wife's feeling for Ben and Ben's feeling for Keefer's daughter, and through the guilty parties, the two Dorson brothers, who in age come between the hero and his two father-figures. They are, of course, the Oedipal hatreds repressed in the spectator who recognises his better side in the hero. To compare this complexity with that of Greek tragedy is not a figure of rhetoric. Freud drew from Greek tragedy the schema for relationships which Hollywood scriptwriters quite consciously drew from Freud, while the scriptwriter of *Swamp Water* sub-sequently approached Greek tragedy through his version of *Mourning Becomes Electra*.

Apart from being a specimen of the Deep South poor white genre, a near-Western, and a *film noir* in the general sense, *Swamp Water* is also a murder mystery, whose plotline is roughly transposible into terms of the city jungle (although a real equivalent of Keefer's resurrection becomes less credible there). But the story draws much of its meaning from the context of the rural myth, with its abrasive interactions between toil, trade, indi-viduals, the family, the community, and exile.

Renoir's achievement is the film's retention of ordinary human relation-ships; of people as mixtures of toughness and weakness, of good and bad. The Dorson brothers do not become substitute scapegoats for Keefer; the solution of this particular crime will ease the atmosphere and Ben's own position, and so was worthwhile. But he retains a certain bitterness; and the overall atmosphere of the community will probably not change.

In some ways the community is a series of traps, and like *La Bête Humaine* this thriller has a bleak, deadpan style. At the same time, the visual grouping of the protagonists sometimes recalls stiffer, more guarded versions of groups in *La Règle du Jeu*. It is almost as if Ben were willing himself to reach out across the angularities of the earlier film, and bring into existence a sobered, grudged interaction corresponding to the only too giddy farandole of the later film. The film seems to be hesitating between two views. The first sees society as egoistic plots and needs where, at best, alliances and ex-changes for the purpose of self-gratification are possible, although not to be too far trusted. The second allows for an effort of will or of sacrifice by which the separation is reduced, or rendered less harsh, but the process is tortuous. It is almost as if Renoir were rethinking his view of individual egoism and its social relationship, perhaps through exposure to the optimistic American assumption that individualism and the general good are easily compatible, and a desire to show that it's not so easy, and perhaps through the shock inflicted by the Popular Front and the fall of France to his confident ex-pectations that somehow "fraternity" would prevail.

Swamp Water proved unexpectedly successful at the box-office, possibly because Renoir's "soft" sense of everyday vulnerability and his hard realism made themselves felt alongside the "action" ingredients. At its Paris premiere in 1948 it was booed, probably because of the French reaction to *This Land Is Mine*, Renoir's subsequent film, which had reached Paris first.

This Land is Mine
(Vivre Libre)

After *Swamp Water* Renoir and Fox decided on an amicable waiving of his contract. Renoir attempted to interest producers in a version of St.-Exupéry's *Terre des Hommes,* but to no avail. He discussed the possibility of a film starring Deanna Durbin; later, he spoke respectfully of the star's talent, adding, "I was scarcely gifted for the genre." His real objection was the studio system. "What people say about the tyranny of the big studios is sometimes true, but it does depend on individuals. Personally I could have worked under the worst tyranny in the world, and even in a very agreeable way, had I possessed the gift of foreseeing what I want when on the set. I don't possess it." On the Durbin film, "a smile and a wink on the side were the subject of deliberation between ten people around a green carpet. It was difficult for me to work under such conditions." However, he "had all the Deanna Durbin films projected . . . and those with Henry Koster were clearly superior to the others."

RKO Radio, however, agreed to finance and distribute a film for which Jean Renoir and Dudley Nichols would act as their own producers. Although they hadn't complete independence, they nonetheless secured a greater control than Renoir had enjoyed at Fox. And another project had formed in Renoir's mind.

All Hollywood's hasty, melodramatic tributes to the Resistance did nothing to explain to the American public any reasons for France's sudden collapse, nor the complexity of the situation in which some decent Frenchmen felt they should support a collaborationist government. This historical void left a kind of blanket contempt for France and the French which Renoir found painful. "This film . . . was made uniquely for America, to suggest to the Americans that daily life in an occupied country was not as simple as some people might assume. . . . I thought of Daudet's *Contes du Lundi,* and it was while telling Daudet's story to Charles Laughton that I had the idea. . . . "

Renoir's collaboration with Dudley Nichols was "very close—we shut ourselves up in a little room, him, my wife, who was helping us, and myself . . . " It was as didactic a film as *La Vie Est à Nous*. "I shaped and I storyboarded the film, like a commercial film, so that if the need arose I could modify the cutting and work out, via previews, the effect on the public whom I wanted to convince . . ." To convince, not only emotionally, but to analyse and to explain. *This Land Is Mine* was to be a clarifying, linear film. Accordingly, the style features "more reverse angles, fewer one-shot scenes."

The film was to mediate between French realities and American assumptions. A completely "authentic" film would remain simply foreign, especially given the American tendency, commented upon by various sociologists, to repudiate, ridicule or despise the "immigrant father". Hollywood's usual strategy was to over- Americanise everything foreign. Renoir's task was to do so in such a way as to respect those alien realities to which attention had to be drawn. Its primary concern was not to be a suspenseful melodrama, not to portray Resistance matters with an authenticity which would satisfy the French, or the ideal, spectator. It had to explain "neutralist" hesitations at a period of peak war effort. It had to explain them to spectators who had hardly known war, let alone Occupation. It had to explain a different social background to an audience which was used to believing, expecially in the cinema, that every individual is able to make himself free from social pressures, and is only a man insofar as he asserts himself against them. That audience not only took heroism for granted, but was relatively quick to allow abstract causes and connections between scenes to slip out of focus, while making a very direct, personal, individualist involvement in the immediate situation.

Thus realism, in the naïve sense, is as irrelevant to this film's purpose as to Brecht's. Arturo Ui is neither Adolf Hitler nor Al Capone. He is a kind of "transitional" figure between the two, invented in order to indicate the growth points of Fascism within American capitalism. In just the same way, Renoir's opening title, "Somewhere in Europe . . . " warns us that his film is to function at a certain level of generalisation, and therefore of infidelity to the particulars of any one country. To an English spectator, the street-signs are jarringly American: "Buy Defence Bonds", "City Hall" and so on. Given an American audience, their *raison-d'être* is obvious. The town is neither French nor American, but a mid-Atlantic equivalent between the two. It is almost as much about how Americans *might* react, given a French social situation, as about anywhere in Europe.

Brecht's play is clearly stylised, sardonic, ironic and condemnatory, i.e. more to critical taste, than Renoir's film, which is less clearly stylised, and more explicative and exculpatory. (It's not, at bottom, as sentimental as certain details might suggest; that everyone has his reasons is precisely what's terrible). But it is merely snobbish to idolise Brecht while dismissing the Renoir film because it parallels Brecht's procedures, in a style which happens to resemble the *naïve* inauthenticities of other Hollywood war films. As James Agate put it, "The film critic wants a picture to be so good that it will stand up to educated taste, whereas the aim of the film producer is to produce something which cannot be defeated by lack of taste."

We cannot here discuss the question of how far and in what ways the two purposes are incompatible, or what grounds exist for believing that many commentators, not only on movies but on the mass media generally, are wrong in assuming as readily as they do that what's artistically good must be all but universal in appeal, and that the hierarchy of cultural quality is an uncomplicated affair. It's a correlated question whether or not, in *This Land Is Mine,* Renoir makes the wrong kind of compromises. But it would be absurd to assume that the problems were unreal, or that another answer was self-evident, or that "Hollywood" was simply and solely responsible. In the end, the film nearest in style and spirit to Renoir's is Hitchcock's *Lifeboat.* It is also an Occupation story, in which the "occupied" are Americans, in which basic social conflicts are asserted (notably between the Communist shop steward and the businessman) and which contemporary critics disliked for much the same reason: the superficial implausibility, and the contrast of impressive Nazis with weak, disunited and collaborating democrats.

8500 feet long, *This Land Is Mine* was shot entirely in the RKO Radio studios. Charles Laughton plays Albert Maury, a middle-aged school-teacher in a provincial town. He is narrowly preoccupied with his tight, modest, mediocre, egoistic way of life. By temperament he is timid and respectful of law and order. He is spoiled and smothered by a widowed mother (Una O'Connor). He refuses to involve himself in activity against the occupying enemy. He refuses to read the newspaper and docilely obeys orders to tear subversive pages out of schoolroom classics. But he nourishes a secret love for a schoolmistress, Louise Martin (Maureen O'Hara). Her fiancé, Georges Lambert (George Sanders), an engineer, feels that, tragic as France's defeat has been, it is a heavensent opportunity to put her politico-moral house in order. He is both a patriot and a collaborator—a Vichyite. But the Resistance will keep blowing up trains, until the German commandant (Walter Slezak), though personally humane, is forced by the logic of his situation into taking hostages—Maury included. Georges, also trapped in his turn by the pressure of his commitment, denounces his brother Paul (Kent Smith) as a member of the Resistance, and Paul is shot down by the Gestapo. Georges commits suicide. Maury is accused of his murder. His mother, attempting to save him, accuses Louise's brother, a "common" signalman, and a resister, and therefore disposable and guilty. But Maury turns his defence into a rousing denunciation of collaborators and tyrants alike. The court frees him, and next day, in his classroom, he reads the Declaration of the Rights of Man to his class. The Gestapo arrest him before he has finished, but Louise continues the reading.

The objections to such a scenario are only too obvious. James Agate uses words like "disconcerting tendencies" in its understanding of collabora-

tionists, queries the credibility of the characterisations, dismisses the plot as "dull, prolix and unamusing", and finds Laughton's performance "for the most part . . . boring, unattractive and even unappetising." Objections along these lines abound in contemporary criticisms. It's certainly hard to accept Maureen O'Hara's glycerine tears, or the painlessness with which a potentially challenging scene where Allied bombers pour their tonnage of T.N.T. onto French schoolchildren is turned into acceptance by a remark about "our friends in the sky." (At the same time, this is a wartime film, not a postwar film, and the mere presence of such a scene is exceptional.) If Laughton's performance re-sensitises and re-energises the quiet rhetoric of his "declarations" it is at the price of a Franco-American-Yorkshire potpourri which fascinates and moves without exterior realism. One cannot but query such trial scene rhetoric as "Who started that laugh?"—"I think—it was . . . the unknown warrior."

All too obviously it is not only the American spectator but Renoir himself who labours under the disadvantage of not knowing what the Occupation was like. He was caught on the awkward side of a controversy which raged, not only in the press and movies, about whether all Germans were bestial, or only Nazis, and whether much propaganda about Nazi atrocities wouldn't turn out to be as false during World War II as it had during World War I. It may well be that Renoir (whose long historical sense is confirmed by his recourse to the Boulanger affair as basis for *Eléna et les Hommes*) began thinking back to the last occasion on which there had been a German occupation of a defeated France (1870). He then crossed it with his experience of German aerial antagonists in early 1914-18. He is, of course, "defending" a German general, not a Nazi one, and no doubt the film seriously underestimates the extent to which the Gestapo, and their French allies, controlled nominally "independent" Vichy French courts. The Judge's complaisance is, nonetheless, some sort of metaphor for the type of independence which the best elements among the collaborators were attempting to retain. Agate's apparent insistence that all Petainists must be shown as throughly wicked instead of politically wrong helps demonstrate just how precious, in its time, was the film's interior realism—its anti-Manichean sense of socio-political tensions. It centres on a quietist and associates his stance with the middle-class values which he dispenses in the schoolroom. The advocate of active collaboration is middle-class also: George Sanders feels that the Occupation, however humiliating, offers France a paradoxically heavensent opportunity to restore an idealistic, authoritarian and traditional patriotism. So far as Petainist propaganda was concerned, Renoir had done his homework.

The scenario shows considerable ingenuity in relating the French characters to familiar and acceptable American movie types. Maury, in American terms, is a male schoolmarm—a decade later, he might have been played by Clifton Webb. The opportunistic Mayor transposes the familiar American type of corrupt sheriff or political boss from the Capra movies. A third collaborationist is the possessive Mom, and here, too, the film finds an overlap between the tight family orientation of the provincial French bourgeoisie and the fiercely individualist American matriarch whom we find in, for example, *Wild River*. (The performance is less assured than the conception, maybe further perturbed by Renoir's hesitation between dramatic intensity and emollient caricature.) Class tensions exist, but without Manicheanism. Maury is balanced by Louise, Georges by Paul. The fraternal antinomy between the last two expresses that fascinating bifurcation of middle-class idealism into conservative and radical forms. By class origin and in a certain infantilism and hermetism, Maury recalls Lange. He also devolves from his ivory tower. He prolongs Legrand in *La Chienne* and Louis XVI in *La Marseillaise*. Both are preoccupied with little personal comforts and subject to unappetising gynocracies. They are the anti-Boudus—the Lestingois. In build and style, Laughton recalls Michel Simon and, says Truffaut, ever-anxious to discredit anything as committed as moral purpose, "not only the Pierre Renoir of *La Marseillaise* but the director."

This must be the only wartime Resistance film in which our principal identification is with a political indifferent, and the only Hollywood film, even including comedies, whose hero is more frightened of Allied bombs than the schoolchildren are. It is also the only American film whose ideas of

Occupation realities are of even the slightest interest. Less severe, the film's moral structure anticipates the fascinating, awkward films of Losey's last American years—a gradual realisation of unaware sin, a slow, painful revulsion from the subtle complacency which made it possible, and a last sacrificial gesture.

As in *Swamp Water,* animals abound. Maury's saving little defiance of his mother consists in taking in next door's stray cat. The railway yard assistant superintendent fondles the pigeon which he will shortly convert to pie. Through this marginal bestiary, Renoir maintains that tenderly tragic sense of life and its derisoriness which was less easy to intricate into the story, especially given the American moral climate which still opposed both its optimism and its puritanism to all that in Renoir is promiscuous, amoral and antitragic. There too, perhaps, lies a reason for the replacement of Renoir's French lyricism by the dry, linear plots of his American films. The intricacy of the action becomes a network of surprises and paradoxes, which, without quite contradicting, nonetheless confuse and distend the fundamentalism implicit in the American taste for melodrama. When American films of the period become as complex, it is almost always in the dark, brooding paranoid mood of Preminger's *Laura* and Siodmak's *Phantom Lady.* Renoir's studio films exist in the light of moral everyday.

Visually, the film is characterised by white, flat, even lighting, with neither heavy shadows nor close moulding of form, over open texturally undifferentiated space. By 1973 it's as easy to feel the plaster of the sets as that of Meerson's décor for René Clair. Empty space is conspicuous also, almost as if Renoir had set everything up to accommodate the depth and flow of *Boudu.* Yet action and acting, being American and thus tight and terse, show little or no sign of actually overlapping into that space, which thus remains blank and loose rather than charged and dynamised. The townscape, featuring prominently in each scene, points to the fact of social network (against individualism). For the film's emphasis lies on the network of connections rather than any one climax, and architectural features become the natural markers for reminding us, during one scene, of something that has gone on before, or of the next corner around which other events may be taking place. As in *Diary of a Chambermaid,* this film's spiritual "twin", Renoir underplays obvious high points, while hingeing the plot on direct discussion and discovery of underlying relationships. Occasionally, he comes near the use of grids of space which, light and texture apart, recall Fritz Lang—notably in two pursuits, over rooftops and across the shunting yard.

Financially successful, and, it would seem, effective in America, the film should, as Renoir observed, never have been shown in France. Not only was it the first of his Hollywood films to be shown there after the war, but it was dubbed into French (!), and went the rounds at a time when French critics were urging a struggle, more patriotic than Communist, against Hollywood, not simply for reasons of cultural chauvinism but because of an absolutely realistic and well-founded fear that Hollywood would use its five-year backlog of movies for "dumping", thus depriving the French film industry of its home market, and menacing its very existence. That Renoir's films should be part of such a campaign was a bitter irony. The film also offended prevalent critical preoccupations about the exterior realism which ten years earlier Renoir had helped to pioneer. Worst of all, it misrepresented Occupation realities by its *relative* realism, in a way in which the completely stylised Hollywood absurdities did not.

The political wounds were, in 1946, even more gaping than they had been when *La Règle du Jeu* was booed into automutilation. Renoir's kindness towards collaborators, neutralists and hesitants (whatever its intentions and its maturity in an American context) could provide comfort to the collaborationist ultra-right, which was desperately trying to regain political respectability. That this interpretation is justified is suggested by the emphatic defence of the film by Bardèche and Brasillach, who, obviously, agree with me in finding it infinitely truer than so many post-war French films about the Occupation, and they can find in it only one flaw, namely, its appeal to the Declaration of the Rights of Man: "its loftily Republican sentiments incline one to smile . . . " Well might Brasillach smile. During the Occupation, he had *advocated* the shooting of civilian French hostages by the Nazis, and was himself tried and shot by his countrymen when their turn came.

Nor were Renoir's old friends exactly delighted at the film's silence about the role of the Communist party in the Resistance, which from 1941, was a major and a courageous one. Even the cautious Hitchcock had assigned a prominent role to Communism in *Lifeboat*. Maybe Renoir's experience of the French Communist party included a sharp recollection of its opposition to the war against Hitler from the signing of the Hitler-Stalin pact until Hitler's attack on Russia; and he felt, quite reasonably, betrayed by it, after having given his cinematic efforts on its behalf. And he was right in assuming that, even if Stalinism had performed yet another of its monolithic pirouettes at the precise moment at which Russia was threatened, the real spiritual initiative for the Resistance had come from the French workers as French workers. Unfortunately for Renoir, the Party's subsequent role as organisational backbone of the Resistance was generally considered in France to have more than redeemed it. Renoir's omission seemed to associate him with America's anti-Russian, anti-Communist Cold War policy. Objectively speaking the film must indeed have functioned in this way, and thus offended even those Frenchmen of the centre who wanted to pursue an independent patriotic line, and not a supinely pro-American one.

The film's sympathetic regard for blackmarketeers (poachers!) as saboteurs of the Nazi economy was just as unfortunate. Much blackmarket activity was not inspired by the Resistance spirit, but by capitalist profiteering of the nastiest kind, and in many ways helped the Nazi system. Worse still, blackmarket activity remained a major political problem in postwar France, long after any excuses about "patriotic sabotage" could possibly be retained, and during this period the ex-collaborationist right was the beneficiary, at the expense of the Resistance poor. And it was because of anger over the last point, that in France the film was withdrawn from public exhibition.

Salute to France

Renoir's next film was a short produced in 1944, made for an American government agency and running 1665 ft. Renoir described its scope and purpose thus: "*Salute to France* cannot be considered as mine. In the course of my life, I've made a quantity of films, more or less propaganda, in the aid of various causes, or, very often, to help teams of technicians who had become my friends after having worked on my films, and who said to me, "We're making such and such a film, come and give us a hand." For *Salute to France*, some friends were working at the Office of War Information in New York, Burgess Meredith for example, and Philip Dunne. . . . They said, "You should come to the Office of War Information and help us to make a film for American soldiers, to explain to them that in France you drink wine, you do this, you do that, so as to avoid conflicts, which are inevitable anyway. . . . I felt that I could hardly say no, it was my way of paying what I owed to the American government and the French government; I went there and I participated on the film . . . there's a little of myself, but very little. . . . I offered the Americans my familiarity with France and some technical advice."

Cauliez: "On the deck of a troopship sailing for Europe, there are, notably, an American soldier (Burgess Meredith) and a French soldier (Claude Dauphin). This Franco-American dialogue articulates a rather boy scoutish affair . . . " Louis Marcorelles adds that Dauphin acts quite straightforwardly as a spokesman for French *douceur de vivre*, although the film ends on a more disquieting note: what will have become of France after the Occupation and Liberation? Marcorelles supposes that Renoir's gift for casting against type lies behind Meredith's fine smile, more Broadway intellectual than John Doe, and affectionately recalls a shot of him floundering about under all his kit. The film was sufficiently attractive to American taste to enjoy a public release through United Artists.

"Subsequently I shot a quantity of little films for the government on the training of recruits. I don't know what's become of them."

The Southerner
(L'Homme du Sud)

In 1944, Jean Renoir, without renouncing his French citizenship, became an American citizen, married Dido Freire, and settled in his villa on a hillside overlooking Hollywood. Unkown to him, his divorce from Catherine Hessling was not valid in the USA, and he had thus committed bigamy. That Renoir's request for American citizenship was connected with more than a desire for certain minor conveniences, or politeness to a country which had placed a passport at his disposal, is suggested by his testimony in 1951 that "Something happened to me . . . in America . . . I was to meet some people who were very important to me . . . it seemed to me that I was born a second time." Exactly what happened, he doesn't say, although from a quotation cited in full later, it disposed him to offer his fellow men love rather than sarcasm, and it involved him in a loss of certainty, which turned him aside from the offering of solutions, as he tried to do in the '30s. This seems to be reflected in the relative bleakness of tone of his feature films. Much later he remarked that the Americans of today were like the Frenchmen of 1910: "That's my epoch." The context of the remark suggests an atmosphere of straightforwardness, of ingenuousness, as against political (and therefore intellectual) rancour. Renoir's next feature, *The Southerner*, reflects something of this ambiguity, perpetuating the "arduous optimism" of *Swamp Water*, and positing co-operation on an individualist basis.

Another immigrant to Hollywood, Robert Hakim, first drew Renoir's attention to George Session Perry's novel *Take Autumn in Your Hand*. He showed Renoir a scenario which was suitable for low-budget production, but with which Renoir was not altogether happy. Instead Renoir returned to the source material, elaborating a different scenario on which he consulted William Faulkner and which he showed to David Loew. Loew joined Hakim and Boris Morros to form Producing Artists Inc. and back the film. But the stars whom Loew approached found the material too offbeat, and United

Artists refused to involve themselves in a film with relatively little-known leads. Loew, however, had a substantial financial interest in thirty of their films, and threatened to transfer them to Columbia. Renoir promptly found himself enjoying creative liberty and a none too exiguous budget. About 60% of the film was shot on location in California (not in the overt setting, which is Texas) and the completed film (7873 feet) was premiered at Beverly Hills on April 30, 1945.

Tim tells the story of his friend Sam Tucker (Zachary Scott), who for years had scraped a living as a migrant cotton-picker. Then Sam's Uncle Pete, dying of sunstroke in a cottonfield, urges him to quit toiling for others, and stake his savings on his own smallholding. At Pete's burial, Sam and his wife Nona (Betty Field) decide to take the plunge. Sam quits the work-camp in his truck, with Nona, two young children, Jot and Daisy, tetchy Granny (Beulah Bondi) and dog. He has been able to lease fallow land against rent in kind; but their new home turns out to be derelict, and Granny refuses to leave the truck, despite an approaching storm (eventually getting herself soaked as well as chilled). Sam takes a fish round to his neighbour Devers (J. Carrol Naish), a misanthropist who grudgingly grants him leave to draw water from his well. His daughter Becky (Noreen Roth) and nephew Finlay (Norman Lloyd) explain that Devers was embittered by early hardships and his young wife's death from exposure.

The Tuckers' first winter is a hard one. Granny's blanket becomes a coat for little Daisy. But appetites are relieved when Sam catches an opossum, and he leaves a bait for a huge, old, cunning catfish, Lead Pencil.

Spring: Sam ploughs his difficult ground, though only with Nona's help. Meanwhile Joy (Jay Gilpin) falls sick with pellagra, for which the local doctor prescribes milk and fresh food. With his friend Tim (Charles Kemper) Sam calls on the community grocer Harmie (Percy Kilbride), who won't allow credit; subsequently Sam bursts out in a saloon brawl. When he begs milk from Devers, Devers gives it to his pigs instead. Nona collapses in the field, and Sam prays.

At length, Harmie, who has fallen in love with Sam's widowed mother (Blanche Yorkie) sends them a cow. She visits them, nurses Joy and gives Sam courage to refuse the factory job offered by a friend. Sam catches Finlay foraging in his vegetable patch and complains to Devers, who goes for him with a knife, only to get tossed into his own pig pen.

Washing his wounds, Sam sees the set fishing lines twitch, and peers down at Lead Pencil, hooked at last. Two bullets from Devers narrowly miss him. But Devers forgets his revengefulness in his excitement at the chance of catching their common enemy. Sam allows him to brag of having caught it—in exchange for fresh vegetables and continued permission to use the well.

As a good harvest looms, Ma and Harmie fix on a date for their wedding. After the wedding breakfast, however, a sudden cloudburst devastates the cotton crop, floods the vegetable patch, and scatters the animals. Tim nearly drowns while rescuing the cow and for a few seconds Sam hesitates as to whether to rescue his cow or his friend. But the women have begun to put the house to rights. Sam, Nona and even Granny set to ploughing the land for a new crop.

"The most interesting film I've made here. Another story too simple to tell. A poor family is born, lives, dies . . . " Renoir returns to regional, rural America, for what, with *The River,* is his only film to celebrate family virtues—although it significantly extends them. Ironically, the title of his previous film might have served for this, suggesting that Renoir's peasant and patriotic atavisms are chameleonic precisely because they are as deep as they are. Affinities and contrasts with *The Grapes of Wrath* and *Tobacco Road* are ineluctable. Renoir's film is less heroic and more realistic in the tone with which it confronts its characters' vicissitudes and bitternesses. The comparison with Clarence Brown's *The Yearling* hardly needs comment.

Social consciousness in the overt sense seems absent. Renoir has acquiesced in the usual mythic apparatus of economic individualism, good neighbourliness, pioneer puritanism and a timely appeal to the Deity. Even if one accepts this political structure, an important distinction remains; nothing in the film allows them to be taken for granted, or assumes that they exist on tap, which is when they become mythical in the cheap sense. Almost every scene suggests an ingrained reluctance to give, an indifference like callousness, as the social norm. Devers is not a scapegoat for society but a representative of it. Although he has survived as an individualistic economic unit, he has become stunted as a man. The eventual reconciliation of the men is the result of a dishonest deal and it is not allowed to obliterate our sense of the hard-hearted hermit he has been for so many years and which essentially he is still. The happy end is not proposed as compensation for a wretched life, in the way which comes so easily to heirs of the puritan notion of salvation as a total redemption outside time. Although some of Sam's difficulties are solved when the grocer falls in love with his mother, the overtones are none too sentimental, since he earlier refused Sam's children the milk they needed to preserve them from malnutrition. Everything is a matter of bargains, love included.

In itself, this could be given relatively complacent, right-wing or pointedly apolitical interpretations. Maurice Scherer and others see the change in Sam's fortunes as hingeing on the appeal to God. The scene is presented as a climax and the thought must occur to many fundamentalist minds, although one is surprised to see such unsophisticated Protestantism taken seriously by Champs-Elysées intellectuals; Dreyer would hardly have countenanced this sort of cash-register Christianity. Again, the eventual outcome of the chain of reciprocations might seem a vindication of enlightened self-interest or even *laissez-faire* in the style of Mandeville's *The Fable of the Bees*. Yet the temptations to misanthropy are too obvious and too odious for the spectator to emerge reassured. It is not simply the common casting of Zachary Scott which evokes Buñuel's *Island of Shame*—a very Marxist variation on the same themes of territoriality, and of subsistence, and with a very cagey approach to the mutually satisfactory reconciliation of interests. Roger Boussinot spots the insinuations in Renoir's film. Sam has a real chance only once "their misery and courage move a remote cousin, a worker in the town, and a household of small shopkeepers. . . . the alliance of the worker, the small tradesman and the peasant . . . becomes a condition of their happiness." In other words, "good neighbourliness" is inadequate if it isn't extended into an equivalent of a Co-operative, of a poor whites' "Popular Front". A Popular Front against whom? Renoir is tactfully silent, where Ford in *The Grapes of Wrath* is not. But his picture of the poor whites' struggles against their own individualism, and his daring to indicate the presence of poverty in America, didn't pass unnoticed. It was banned in Tennessee and provoked attacks throughout the South on its "sordid" picture of life.

Renoir's tone establishes something of a holding centre—or hub— between the pseudo-tough approach to pioneering (the *Red River* Western), the fundamentalist-humanist epic (John Ford), the mysticism of will (King Vidor), and the rustic morality of William Wellman and Henry King. Eric Rohmer suggests that the film is impregnated with the poor WASP ethos and with the Puritan notion of dominating Nature (although one might

wonder whether Puritanism isn't more concerned with hard work in itself
and success as evidence of God's favour, which are rather different). At any
rate, for Rohmer, this metaphysical dimension is such that "behind appearances—which it's permissible to find greyer than usual—there looms the
shadow of a great moral or metaphysic idea . . . an explicitly evoked God
for Whom Renoir's work had previously shown little concern." Alterna-
tively, Renoir may have been showing the same respect for the idea of
God which he had shown for the dissenting priests of *La Marseillaise* and for
the Hindu deities of *The River*. If Sam's call on God is a matter of mastering
Nature, the answer he gets is an emphatic No!, for God's eventual reply is
the flood, a more devastating manifestation of Nature than anything that has
gone before. Rather, Sam's call on God is an acknowledgement of the helplessness of individual effort. The Protestant argument would involve the
theme of moral purification; God stays his hand and gives Sam a chance,
indirectly, through human emotion; the flood is a climactic testing; will Sam,
by saving his friend, repay his debt to God, through man? The interval
between Sam's plea and the flood camouflages this somewhat and demobilises
the counter which is second nature to any intelligible Protestantism, being
in any case adumbrated in the Book of Job. So the film is non-committal:
co-operation never quite becomes a Co-operative, and God may or may not
exist to answer. But about the radical necessity for human solidarity for
subsistence (on Sam's side), a minimally decent humanity (on everyone
else's) and any social satisfaction (on Devers') the film is not equivocal.

Armand Cauliez describes the scenes of work in the fields as "part-documentary, part-poem", while James Agee underlines the film's double-edged relationship with documentary realism, but thinks the depiction of field-work is merely "token" and the acting inaccurate. "Physically, exclusive of the players, it is one of the most sensitive and beautiful American-made pictures I have seen. There is a solemnly eager, smoky, foggy 'possum hunt which may have been studio-faked for all I know; it gets perfectly the mournful, hungry mysteriousness of a Southern country winter. There is an equally good small-town street; I have seldom, in a movie, seen the corner of a building look at once so lonely and so highly charged with sadness and fear.

"Yet warmly as I respect the picture's whole design and the many good things about it, I saw it with as much regret as pleasure. The heart of this kind of living is work; and the picture should have made the work as immediate to the watcher as to the worker in all its methods, meanings and emotions. It offers, instead, mere token shots of work; and in these, too often, the clothes aren't even sweated. . . . I don't so much mind that the dialect is very much thinned out, or even that it lacks uniformity. . . . But most of the people were screechingly, unbearably wrong. They didn't walk right, stand right, eat right, sound right or look right and . . . it was clear that the basic understanding and the basic emotional and mental—or merely human—attitudes were wrong, to the point of unintentional insult.

"To cast and realise such a film correctly would be . . . one of the hardest conceivable jobs; but when has that stopped being an artist's responsibility? The one person in the film who for all his minor mistakes is basically right, in everything from cheekbones and eyes to posture to spiritual attitude, is Zachary Scott; he was born in Texas. J. Carrol Naish is no Texan, but he is such an observant, disciplined and clear-spirited actor that he comes close to making up the difference. I have no desire to go into unkind detail about other players such as Beulah Bondi, Betty Field, Percy Kilbride, Blanche Yurka, Norman Lloyd and two dreadfully miscalculated children, but I'll have to a little, to make my point clear. Percy Kilbride is a wonderful player of certain rural types, but it is hard to imagine him much South of Connecticut or much West of the Hudson. Betty Field clearly and deeply cares for the kind of regional exactness I too care for; but her efforts to disguise the fact that she is an intelligent, sincere young actress who feels sympathy and respect for a farmer's wife are as embarrassing as mine would be if I tried to play Jeeter Lester. Beulah Bondi, an actress I generally admire, demonstrates merely how massively misguided, and how smarmed with unconscious patronage, the whole attitude of the theatre has always been towards peasants. I don't want to go on. I am afriad that in my objection to this kind of inaccuracy there are streaks of parochial pedantry and snobbery. But mainly, so far as I know, my objection comes out of a respect for people. If you are going to show real people, in a real place, I think that you have to know how their posture and speech and facial structures can alter even within the width of one country; that you have to communicate the exact beauty of these minute particulars without their ever becoming more pointed to the audience than to the people portrayed, and without a single false tone; that if you don't you are in grave danger of unconscious patronage. You don't see or appreciate or understand your subjects as well as you think you do, you stand likely therefore to be swamped by your mere affection or respect, and so perhaps should give up the whole idea. . . . "

Richard Winnington, in England, notes, "I cannot let pass this short review of a fine and beautifully acted film without referring to the superb playing of the grandmother by Beulah Bondi. It merits at least a couple of dozen Oscars at current rates," while Roger Boussinot praises the "astonishing couple formed by Grandma Tucker (Bulah Bondi) and his little daughter (Jean Vandervilt) . . . " Rivette speaks of a legitimate "theatricalisation" of its pictures of work. Cauliez justifies the most theatrical gesture (Nora, weeping, pressed against the earth, while Sam turns to the sky) by other references: "It's a 'canvas', an anti-Millet. . . . Sam's prayer evokes an Old Testament prophet battering at God . . . " Claude Mauriac, however, queries Agee's acquiescence in physical realism: "The banks of this American river . . . strangely resemble the banks of the Seine and of the Marne."

Clearly, even exterior realism isn't a self-evident quality. And it is impossible, here, to follow all the ramifications of all the arguments involving Agee's thoroughgoing naturalism and Renoir's own distinctions between exterior and interior realisms. The naturalistic assumption is that

a work of art will be universally eloquent if it works its way towards the general truth through an absolute fidelity to particulars. At its naivest, documentary fundamentalism, it all but equates fidelity to particulars with general truth without even asking: "But *which* particulars, and what of abstractions, invisibles and generalisations?" At any rate, the discrepancies between Agee's response and the European critics' would suggest that an exact particular is not only not an indispensible prerequisite but may fail to be recognised as such; fidelity to an alien culture may seem "absurdity" to spectators who know too little of it. If particularity to historic-geographic reality were essential, then neither expressionism nor, say, the Western, could aspire to artistic merit, since both reject historically localiseable specificity. Conversely, the extent to which naturalistic exactitude can skirt, omit or obscure centrally relevant particulars is exemplified by the long and continuous connections between the documentary movement and propaganda and public relations purposes. Hitchcock remarked that America is an agglomeration of cultures so divided that any naturalistically regional film would be incomprehensible to, or remote from the interests of, or derisively received by, almost all other sections of the audience. And it can be argued that many characteristics of Hollywood and the American mass media generally (in particular the high degree of stereotyping) owe a great deal to this "invisible" diversity. It is also arguable that this was truer in the '40s than since, although one may also wish to maintain that it is only since *On the Waterfront* that Hollywood began to rediscover America. No doubt, too, cinéma-vérité affords subsequent support against Hitchcock's remarks. But to erect exterior realism as sole criterion for interior realism would be to negate not only the first sixty years of the cinema's history, but the even longer heritage of other media.

Certain intimacies seem particularly trenchant. The confusions of the ordinary man are evoked with a tender and a tragic irony when the mealtime discussion as to whether vegetables cause or cure spring sickness comes so near the truth. And as Becky holds yet withholds the can of milk Joy needs to live, is the expression on her face caution, or timidity, or a natural callousness? How enigmatic is she to Sam, and Sam to her? The ambiguity is matched by a transient expression on Sam's face as he has to abandon his cow, now his family's sole livelihood, to save Tim, who is merely a friend. As Lange all but becomes Batala, so Sam almost becomes Devers. But he resists the temptation of property.

Cauliez points out how Renoir, as often, "sums up in one image the lyrical key of the work: the porch (a sort of intermediate zone between the family interior and the agricultural exterior) reunites the couple, at the intersection of love and of work, and forms a sort of biblical 'beach', comprising the meditative and the perennial. . . . " The still which, so often reproduced, has become almost the emblem of the film, illustrates Renoir's self-effacing skill at locating each person within free space without denying the group, of so combining establishing and reaction shots as to replace the "ping pong" rally of reverse angles with a continuous solid entity. The porch implies the whole house, the facing space an endlessness of desolation, both within a tight, bold composition.

United Artists disliked the film over which Loew had forced their hand. It had also to overcome a change in public preoccupations since *The Grapes of Wrath*. Wartime prosperity and patriotism ushered in America's two decades of near-silence about her poverty-stricken subcultures. Banned in Tennessee, and widely denounced throughout the South, it was nonetheless a financial success, on the modest but satisfying scale of Vidor's *Our Daily Bread*. It was well received in England, surviving critical prejudice against American regionalism. It was awarded the Grand Prix at the Venice Festival in 1946, but United Artists, perhaps influenced by the post-war concern to foster a positive image of American capitalism, perhaps perpetuating a vendetta against the "artistic" film, even at their own expense, in a way which was characteristic of Hollywood at the time, perhaps fearing that its subject matter was too alien to interest European audiences, delayed or minimised its European release, until after it had featured at the *Festival du Film Maudit* at Biarritz in 1949. It was premiered in Paris in 1950, and Renoir reports that it failed at the boxoffice there, owing, he felt, to its incompatibility with the then preconceptions of the French public concerning American life.

Diary of a Chambermaid
(Journal D'Une Femme
de Chambre)

Of *Diary of a Chambermaid* Renoir said in 1957: "I shot it at the beginning
of a period when I was seeing things in a more concentrated way, more
theatrical, with fewer reverse-angles . . . I saw the scenes rather as small
groupings, added one to another—scenes which would almost be sketches,
that is to say, outlines . . . My first project had been in silent days, and
at that time I saw it very romantically, in the style of *Nana*. . . . I revived
the project, because I very much wanted to make a film with Paulette
Goddard . . . " Unlike Buñuel's subsequent version with Jeanne Moreau,
Renoir's film relates only indirectly to its source, the novel by Octave
Mirbeau (who had championed the work of Renoir *père*). The film is derived
from it via a French stageplay and a screen adaptation by Burgess Meredith,
the film's co-producer and male star. Hollywood was still under the sway of
the Hays Code, and Mirbeau's study in the furtive decadence of the provincial bourgeoisie had to be profoundly bowdlerized.

The film was produced by Meredith and Benedict Bogeaus. The latter
"who was the proprietor of an independent studio which functions like the
studios in France, that is to say, which leases its facilities to individual
producers, and doesn't even include sound . . . " (Other features of the
time with the Bogeaus name include *The Macomber Affair*, *On Our Merry
Way* and a number of Allan Dwan movies). Renoir shot "in complete liberty
with much improvisation"—the climactic lynching sequence was invented
on the set. The film ran 7640 feet.

The story is set in the early years of the century. Celestine (Paulette
Goddard) leaves Paris to take up employment in a provincial mansion. She
is met at the station by the majordomo, Joseph (Francis Lederer), a smooth,
dangerous character whom she rebuffs. Sick of the inconsequential life she

has been leading, she has resolved to turn gold-digger, and hook one of her betters.

The state of affairs in the Lanlaire household is none too propitious. Madame Lanlaire (Judith Anderson) rules not only the servants but also M. Lanlaire (Reginald Owen) with a rod of iron. She reckons that a pretty domestic, if under strict surveillance, will help keep her gentle tubercular son Georges (Hurd Hatfield) under her roof and thumb. But though Celestine takes a liking to him, the young man flees, fearful of a relationship doomed by his own ill-health. Celestine makes the acquaintance of Lanlaire's neighbour and old enemy, Captain Mauger (Burgess Meredith). A stalwart radical and Republican, at daggers drawn with the Royalist Lanlaires, he seems the epitome of liberty, joyously eccentric and egalitarian. He munches flowers to test their nutritive capacity, he hurls his rubbish onto his neighbours' flowerbeds, drops stones into their greenhouse, fondles his pet squirrel, and sleeps with his stout maid (Florence Bates), who mothers him and calls him her baby. Celestine is more profoundly intrigued by the sombre Joseph, eventually agreeing to marry him and help him set up a café in Cherbourg, where at last he will be his own master. But Joseph is impatient. After murdering Mauger for his money and stealing the Lanlaire silver, he attempts to drive through the crowds as they celebrate Bastille Day. But when Georges loudly proclaims his gift to the populace of his family's silver, they turn on Joseph. Celestine and Georges can face the future together.

254 • *Jean Renoir*

Whatever the promise of its title, the film's real themes are avarice and equality. Celestine, the lower-class girl making good, is a soul-sister of Nana—more womanly, more aware, less grasping, a champion of her downtrodden colleague Louise (Irene Ryan). The rigid hierarchy of the conservative home finds an apparent converse in Mauger. Their radical enemy is childlike, loveably eccentric, seemingly progressive, audacious, empirical—and yet, oddly, nonviable. He unintentionally holds his pet squirrel too hard, killing it. Its name is Kleber, which just happens to be that of the brilliant young general and protégé of Napoleon, whose patron eventually abandoned him in Egypt. Mauger's own military rank isn't just an accident, Napoleon having bequeathed to France a tradition of Republican militarism, which, by the time of the Dreyfus affair, had been all but wiped out by the subsequent association of army officers with higher social classes and right-wing circles. Mauger dismisses his elderly maid for Celestine with scarcely a shrug of sympathy for her. His empirical openness is divorced from any proper scientific rigour or social utility; munching rose-leaves recalls, if anything, Symbolism. He pelts the old order with rubbish (uselessly, since it's defeated anyway; he's a sterile muckraker). Far from being just a weird oddball, he has a specific social meaning. He incarnates the Radical Republicanism which is the heir of the Enlightenment that inspired the French Revolution. By Mirbeau's time, it had assumed its merely reformist position vis-à-vis the newer left-wing parties. Thus he proves a force at once spent and immature against Lanlaire's valet, the servant-turning-petit-bourgeois whose loyalty and subservience are merely a mask for a cold cruelty and avarice which matches his master's. He seeks to acquire both fortunes in a lust for status, as reactionary as the ethos of Vichy France. He is wily, resourceful, pitiless, nearly triumphant, and in all these respects he recalls the Fascists of *49th Parallel, Foreign Correspondent* and *Lifeboat*. But the ailing, sensitive, ever so slightly masochistic Georges finds the only answer. Against tyranny he motivates the masses. He appeals to something more definite and down-to-earth than their much-abused altruism, and he legalises the revolution which he also provokes. The film retains the stress on meanness prevalent in Renoir's American films insofar as Joseph is the only male strong enough to constitute an antithesis to the trio of managing women—Mme Lanlaire, Mauger's maid and Celestine. Thus the film blends with Renoir's old theme—the hierarchy-dissolving interplay of masters and servants. Mauger himself gambols like a faun through his garden, half-Puck, half-Boudu. Every 14 July, the Lanlaires, in sepulchral defiance, like something out of Edgar Allan Poe, draw their heavy curtains, bring out their silver and toast "Death to the Republic!" They are crushed by their past; Mauger's irreverence is, in the end, useful only in insisting on the possibility of an alternative. But the only viable alternative for France, deeply divided as she is, is a sacrificial, convulsive, regrouping of the best of the old order (Georges) with all that is generously individualistic in the people (Celestine),

together with what may look like a revolutionary mob. But this is not a mob. It is a patriotic, holiday crowd, and its fault is not its propensity to riot but the fact that it has to be shouted at, taunted, whipped out of its passive insouciance. Georges laments that he has never been able to make contact with the village folk (in which sense he is, like Octave, *un raté*). But Celestine can do it, with him and for him. And both are powerless without the crowd. If the redistribution of silver is taken literally, the film's moral is almost a sort of volunteer Socialism. Certainly its social message is that of the potlatch against acquisitiveness. In counting on the crowd, it perpetuates the activism of *La Marseillaise* and *Le Crime de Monsieur Lange*. Doubtless Renoir demonstrates his usual tact in contrasting realism with royalism rather than with less extreme attitudes, and showing a holiday crowd rather than a Socialist one. All of which is normal procedure in entertainment and propaganda films alike.

Possibly the film's political overtones are masked for American spectators by a superficial resemblance to a cycle of films set in sombre middle-class mansions, dominated by matriarchs and the past, from which a younger generation struggles to escape (*Rebecca*, *The Magnificent Ambersons*, and *The Little Foxes*, although in the last it's important that it's a banker's family).

Mauger kills his pet squirrel. Joseph drives a needle through a goose's brains to tenderise its flesh. "Perhaps they're murdering somebody!" wonders Celestine, as she hears its squeals, and this line of dialogue marks the closest intersection of three motifs: Renoir's interest in food, his use of cruelty to animals to establish a disconcertingly unjust universe, and the trend in American movies of the era to verbal sadism (e.g. in Fritz Lang's *Clash by Night*, Robert Ryan expresses the desire to stick pins all over Barbara Stanwyck and watch the blood run down). Mauger eats roses, won't contribute to the 14 July feast. Georges enjoys snacks with maid and cook and always hunts without cartridges (a habit curiously "prophetic" of Buñuel's, who was subsequently to direct another version of Mirbeau's novel).

Paulette Goddard smoothly and irresistibly Americanises Celestine. Less brash in her energies than she might have been with La Cava, Sturges or Wilder (all of whose versions of the subject are worth visualising), her go-getting seems less the fruit of bitter experience than an *a priori* expression of spontaneous energy. She firmly champions the plain and downtrodden Louise (Irene Ryan), although American films, as the much-mocked-at spinster in *On The Town* reminds us, tended to perpetuate a nineteenth-century derisiveness about ugly old maids. Mauger, a somewhat "American" optimist (ever-youthful, pragmatic, fun-loving), locks *his* old maid-servant up in the cupboard. But if he's Bouduesque in this way he's not quite Bouduesque in another. It's because he goes back to his house for his money that he runs into Joseph stealing it, and it's because he's locked his maid up that she can't come to his aid or call for help. Because his freedom

is merely a parasitic irresponsibility, dependent on private means, it leads him to his death.

On first meeting Joseph, Celestine tells him he has a face like death. Yet real feeling throbs in his voice as he urges Celestine to believe that they are of the same species. And they are both devoted to ambition, which, given Renoir's vitalist hedonism, is at once an expression of life-force and a biological perversity—a waste, a fetishism, therefore thanatonic. The union of Celestine and Joseph is as "natural" as that of the too-experienced woman and the too-brutal man, in *Stagecoach*, *Bus Stop* and *The Big Heat*. Another "American" theme appears when Madame Lanlaire employs Celestine's sexuality to keep her son at home, even though she also believes that sexual excitement might kill him. As Celestine reads the consumptive youth to sleep, she is required to wear the same dresses his mother wore in her youth. This necrophiliac transvestism echoes Hollywood's '40s Freudiana, which centred on mother-figures rather than, as in the following decade, father-figures. But Renoir takes the perversities far more lightly, as, rather than locking his characters up in heavy atmospherics, he brings them in and out of their weaknesses and their normalities as swiftly as one walks through sunshine and shadows. Renoir's matter-of-fact lightness may well have intrigued and exhilarated spectators used to a more solemnly hypochondriac tone.

André Bazin does full justice to the film's *theoretical* profundity when he observes: *"The Southerner* is admirable, but *Diary* is, I think, even more beautiful and pure. Renoir satisfies unstintedly and in a dazzling unity of style one of the propositions which is fundamental to his inspiration: the synthesis of the comic and the dramatic. *La Règle du Jeu* was still only a 'gay drama'; *Diary* is a burlesque tragedy, at the borders of atrocity and farce."

Yet *Diary of a Chambermaid's* sprightly skeleton carries incongruous flesh. Paulette Goddard alludes to both an American brashness and a French knowingness, but fulfills neither, still less exploring the interactions between them. Burgess Meredith, too, recalls, in his eccentricities, Boudu, and in his clumsy goodwill, Octave, and even a sort of proto-Jacques Tati, but he also relates to S. Z. "Cuddles" Sakall, a character actor whose sub-star status in the late '40s is incomprehensible unless one bears in mind a theory of Geoffrey Gorer's whose application to Hollywood trends and cycles was adumbrated in *The Crazy Mirror*. From *Little Caesar* on, the application runs, a certain kind of character-actor incarnated the non-WASP, Jewish or Central or Eastern European father in those aspects which the younger generation, better adapted to American speed and conformity, saw as a mixture of the paternal, the friendly, the ludicrous and the sinister. Early representatives of the type included George Bancroft (the Irish father), Emil Jannings (the German father) and Lon Chaney Sr. (a kind of pantechnicon misfit). With *Little Caesar* and *Scarface* Edward G. Robinson and Paul Muni inaugurated their long line of mainly Latin father-figures, more or less benevolent. By the mid-'40s the type was moving into the grandfather category, and by the epoch which produced the dotty music teacher of *A Song to Remember*, Burgess Meredith's capering madcap was less uniquely eccentric than may now seem, since the rehabilitation of non-WASP father-figures via, notably, Anthony Quinn *(Zorba the Greek)*.

Meredith's Mauger provoked widely differing reactions among French critics of the time. Paul Gilson compares him to Chaplin. "At the end of the film he is no more than a broken puppet whose watch swings at the end of a golden chain and who mimes a last jig on the shoulder of his murderer . . . " Georges Sadoul: "This actor who once had talent is today no more than an embarrassing puppet whose desire to seem intelligent, not to say intellectual, has plunged him into a stiff and unsubtle affectation." For Gilson, Renoir's actors play with such truth that they seem to be acting in the American version of a French film.

In a sense, this ambiguity as to reality is a function of the film's relative estrangement from it. A critic objected that "there is not one genuine outdoor shot", to which Brunius made the sensible reply: "If one accepts the fact that it is *impossible* to reconstitute an authentic French atmosphere abroad (I should know; I have worked as French adviser on several British films), if one imagines the *Diary* as taking place in an imaginary country, it must be admitted that it is an admirable film. I still do not understand how a French atmosphere would have improved it. The subject is universal."

But a discrepancy does perhaps run deeper than questions of exterior realism alone. Bazin's preference for the film even, it seems, over *La Règle du Jeu*, is countered by those critics for whom it "wavers between comedy, farce, slapstick and melodrama without achieving success in any of them". Exterior incongruities like its Franco-American grafts and its tragi-farcical tone generally left critics dissatisfied and patronising. Occasionally its long shots, with characters running amidst plaster sets, evoke René Clair, although even those characters of Renoir's who are caricatures have a dramatic complexity unlike Clair's piquant ciphers.

Renoir testified that "the film wasn't particularly successful when it first appeared" but added "it got its own back later . . . it's one of the films most in demand on American TV." At one time he said he'd willingly pass the sponge over all his American films except *The Southerner,* at another he acquiesced in the then general opinion that this subject shouldn't have been made except in France, and at another he stoutly maintained, "I'm very proud of it." Maybe the best summary of this dissatisfying, unfailingly fascinating film is Maurice Scherer's first critical assertion of Renoir's American films as the equal of his French. He sees *"Diary* . . . for which I don't conceal my secret predilection and which I consider (*pace* its *auteur;*

but must one take him literally?) as one of Renoir's most personal films (for Flaherty might, at a pinch, have made *The Southerner* and Stroheim, *Nana*). I see first the *summa* of a thousand antecedent motifs, and the lover of cruelty who is sufficiently refined . . . not to be satisfied by a merely exterior violence, will find himself satisfied more than anywhere else . . . *Diary* is perhaps the only film I know (I really see only *The Last Laugh* to be placed alongside) to uncover for us so limpidly, with the aid of neither commentary nor artifice, that sort of feeling that one likes to hide away in the deepest part of oneself—not only repressed humiliation, but the disgust and the weariness one has of oneself . . . no one more than Renoir could feel anything but repugnance for the cinema of 'allusion' so dear to our lazy film-makers. But the worth of such a film is precisely that the transparency of the gesture should have issued from an apparent opacity, postulating that mystery of interior life which three centuries of investigation in fictional form leave us still so inept to pierce . . . "

The disgust and lassitude which Scherer senses loom large among the themes of Renoir's subsequent film, *Woman on the Beach*. There too we find a terseness of emotional notation which is the antithesis of the earlier, lyrical Renoir, but which remains with him even as he leaves Hollywood. The camera is not subordinate to Celestine, who is merely *prima inter pares*. It watches a sort of hornpipe, or, as Gilson puts it, "these characters . . . seem to improvise the figures of a quadrille before entering together and frenetically on the dance of death . . . One can see it as a coconut-shy whose dummies sometimes fall backwards into a pool of blood. . . . "

The Woman on the Beach
(La Femme Sur la Plage)

Renoir's next film was "made at the request of Joan Bennett, who said, 'They've asked me to make a film at RKO, I've two or three scenarios, come and make it with me.' At first the producer was to be Val Lewton . . . Then other projects interested him more and I practically became my own producer . . . I've never shot a film with so little written scenario and so much improvisation."

Renoir was intrigued by "a love story in which the attractions were purely physical, in which feelings wouldn't intervene at all . . . I made it and was very happy; it was rather slow maybe (so) . . . we arranged some previews. It was very badly received and we returned to the studios pretty depressed . . . I was the first to advise cuts and changes. I asked for a writer as collaborator, so as not to be alone . . . Joan Bennett's husband (Walter Wanger) . . . came to showings and gave me his point of view . . . I reshot numerous scenes, being very prudent. About one-third of the film, essentially the scenes between Joan Bennett and Robert Ryan, and I put out a film that was neither flesh nor fish, that had lost its *raison-d'être*. I'd let myself be too influenced by the Santa Barbara preview . . . I'm afraid I was too far ahead of the public's mentality . . . " The final version ran 5944 feet (71 minutes) and had its premiere in 1947.

Riding along the beach, Coastguard Scott Burnett (Robert Ryan) encounters Peggy Butler (Joan Bennett) breaking wood from a wrecked ship. After their first insulting exchanges, he softens sufficiently to confess that, law and property rights apart, that ship, for him, is sacred, as a symbol of the frightening yet beautiful dreams which have haunted him ever since his own ship was torpedoed and he had to accept non-combatant duty. In the dream he relives the explosions, and sees himself drifting across the seabed towards a young woman in flowing white beachwear. The woman has the features of his fiancée, Eve Geddes (Nan Leslie), who is too gentle and cautious to marry him in haste, as he asks.

After a second meeting, Peggy introduces Scott to her husband Tod (Charles Bickford). This gaunt, craggy, surly figure is a celebrated artist, but now blind and embittered, particularly towards Peggy. His presence persuades the suspicious Scott that his blindness is only a pretence. Scott leads him to the edge of a cliff and is still unable to decide whether his suspicions are unjustified, or the other's nerve imperturbable. He is puzzled by Tod's friendliness, and suspects him of some strange strategy, or sinister pleasure, in his relationships with a man whom he may believe to be his wife's lover.

On his next visit, they embrace within the ship's hulk, to be disturbed by Tod, tap-tapping at the shell of the wreck with his stick. The two men go fishing, and Scott provokes a tussle in the boat. He realises that although Tod is indeed torturing Peggy with his sarcasm, he is also paying her back for having married him for his fame and money, and then blinded him by a glass flung in jealous anger and aimed either badly or only too well. Husband and wife are locked in their ambivalence, and Scott can never be more to Peggy than a friend.

Confused, disillusioned, he returns to Eve and her father's boat-building yard. Summoned by an urgent call from Peggy, he goes to find Tod's house burning, together with all the paintings in it. Peggy leads Tod to safety, thus putting an end to both men's suspicions, and to Scott's hopes. Scott bids her farewell, with affection rather than bitterness, and returns to Eve.

The Woman on the Beach shares various motifs with *La Nuit du Carrefour* and with *La Bête Humaine*. It shares them also with many Hollywood *films noirs* of its period. As its psychologically disturbed hero, tortured and torturing, Robert Ryan relates to his sadistic misanthropy in *Crossfire* (where again he is caught in the demobilisation doldrums) and *Clash by Night*. Joan Bennett, the tramp who mesmerises the middle-aged intellectual and the tough vulgarian alike, recalls her roles in *Scarlet Street* and *The Woman in the Window*. She becomes jealous of an attachment developing between men whom she intended to be rivals for her (like the heroines of *Gilda* and *The Outlaw*). The apparent opposition of the ordinary guy and the megalomanic intellectual recurs in *Laura* and *Phantom Lady*. Dreams loom large in the action, relating to the past (as in *Spellbound*) yet having a prophetic role, prompting towards destiny (as in *Portrait of Jennie*).

The atmosphere seethes with suspicions, confusions, and resentments. All three protagonists are dominated by memories which are painful and sterile. Tod clings to paintings he can no longer see. Only by burning them can he, at one stroke, throw off his nostalgic bitterness and enable his wife to prove her love. The coastguard is deranged by the war wounds which left him his nightmare and all that it represents. Peggy resents being deprived of her gold-digger's dreams: champagne parties, the gay life. Each unfulfilled ambition has bred its spurious hope. Tod tries to write instead of paint, but furiously admits that his prose is sententious. Peggy is tempted by a nice, tough, uncomplicated guy. Scott is tempted by the *hope* that Tod is guilty of something—so that he can "rescue" Peggy. Tod, destroying his paintings,

destroys both their dreams. But to his renunciation and/or liberation she adds hers. Scott renounces his perverse hopes of Tod's guilt, and her. Then she calls for help, and he comes—abandoning himself to fate, sacrificing his peace of mind. He accepts what the American film hero of the '40s accepted so rarely, not only his own weakness (his trauma), but defeat, and a real, sober, everyday hope.

The past is evoked obscurely and pervasively in dialogue, except for its recapitulation in Scott's dreams, which we share presumably because he is our identification figure. The wrecked ship lures him from the boatbuilding yard to Peggy, who gathers its wreckage. Her bundle of firewood prefigures the final blaze of pictures, of house and property. So does the lighter which Scott moves to and fro before the blind man's eyes.

Peggy, squatting and muffled in dark clothes, contrasts with the flowing white of Scott's dreamfigure. For the latter is unreal—a mermaid, a *fille de l'eau*. Scott is a gamekeeper, and tainted, like Lantier, with a secret violence. Peggy, caught "poaching" firewood, is a "tramp" in two senses: gold-digger and rag-picker. Like Boudu, she refuses to be grateful for being kept. The renunciation of art by an artist self-condemned to social reclusion recalls *La Chienne,* perhaps even Octave.

The tight, tense deadpan, which might at first seem the antithesis of Renoir's style, gradually reveals itself as Renoir in another key-signature. All the moulds of the *film noir* are filled with material at once subtler in its violence, finer in its nuance, and warmer in its tone. Because they are seen through the coastguard's eyes (or, more accurately, because they are matched against reaction shots of the apparently most ordinary guy), the couple in their clifftop house seem ominous, even monstrous; murder à la *Double Indemnity* is in the air. Yet their relationship is not so strange, its mutual conjugal torturings are not so far out of the ordinary. A blind husband refuses to be jealous of his wife's flirtations, and adopts the apparently more positive tactic of moving in a friendly yet imposing way on an intruder—whom in any case he likes ("birds of a feather"). The wife relishes the reassurance of flirtation, and being lonely, drifts towards taking an affair more seriously. The gloom is pervaded by a drab, yet tenacious affection.

The typical crime thriller ends with a dénouement in whose light every detail in the story changes its meaning. Apparently innocent or enigmatic or ominous acts become clarified with a clearly guilty intent. *The Woman on the Beach* is a crime thriller whose final twist is that there was no crime, no thought of crime, except in the twisted mind of the detective. In *Laura*, in *Phantom Lady,* in *Kiss Me Deadly,* the artists, the intellectuals, the sophisticated ones, are guilty. Against the anti-artist, anti-intellectual animus with which the *film noir* presaged a far from incidental aspect of McCarthyism, Renoir insists that the most sinister "creative work" is performed by the devious, obsessive and sadistic paranoia of the ordinary guy in uniform. A war trauma is a tactful excuse, or extenuation. Scott is infuriated by all that wanders freely in that transitional zone where day becomes night, land becomes sea, dream becomes reality, past becomes present, and driftwood becomes firewood; where it is possible to befriend one's wife's lover and where suffering becomes bitterness rather than being denied in the name of a confident optimism or sharpened into aggression. He fears those nuanced, sad, sometimes morbid complexities, an awareness of which distinguishes adult mellowness from infantile fundamentalism.

It's never quite clear whether the artist is unaware of the coastguard's tests, which stop just one lucky step short of manslaughter. Perhaps Tod possesses, as in myth and movies the blind so often do, second sight. But

his sophistication confers on him no general immunity from the follies to which flesh is heir. He in his turn was enthralled and frustrated by the female who destroyes him as an artist and half-destroys him as a man. He is purged by his renunciation, as Nana by her disfigurement.

The dialogue is cryptic. "My paintings are my eyes" implies, given the full range of dramatic irony, "I was blind even when I could see", i.e. "In blinding me she compelled me to face reality." "There's a saying among artists; you're never rich until you're dead." The bitterness inculpates not only a philistine society, but hints that Tod's own self-sacrifice for immortality is a kind of obstinate self-murder (corresponding to the coastguard's recurrent dream of dying), and that he is as worldly as the suspected "tramp" he loved. For if her champagne parties were only a brittle, superficial commensalism, they are to a profounder sociability as the artist's megalomania is to his art. The spiritually false form of the activity resembles the truthful one so closely that only tragedy can liberate the latter from the former. All the characters are blind. The artist, who is everyone's victim and his own executioner, "wins" in that he retains the woman's love and resolves the situation.

It is important to accept what is American in Renoir's American films, since he has accepted it into his work. It is as inseparable from them as the political issues of the '30s are to *Le Crime de Monsieur Lange* and *La Vie Est À Nous*. Once one has traced the American, or at least the Hollywood, aspects of the film, then its similarities with Renoir's earlier films emerge more clearly, but without reductionism. The contrast of setting and dialogue, the camera's oppressive immobility, all contribute, according to Cauliez, to "an interiorisation of form . . . to the advantage of a profoundly implicit nostalgia—a Bovaryism completely dreamed." Bovaryism in a purely American sense, of course, as the heroines of King Vidor's *Beyond the Forest* and Arthur Penn's *Bonnie and Clyde* are Madame Bovarys. But each of Renoir's figures, imprisoned in his obstinately lonely dream, comes to life through his nightmares, and escapes to a freedom which is not self-assertion.

The film is the spiritual negative of the American *film noir* of the epoch in another sense also. One can hardly claim that the Hollywood scriptwriters, or indeed their critics, were altogether innocent of psychoanalysis, and, in these terms, the painter is the father and the coastguard is the son, trying to snatch both the former's spiritual authority and his woman. In their *Movies: A Psychoanalytical Study,* Martha Wolfenstein and Nathan Leites analyse all American A-feature melodramas with a contemporary setting between the latter part of 1945 and 1949. They can find only two films whose manifest content expresses "the insight that the father-figure is dangerous only in fantasy." Of these two films, one, *The Web,* only modifies but does not negate the usual pattern. The other is *The Woman on the Beach*. Meanwhile, "In French films dealing with familial themes (which are usually less disguised than in American films), the central conflict tends to be a love rivalry between an older and a younger man. The two men are usually on friendly terms; there are rarely any violent hostilities between them. One or both of them suffer a severe love disappointment. A major plot type shows the older man falling in love with a young woman who might more appropriately pair off with the younger man. This love of the older man is a misfortune for all three, but he is hardly to blame. . . . American films are preoccupied with who is to blame for a crime of violence. French films tend to express the feeling that no one is to blame for the conflicts that arise from misplaced love."

Superficially one may see Joan Bennett's Peggy as another deadpan vamp, less emphatic (and therefore less satisfying), than in *Scarlet Street* and *The Woman in the Window,* but the gradual revelation of levels and ambiguities reveals several actresses in one. Her quiet, dark, muffled figure recalls Simone Simon in *La Bête Humaine*. She retains something of the plucky cynicism of the "confession" heroines of the early '30s, as do two other vamp-victims

of the '40s misogyny, Margaret Lockwood and Jane Russell, whose common origin is Hedy Lamarr. Joan Bennett suggests at once the Slav *femme fatale*, the Irish colleen, and the coolly tough sophisticate. Between Garbo and Novak (throughout, in fact, the deadpan '40s), Hollywood was extremely reticent about non-WASP origins and styles, and Joan Bennett's brooding assurance endowed her with a quiet alienation earthier and more amiably knowing than Novak's. She relates both to a pre-immigration peasant atmosphere, and the socio-psychological crisis of which Novak and Brando (with their conspicuously non-WASP surnames) are subsequent expressions. It's interesting to transpose the film into Hitchcock terms: casting Kim Novak for Joan Bennett, James Stewart for Robert Ryan, James Mason for Charles Bickford, and Barbara Bel Geddes for Nan Leslie.

The settings recall *La Bête Humaine;* the wooden hall for the coastguard's dance, the wooden houses. Peggy steals bundles of wood from the wrecked ship which is a *bateau mort-ivre*, stranded on a *plage des brumes*. The beach, at night or in mist, is agorophobic through its implied expanse and claustrophobic in its darkness. As Rivette observes, the film is Renoir's closest approach to Fritz Lang—who returns the compliment with *Clash by Night*, another film about America without chromium plating, the wooden America of the coast.

The mist gives this *film noir* a curious softness, contrasting with the rugosities of dunes, of cliffs, and of Charles Bickford's physiognomy. Yet the waves are metallic, restless. Perhaps the physicality for which Renoir strove is, at least in the release version, a little too reserved for a public conditioned by the cleavage of Jane Russell. The overall effect seems less that of a diffuse but insistent sensuality than of a potential dream (beach, falling, drifting . . .) and a stiff resistance to it by a core of watchful censor within the dream.

Jacques Rivette: "It is . . . the conclusion of what one dares not call Renoir's second apprenticeship . . . all technical virtuosity seems abolished. The camera-movements, rare and brief, decisively abandon the vertical axis of the screen image to one continuous plane and to the classic reverse-shot." One may wonder how far this represents a surrender or a response to a Hollywood style. It probably represents both processes at once. Rivette rightly notes that it forms the basis of Renoir's future style (for Bazin's celebration of Renoir's camera-movements is altogether retrospective). "Henceforward, Renoir states facts, one after the other, and beauty, here, is born of intransigence; there is a succession of brute acts; each shot is an event." And this, it must be said, isn't unique to Renoir, but a perfectly conscious Hollywood principle allowing a certain variation while still remaining valid: the principle of "one shot, one point". Even in *The Woman on the Beach*, the nuances within the acting counterpoint the syntax, giving it a brooding insistence and a slow, foggy rhythm. As Rivette puts it, the following films, "as rich in ornamentation as they may seem, by contrast with this paring-down . . . take this style as their armature . . . "

For Rivette, it opens a trilogy of masterpieces, and is no more disqualified by its mutilation than is Stroheim's *Greed*. It returns, curiously, to Renoir's silent-era aestheticism, with its studio artifice, its atmospherics, its dreams, and its bitter pathos of confusion, frustration and death. Like the work of other Hollywood expatriates (Siodmak, Lang, Welles, Dmytryk) it unfolds the expressionist visions behind the *film noir* deadpan.

The *overlay* of life and dream recalls that of *La Petite Marchande d'Allumettes*, though in a very different sense—matches/firewood, delirium/dreams . . . One thinks also of *La Fille de l'Eau*, but the moral guardian on horseback renounces his dream-woman. It is as if Renoir, at the end of his American career, has returned to the beginning of his French career and now looks back with a certain detachment, resignation, abnegation and calm, to his involvements then.

Interlude: Hesitations

While Renoir's American films were appearing, the critical consensus diagnosed yet another sad case of the Hollywood studios cramping, bowdlerising and, finally, smothering a European talent. A single lyricism, external realism, and an absence of Hollywood elements loomed too large in their canons. Since then, the case of "Renoir Américain" has been reopened. A common assumption is that version of *auteur* theory which assumes that Renoir is Renoir in Hollywood as in Paris. Maybe the truth lies between the two extremes. Though most of Renoir's Hollywood films are less successful than most of his French films of the '30s, they are still considerable artistic achievements. Nor are they impersonal. They are an expression of Renoir's developing social thought, and of his concomitant movement away from "the shock of lyricism" to a more detached, contemplative attitude.

He seems to be pursuing a series of reflections on the nature of society, the intricacy of relationships, and the need for an effort of sacrifice, before the individual can acquire, not what he thinks he wants, but what he really wants. The theme is distinct from that American perennial, the idealistic moral innocent discovering the world's corruption or its moral complexity. From the beginning, Célestine is no less corrupt than Chesnaye. But where the dance, the interlacing of partners, in *La Règle du Jeu* is confounded by an ugly fact irrupting from outside the dancers' social world, the Southerner, alone, is helpless not only before the more spectacular unmercies of nature but before quieter evils, like the malnutrition of his children. Against them he must appeal to a multiplicity of generosities and pacts. Maury's resigned love for Louise draws him towards martyrdom. In one sense, this represents a recovery from the social pessimism of *La Bête Humaine* and *La Règle du Jeu*, and brings the academic-romantic affirmation of *La Tosca* down to earth. From another angle, the stress on tortuousness and the transformation of purpose heightens their criticism of American individualism and optimism, like their refusal to melodramatise the pain and menace, and their refusal to sentimentalise away the egoistic element in relationships.

Figures corresponding to Michel Simon's amalgam of the free (Boudu) and the hesitant (Legrand) abound (Keefer, Maury, Devers, Mauger, Tod) but the emphasis lies in the ill-foundedness of their excessive suspicion and self-isolation. In *Swamp Water* Dana Andrews, whom one may regard as a transposition of Gabin's qualities, reconciles the "fauve" Keefer with society, but only by risk and sacrifice; while Lestingois, with his complacency and hypocrisy, fails to "save Boudu". Of Renoir's "eternal feminine", there are two reincarnations: Paulette Goddard, whom Renoir had admired in her earlier films, is a compromise between the quicksilver celerity of Catherine Hessling (especially her guttersnipe in *Modern Times*) and a steadier energy. As the *Woman on the Beach*, Joan Bennett recalls the vamp of *La Bête Humaine*, but matured and half-reconciled with a husband who has the ill-directed strength of a Lantier or a Schumacher. The theme is reiterated by the reconciliation of Tod and Scott. Scott, renouncing the woman he loves, leaving her to the man whom he hated and whom he has finally come to appreciate, seems to mark the end of a privileged nightmare that began with *La Chienne*, perhaps even *Nana*.

It is no easy matter to decide how far "Renoir Américain" is the Renoir of the '30s who has evolved, after the shocks of 1938-40; how far he is "Renoir Américain" responding to the authentic cultural characteristics of America; and how far one must think of "Hollywood Renoir". For it's only too easy to confuse: (a) American tastes as they actually were, while conceding some sort of highest common factor for regional variations, (b), American tastes as they might have been if American audiences had not been influenced in their expectations by the strategies which Hollywood developed—strategies arguably geared to lower common denominators rather than higher common factors, (c) the diversity of intuitions and theories, within Hollywood, as to what public taste was and how it might be satisfied, and (d), Hollywood's retorts to critics, particularly the middle-brow uplifters of the sweetness-and-light brigade.

Certainly one must beware of seeing "the Hollywood system" as more monolithic than it was. Renoir found champions in Zanuck over *Swamp Water*—an executive producer against the front office—and in David Loew over *The Southerner*—a financier-producer against distributors. RKO Radio gave him a free hand with *This Land Is Mine*.

One might, however, sustain a radical criticism of the system's effect on Renoir by postulating that the very responsiveness which enabled him to come as close to the real America as any American director had ever come, also rendered him vulnerable to a kind of "pre-compromise" with Hollywood, making the most of its latitude, but still forcing him to develop in certain directions rather than others. This might be true even if one saw Renoir's American films as largely reactions *against* Hollywood cliché or American assumptions—like *This Land Is Mine* and *Woman on the Beach*—or if one saw Renoir as using Hollywood conventions as stalking-horses for altering those assumptions.

Interlude: Reorientations

Had Renoir's problems been merely a matter of the rigidity of Hollywood as against the more elastic French system, one would have expected him to return to France as soon as possible at the end of the war. After all, neither René Clair nor Julien Duvivier, whose Hollywood careers had run a great deal more smoothly than Renoir's, wasted much time before resuming work on their native soil. Yet Renoir waited ten years before filming once again in France; and the difference is all the more remarkable in view of his previous insistence on an artist's need for deep cultural roots.

Clearly the real reasons for Renoir's delayed return might be family or personal matters which have nothing to do with criticism. But the course of his work makes it reasonable to extrapolate some possible reasons, of a semi-professional, semi-personal nature, and combine them into "une fantaisie dramatique".

First, Renoir may have recognised that that sensibility which, in the '30s, he had taken to be rooted in France, was really so generalised as to be nomadic. His French career had already been characterised by its variety of social settings and types. Renoir's real dependence was on friends, the nearest and closest of whom were now American (he has mentioned Charles Chaplin, Clifford Odets, Eugene Lourie, and Dudley Nichols).

He might have feared that to return to France would be to immerse himself in the bitterness of the aftermath of the Resistance and the hardening of the Cold War. The latter provoked further problems of loyalties, as between his American friends and those French friends whose allegiance was still with the Communist Party, which, from America, he sensed as Stalinist more clearly than they.

His reasons for hesitation would be strengthened by the extent to which his work was moving away from its earlier oscillations between anarchism and a more direct, emotive involvement with "les copains", towards a more philosophical contemplation of the individual and his often oblique alliances with others—a sense which is one of the most bracing aspects of his American films, sometimes foreshadowing Losey's. It can perhaps be seen as a compromise between a certain pessimism, and the type of liberalism which appeared in Hollywood in the '40s and which, in the hands of a Richard Brooks, a Dassin or a Losey was not at all as sentimental as it is sometimes remembered, since it had the pressure of hard-headed individualism to deal with. Even so, it had to cede to that individualism a focus on individual choice rather than a collective sensibility.

Renoir's increasing detachment may have also been fed by a style of life very different from those evenings around the stove in *La Nuit du Carrefour*, by the "Marienbad" aspect of Hollywood. The philosophical withdrawal and the interest in the internal images of memory which loom so large in his next four Technicolor films, aptly grouped by Cauliez under the title, "The Colours of Time", would have rendered specifically French, topical subjects unnecessary to him—more of a hindrance than a help. When Renoir finally returns to film in France, it is to the France of before his childhood, imbued with a gently sceptical nostalgia, and a sophisticated sense of political ironies and equivocations, reminding us just how often Renoir's films had been in ideological and political trouble.

Meanwhile, the Hollywood atmosphere itself was becoming uglier, with Cold War tensions and witch-hunts in the air. "To clear a path through the jungle it is advisable to feel one's way with a stick to fend off any dangers. Sometimes the stick meets a solid branch and breaks in your hand; sometimes it resists, and your arm remains numb. That's more or less what happened to me during the last few years. I didn't want to remain static. But the needle of the compass I was consulting was haywire and it was very difficult for me to see my way. In fact I'm very proud of it . . . It proves that I hadn't lost contact with our unstable world . . . "

That is roughly the atmosphere of *Woman on the Beach,* while the resolution of the bewilderment is indicated by the acquiescence at the end of the film, and which imbues the whole of *The River.*

After the débâcle of *Woman on the Beach,* he founded a company called Film Group with the purpose of shooting low-budget versions of theatre classics. As usual, he looked simultaneously for an antithetical inspiration. The classics were to be acted by the young theatrical companies whose experiments with theatre-in-the-round and The Method were intriguing Hollywood (and which, with the advent of Elia Kazan, a few years later, would begin to transform it). Thus what looked like a retreat into the past might equally have been a leap into the future; and the interaction of Renoir and these young collaborators might well have resulted in something far from uncontroversial. The banks however were hesitant, and funds were unforthcoming.

The River (Le Fleuve)

" . . . and one day, by chance, in the book pages of *The New Yorker*, I read a review of a book by an English author, a woman, Rumer Godden; and the name of the book was *The River*; and the critic said something like this: that from the point of view of style, at any rate, it was without doubt one of the best novels written in English during the last 50 years; and he added that, probably, it wouldn't make a penny from the public. It was sufficiently exciting for me to buy the book . . . and having read it, I was convinced that here was a first-rate movie subject. . . . I wrote to her that I thought her story was a great inspiration for a movie, but not a movie story, and that she would have to rewrite it with me, modifying the incidents and perhaps even the characters . . . and she replied . . . that she agreed, and I found myself with an option on *The River*; and I went to see a lot of people, and I couldn't interest anyone in my project . . . because a film on India . . . suggests cavalry charges, tiger hunts, elephants, Maharajahs; and they told me, 'after all, one must give the public a little of what it wants'."

Renoir, however, refused to give up. Meanwhile Kenneth McEldowney, an ex-florist from Los Angeles who had served in the U. S. Army Air Force in India during the war, had been promised money by some maharajahs to make a film about India. In one version of Renoir's story, a niece of Pandit Nehru advised McEldowney to look through the novels of Rumer Godden. In another version, the Indian government persuaded McEldowney not to make an Indian-language film, and Nehru's sister directed his attention to *The River*. At any rate, McEldowney found himself confronted by Renoir, who was already in possession of the option, and asked him to make the film. Renoir came to India in reconnaissance in 1949, and returned to write a scenario with Rumer Godden. She accompanied the film on location, and helped him rewrite during shooting. Having been a dance-teacher, she also helped Renoir rehearse his young amateurs (notably Harriet, whose story is partly autobiographical). Melanie, the Anglo-Indian girl played by Radha,

was a new character, "to bring more of India into the interior of our action"; she substitutes for the novel's diversity of visitors and servants. Radha "made me think of a young Nazimova", and acted as Renoir's social and cultural guide to India.

The River was made by a French director for an American company with Indian finance and counted for British quota. This internationalism indicates the new field opening itself before Renoir's reconciliatory energies. It was all the more important, as both Paris and Hollywood darkened under the shadows of the Cold War, to offer a fratricidal world the prospect of *another* kind of internationalism, a "reconciliation of cultures on a personal scale."

The River was Renoir's first colour film, Claude Renoir's first colour film, and the first Technicolor movie to be made entirely in India. The equipment had to be shipped from Britain. Claude Renoir: "The experiment . . . should have been a catastrophe. It was virtually a matter of sending a cameraman, without experience of Technicolor, to shoot, 10,000 kilometres away, film which would still have to be developed in London, and of which he would receive the first technical results only by telegram. Moreover, he was managing without the colour consultants usually much used in this kind of work. . . . The rushes, for economy's sake, were printed in black-and-white, apart from a few short colour samples which it was wisest not to look at. . . . " Many of the scenes were conceived in one continuous shot, and therefore allowed minimal revision by editing.

The tardy arrival of soundproofed cameras hastened Renoir's tendency to shoot more documentary material and strengthened his still hesitant predilection for voice-over commentary as against conventional dramatic sound. Nonetheless "throughout shooting I have reserved all my options as between a commentary form and direct action." Once edited, a rough black-

and-white print, made from one of the three negatives then still necessary for Technicolor, was previewed in the Hal Roach Studios in Beverly Hills to audiences selected as reasonably representative of American tastes. Their reactions encouraged Renoir to stray further from narrative emphases to the documentary material and *temps-mort*.

"Our drama is based essentially on the classical triangle situation, with Harriet, the Stranger, and India as protagonists." But the eventual rivalry is more complex. The stranger is Captain John (Thomas L. Breen), a young American soldier wounded during the war. He comes to Bengal, partly to convalesce, and to learn the use of his artificial leg. He mostly seeks a reason for living other than the optimism of strenuous achievement, now denied him. Quiet, gently embittered, he fascinates three girls all poised awkwardly and sensitively on the threshhold of adult emotion. Harriet's father (Esmond Knight) lost an eye in the First War, and now manages the local jute-mill. It is naturally with him that the three girls compare their new hero. "A leg's better than an eye!"—"An eye's better than a leg!"—"No, it's not!" "Yes, it is!" Harriet (Patricia Walters) is a shy, poetic girl, her plainness illumined by a radiant English expectation that the world is really as kind, just and responsible as her father. Her friend Melanie (Radha) is the daughter of an Indian mother and an easygoing Irishman (Arthur Shields). Uneasily torn between her double cultural inheritance, Melanie accepts her physical type, and retreats from any romantic passion, with its tensions and its implied wilfulness, to the cyclic ritual of a pre-industrialised world. Their golden-haired friend Valerie (Adrienne Corri), beautifully and imperious, seeks to prove her womanhood and her power and conquer her love-object: "I like to be cruel. No, I don't." Harriet woos her hero with a poem based on a myth, learnt from Melanie, about an Indian maid whose love for Krishna made her a Goddess. One afternoon she sees Valerie win her first kiss and is indignant: "I hate bodies!" As the three girls discover love, so Harriet's young brother, Bogey, confronts a male mystery. Imitating a snake charmer, he ventures to charm a cobra with his flute and a saucer of milk, in a wood which the Indians believe to be sacred, and which is strictly out of bounds to him. One quiet summer afternoon, as his brothers and sisters sleep, he proves too venturesome. After his funeral, Harriet, over family lunch, burst out, "We just go on, eating green peas and roast potatoes as if nothing had happened!" Her mother replies, "We don't go on as if nothing had happened, we just go on!" Harriet, in final protest against injustice, attempts suicide by throwing herself into the river. Fishermen rescue her and Captain John, before he leaves, shares with her what he has learned. With every experience, after every encounter, one dies a little, or is reborn. Harriet sees her Captain John go, but what has passed between them is a precious form of love. "The river runs; the world spins; the story ends; the end begins."

The story is less a subject to be explored than an occasion for "an Occidental meditation on the Orient . . . I wanted to be a witness to a civilisation which wasn't based on profit." The story is tenderly evoked with an unsentimental brevity. The sensuality of the physical world, from the fruit, oils and cloths of the market place, to "the sapphire glow of the Ganges at night", merges with the sensuality of ritual. At the Kali Puja, a mother traces kohl (lamp-black and butter) around her daughter's eyes. The women of the household decorate their floor with patterns in rice flour and water. Harriet attempts suicide during the Divali Festival, on the darkest October night, when bonfires and thousands of candles are lit to aid the sun in its battle against the powers of darkness.

Claude Renoir: "With Eugene Lourié . . . , we chose exterior landscapes, then colours for the decor, then the cloth for the clothes, then in the course of a shot we'd say, "Here, let's put a bunch of mauve flowers in the background, that'll look nice!" And it did look nice! And that's all there is to the famous problem of colour! . . . The most important problem before technicians who want to transpose colour onto a screen is the ability to see and to grasp the colours which surround them in the first place." Jean Renoir: "In Bengal . . . nature divides into fewer colours; compare a tree on the Avenue Frochot with a tropical tree; the second has fewer greens, only one or two shades; it's very convenient for colour movies." William Whitebait: "Colour has never before been so employed on the screen . . . three redheads give an almost pre-Raphaelite tinge to the green arbours . . . the exuberant seasonal rites bring such a throwing of confetti and daubing of

crimson powder as would ravish the soul of an impressionist" (and *a fortiori* a pointilliste) "to say nothing of the forest, the wild river expanse, glittering marriage dances, firework displays, temple decorations and the beauties of dress and floor painting. No film has hitherto *painted* its schemes. Others have hit on a single-tone scheme—Ford's bluecoats, for example, against a Texas land and skyscape—but what else does one remember?"

Renoir's orchestration of Indian colours may seem of purely historical interest now that vastly more sensitized emulsions can effortlessly, and meaninglessly, ornament any platitude. Yet in the twenty years since its shooting began, *The River* remains undimmed. For the relationship between the "slight" story and the cymbal clash of yellow blossom on bronze tray is, in Eisenstein's strictest sense, a "montage" effect. The dramatic and the sensuous are welded, like adolescent vulnerabilities, the gentle violence of tropic sensuality, nature's (deceitfully) gentle detachment, and Renoir's *ulterior* detachment, saddened yet evasive of pessimism because "the river runs . . . "

Harriet's commentary recounts how she was rescued from her suicide attempt even as the flashback shows her slipping into the nocturnal stream. Thus flashback structure reverses chronological order, to sacrifice obvious suspense for an ulterior wisdom. As in time, so in space. The three girls bring their love-offerings to Captain John. A long shot shows him in light grey clothes, in the top centre of the screen. Below him and nearer the camera,

Harriet in a pale blue dress peeps at him amidst pale green and yellow foliage (the fresh, gentle colours express her character; so does her posture— she's caught shyly bending). "Her" commentary ends but the shot is held, and we discover Melanie at the top of the screen in her red sari amidst dark green foliage talking to Captain John (the most detached girl is the nearest to him—to gain something by grasping nothing is the sad privilege of maturity). And then amidst the matt reddy grey of a wall at the bottom of the frame our eye is struck by the wine-coloured dress and flaming golden hair of Valerie. The shot gently equates the girls, softens the competitive tension which they must feel into a wry, perhaps involuntary togetherness. The most acute moments of grief are (in retrospect) not very much more important than the (dramatically irrelevant) fireworks ceremony; red and white kites bobbing against a bright sky are more real than the (half forgotten) suicide attempt. One remembers W. H. Auden on Breughel's *Icarus*:

"About suffering they were never wrong,
The Old Masters; how well they understood
Its human position; how it takes place
While someone else is eating or opening a window or just walking
dully along . . . "

Our heroine's attempted suicide is watched calmly from the God's eye view of her future. "I cannot tell/What then I felt . . . " The ellipse is essential. Amidst the caress of silk, one feels the razor. Poulle speculates whether Renoir's evasiveness before violence may seem more like a certain fastidiousness. It is true that moments of climax, of paroxysm, have less continuity with the remaining 99/100ths of one's life than one's anticipation and recollection of those climaxes. This is not to say that climaxes are *never* moments of truth, and that a cinema of climaxes is false; simply, that there is need for both sorts of cinema, and for that cinema which, like Renoir's, is a strange, yet sensitizing combination of climax and evasiveness. Just this restraint, I believe, constitutes a common reason for disappointment with Renoir's American films. Primacy of the climax is a romantic concept; in classicism, and where realism goes with a sense of the life force as a continuous freedom, every climax is slightly deflated by the sense of its position in a structure, or by its inconsequentiality given the existence of tomorrow.

A similar "democracy" exists among important and "incidental" events within a shot. A postman chats to a friend while in the foreground children rush to and fro across the group. Our eye is drawn by both, the whole scene becomes a precarious happiness, a bouquet of mutually irrelevant existences. On the extreme left of the screen a firework blazes, but most of the screen shows a lively crowd, and the finely balanced rivalry of colour and composition draws the eye searchingly over the entire frame. Such equilibrium often becomes a matter of editing-in-space: compositional predominance guides the spectator's eye around the frame. We find ourselves looking at what seems simply a close-up of an Indian playing a flute. Caught

in the film's meditative tempo, we study the stiff vein on the forehead, the narrowed alert eyes, the coloured turban. The shot is held, and, wondering why, we see the cobra-head in the lower part of the screen. If that cobra had been shown first, we would hardly have seen the man's face as openmindedly as we do. Such visual intricacies explain why Renoir chose to risk so many one-shot scenes, despite probable editing problems later.

However dubious Bazin's arguments about the greater spiritual integrity of *mise-en-scène* over editing, they certainly apply here. More important though, separate shots of charmer and snake would have inculcated an obvious shock rather than our sense of danger held in a constant equilibrium which is everyday life. Is snake-charming any more dangerous than avoiding motor-cars while crossing a road? That piper has the same calm hard pitiless gaze as Pan piping up the storm in *Le Déjeuner Sur L'Herbe*. To attempt, as Bogey did, to master nature, even by befriending it, reveals a child-like innocence, and a natural form of *hubris*. Bogey's death is tragic, in the real sense of the word, and inevitable, for most of us will die thus, in our own little convulsion while all around us others sleep serenely. Bogey's being killed by a cobra is yin to the yang of Mauger killing his tame squirrel. The film ends with another child about to be born—and we recall the rebirth of another victim of snakebite, Keefer, in *Swamp Water*. But since we are in India, a reincarnation holds sway rather than individual immortality (immortality—that notion which ought to be so optimistic, but which, from Lazarus to the ghost of Hamlet's father, so rapidly slides into the sinister . . .).

As Cauliez suggest, Valerie represents the aesthetic and Harriet the ethic (Melanie, one might add, incarnates the religious). The American girl attempts to conquer; the English girl to commend herself by her moralized sensitivity; Melanie to touch, yet renounce possession. The simplicity with which the characters are given these other functions is essentially classical, all the more impressively so in that their human hesitations are not sacrificed to the schematic. Valerie throws the quoits forcefully, between each throw taking two steps back, like a panther crouching before pouncing, keenly calculating her prowess. Her speculative air, as she smokes a cigarette, betrays her uncompleted familiarity. "Captain John, you *must* dance!" she says grandly, and with unconscious cruelty she finds her hero's Achilles heel. Something in her imperious statements seems to hang in the air, puzzling her, as if she began her sentences quite sure of her opinion and of her divine right, and concludes surprised to find herself unsure. Yet she needs an accomplice to liberate her from the immature assertiveness of Western egoism. Harriet ventures her moral certainties with a quick glance from shining little eyes to see her interlocuter's reaction; she and Captain John share their sadness wthin the warm circle of lamplight in a communion perhaps closer than Valerie's first kiss. It is Harriet's sadness which gives him a sense of having something to give after all, and so helps him to find himself. Melanie, meeting Captain John, stands nervously still till her father signals to her to sit down opposite him. After a careful sip of whisky, she pulls a face. All are defeated, gently, by a man whose weaknesses undermine his Western rejection of acceptance. His is a second adolescence, by which they are hurt and freed.

Captain John, immobilised, pallid, hesitating between bitterness and acquiescence (his two alternatives) finally achieves a quiet fatherly strength. Cauliez notes that he, rather than Melanie, expresses the Indian philosophy. Melanie's father, already adapted to the East, offers us another link—that of the Irishman, whose poetic blarney and folk ways are another form of waywardness vis-à-vis industrial rhythms and rationalist routines. Bogey's

is a tragic destiny, the manipulating, secularising West breaks the rules of the game. The child who replaces him is a girl. The film is less a repudiation of maleness, which is celebrated in its erotic form in Krishna's dance, than a repudiation of the Western edge to masculinity.

The River forms, with *The Woman on the Beach* and *French CanCan*, a trio of meditations on the theme of time (or more exactly of memory) and of space (or more exactly of detachment). The themes are not unique to Renoir. The '20s had its avant-garde idioms for subjective realities (quick cutting, hazed images). They lapsed somewhat in the socially tense '30s, but Carné's (or rather Prévert's) *Le Jour Se Lève* and Welles's *Citizen Kane* sparked off the charactheristic '40s idiom: a strong narrative told in flashbacks and "revue et corrigé" by its intersection with an ongoing dramatic narrative present or commentary. *The River* is transitional between their '40s idiom and the '50s sense of foreground-background interplay represented by, say, Ophuls's weaving camera. *The River* uses a basically motionless camera, but the eye moves, sometimes in closed circles, around the foreground-background. Cinemascope and so-called "wide screen" introduced no new possibilities, but made those which Renoir had already explored more obvious to more directors.

The shift of idiom was noticed, partly understood and partly distorted, by Bazin, who tended to confuse Renoir with Rossellini. Certainly *Stromboli* (1948-9) recalls *The River* insofar as it turns semi-documentary neo-realism, a largely improvised script, and the theme of a woman's adaptation to a pre-industrial culture, towards spiritual rather than social ends. But Renoir, less disposed than Rossellini or Bazin to a Christian metaphysic, did not suppose a simple correspondence between interior and exterior reality, and relished artifice, coming nearer the worldly ornamentation of that other sceptic, Max Ophuls. " . . . one thing which continues to fascinate me, when I shoot

a movie in colour, is to cheat with nature. In *The River*, for example, with Lourié, we had to pay out a fortune on paint; green, for the trees of Bengal! We went out strolling with large cans of paint and we changed the green, completely!" No paradox is involved in a procedure quite as ordinary as facial cosmetics; all the same, its unabashed application to landscape preludes Ophuls's lavish repainting of roads in *Lola Montès,* another essay in space-and-time, on meditated experience. Resnais' *Hiroshima Mon Amour* inaugurates the dominant meditative style of the '60s. Flashbacks lose their quotation marks, are parachuted into the present tense, and so imply a stream-of-consciousness continuity. Too often, however, the initial inexplicability of the reference draws attention to the disruption of tenses, or moods, and so prevents the past-present, reality-unreality, subjective-objective intersections from being as self-effacingly functional as those of verbal language. The jolt of enigma or contradiction performs a different purpose, creating a sense of the arbitrary, the enigmatic or the unreal, and therefore of the mind's only partial and provisional grasp of the world around, or indeed of itself. Much in Renoir (as in Resnais) can be related to Bergson. His handling of consciousness and time presupposes an instinctual drive providing sufficient continuity and meaning, and so can be opposed to the solipsist use of stream-of-consciousness devices in Robbe-Grillet, whose minds are less instinctual even than Kafka's, and contrasted to the nobly pessimistic disruptions of consciousness in Resnais. Yet *The River* approaches the '60s style in its inconspicuous use of the flashback-commentary "timeslip", its essentially anti-realistic use of the ellipse, and its responsiveness to the distortions wreaked by the selectivity of memory.

For the Surrealists, Ado Kyrou: "I am unmoved by Renoir's American films. All the characters play by the rules of the game, they love without revolt, they prefer the placidity of the hearth to passion. *The River* is more interesting, even though there appears a pantheist humanitarianism which eliminates passion and revolt, to the advantage of acceptance and resignation. Some beautiful images of young girls at the mercy of love, a dazzling sequence of kite-flying in which Renoir unveils the cruelty of young girls discovering love, enable one to forget the general theme."

A list of the themes on which the film doesn't touch can be extended almost to infinity. Notably it doesn't touch on the tensions underlying the Hindu-Moslem massacres which were flourishing during its preparation and which might be considered a melancholy comment on Renoir's search for an Indian example of transcultural fraternity. Whence Marcel Oms: *"The River . . .* is only a long slow hymn to the glory of the Eternal. The misery and overpopulation of India are not seen. . . . Moreover, the film is set in the society of European colonists. . . . Renoir has preferred the fruitbasket of Rabrinadath Tagore to the anti-colonial protests of Gandhi." Must we condemn Auguste Renoir for painting beautiful women without reference to the causes of World War I, the exploitation of female labour among the working-classes, and the rise of the suffragette movement? Hasn't Jean Renoir's art always been engaged, by the didactic purpose of its counter-examples, in offering an alternative philosophy to the destructiveness perennially in vogue, and sometimes rightly, but rarely, surely, to the exclusion of all other temperaments and modes?

The film was awarded the First International Prize at the Venice Biennale in 1951. Its continuity was not immediately understood. For one English critic it was "like rambling through the family album of an exceptionally gifted photographer", while for another the plot was "a rambling clothes-line on which to hang some pretty and some limp strips of celluloid." Fortunately such imbecilities were not matched by Rank's circuit bookers nor by the general public. *The Observer's* critic found the film "as finely spun as a spider's web outlined in hoar frost." (!) William Whitebait compared it to "a Chekhov play, barely sketched in, of childhood merging into ado-lescence" and to E. M. Forster, for its querying of Western values. "It triumphs, as did *Louisiana Story* in its identification of a landscape with childhood haunts; and it is hardly accident that a great river should have inspired both films. But Renoir's story, however lightly touched in, is rather more complex and shaded. . . . "

The Golden Coach
(Le Carosse D'Or)
(Il Carozzo D'Oro)

The financial success of *The River* throughout the world, especially in view of its originality of tone and topic, restored to Renoir his pre-war eminence as an international film-maker. Anglo-Saxon critics loved the film's combination of idyllic documentary à la *Song of Ceylon* and idyllic childhood à la Rumer Godden. It seemed to give a new dimension and tone to neo-realism. In the eighth issue of *Cahiers du Cinéma* Maurice Scherer began the rehabilitation of "Renoir Américain", while André Bazin made his brave and ingenious bid to reclaim Renoir's Heraclitean paganism for a kind of crypto-neo-Platonist-cum-phenomenological Christianity. Slowly British colleagues realised that Renoir's "lack of concentration" was a matter of, metaphorically, a deeper focus and a wider-angle lens.

Quite apart from Bazin's metaphysics, the film's influence seems to have spread from Vadim's *Et Dieu Créa La Femme* (its disposition of separate characters within the same shot and in its fondness for "irrelevant" background and action) to *Shakespeare Wallah* (as James Ivory testified) and perhaps Wolf Rilla's idyllic colonial sunset, *A Pattern of Islands*. It anticipated the cinema of philosophic time, established as fashionable in *Hiroshima Mon Amour,* collaterally with the different idiom of Ophuls' *La Ronde.* Following the film's success, and a gradual eclipse in left-wing militancy with, in consequence, an apparent healing of the political breach, Renoir returned to France with film projects in view. He commented that, when he met his old friends again, they resumed their conversation, not where they left off in 1940, but where they would have continued had they never parted; and this sense of the world's oneness is a rather beautiful one, although it doesn't refer to the disappointment expressed over *The River* by his old left-wing colleague Jacques Brunius.

Less with Renoir than any other director does a choice of subject indicate what propositions might have emerged from its final form. Nonetheless, a move towards an "American" optimism, to something like the "fantasy of goodwill", and towards the French centre-right, may have underlaid his particular interest in filming Jean Giraudoux's *La Folle de Chaillot,* a subject which nearly twenty years later finally saw the light of celluloid in the hands of Bryan Forbes, a British convert from sarcasm to right-wing sweetness and light. Renoir dropped the project, and four subsequent ones. One was an original outline entitled *Paris-Provence* and published in *Cahiers,* with a view of ordinary people as old-fashionedly innocent as in the pre-Occupation films of René Clair. Its development and its actors might have transformed it, or it might have acquired a beauty to which its archaisms were irrelevant or contributory. Another project was an original story, written with Dudley Nichols, entitled *Les Braconniers* (The Poachers) and set to star Danielle Delorme as a girl who shares her house with the denizens of a Boulogne forest a hundred years ago. A third project was a version of Turgenev's *First Love,* and a fourth was a film about Van Gogh, abandoned in view of the three other adaptations also under way (by Jean Aurenche in France, Cesare Zavattini in Italy and Vincente Minnelli in America). Renoir returned to his California home and friends. Once again, however, the road between Hollywood and Paris ran through Rome, an itinerary coinciding with Renoir's sharpened feeling that Italy constituted the main trunk of European culture.

The *commedia dell'arte*—that junction of spontaneity and classicism, of folk, bourgeois and even court culture—had interested Renoir in silent days. Around 1939 he had thought of Merimée's story as a possible basis, but the film eventually came to him via an adaptation by Visconti, and his interest was clinched by the chance of directing Anna Magnani. "I was convinced . . . despite her usual style, despite her reputation as an ultra-romantic, naturalistic actress, that I could achieve with her a little essay in classicism; and that was my guideline; what replaced India for me . . . was my admiration for . . . Italy before Verdi and romanticism." With co-scenarist Giulio Macchi as his cultural "guide", Merimée's story was reduced to a scaffolding, and the dialogue left to be improvised during shooting.

As in *The River,* paradoxes of nationality abound. Although the film counted as a Franco-Italian co-production, it is usually considered as an Italian rather than a French film, shot as it was in Rome and with a largely Italian cast. Nonetheless, Renoir considers the English version as the original, since Magnani and most of the actors played in English (certainly the French dubbing seems conspicuously less successful than the Italian, and Renoir has since been caustic on the subject of dubbing). Shooting began at Cinecittà on February 4, 1952 (saddened, for Renoir, by his brother Pierre's death in March). The film was premiered in its French version in

February 1953, although substantial cuts later reduced the English version to 100 minutes.

"In Merimée La Perichole is an actress. In my film Camilla is the actress. In the play, the golden coach symbolises worldly vanity, similarly in the film.

The conclusion is likewise brought about by the archbishop. From these few points, my collaborators and I invented a story which might be called 'the actors, the theatre and life.'" To Merimée's bitterness Renoir preferred "the light, edgy, stinging, derisive tone of Italian comedy." The first film treatment underwent progressive alteration. According to René Vidal, the film originally opened in Venice, and included sequences showing Guido (subsequently Felipe) among the Indians, deliberations concerning the baptism of an Indian chief, and an accident to the coach. The play occurred near the beginning of the film, to be followed by the deliberations of the Council, and a study of the effect of a colonial war on the finances of a little kingdom.

The final version, however, begins as a *commedia dell'arte* troupe arrive in a Spanish colonial town in Peru. Their unhoped-for success is not so much the triumph of their art as that of their leading actress, Camilla (Anna Magnani), who triumphes in a duel for the audience's attention and respect against distinguished spectators. Three men, Filipe, Ramon and Ferdinand, court her. Felipe, a young nobleman, becomes her business manager but eventually leaves as a soldier to fight the Indians. He returns, fired with admiration for the "noble savage", and hopes to carry Camilla off to a simple, natural life away from the artificiality of stage and court. Ramon, the reigning bullfighter, realises he must come to terms with a redoutable counter-attraction. He woos her, imperiously, possessively, and with the murderous jealousy of a patriarchal code of honour. Her third suiter is the Viceroy Ferdinand (Duncan Lamont), who agrees to provide the proof of love Camilla demands. The bourgeois-minded citizens of his council of state have reluctantly agreed to vote their aristocratic leader the funds for a golden coach which he has considered necessary to his person and his office. He will give it to Camilla, as she demands, even when the result must clearly be loss of office. Camilla, realising that her love is unworthy of his, renounces him, and she spares him all the sacrifices arising from his gesture by presenting the coach to the Bishop. The Bishop announces that the coach will be used to carry the holy sacrament to the dying, nobles and commonalty alike.

If the coach is worldly vanity, then worldly vanities are theatre. The Viceroy wants it to impress not only the people but his peers, and himself. Business of state is show business. The bullfighter mentions to Camilla that they would more than double their audiences in partnership. He makes a posture out of what he is—a childishly simple soul, determined to slaughter all rivals, if they're men, and conquer by possession, if they're women. His active, arrogant egoism is matched by Felipe who sincerely and quietly slides down the social scale: nobleman, bourgeois, soldier, settler, then brother to the noble savage. The roles Felipe plays for real also betray a certain passivity, an inability, for all his manoeuvring, to assert himself as himself. With sincerity goes simplicity, an *absence* of theatre—which is a kind of banishment. . . .

Le style, c'est l'homme; le style, c'est du théâtre. Since all communication (even with oneself) is theatre, the theatre both infiltrates life and undermines it. The condition of the Viceroy's relative freedom is his ironic sense of life as style, as a game that can only be won by knowing, even if you choose to break it, *la règle du jeu.*

Camilla alone will stake little on—real or apparent—love. She knows no reality but the theatre's, desires no love but that of an audience. Her enjoyment of its admiration is vanity, and it's so misguided as to be a religion: *vox populi, vox Dei.* Her farewell to the Viceroy is interrupted as soldier and bullfighter burst in duelling, bringing with them the absurd theatricality of a game played in deadly earnest. She angrily quietens them. The Viceroy aligns himself in defeat with the other two, so suddenly the three have become, not simply her suitors, not simply an audience, but her judges. They turn and go, leaving her to her vocation, and her fate.

The Viceroy, the Council, the bullfighter, Felipe, and the Bishop represent codes of honour: the aristocratic, the bourgeois, the warrior's, the moral, the vocational. Each is some way involves or encounters its own antithesis. The aristocrat and the bourgeoisie are in uneasy alliance, the Council itself a ludicrous mixture of financial realities and titled pretension. The Viceroy is democratised by an attack on two fronts, from the people's favourite and from the King's mistress. Felipe veers from colonialist soldier to admirer of the Indians. The bullfighter accepts co-existence with petticoat government, and becomes one of a crowd (of three). The Bishop acquires the supreme symbol of worldliness, and pays tribute to it. Camilla's profession, which might seem the apotheosis of life's glitter, is finally revealed as a vocation almost as solitary as the Bishop's. All is the vanity game.

The relationships within the film are a mirror image of those within the play—which thus appears twice: within the film, which is *about* it, and behind the film, which is an adaptation of it. René Vidal remarks that "in the play, Isabelle is Colombine's mistress, in the reality . . . she is almost Camilla's servant." The Viceroy recalls Pantalone, and Felipe Captain Fracasse. Cauliez sees Ramon as the Captain, and Felipe as a blend of Scaramouche and Pierrot, with Martinez combining various valets and the long-winded noble, the Commedia doctor.

The theme rules all aspects of the film's style. In *Lange* there were three pivot sequences (virtually 360° pans) when the world sweeps and spins. In *The Golden Coach,* the three sharp transitions between theatre and reality are not expressed by panning shots. An opening sequence identifies stage and screen by showing us the action from a theatrical seat. (If Camilla is often allowed her own un-theatrical close-ups, it is not simply because Camilla is the star, on whom we turn our opera-glasses, but because Camilla's life-force, craving a reality (that of love) and establishing a real contact with the audience (by turning her back on it) is already refusing to be imprisoned within the illusion, just as it pervades that illusion and gives it its life). The final shot of the coach's departure suddenly becomes as com-

posed, as two-dimensional, as the theatrical stage—but the coach is curiously out-of-key, as redolent of reality as an automobile on a theatrical stage. And the screen asserts itself as the camera tracks back from the stage away from it, back into the audience, an effect which all but brings the screen's edge into the picture.

Another backyard tracking shot marks perhaps the tersest bullfight sequence in movies. In close-up, Camilla—in the audience this time—watches Ramon's danger, and his daring escape; and as she applauds, the camera tracks rapidly back right into the arena to frame Ramon in the foreground. The crossing of the perimeter—or proscenium line—is all the more forceful in that Renoir began by holding the close-up of Camilla through changing expressions, long enough to convince us that we did not need to see, and would not be shown, the actual bullfight. (And, of course, what matters is Ramon's triumph over Camilla's heart). Renoir is also, like Orson Welles, playing a joke on the cognoscenti among the audience. Just as we have convinced ourselves that we had spotted him covering up a small budget by implying a bullfight with one trackback from a close-up, he indulges the luxury of an extensive track revealing the full extent of the set. Ironically, too, the tracking shot "arrives" *after* the conventional emphasis on the point of maximum danger for Ramon.

The story's three-act structure is quite conspicuous. Many scenes are viewed from one side only (as on the stage), the effect being underlined when the décor is "set square" to the screen frame. Or they are studiously sparing of other than small changes of angle (reverse angles being particularly rare). Details and close-ups are inserted with a certain abruptness, particularly when the cut involved a change from a complex of colours to a second complex in which one of those colours suddenly bursts forth closer and nearer. The effect, as of a suddenly sharpened pitch, oddly isolates the two scenes. In colour, in mood, in volume, the close-up often relates to the scene as a whole like a box-within-a-box. The effect implies a certain temporal discontinuity and when a detail is followed by a more general view, it often seems as much suppressed by, as continued through, the subsequently more complex shot. To a superficial glance, the film may well seem cluttered; one might speak rather of an anti-steroscopy (3-D being in its brief vogue at the time). The long or medium shots assert an objective, meditative, *classical* view of the characters in their complicated little predicaments. The close-shots have a passionate subjectivity, giving us a romantic view. The two views slide through one another, never quite merging. The images are occasionally rococo (pattern in a flat plane), although always vividly un-balanced, while Renoir tirelessly turns complexes of décor into gentle little mazes (a duo in and out of doors, Ferdinand marching between three rooms, a conversation among the hung sheets which so often recur in Renoir, like a proliferation of screens among the screen), and one recalls the neo-classical vogue for the maze. The few "set square" images are all the more con-spicuous in that they have to work against the energy generated by their more turbulent neighbours. Rococo depth—a succession of facing planes in parallel, laminated like the slices of a loaf—interacts with a gentler uneven-ness, a succession of restless diagonals, which honeycomb space with little perplexities.

Colour is carefully graduated. The theatre is sharp, clear, vivid, with reds and yellows. The colours of the court are pastel creams and rose. The Indian peasants, in their packed mass, are tight, savage, like glowing ashes (how Renoir cherishes the discrepancy between the obsidian closure of their faces under their hats and the loose, flowing, amiable play on stage). A high nervous tension keys the hues of Camilla's broodings, as when her black dress appears by the golden coach, with its beige curtains, and its roof shines with a trapezium of green light. Black, negation of the spectrum, is imposed by the King's mistress, by the Bishop, and by Camilla herself during her last scenes; black is the colour of absolutes: the scattered seed of these funereal blossoms in the shadow in the corners of her dressing room, the "porch" between theatre and night, the illusory and the nomadic.

Colour, however controlled, is also a source of visual instability. " . . . the pastel blues of the Viceroy's garb, the black and russet of the Consul, recall the verses of Racine." Jean Demonsablon's comparison may surprise the Anglo-Saxon reader, if, at least, he sees Racine through the eyes of romantic criticism, whose over-facile contrasts with Shakespeare associate Racine with the neo-classical notions of Greek statuary as cold white marble. But, just as the Greeks painted their statues in bright colours, so, as Barrault has insisted, the real colour of Racine is blood-red. Colour here is a baroque constituent, in its forceful counterpointing of purely spatial perspective by every resource of colour. Sometimes a bright background flattens the perspective, or a matching of foreground and background colours confuses it, or a shrilly coloured detail insinuates itself into our attention. Thus colour pixilates the sense of order and the characters' subjectivities, and mediates between them in a capricious way.

The film possesses a joyous sadness (but not a sad joy) akin to that of Franju's *Judex,* another tale of characters whose past-in-our-present becomes a subjunctive mood of craved dreams, of nostalgically remembered childhood art, or semi-fictional beings. This paradox, which has revolving doors permitting continuous antitheses, can be entered from either side. Fictional genres and worldly codes are charades which permit and invade life.

The intersecting dimensions of screen, theatre, ceremonial and polite restraint, find their natural complement in characterisation which is a bas-relief. Often indeed, the human face is, not actually eclipsed, but challenged by the chop and change of compositional colour scenes notably more unsettled than those of *The River*. These individually intricate colour schemes, following in succession, oscillate between dramatic and visual centres of focus, between stability and instability, between the eye's longing to linger and the story's rapid rhythms, weaving an optical world to which it is by no means incongruous to extend the term: fauve. Our pleasure in a colour patchwork, a kaleidoscope, as refreshment of the spirit recalls Matisse. Far from being abstract, the film's colour provides much of its sense of spiritual joy. But many colour schemes also have an acid luminosity, a quietly scathing virulence of hue, recalling a certain astringency in the work of Renoir *père*.

In *The Golden Coach,* as in *French Can-Can,* later, the serpent's tooth is money. Only the bourgeoisie can afford to pay for their seats at theatrical attractions. The elderly Councillor's boring story has a bloodcurdling moral. Extolling the exemplary patriotism of his ancestors, he recounts their self-sacrifice, pawning their family plate. Shortly afterwards, in their capacity as justices, they find the pawnbroker guilty of usury and burn him alive. Thus the plate is returned to its rightful owner, constituting yet another proof of the protection of the righteous by divine providence. The gold of the sacramental coach is the apotheosis and transcendence of the financial theme. God's in his coach, all's well with the dying. Yet a child is convinced that Felipe is "le roi", and the faith of this soldierly chameleon is in man, and the assertion, not of his lowest common denominator (mobocracy) but his highest common factor (in the tribe, each individual shares sovereignty). Renoir's tender bitterness arises not in a pessimistic obliteration of hopes, but in his balance of idealism and—acquiescence. Felipe recalls Jurieu, his idealistic, childlike energies cast out by the complexities of all but an ideal code. The rapid surrender of the Viceroy recalls the contrast between the mountain fugitives of *La Marseillaise,* and the exiled aristocrats of Coblenz. As so often in comedy, the contrast is relative rather than absolute. Both men surrender, both men lose. They must smile; for not to smile is to lose even our consolation prizes; it is a futility, a romantic protest, or suicide. Vidal compares the film's humour to Voltaire's. That its tragic possibilities are alleviated is a matter of good luck and quick wits, i.e. of evasion, but not of illusion.

It is still too easy to assume that any bright and rapid movie must be cheerful, that *lacrimae rerum* lie only in tragedy. One can take too complacently the potential force of Bazin's remark that Renoir's paganism has deepened into a Franciscan serenity. The term Franciscan suggests both the consolations of faith and the asininity of St. Francis à la Rossellini. But even if we restore to Franciscanism its austere dignity, and even if the film's sense of relinquishment and acquiescence evokes the nomadic aspects of monasticism, any Christian sense must be dissipated by the worldliness, and the sense of theatre as all the consolation there is. Renoir's affinities are rather with Greek paganism; with his cult of Dionysius-Pan, the "canine" lifestyle of Diogenes and Boudu, the chameleonic ideology of the Sceptics (with whom Renoir shares a refusal to be sceptical about the senses), the less pessimistic aspects of the Epicureans (notably in his elevation of friendship and in a sensuousness suggesting a soul diffused throughout the body), the self-flight of Lucretius, the natural egalitarianism of Stoicism, the apathetic indignities of cynicism. In many ways, what is usually referred to as Renoir's Rousseauism is more akin to Stoicism (whose influence, from the Renaissance on, does, of course, constitute part of the cultural background to Rousseau's thought). Camilla's gift of the coach to the Bishop is an acceptance of religion in its most establishment and exterior form (parade); the form, that is, which non-Catholics are least likely to revere or to accept at face value. Perhaps the gift carries an overtone of that nineteenth-century Romantic view that the feudal church was intended to champion the mass of poor believers against the feudal aristocracy. But it's more in the spirit of Renoir, and of the film (in which not a grain of specifically Christian sentiment appears), to take an interpretation which is tolerably bleak. If Camilla immures herself in showbusiness, showbusiness becomes a pawn in power politics. It's redeemed, to some extent, by the *this-worldly* consolations offered by the Last Sacrament: consolations necessarily brief, merely illusory but preciously symbolic.

Choreographically the film is as intricate as *La Règle du Jeu*—the informal Renoir maze of optional openings rather than alleyways is asserted by complexes of rooms, by sheets hung up to dry (the laundry theme), and made linear in the Council Chamber sequence with three rooms in a line, like three boxes. Renoir: "The influence of Vivaldi proved decisive in the final stages of editing", imposing "a side which is not drama, not buffoonery, not burlesque, but a sort of irony which I tried to bring as near as possible to that rather light spirit which one finds in, for example, Goldoni . . . " This play of levels is parallelled in levels of characterisation. Renoir requested a discreet overacting to give many of the non-theatrical scenes an insidiously theatrical air, often sharpened by colour plumage.

Thus the characters, however intricate their twists and turns, become threads in a tapestry which evokes Von Sternberg. So does the stress on insolence and correctness, on honour and self-abasement; and the confrontation of a magnificent *femme fatale* with several mere males. Certainly, Renoir's key is that of overflowing generosity, where Von Sternberg's is that of prickly, retreating pride. And this difference affects the attitude to actors. Renoir's heroines are unintentionally destructive, by a responsiveness

to life which slips into promiscuity, Sternberg's are unconcernedly destructive and compound their infatuation with a callous air. Yet there are, after all, parallels, and contrasts, between *La Chienne* and *The Blue Angel*, as there are between *The Golden Coach* and *The Scarlet Empress*. And isn't *Blonde Venus* a relative of *Nana* and *Boudu*?

The film's structure is an unstable equilibrium, between purpose and impulse, state and enterprise, nomadic artist and hierarchic aristocrat, reality and unreality. The result is an interchange of antitheses, a—not always discourteous—exchange of positions and orientations, in brief, a dance. Precisely because Renoir's is an art of balance, of reciprocation and exchange, it evokes films whose affinities only become evident through it. From the men's viewpoint it's a vamp story. From the women's viewpoint it's a tragedy about men's subtle inadequacy. Yet precisely because it's both of these things, it's neither. In one sense it recalls Prévert's *Les Enfants du Paradis*, in another George Cukor's *Heller with a Gun (Heller in Pink Tights)*. The game of *films imaginaires* retains its fascination. Let us enjoy Renoir's Technicolor version of *Les Enfants du Paradis*, and his *Heller with a Gun*, with La Magnani for La Loren, and a more complex view of the Indians. . . .

In *Nana*, Renoir's earlier version of the story of the actress and her suitors, Catherine Hessling's personal style embodied (that's the word) the intrication of impulse and art(ifice). And this keys my acquiescence, from another angle, with Pauline Kael's answer to the question whether *The Golden Coach* contains Anna Magnani "or is exploded by her. But as this puzzle is parallel with the theme, it adds another layer to the ironic comedy. . . . Magnani with her deep sense of the ridiculous in herself and others, Magnani with her roots in the earth so strong that she can pull them out, shake them in the face of pretension and convention, and sink them down again stronger than ever . . . is the miraculous choice that gives this film its gusto . . . " Renoir: "Anna Magnani is the complete animal—an animal created completely for the stage and screen . . . Magnani gives so much of herself while acting that between scenes . . . she collapses and the mask falls. Between scenes she goes into a state of depression . . . " Camilla's tragedy is, as Cauliez notes, that she combines in herself devotion, energy, and aristocratic intelligence. Each of her suitors possesses one quality, without the others. A discrepancy of character essential to the theme unjustly eclipses the very real finesse of two admirably muted performances, Georges Higgins' Martinez and Duncan Lamont's Viceroy.

Several of the minor roles are conceived in a spirit of agreeable caricature which adapts them well for the ensemble while depriving them of much individual interest. What I take as part of a whole battery of disjunctions indispensible to their total context, might seem to some a surrender to facility, as prefigured by the grandmother in *Partie de Campagne* and the police-chief in *Les Bas-Fonds*. Renoir's respect for the rhythm of each person's movements is difficult to square smoothly with the search for an overall rhythm necessary to comedy. Here the story's obvious suspense ("Will the public like the show?") is fragmented out of existence by the film's visual complexities and by what may look like dramatic ornaments but are really ramifications of the theme's ironies (e.g. a running gag, with a very gently cruel touch, about a child's eagerness to somersault onstage). *The Golden Coach* was found by all but Renoir's most fervent admirers to be distinctly puzzling. If critical impatience with Renoir's film was mitigated by a general affection and respect for the director of *La Grande Illusion* and *The River*, that of even the educated public, which had yet to accept directors as superstars, was not. The fortunes of the English version were further depressed by cuts imposed as a result of the poor reception accorded the initial dubbed version.

Jules César

The commercial infortunes of *The Golden Coach* again laid on Renoir a certain pressure to re-establish himself as a commercially viable director. Renoir began writing a stage-play, *Orvet*, work on which was interrupted, first by preparatory work on *French CanCan* and then by his first venture into theatrical production, in circumstances and a setting akin to the stage-reality paradoxes of *The Golden Coach*.

Now he agreed to produce a translation of Shakespeare's *Julius Caesar* in the Roman arena at Arles, as part of the town's 1954 Festival. The cast was headed by Henri Vidal as Caesar, Paul Meurisse as Brutus, Yves Robert as Cassius, Loleh Bellon as Portia, Jean-Pierre Aumont as Marc Antony and Jean Parédès as Casca.

Pre-rehearsals were held in Paris. Otherwise, the play could never have been rehearsed in sequence, since Renoir had plans, in the event only half-realised, for using groups of spectators to double as the crowd. The one dress rehearsal was disrupted by a corrida, while "for the citizens of Arles, the performance of *Jules César* was not primarily a theatrical event, but a regional fête." (André Bazin). Thus art, again, merged with "sport". The piece was played on 10 July 1954 before eight or ten thousand corrida enthusiasts. Initially "guffawing and boisterous, they responded more fully to local faces among the actors than to the characters and the whole atmosphere must have resembled that of a Peruvian audience before the *commedia dell'arte*." But, continues Bazin, "At Casca's first monologue, admirably nuanced by Parédès, the tone of the applause changed . . . I could locate, to the nearest second, the crystallisation of this meridional crowd into an Elizabethan public." As floodlights replaced the final curtain, Renoir mistook the crowd's call for "Re-noir" as demands for "le noir!" and tried to dim the lights before being persuaded to take his bow. But "he eventually appeared on the proscenium, enormous and more gammy-legged than ever, plunging towards the microphone in acknowledgements almost burlesque with emotion, and I thought of Octave embarrassed by his bearskin in the Grand Salon of the castle in *La Règle du Jeu*."

Orvet

The shooting of *French CanCan* was completed in December 1954, but the film was not premiered until May 1955, so that the play *Orvet* is chronologically his next piece, having its first night at the Théâtre de le Renaissance on 12 March 1955.

In 1924, *La Fille de l'Eau* had involved the son of an automobilist, played by Pierre Champagne, and a poacher. After the subsequent automobile accident, when chance, sadly, imitated art, art returned the compliment: poachers feature in *Toni*, in *La Marseillaise*, in *La Bête Humaine*, in *La Règle du Jeu*. When Renoir first saw 13-year-old Leslie Caron in London's Victoria Station he had been struck by her resemblance to the fourteen-year-old daughter of one of of the poachers who found him in the wreck and whose friend he had subsequently become. When Renoir found Leslie Caron again in Hollywood memories were revived once more. *Les Braconniers* had featured a secondary character called Orvet, but now she was to be the play's heroine.

The substitution of personalities, the intersections of art and life (the former so often prophetic rather than reflective) are the play's theme. "Once the play was written, I tried to make a film of it. . . . Whichever way I turned it, I could do nothing with it; it has a theatrical convention as basis." Even so other alterations followed: "in the last version but one, the characters were real, and the hero was not an author . . . I also modified my piece because I absolutely had to have Paul Meurisse" (whom Renoir had met on *Jules César*) "and my first character had been much older. It was really the story of a very old man and a young girl." The scene where Orvet dances in shoes was invented on the last day of rehearsals. During the run's first week, the text "changed every night, for the greater convenience of the actors"—the published version being the final one.

Act One: Hoping to drown an unhappy love affair in creative activity, a writer named Georges returns to his country villa. The promise of imaginative toil blinds him to the proffered consolations of his housekeeper, Madam

Camus. A robust young widow, she too is in search of heart's ease after the elopement of her virile but fickle gigolo.

Georges plans a play based on Hans Christian Andersen's story *The Little Mermaid*. Its heroine falls in love with a young Prince, follows him to land, and endures an agonising "transplant" of legs for tail. When he loses interest in her, she pines away; her sea friends press a knife into her hand, saying that only his death will save her life.

Georges finds his mermaid, when Orvet, daughter of a local poacher, Coutant, ventures into his room to sell him freshly gathered mushrooms. Coutant tries to snatch from her the watch she has stolen from a writer, Oliver. Oliver cannot bear to denounce her, while Orvet for her part is fascinated by his telephone and his typewriter. To thank him for his silence she offers first to cook him a pheasant, and then to sleep with him. Oliver is taken aback, not to say shocked, but she reassures him; he has a special privilege, being the first man to have kissed her on her mouth.

Act Two: Georges is in love with Orvet and perturbed by Olivier's success. Their creator becomes a paternal, ironic and increasingly jealous witness of their happiness. Meanly, he concocts two new characters—a manservant called William, an old maid named Clotilde. He hopes their imposing concern for convention will dissuade Orvet from following Olivier to Paris. But William's previous masters were titled rascals, so he's indulgent rather than moralistic, and Clotilde falls for Coutant. Thus both Georges' would-be puppets turn against their master. In a desperate *coup de théâtre*, he summons forth Orvet's ragged forest friends to plead with her to stay. Among them, her resurrected dead sister Berthe begs for another chance of life. But Orvet hesitates just long enough between guilt and selfishness for Berthe to relive her death; and Orvet is free to leave with Olivier.

Act Three: Clotilde's passions have wearied even Coutant. Self-protectively opening the newspaper, he reads of Orvet's triumphs in fashionable society. But Orvet herself returns disillusioned. Olivier has tired of her and now loves a woman of his own class. She begs Georges to restore Olivier to her but he cannot. His story is now quite out of his control. He can only urge Olivier to make Orvet happy, or at least to spare her the truth of his indifference to her. Orvet is only narrowly saved from suicide. Olivier and Georges each beg her to kill him, seeing in their own deaths her only chance of happiness. Georges will confer upon them "the most beautiful present an apprentice-creator can give his creatures: I will choose the moment, when you believe in the illusion of happiness, to restore you to nothingness . . . "
He would be grateful now for the consolations of the good Madame Camus, but too late. Instead, the real Orvet returns.

The play's themes recall Pirandello (an author in search of his characters . . .) and Giraudoux (with its transcribed myth, its wistfulness, its image of a feminine spontaneity like innocence). It is a conventionally constructed, charming, theatrical evening out; yet it involves such effects as the author-within-the-play inventing an author-in-the-third-degree, sitting

amongst the audience and calling down the curtain. Its paradoxes of inex-
istence evoke the theatre of the absurd; yet it affirms, despite all these lacunae,
the possibilities of some consolatory meaning. Renoir's direct exposition of
his themes contrasts with the enigmatic forms favoured by his younger contemporaries.

Perhaps, in the end, it is the equivalent of *La Fille de l'Eau,* an
"apprentice-creation", more sophisticated than it seems, in a new medium by
a creator already established in another. It certainly throws a new emphasis
on certain themes and connections glimpsed throughout his films, but sub-
sidiary within them. A mermaid is *une fille de l'eau* and Renoir equates
Orvet's forest with a submarine world (the mushrooms she collects are
likened to coral). The references to snakes culminate in her name (literally
slow-worm or blind-worm), perhaps best translated by grass snake (harmless
and vulnerable). The meaning is made explicit: "Tu n'as pas volé ton
nom! Un vrai petit serpent! Ça se glisse partout ou il ne faut pas!" The
old woman who sees Orvet's "other" future, if she stays in the forest, is
called Ma Viper. A mermaid's tail recalls a snake, and the transition from
barefoot urchin to elegantly shod mondaine is likened to a snake's sloughing
off its old scales. Bogey lures a cobra with milk, Sam Tucker's grandmother
is lured among the snakes by the prospect of delicious grapes. The same
complex of ideas recurs as the snake-girl gathers mushrooms with which
Georges promptly thinks of poisoning everyone, himself included. Snake
and mushroom are perhaps Renoir's symbol for something more often
expressed in his earlier films by the action of the plot; a quietly insidious
tragedy which none of the characters desires, yet which in the nature of things
quietly insinuates itself and strikes, abruptly and gratuitously. Against a
caprice without malevolence, no defense is possible. In terms of the plot of
La Règle du Jeu, Octave is almost a snake—wise, persuasive and treacherous. Visually, too, he is stripped of his skin by a vamp in a situation which is
a coil-within-coil of confusions. The extremely paradoxical equation of
lumbering bear, limping man and snake, is rendered less improbable by the
extraordinary transformations, based on movement, as Catherine's rival
lovers pursue her through the nightmare of *La Fille de l'Eau*—and Orvet, we
remember, exchanges her scaly tail for legs. If we accept, as we must, these
choreographic "puns" and play with names and metaphors, we may postulate
another connection. Ma Viper describes her friends as "nous de la cloche";
cloche suggests *clochard* (beggar, i.e. Karen), *cloche-pied* (lame, i.e.
Renoir, Cabuche), and *cloche* (cracked, feeble-minded, i.e. Boudu).

As in *Le Carosse d'Or,* art and life take it in turns to swallow one another.
The obvious antagonism of nature and machines, of innocence and literacy,
is deftly avoided by Orvet's immediate pleasure in telephone and typewriter,
and by a brief preoccupation, borrowed from *La Chienne,* with water-heaters.
Madame Camus is as blessedly "transparent as rain-water". Like Sam
Tucker, Orvet hunts a pike. She calls it Philippe—after Philippe-le-Pied-Bot,
i.e. Club-Footed Philippe—another limping man; perhaps Olivier is Octave,

as Georges is Jean. Georges tells Oliver: "You are writing a book . . .
so you are seduced . . . provisionally seduced; but it'll pass . . . "
Like Valentine, Orvet's amiability is associated with a prostitution for
gratitude, a sort of "hospitality prostitution". Georges suggests the theo-
logical impossibility of a Christian God in Renoir's world. But soon he is
trapped by his own play. He cannot but confer autonomy on his creations, be
reduced to the role of a helpless spectator, to self-abnegation, to a self-
sacrifice which is a painless abolition. The devout may take it as an allegory of
modern theology's discovery, one hundred years after Nietzsche, of the death
of God.

In-jokes abound. About exterior realism: "A mermaid is a sort of fish.
You should go off and write your play by the seaside!" While the real author
(Georges) plans a fiction to console himself for real disappointments, his
fictitious hero, Olivier, plans a documentary on forest life. Before she took to
begging, Ma Viper was a cinema usherette (French usherettes being notorious
for insisting on tips while groping spectators fumble in the dark). The guests
at a high society reception include not only a certain Baron Braunberger
(another Jewish nouveau-riche aristocrat!) but "the film director Jacques
Becker". A garden party given by the Prévert brothers is announced in the
(rightwing) *Figaro*. In *Orvet* we see also the first appearance of a theme which
is new and surprising, but which is to reappear: that of body versus mind,
and of the mind's happily unavailing efforts to become independent of the
other. Georges, ignoring Madame Camus, lingers too long in his cerebral
no-man's-land. Ma Viper asserts that so long as Orvet goes barefoot,
ignoring physical discomfort, she will be a "spiritualist". But as a woman of
the world whose mind is constantly conscious of her beauty and comfort,
she will become a "materialist".

When Georges observes that "a comedy is an uncompleted drama" he is
in effect defining the play's chosen limits—even if his definition exists only
to blur itself. The aesthetic interplay is criss-crossed, rather than extended,
by the triangle Orvet-Olivier-Georges and by the somewhat archaic theme
of pure love negotiating the hazards of sophistication. Orvet's dialogue strays
into the limpid, resilient simplicity which, after Giraudoux and Anouilh,
can seem a little too familiar. Thus the play reads as a fascinating lightweight,
yet one which in performance might take on a certain gravity.

At the time, the play was championed principally by men of the cinema,
notably Bazin and Rossellini. The complete moral victory which *Orvet* allows
to life at the expense of art gives an early clue to Renoir's subsequent
direction. Others will see the first assertion of an aesthetic philosophy which
reaches its fuller flowering in *Le Déjeuner Sur L'Herbe*. My personal
predilection would be to interpret the play as a description of art as an important prologue to a conversion—a kind of *reculer pour mieux sauter*—whose
pessimistic aspects should not be glorified out of existence (as by art
fetishists they regularly are), while wishing that the play had had as cruel
an end as that which *La Petite Marchande d'Allumettes* eventually acquired.

French Cancan

Originally destined for direction by Yves Allégret, the subject, or rather title, which was all the producer insisted on, was offered to Renoir. "It corresponded to a great desire I had to make a film in a very French spirit, which would allow an easy and convenient contact . . . between myself and the French public. . . . It was simply a question of providing a certain type of spectacle and keeping the title. Since 1924 I have been haunted by the idea of making a cinematographic opera. I had two or three songs to write in *French CanCan*. It pleased me enormously, it was a little step towards this old dream . . . (which) will probably never be fulfilled." Pierre Kast, then *Cahiers* critic and Renoir's assistant, recalls the pains taken by Renoir to construct a scenario "without suspense," to "speak" his dialogue rather than write it, to visualise "a film-tapestry where around the feet of the central characters, rabbits and monkeys would disport themselves and sentimental little flowers would grow, as indispensible to the film as the intrigue itself . . . ", to hit on the "good humor, insolent or light, violent or tender, with which Renoir wished to imbue it."

Shooting began at the Francoeur Studios, Saint-Maurice on October 4th 1954 and concluded on 20 December. The film was premièred in May 1955, shorn of a few scenes, notably one of Van Gogh, Pissarro and Degas at a café table. The English 35mm release lacks several scenes which later appeared, without subtitles, in 16mm versions. One concerns the financial intrigues behind show business, another is a song by Philippe Clay which depends on a staccato verbal delivery.

Paris in the 1880s. At his small but fashionable cabaret, *Le Paravent Chinois*, impressario Danglard (Jean Gabin) employs such acts as a whistling clown and a belly dancer, La Belle Abbesse (Maria Felix). In the course of a visit to the nearby village of Montmartre, Danglard and friends drop in at *La Reine Blanche* and join in the *chahut* with the artisans and riffraff. Its proprietor persuades Danglard that fashionable people are beginning to show an interest in low life and that *La Reine Blanche* could be quite an investment. Danglard flirts with a little laundress, Nini (Françoise Arnoul), to the fury both of her boyfriend Paolo, a baker's assistant, and La Belle Abbesse. The latter's reaction provokes the hopes of an officer admirer and the resigned cynicism of her protector, Baron Walter. He draws the line at her public predilection for Danglard, who thus finds himself with a leading lady but no more than a little loose change to offer his creditors. Nonetheless the bailiff's man (Philippe Clay) avows his ambitions of going on the stage as a contortionist, and joins the artists. Eventually La Belle Abbesse and Walter are reconciled. In return for the former's public discretion, Walter will build a lavish new music hall, the *Moulin-Rouge,* on the site of *La Reine Blanche.* He even secures a cabinet minister to lay its foundation stone, although the ceremony is ruined when La Belle Abbesse, seeing Nini by Danglard's side, attacks her. Paolo pushes Danglard down a hole and severely injures him. This time Danglard alienates both Walter and La Belle Abbesse, until he accepts the latter's terms. Gradually, in rehearsals, the chahut begins to evolve into the cancan. A Balkan prince, Alexandre (Giànni Esposito), falls in love with Nini and acts as their angel, until La Belle Abbesse reveals that Danglard has been Nini's lover all along. Recovering in hospital, the prince asks her only to give him some "false memories" of happiness, and Nini has to renounce both Paolo and the prince for the dance, even though the uncertainties of showbusiness may condemn her to finish, like the old rag-picker Prunelle, in the gutter. On the opening night, she realises that Danglard has forsaken her for his new discovery, Ester Georges, a maid-servant whom he presents as a streetsinger. She refuses to go on, although implored by all, including La Belle Abbesse, until the last moment. Danglard, alone behind the scenes, hears the audience's roars of approval as the cancan reaches its climax, and ventures forth among the spectators, where another girl catches his eye.

The film's Paris is essentially nostalgic, and like most nostalgias is based on historical realities. The cancan was a development from the working class *chahut* (cf. Seurat's painting of that name), itself a development out of the *polka-piquée,* popular from around 1845, in which the dancers kicked their legs as high as they could and the ladies showed not frilly lace, which they couldn't afford, but their best cottons. Around 1850 the *polka-piquée* was combined with the quadrille. It is the latter, quieter movement which Danglard sees at *La Reine Blanche,* the faster passages being suggested only, presumably to avoid anticipating the film's climax. The *Moulin Rouge* was opened on the site of *La Reine Blanche* in 1889 (as late as 1902 Montmartre could boast four entertainment venues housed in or inspired by old mills). At the *Moulin Rouge,* dancers in their street clothes mingled with spectators and until the dance began it was difficult to tell who was which. Nini's lessons at Madame Guibole's school (*guibole* being slang for "stump") may have been suggested by a well known Nini of the epoque, Nini-Patte-En-l'Air, who ran a dancing school, allowing wealthy men about town to watch rehearsals, and to encourage her girls "with valuable suggestions".

As in *The Golden Coach*, art, disrupting life, substitutes itself for it, and makes demands on its privileged acolytes as tyrannical as those of religion. But if in *Orvet* the emphasis falls on art as *merely* part of life's processes, in *French CanCan* art is neither a means of, nor a substitute for, life, but its apotheosis. Danglard is Camilla's masculine counterpart. He has three mistresses, but is wed to the music hall. Camilla has a feminine counterpoint in Nini, who too has three lovers. Something of Camilla's imperiousness appears in La Belle Abbesse, who likewise has three lovers. They and their lovers must accept jealousy as best they can, for the sake of a dance which

is a privileged disruption of life. As the *commedia dell'arte* shatters the social hierarchies, the dance disturbs what Danglard describes as the bourgeois domestic ideal, with its possessive view of relationships, as distinct from his own participative life-style. Danglard's aristocracy is a personal one: "T'es un prince", says old Prunelle, at a courteously spendthrift gesture.

The whistling clown articulates no words at all, but has, nonetheless, *"le coeur d'un poète, le gosier d'un merle"*. His is the sincerity and nervousness of the true artist. Danglard reassures him that every spectator will give him rapt attention, and, while he performs, strolls among the audience, chatting affably to all. As the dance nears its climax, Danglard sits behind the stage, speculatively lifts his middle-aged leg and lowers it at a glance from a passing cleaning-woman. As his creation welds artists and spectators into an illusory, Dionysian unity, he remains sedentary, excluded, yet fulfilled. Then he mingles with the spectators, delighting, both paternally and egoistically, in their delight. He spies a pretty girl and begins wondering what he might make of her. A man protests: "Monsieur, vous bloquez ma vue" (ungratefully, no doubt, but also a nice comment on *auteur theory,* on the artist's role as medium rather than monument).

In each case Danglard does little more than appreciate a talent, train it and frame it. He first heard the clown whistling on top of his ladder while working. His cancan is based on *le chahut.* His so-called "flower of the paving stones" was spotted singing while dusting a picture in a neat bourgeois interior.

For years Renoir has studiously referred to his art as "mon métier", i.e. his craft. But if the unfine arts of giving coarse pleasure also involve a creative mystique it is not only because showbusiness is discipline but because "mere" pleasure has a radical human meaning. The prestige art gives with one hand it takes away with the other. "Chez les artistes il n'y pas de drames; il n'y a que des scandales. . . . "

If the dance is a mystique it's simply because everything worth doing needs to override other human claims. Quite possible Paolo's Jeremiads are correct: the public's favour will prove treacherous, and Nini be left in the gutter, like Prunelle. Equally, of course, the dance can prove an escape from the lifetime of drudgery in the laundry (at the thought of which Nini's friend, failing her audition, bursts into tears). The essence of the dance is that it is a gamble, a self-abandonment, like that of *la fille de l'eau* to the elements. One goes *au fil de l'eau,* with the stream. Danglard, too, feels the bourgeois temptation, though at the moment of truth he sells the cabaret which, like a canny peasant, he was saving for his old age. The artist(e)s are aristocrats, in poverty as in success.

The religious metaphor in *Le Carosse d'Or* yields to the military one in *French CanCan*. Danglard describes Nini as *"un bon petit soldat";* the Prince evokes *"la campagne du Moulin Rouge"*. Both understand *la règle du jeu,* with all its bracing irony and self-disregard. The Prince and Paolo are both prisoners of their status and make themselves unhappy. The former begins by envying those who have worries—and Nini so gratifies him that he puts a gun to his head. Yet the clumsiness which betrays the masochism of privilege also saves him from despair—for such masochism is also a longing to be changed, that is, to survive. It is no more masochistic than its apparent opposites: Paolo's threats to kill Danglard very nearly come true. Probably he hasn't seen the hole into which he pushes Danglard, but like the prince, he is accident-prone. Often in fiction, the accident is the expression of either fate, or a character's unconscious intentions, or the author's (and audience's) ideas of the morally significant consequences of certain attitudes. The prince isn't quite suicidal and Paolo isn't quite a killer, and their beliefs are what Sartre, more Puritan than Renoir, could stigmatise as "bad faith", but without which human nature as we know it can hardly be conceived. Baron Walter as a financier is accustomed to gamble: though money is his game, his soul is not an altogether bourgeois one. Yet he attempts to appropriate La Belle Abbesse by money. He fails but accepts, like Danglard, the rules of the game. He will finance Danglard (no great altruism, profit is his motive); his mistress, in return, will manage her infidelities to him discreetly (vanity is more than reality). In *The Golden Coach*, the victory is subject to his council. Here, Danglard, "le prince", is subject to his backers who are half-aristocratic, half-bourgeois.

For Danglard the Moulin Rouge is a splendid machine to be put at the disposal of absolutely anyone—lowlife for high society, highlife for small purses—in other words, it's a golden coach. Walter corrects him. It offers only "the *illusion* of high life—I believe in the social value of illusions . . . ", i.e., the entertainment industry is the opium of the people. The interaction of Danglard's and Walter's world is neatly expressed in an apparently unconsidered scene where, a few seconds before curtain up, Danglard asks his three financiers to help him lay a red carpet properly. One stammers that copper's crashing in New York, and panics. Walter doesn't: "We'll make more from the Moulin Rouge than Danglard will . . . "

If love is really a courtly dance, a quadrille, a criss-cross and exchange of soft smiles and hard slaps, political alliances are equally shifty. At his opening Danglard welcomes sailors from the Russian cruiser *Prince Orloff,* moored off Brest, in honour of the Franco-Russian alliance. The first part of the show is built around the Russian bear and Catherine the Great. By 1955 France, Cold War notwithstanding, had begun to resume her traditionally amiable relationship with Russia—whether Tsarist or Communist. The Franco-Russian alliance was actually signed in 1894 and the Russian fleet paid a visit to France in 1892, so Renoir has gone to the trouble of moving these events a few years in time to accommodate them within his story. Given the dissensions evoked in *Le Crime de Monsieur Lange,* the Tricolors lining the walls of the *Moulin Rouge* evoke a vanished unity: the patriotic joy of *la belle époque.* From the later 1870s until 1914 the French were confident and ready for a return match with Prussia. In 1913 Renoir became a cavalry officer; and if he ridicules the officer here, the Tricolors are paraded with a wistful, fond, irony.

Nationality is somewhat whimsical. At a cabaret called *The Chinese Screen,* La Belle Abbesse performs an Egyptian belly dance, talks about her Spanish father, subsequently reveals that she was born in Montmartre, and finally appears as Empress of Russia. Just as Nini dispenses to her prince his false souvenirs, Renoir gives us some. She takes him around the cabarets and the stars of the 1880s are impersonated by those of the 1950s. e.g. Yvette Guilbert by Edith Piaf. Given Piaf's celebrity the pretence could hardly be more obvious, and is underlined by placing a much-loved "city sparrow", ex-prostitute and drug-addict, before a backcloth representing a romantic lake and Greek temple. Renoir shows none of these numbers in full, fading out a moment or two after we have settled down to it, thus giving the sequences the quality of memory, fragmentary and elusive. Ester George sings to the Moulin Rouge spectators lyrics whose sexual and social persona demands that Danglard sings them to her. Hidden on stage he listens to her in the auditorium. Their half-real, half-unreal emotion prevails in our attention over the altogether real feelings of Nini, as she peeps at peeping Danglard. The words celebrate a literary theme of the period, the beautiful febrility of a starved or tubercular girl. We may recall also the illnesses of

la fille de l'eau, of Nana, of Madame Bovary, and Berthe in *Orvet* complaining to the author about her death by peritonitis. Cauliez describes the song as "a sort of abcess of fixation" and adds "the author hopes that, in time to come, it will be mistaken for a song of the period . . . " So beautifully sad a past is an illusion, as showbusiness is an illusion, and if such illusions haunt us, it is because they express inalienable spiritual realities. *French CanCan* comes near being a Symbolist film. Only in art can lie cut lie and life look like itself. If our link between impressionist paintings and Symbolism seems strange, it is worth remembering that Verlaine was sometimes called an impressionist too.

The same effect determines the almost painfully abrupt cut from the height of the dance to the last shot of the dark street outside. The bright beautiful colour schemes, the pristine freshness of the passers-by, are all nostalgic rather than documentary. As in *The River* and, in their very different idioms, Sternberg's *The Saga of Anatahan* and Dreyer's *Gertrud,* the film's images are those of a past reality, selective and heightened, as subjectively real, that is, as superreal, as moments polished by memory. Up to a point, the evocations of impressionist paintings may gently remind us of the realities behind art (for moving photography is, by convention, more "real" than painting). But these paintings are in no way undermined or "explained". The effect is rather of a "double medium", of art as memory as life, neither discredited by reality nor impersonating it, but existing in symbiosis with it.

By Renoir's usual standards, the acting is schematic, linear, even superficial. The story passes lightly over its considerable possibilities of being harrowing, cynical or cruel. Thus La Belle Abbesse brings Walter to his rival's hotel bedroom to declare his surrender of, at once his mistress, his pride and his purse, with the deliciously perverse declaration, "Here's a repentant sinner who has come to make his excuses." Thirty years earlier, Nana might have treated Muffat thus, to harrowing effect. Since *le style c'est l'homme*, Walter's style is as significant as his real feelings—it is part of his choice, of his freedom, of his spiritual resilience. Danglard, too, achieves an admirably ironic gesture of surrender to the same *femme fatale*, La Belle Abbesse. It's his ability to borrow from one friend to give to another even when both know he's broke that draws forth from Prunelle the gently envious "T'es un prince", but the words are, for us, a tribute to the ruling spirit which is the real secret of his "aristocracy". Its *règle du jeu* is an amoral generosity (as opposed to prudence or meanness), and is suicidal, just as resilience without sensitivity (Paolo) is philistine, and no less self-defeating. Danglard breaks hearts galore, Nini's tenderness is almost callous, while La Belle Abbesse is rightly described by Danglard as *la reine des garces*, yet even smashing the show and goading Alexandre to attempted suicide is forgiven in the end. Selfishness, even a search for sweet revenge, may be a sin but it is an inalienable one, and it is the ability to forgive real wrongs which characterises Renoir's magnanimous man. The real disqualification is an absence of generosity, an inability to be appropriately insincere, to lose the step of the dance; and the dance is beautiful just because feelings are involved. The moral person is not the person who takes such care not to hurt others that he crimps his own life-force, but the person whose warmth helps others lift themselves over their hesitations and fears. Film criticism, frequently puritan in background, is apt to underestimate the ordinary man's sense of personal style as "content", not only in actors but in people, and in deed as well as gesture. The issue underlines the discussion between the two seducers in *Partie de Campagne*. It exists, above all, in those moments where, if the dance is to continue, a good grace must prevail over resentment in defeat; more than an index of generosity is provided by just such grace, and that is one reason why *French CanCan* is a film without suspense. Whether or not the show goes on is quite secondary to our observation of life style, particularly in defeat.

Such suavity is not necessarily inimical to dramatic intensity, as Ophuls proves. But Renoir wishes to make it so. The film's nostalgic intricacy and sensuousness require the distillation of drama to anecdote, and anecdote to the essential phrase or gesture. Walter's "I adore your violence, but not in public", his mistress's towering with swelling breasts and fine rage over the little bailiff—are all we need to "see" scenes which Renoir omits.

In the absence of a fully unfolded intensity, this drastically discontinuous narrative is authenticated by a delicacy of acting thrown into relief by the detail's bright superficiality. The balance is a fine one. Renoir found it with the simpler plot and visuals of *The River,* but confused many spectators in the course of *Le Carosse d'Or.* When Danglard proposes a revival of the *chahut* to the old dancing mistress, the plump stubby woman elbows a fresh strapping young girl aside, displaces a chair, pulls up her skirts, struts spiritedly, highkicks, and proudly subsides into the splits position before her body wilts. The gesture occupies a few seconds of screen time, and part only of the screen. Yet the older dancer's response to a rhythm loved in her youth, her sudden delighted impulse to fling aside the asperity of years, of which her voice has given ample evidence, are all intensely communicated.

Just as dashingly, Renoir orchestrates the movements of successive candi- tates at the audition. As the girls line up for the first rehearsal, one might ex- pect as clear a view of their movements as possible. Instead Renoir obscures much of the gay moving mass by Danglard's static back, and for good reason. So long as the exhilarations of achievement suddenly exploding over aching fatigue is sufficiently vivid, the contrast with the static, the judicial, can only sharpen it. At the same time, we are gently reminded of the essential ambivalence of any collaboration. In every scene, and in very nearly every shot, just some such dialectic is established, in a way to which Eisenstein's theory of montage, in its mature form, has classical application. From the encounter of antithetical elements, a third element is generated which is quite different from the sum of their parts.

The complexity is possible only because Renoir's eye for the eloquence of gesture is as sure as it is. Nini's first experience of love with Paolo is communicated in virtually one shot: they lie among the warm bread, after- wards. She cradles his grateful, slightly bewildered face, her body still softened by love, her mind's eye already focusing on Danglard. Retrospec- tion, anticipation, the perfidious fluidity of feeling—the dramatic content of the shot can be as radically cynical as the sensuousness of loaves, bodies, kind faces can be consoling. But this might be a scene from *La Ronde,* and the structure of contradiction hung on this one, apparently simple, senti- mental shot, would be nullified without the eloquence of face, of posture, and of atmosphere.

Although the film depends on movement, the tendency to reduce each scene to one moment takes us towards a syntax like that of impressionist painting, which must also polarise movement and change around one moment in time. The scenes on La Butte may evoke Utrillo, the gently animalesque postures of the aching dancers recall Degas, while La Belle Abbesse receives her military lover in a room decorated à la Delacroix in the style of a Moorish odalisque. Leprohon relates the façade of *La Reine Blanche* to the style of Pissarro, and the woman leaning against a post within to Manet (how delight- ful to come across a Manet "behind the scenes" of a Pissarro). Bazin stresses Ester George's duster whose "bright yellow patch is waved for a second before disappearing. Clearly, this essentially pictorial shot has been conceived and composed around the *momentary* apparition of this yellow patch whose harmony supposes a before and an after. But there's no doubt that this event is neither dramatic nor anecdotal; its appearance remains purely pictorial, it's the red area of Corot, but in eclipse!" "Renoir . . . continues painting, he does not imitate it" (Leprohon). Certain *hommages* are Symbolist in their nostalgia, impressionist in their palate, in the invigorating shock of colours. Renoir could too easily have imitated, say, Degas's *La Répétition*. All the elements are there; the clusters of girls dancing or resting, the expanse of pink-brown floorboard, even the "slice of life" photographic casualness. But the cinematic equivalent of its spatial composition is the sequence of contrasts, in time, movement and space. The long scene outside Nini's dressing room is something of a *morceau de bravoure*, what with its "crossroad" of corridors, to the complexity of whose asymmetry is added a staircase in left foreground (introducing a fifth, vertical "road"), various invisible (sideways on) doors from which startled heads may pop out, while a foregound space-within-a-space is later marked out by the mass of dancers flanking Danglard. As he harangues Nini, the familiarity of his argument allows our eyes to stray over their silent, reproachful faces. Directly behind Nini's mother, pale and plain in street cothes, towers the most sumptuous creature of all, La Belle Abbesse in her gold satins.

A similarly sophisticated sense of the diversification and development of colour and space governs the *Moulin Rouge* première. The red curtain lifts to show another plane behind it, parallel to it but paler (grey), and consisting of men dressed as cossacks, immobile like toy soldiers in their boxes but neatly stacked on two vertical levels. Within this shallow depth, action (Casimir's song about *La Belle Catherine*) is lateral (from side to side of the screen). Gently Renoir introduces the visual modulation, a "reverse angle" combined with an increasingly elaborate twist. This develops through the back-to-front itinerary of Ester George and the strong diagonality (i.e. transition between laterality and depth) in the shot of Nini and Danglard peeping at her from each end of the curtain. Eventually, the spatial areas are merged. First, members of the audience are urged to sit on the stage. Finally the cancan girls burst through postures, shin down ropes, storm into the very centre of the audience, and form a square, into which spectators finally run, and break open.

Renoir regularly follows a long shot whose main lines are "flat" (180°) to the camera, with a close-up set at a light diagonal—creating a gentle perspective agitation, ripples to criss-cross the other visual elements.

The careful orchestration of space is matched by that of colour. Bidding farewell to her Prince, Nini pauses, her hat with its pink roses by the bare laths in a peeling wall. The contrast is elegiac—beauty/decay, wealth/

poverty. Claude Beylie takes up Bazin's remarks about the yellow duster: "This same yellow (nuanced to cream or saffron, and consequently rather different from the golden yellows of the final bouquet) reappears . . . at two other moments . . . with the same radiant suddenness. It's the colour of La Belle Abbesse's gloves, discovered by Prunelle. . . . And it's also, at the beginning of the film, the hue of the carriage entrance before which Danglard stops while watching Nini skip on La Butte. If I'm not mistaken, these three yellows, conceived not only in terms of their momentary sparkle in each sequence, also have a very special significance; they are the lucky colour of the three women . . . of whom Danglard has made, or will make, stars (the least pure of the three belongs to the waning star)".

Paul Dehn admirably evokes the film's colour-energy. "Jean Renoir swallowdives from the historical springboard of the Moulin Rouge's opening in 1889 into a fairytale Paris. . . . the dive throws off a fountain of painterly damson-coloured corsets, herbaceous hats, milkblue skies, cloaks of goldest lamé, and vermilion passion couches. . . . the lacy skirts of the dancers surge towards us as prettily as the surf on a windy Edwardian day at Deauville." Yet the riotous colour carefully codes character. Thus Nini's pastel clothes go with the more sullen, worldly, "hardheaded" red of her hair. The yellow tuckover of blanket in the Prince's hospital bed expresses perfectly his physical, perhaps his moral, weakness.

Composition is based on colour rather than line. Schematically, Renoir divides the screen into two basic areas, one of each colour, e.g. green and pink, ensuring that the boundary between them is not over-simple, and puts before those backgrounds clashing variations of each of the two basic colours. Thus, a pink background might call forth brilliant splashes of two different reds. In addition a spot or splash of a third colour adds a lively dissonance, a casual air.

Many shots take this basic scheme further. A shot of Danglard and a servant talking to the bailiff's men has the latter in black before rich red plush curtains. Danglard, dressed in pastel shades, stands against a cooler wall, while his servant sports a yellow waistcoat. Certain harmonies are cherished for their current antisentimentality, e.g. Nini, under a cherry tree in blossom, with white-pink blossoms on her hat.

Hardly has the whistling clown with his white mask, and flowing white cap disappeared behind the briefly closed red plush curtains, then out rushes Casimir in blue velvet. The flowing white hits not only the red plush, but also the long-limbed electric blue. The energetic extrovert replaces the sensitive introvert. The red curtain, too, regains its sullen mysterious fire as the mystic barrier which this dance will penetrate.

The cancan sequence contradicts all the textbook rules of its day. It should, so the old saws run, be handled in terms of quick, dazzling cuttings between bold startling close-ups of boots, garters, thighs, lace drawers, laughing faces, perhaps itself panning and tracking to join in the dance. If my

memory serves, such an approach, more restrained, works admirably in
Pabst's *L'Atlantide*. Renoir's approach is quite different. There are relatively
few close-ups, and they are (1) played off against long or "double-centre"
shots, and (2) used to conclude, to decelerate, the whole sequence before its
abrupt "curtain" (outside, night). Rather, he shows us the girls as a group,
so that between the pastel walls, with their Tricolors, and the girls in their
bright whirling dresses, there is a mass of male spectators in black evening
suits and white shirtfronts (diversified of course by buttonholes and the women
among them). But their black is the sinew of the sequence. Gradually the two
groups merge but never so completely that the climax can't be helped by a
line of black top hats fountaining up on waved arms over black lines. When
the camera cuts into details of the girls alone, it does so in such a way that we
see two or three girls asymetrically disposed. Schematically: one spins, with
lifted leg, one cartwheels, one does the splits. Helped by the movement, the
colours and rhythm take in their stride a further counterpoint: Danglard,
alone. So strong and exact is the transfer of energies from the rapid to the
almost motionless that, at each viewing, I found myself tensing my jaw a
second or two before Danglard does just that.

Visually the film fits R.H. Wilenski's distinction between romantic painting (built around radiations and gradations from one central point) and classified painting (characterised by an overall balance between contrasting elements). On the dramatic level also we are not so much split between, as
spread over, the network of tensions formed between three people with three
lovers, as well as our other friends and *alter egos*. Their close-ups fill the
screen in quick succession as the cancan ends: among them, Paolo (quietly
embraced by Nini's friend), Danglard's new recruit, Walter, Mme Guibole
and her placid white-haired husband, Oscar. As the curtain descends, a harsh
cut whisks us into a long shot of the façade, before which a drunk staggers
about in the street and, almost falling, takes, by visual pun, a bow. He is
out in the darkness with us, expelled from his own film, from *la belle époque*
of his own childhood; we think also of Bazin's impression of Renoir's bow in
the arena at Arles.

Other old friends are here, motifs so tactfully disguised as to come as
freshly as ever. As Ester Georges sings her street-song, a hurdy-gurdy
appears on the orchestra's balcony. Since Renoir appears in the guise of
Danglard, Oscar, an anonymous drunk and a bear, must we exclude dream-
garbled recollections of another dancer: la petite Catherine for La Grande
Catherine, and even Oscar's doll-faced wife, Madame Guibole? Sarcastically
Renoir kidnaps elements from two films set in much the same time and place:
Huston's *Moulin Rouge* and Becker's *Casque d'Or*. Huston's (or rather
Hollywood's) moralising about artistic promiscuity leading to tragic loneli-
ness, and his subplot about a loose-living dancer who ends up in the gutter,
are put firmly in their place, that is to say, in the mouth of Paolo, whose
every intervention in this film is mistimed and misplaced. If Paolo is the

spokesman for middle-class morality, he corresponds also to the honest artisan (Serge Reggiani) who is the hero of Becker's *Casque d'Or,* an almost equally pious tragedy, the parody of whose principal characters is continued through Paolo's acquaintances: a slack-mouthed, weedy, swaggering, thief, and a golden-haired but boring and dim-witted moll.

The scintillating phalanx of "bons petits soldats" lead their commando raid on the black, male, bourgeois order. Ravished, its victims hold out their hats to be sent flying by these highkicking centauresses, lie down side to side to be jumped over, behave with a joyous, drunken, clumsy, fraternal abandon. Renoir makes sense of the cancan and its social significance. The dancers unleash the insolence not only of proletarian energy, but of the aggressive female, and storm the 19th-century bourgeois male patriarchy like the light brigade of sexual suffragettes which they are. As they sport the sweet dynamism of thighs long smothered under petticoats and startle the exhilarated male in a massed scissors-splits which is, of course, a kinaesthetic equivalent of crutch photography, the suggestion is that the erstwhile weaker sex won't henceforth find the erstwhile lord of creation too hard a nut to crack. A river of feminine energy flows devastatingly, but not destructively, through society.

I find the film irresistible in its intellectual intricacy; visually so contagious that on several occasions a mild but significant "mescalinisation" of colour perceptions has continued for an hour or so after seeing the film; and emotionally moving, given its astringent sense of life as dance, and the real tenderness with which so cynical, or pessimistic, a point is made. If *French CanCan* is poignant, it may be because it catches a certain conjunction, a certain stage, in Renoir's withdrawl not only from contemporary realities, but from reality itself, into a philosophical and a theoretical world.

Premier Plan suggest that the always influencable Renoir was corrupted by the hero-worship of his young critical admirers. At any rate, essentially isolated intellectuals, living in theoretical worlds, are central in *Orvet,* in *Le Déjeuner Sur L'Herbe,* in *Le Testament du Dr. Cordelier.* Danglard's "Symbolist" world relates to theirs, but it also relates to the *retrospective* worlds of *Renoir Mon Père* and *Les Cahiers du Capitaine Georges.*

Eléna et Les Hommes
(Paris Does Strange Things)

The financial success of *French CanCan* ensured a smooth passage for Renoir's next project. "For years I have been dying to do something gay with Ingrid Bergman. I wanted to see her laugh and smile on the screen, to let the audience enjoy the kind of uncomplicated sensuality which is one of her characteristics." "I even went to America to discuss one possibility; it was then that Mel Ferrer expressed the desire to act with her." Meanwhile, Renoir had also "written an absolutely caricatural story about the adventures of General Boulanger. My God, the producers were scared—so I altered it and Jean Marais played no particular general." The two stories merged. As the project developed, the first aspect came to predominate. "The only reason for *Elena* is: Woman . . . represented by Ingrid Bergman. Around that I constructed a satire, I amused myself with political matters, affairs of generals. I tried to show the futility of human enterprises, including the enterprise which we call patriotism, and then to have fun with some ideas which have become the serious ideas of our time. . . . I attached myself so much to the feminine character that perhaps I rather neglected the other." At any rate, Renoir introduced the finished film as "a reaction against the sordid and degraded realism now in fashion."

The film was a Franco-Italian co-production, shot in Paris between 1st December 1955 and 17th March 1956. It was to be shot in two versions, French-speaking, with English-speaking actors in the secondary roles. In the event they proved unavailable, and the French actors' English was so unsatisfactory that Renoir found himself simplifying both the situations and the dialogue. Conversely, Ingrid Bergman's French was as yet scarcely adequate for the French version, especially since when she went home in the evenings Rossellini spoke to her in Italian. Such was the havoc wrought by language problems that Renoir described the shooting as "one long nightmare".

The story returns to the epoch of *French CanCan*. Elena (Ingrid Bergman), a Polish princess living in Paris, walks out on her lover, a somewhat self-important composer who, irritated by the cheerful noises of the 14th July crowd in the street below, tries to drown them with his piano solo. The crowd are enjoying not only the national day, but the triumphant parade of General Rollan (Jean Marais), their military hero. Elena sallies forth alone to lose herself in the general gaiety. She makes the acquaintance of Henri de Chevincourt (Mel Ferrer), an amiable, indolent, none too wealthy aristocrat. Like her, he enjoys the warmth of crowds. He believes the common people should have more leisure, and, like them, he admires Rollan's dash. He involves himself in an altercation with a shrewd, vaguely left-wing critic of the general.

Nonetheless Elena decides to renounce her romantic ideals and prudently exchange her title for a fortune in marriage. Her admirers include Michaud (Pierre Bertin), a wealthy if ludicrous shoe manufacturer, and she accepts his invitation to spend a day in the country hunting. There she encounters Rollan, now minister of war, directing the manoeuvres which are his spirited reply to German threats about a runaway balloon alleged to have been spying.

Rollan, a straightforward hero, is tempted to defy the government's wiser, only apparently pusillanimous, reaction to German sabre-rattling. He is also being egged on by right-wing extremists and partisans of "order" who see in him a popular figurehead whom they can use to destroy the Republic. The myopic shoemaker finances the cabal in exchange for promises of a protectionist policy. "La Polonaise", in her naive, warmhearted, romantic way, urges Rollan on, and sees herself as the inspiration of this handsome man of destiny. Meanwhile both Michaud's son and Rollan's aide, Hector, clash over Elena's maid Lolotte (Magali Noel), thus ridiculing both bourgeois hypocrisy and military notions of honour.

Henri comes to realise the true nature of Rollan's supporters. Rollan, through his love for Elena, realises the emptiness of power. He also realises that it is not her hero whom she loves, but his heroism. His political victory could only be hollow, so he renounces it and makes a sensibly ignominious escape with the help of gypsies, among them the singer Miarka (Juliette Greco). Elena, disillusioned, falls in with Henri's scheme for abetting Rollan's escape. He dons Rollan's uniform and stands facing Elena where their shadows, projected by an oil lamp onto the curtains, will seem to the crowd below to be kissing. The crowd is disarmed but instead of being disillusioned, it is delighted, and men and women by contagion kiss blithely. Thus Rollan, in *absentia,* via his stand-in, exalts love above patriotism and sets an amorous example instead of a military one. Elena recognises the sincerity in Henri's kiss—and the false embrace becomes reality.

The film completes Renoir's quartet of colour "tapestries", on the common theme of living as letting go. The tone throughout is tender but detached. All are concerned with apparent reality, with fictions and with personal style. In *Elena et les Hommes* the fictions and style are those of

political man. Rollan commences as Hotspur, continues as Hamlet, and concludes as Pépél. The bugles of honour and commitment find their answer in the silent faces, the "words without story", of the gypsies, those with no stake in established society (like the Peruvians). The crowd, crying for war, more in misled exuberance of spirit than in meanness, will get its war—in 1914.

The kiss is an ideal work of art, it is influential (averting a revolution), anonymous, and undetected. It triggers off a crazy sanity in the imaginations of its audience, and it goads them to a similar frenzy. It emerges, also, from the personal humiliation of all concerned. Rollan has lost his place in history, as she has sacrificed her romanticism about honour (and she is saved from yielding to bourgeois prudence). She yields to the sincerity of a spiritual and political also-ran, Henri. In the arms of the woman he loves, Henri is another man's stand-in, his shadow: the ghost of a lie. But with good grace he plays the game and from a generosity which is not unnaturally hypocrisy, a sufficient sincerity emerges.

The shadow-play has two antitheses: first, the self-centred composer who strives to exclude the mob; and second, the extremist triumvirate of the Rollanist movement (three sly men, introduced, respectively, as the movement's brain, eyes and heart). A third motivation for political activism, expressed by the shoe-manufacturer, representative of the profit motive, though personally more ludicrous, is less rapidly dispatched. In the end the gypsy's (or mermaid's) song is the bedrock of art, its simplest and most insidious form. It is heard only by those with ears to hear (like the whistling clown's). The nation's leader is almost a woman's puppet: he is man enough to shrink in stature. Elena, who craved a hero, settles for an agreeable mediocrity. He makes all the crowd's mistakes, except that he is more privileged than the crowd, and therefore more detached, and more involved. He has lucidity while the crowd has only instinct, but their responses are parallel*. Embracing him, Elena is embracing Everyman. Her purgation is a gentle one: yet as Truffaut observes, *"Nana rime avec Elena"*. Not that even the right choice is ever without sting. *Cahiers* wondered whether the conclusion is "optimistic or pessimistic, or between the two . . . the shot where she plucks her daisy and . . . of her daisy fallen on the ground, are heartbreaking shots." Renoir replied: "That's what I had in mind. I thought that this creature made for joy in the streets, for the joy of all, would finish flatly in the arms of this man, that her role now was concluded, that the curtain was about to fall on this marvellous performance which she gives the world. . . . " Baudelaire already spoke of *la sainte prostitution du théâtre;* its counterpart is *le saint Don Juanisme du metteur-en-scène*— Danglard is *un Prince,* that is to say, a Viceroy. The interchange of street and theatre provides the clue to Renoir's "cloister and the hearth" alternations of neo-realism (into the street) and studio artifice, of populism (or Popular Frontism) and a generous aestheticism (the unself-conscious artist as unself-conscious aristocrat). Rivette quotes Baudelaire's phrase about theatrical prostitution in connection with *French CanCan,* and it is in the window of a brothel that Elena's shadow-play occurs.

In discussion with the director, Rivette and Truffaut suggested that the film divided into three acts, each with its distinct style: spectacular comedy, satirical vaudeville and, as they hesitated, Renoir offered, sentimental confusion. (Cauliez described the whole as a *commedia all'improviso,* whose first act is a cavalier comedy, its second caustic burlesque, and its third a lyrical vaudeville). His interviewers suggested that this rich diversity of styles confused spectators as *La Règle du Jeu* had done seventeen years earlier. But Renoir was careful to stress the difficulties in which he had found himself.

Sensitivity, freshness, generosity, distinction, Ingrid Bergman can bestow upon her Elena, who is to Nana as a kindly mother to a fractious child. Otherwise, her role as a courtesan is very much a casting against type. Theoretically, her own private discrepancy of head (intention) and heart (screen personality) could become a source of suspense. But (1) Ingrid Bergman-Elena is too abundantly immune to her nominal temptations (calculation, prostitution, etc.) and (2) the lovers who represent them are caricatural and unreal. In contrast, Katherine Hepburn in *The Philadelphia Story* is real

---

* Renoir does nothing to head off the implication that superior insight depends on privilege—and no doubt privilege can help as well as hinder. In an American comedy, Henri's affinity with the crowd might have been asserted by making him a reporter—though that mightn't be without its sentimentality. Renoir might have made him, and the gypsies, spokesmen for two aspects of the life—its commitment (bewildered) and its anarchism-cum-internationalism.

and complex enough, i.e. she *might* have chosen the wrong man. In *Elena et les Hommes* the shoemaker is impossible, Henri isn't particularly right, Rollan isn't particularly wrong. That suspense *per se* disappears, is unimportant, and *The River* and *French CanCan* were as deliberately void thereof as nostalgia should be. What is deficient here is insight, i.e. interest, i.e. inner realism. Where the characters of *French CanCan* reveal aspects of one another, Elena remains one film, and les hommes another.

It's curious that Renoir, as an inspired caster-against-type, should have achieved this cross-purpose with a star who made every effort to escape Hollywood's casting her against type. When it didn't cast her as St. Joan or a McCarey nun, it cast her as prostitutes and drunks, and this couldn't be further from being the tribute to her acting ability that it seemed. It was precisely her obstinate radiance which excused and endeared her tarnished characters to the ultra-squeamish Legion of Decency. And her absolutely justified feeling that she wasn't being allowed to play any roles profoundly seems to have helped bring her within the ambit of neo-realism. Possibly Rossellini's semi-mystical variety of neo-realist theory, very close to Bazin's, whereby the camera would somehow reveal what was spiritually there, in actors, in landscapes, in reality itself, appealed to a star who felt that deeper and sadder, more serious realities might thus be revealed to herself, or liberated within herself. Renoir's interest lies not in the Hollywood aspect of Ingrid Bergman's radiance (which is a kind of pseudo-ratification, by an authentic spirituality, of the *Reader's Digest* ethos) but in that quality of buoyant earth-mother which expresses itself in middle-class terms as spirit-

edly as it would in any other. "I thought a great deal of Venus and Olympe . . . but perhaps of a Venus rather as Offenbach might have seen her . . . " When Ingrid Bergman came to Paris "we gave her a laughing cure. Every evening she attended a different theatre, where comedy of one kind or another was showing." By a sad irony, Elena's very affability became one-dimensional, perhaps because in the general confusion Renoir adhered more rigidly than usual to his schema of mood.

One can imagine an Ingrid Bergman who compromised between the imperiousness of La Belle Abbesse, Christine's gift for warm friendship, and the warm sensitivity of Catherine Rouvel, in *Le Déjeuner Sur L'Herbe*. Perhaps the clue to her interest for Renoir lies in some sense of Elena as another Christine—a "perfect woman, nobly planned/To warn, to comfort and command,"—finding herself lured into the equal, opposite and simultaneous follies of "honour" and coquettish cunning. If she's a Polish princess rather than a French one, it's not just because she seems to have had a Polish original (Missia Gidebska, to whom several pages are devoted in Renoir's biography of his father), it's also because, whereas the French aristocracy defined itself in relation to a court and a bourgeoisie (i.e. as an aristocracy of taste, etiquette, and a code of privilege—whence its decadence in *La Marseillaise*), the Polish aristocracy retained all the energy of a peasantry-based cavalry caste maintaining itself against Prussia, Russia, Austria, Hungary, and its own subjects, on the Eastern European plain. The same associations inform the characterisation of the dashing princess in Franju's version of Cocteau's *Thomas l'Imposteur*.

Worse, each of Elena's men has a drastically distinct idiom. A diversity of styles is one thing. But the composer is too simply a spoiled child to interest us. The shoemaker is too simply a silhouette from farce, and one can never believe that Elena is looking at *him*. However congenial Mel Ferrer's quietly quizzical style might be to close-ups à la Charles Walters at M.G.M., these multi-centred long shots shrink him to not so much a René Clair pinman as a sugarstick. Jean Marais often rings true. His air of dry disenchantment, of suppressed disgust, of a doomed longing, impatient yet passive, is an authentic modulation of his *persona* in the Cocteau films. Here, too, he is romantic, imprisoned, yearning. Certain graver scenes between Rollan and Elena are all the warmer because each is real enough for us to regret that neither quite sees or knows the other. Yet, if one takes the caricatured roles seriously, the film reveals a startling resemblance to *La Règle du Jeu*. Michaud's son and Hector, both pursuing Elena's maid Lolotte, recall, in naivety, stiffness and mischief, Jurieu, Schumacher and Lisette. Henri, in his very responsiveness, is something of a confidante, both to Elena and Rolland, and so corresponds to Octave. Alas, the caricature which weakens the fringes of *Partie de Campagne* here takes over all the secondary roles. The small parts which in *French CanCan* remained vignettes have become clichés. Even more than in the films of René Clair, the crowd becomes an abstraction (e.g. when it's jolly, everyone's jolly). Perhaps Renoir has paid, after all, for omitting the left. For his film depends on the crowd's extremely implausible switch from blood-thirstiness to amorousness. As its climax it keys all that goes before, and imposes an almost impossible unreality of tone. A more thoughtful finale could have transformed his film.

Yet his variety of frames within frames, the shove and brio of the crowd, the quick, meticulous echelons of actors in depth, the corners of mirrors framing intricacies, exhibit an ingenuity and beauty betrayed by the dramatic content against which it was designed to lean. Renoir and *Cahiers* both compared the gypsy scene with Picasso's blue period. But that inner, independent life which invested the analogous references in *French CanCan* is absent, and if we didn't know of the film's production nightmare we might accuse it of academicism. The most poignant scenes are those in which the human face is none too prominent: a chase glimpsed through doorways, the exquisitely lurid sunset, the military manoeuvres recalling, as Leprohon suggests, the chromo plates in the illustrated papers of the period.

Godard takes up a wry, wise joke of Renoir's—"I'm old now, I play Mozart". "*Elena* is its author's most Mozartian film. Less for its screen influence, like *La Règle du Jeu,* than for its philosophy. The Renoir who concludes *French CanCan* and prepares *Elena* is, morally, very much like the man who concludes the *Clarinet Concerto* and turns to *The Magic Flute.* In content: the same irony and the same disgust. In form: the same genial audacity and simplicity . . . " And that is, surely, the film's spirit, like the Mozartian colour, bright yet mellow, wistful yet supple, even if it occasionally rather than continuously possesses the breath of life.

Because of the political controversies which the film generated, it's worth looking at the original affair and some of Renoir's changes to it. His general view of Boulanger finds some support in D.W. Brogan's account of the general as an essentially moderate figure, uniting across-the-board enthusiasms. André Maurois underlines that the chauvinism which even in its day shocked so many people of the political centre wasn't gratuitously invented by Boulanger, but had objective causes in the European situation. The Schnaebale case was "that of a French superintendent of police, lured across the border by a German colleague and then arrested by a spy." It was played up by Bismarck, who, alarmed by France's rapid recovery from the supposedly crushing terms imposed after the Franco-Russian war, was anxious for a second war, in which respect the Republican government deftly frustrated him. The public, less intelligent, wanted a war led by a soldier. But Boulanger "feared separation from his mistress . . . whom he loved more than anything else, more even than power . . . " His flight was ignominious, not via gypsies but "like some clerk short in his accounts . . . vainly did his adherents follow him . . . his only concern was his tubercular and emotional Marguerite. When she died, he committed suicide on her grave." A journalist of the epoch summarised his career in a phrase startl-

ingly isomorphic with *Cahiers'* and Cauliez's sense of three acts. "He
began like Caesar, continued like Catiline, and ended like Romeo."

Rollan's preference for political irresponsibility parallels Renoir's return
to political innocence—albeit a more cynically lucid one. In his film the
intrigue and the crowd loom quite as large as the purely interpersonal story,
converting it into a comic manifesto—corresponding to René Clair's *A Nous
la Liberté* and *Le Dernier Milliardaire*. Doubtless Renoir hoped that the
Boulanger affair, as the last revolutionary, yet also patriotic, assertion of
the Paris crowd, would allow him to preach reconciliation, and to take by
the horns the bull of political bitterness which he had avoided in 1945. (Even
so, he treads carefully. Rochefort, the left-wing aristocrat and Boulangist,
is dropped, and with him the explicitly left-wing aspects of Boulangist
support. Unfortunately, to *spare* the left of that time, is to *ignore* the left of
the film's own time, and, even more provocatively, to substitute an aristocrat
as a major, finally dissentient, figure). Nonetheless, the intention seems to be
to celebrate a fraternity which has renounced militarism, and to whirl it into
a dance, along with the other preoccupations of his post-war films: The
friendship of rivals in love *(The River)* and in renunciation alike *(The Golden
Coach)*, and all the joys of a joint enterprise which modulates into a Bacchanalia *(French CanCan)*.

The political problem which Renoir takes as his subject, is a hardy
perennial of French politics. Jacques Fauvet speaks of a recurrent Bonapartism: "The extreme right-wing opposition flares up when traditional

parliamentarianism converges with a current outbreak of nationalism. In its purely antiparliamentary form the opposition is chronic, widespread but not always active. In its nationalist form, it is episodic and usually crystallises around a personality, which may not be, as such, exceptional but whose appearance on the national scene always seems providential. At such moments, it appeals to both the people and the army, i.e. is both plebeian and aristocratic. Such moments, violent though ephemeral, have been roused by General Boulanger, the pygmy, and by General de Gaulle, the giant, by Marshal Petain and by Colonel de la Rocque.

"Bonapartism is not Fascism. If the conservatives support it because they prefer it to popular movements or to parliamentary impotence, they soon leave it . . . once the emergency is past . . . Bonapartism is merely the expression of an instinctive protest focused round some personality. It ends in the disintegration of the forces, not in leading an attack." Fauvet was writing, as Renoir was thinking, before the plot of the Algerian generals brought the counter-general, de Gaulle, to power, before, even, such a plot was in the air. Nonetheless, French political memories, as Fauvet also observed, are exceptionally long, and the film depends on the, natural enough, association, "generals . . . militarism . . . right-wing dictatorship."

Doubtless the film's elaboration of the theme of a whirligig of political alliances (already noted in *French CanCan*), intends a friendly message about "la réunion fraternelle de tous les Francais", about patriotism evolving into dancing in the streets and "making love not war". Its political moral is that of the drop-out (Rollan) and the love-in (the crowd's). It is not so much ambiguous as derisive about right-wing extremism, and confident in a humane moderation of impulses which extremists will never quite mobilise. In its comic mode it is as didactic as another essay in enlightened, transformed patriotism, *La Marseillaise*. As left-wing revolution ought to dispense with terror, so right-wing revolution ought to dispense with itself. The appropriate sphere for right-wing anarchism is the private one: pacifistic, fraternal, orgiastic. "Left, right, centre" lose all polarity, as the dancers spin, in a sort of irresponsibility-in-unity, or a political freedom. Not a lunch on the grass, but a dance in the streets—advocating a hope rather like the thesis implicit in Daniel Bell's title of the time, *The End of Ideology* (albeit Renoir's sense of giddiness implies certain irrationalist, anarchist options).

Certainly one could schematise an admirable Boulanger. He realises the consequence of the contradictions within his supporters. He senses the repugnant nature of certain powerful aspects within it. His mediocre blend of deference, duty and decency makes the notion of a *coup* repugnant to him. He likes the common soldier, insofar as he understands him, and therefore increasingly dislikes these right-wing snobs and elitists. What he knows history will despise as loss of nerve is really his mixture of military insight and of commonsense, which surpasses his supporters', and proves stronger than his sense of honour. He prefers a doomed love to a sanguinary glory, and *l'amour fou* to patriotism. This Boulanger—and can we be sure that he is altogether absent from the historical one?—comes within an ace of being a Buñuel hero. Renoir's Rollan is halfway between this Boulanger and history's, except that Renoir is antiromantic about love also.

Whether the film's anarchism is right-wing or left-wing is debatable. In some respects, its interest in aristocrats, and leaders, and a certain emphasis on the crowd's extreme volatility (possibly less derisive had the film not fallen apart aesthetically) brings it politically near certain plays of Shaw's. In other respects, of course, it is hedonistic rather than Fabian, anti-puritanical, anti-utilitarian (life is unreal, life is frivolous . . .). Its omission of a strong left-wing line is doubtless inspired by the general incoherence of the French left, and the bitter divisions between Socialists and Communists. But this gives the film a curious bias: there is *no* left-wing option *at all*. And its nostalgic, yet hopefully didactic quality has another consequence. To propose men's fraternal equality is left-wing, to celebrate it as already existent is right-wing. For if it already exists then class does not. *Elena* says, among other things: "The left is unnecessary. In French history the left has no part. In the quintessential France of my nostalgias, its work is done by aristocrats, unattached aristocrats, by the decent centre within those social classes usually associated with the right, and by the folly of the masses." One may or may not agree with his thesis, but one can hardly argue that it's not both very political and very partial.

Its hopeful anarchism of the centre is as far from the reforming left as from the centrist right. If, as a position, it exists on no realistic political map, it is a common popular, or "folk" spiritual attitude. It certainly marks a sharp move by Renoir towards the right since an earlier encounter between right-wing force and an innocent crowd in *Diary of a Chambermaid*. For if one seriously takes *La Règle du Jeu* as a justly sarcastic piece, then one can't accept *Elena et les Hommes* as a justly indulgent one—or moralising has no place. The OAS was *not* more amiable or less dangerous than the Croix de Feu. Even if the film hinges on Rollan's renunciation, its mellow joviality does much to disarm our antipathy to a military dictatorship. Rollan rhymes with Salan (although, ironically, de Gaulle also deluded his supporters). Which doesn't help the victims of the OAS. Renoir's antennae were very astute—but, by substituting joviality for terrorism, the film could not but come to look like an apologia for a right-wing France, in a way which proved only too topical, roughly coinciding as it did with the upsurge of a right-wing extremism which can't in any sense be described as farcical. By the end of 1953, says René Remond, "The right held both the Presidency and the Premiership; in less than ten years, what a revenge for the humiliation of the Liberation and what a change in the alignment of political strength! It had moved from a feeble opposition to grasping the reins of political power. It had acquired a unity which it had never before attained . . . the year 1954 marked a turning point, for it was when Dien Bien Phu fell . . . and when the Algerian War began. French nationalism which traditionally had defined itself in relation to . . . Germany . . . was now going to define itself in relation to . . . the decolonisation movement. In the Resistance, patriotic feeling was rather on the left; with the colonial wars it seemed to return to the possession of the right, which made good use of this identification. Military defeats and diplomatic concessions revived patriotic sentiment and then exasperated it. At this point there reappeared a phenomenon already seen several times since Boulangism . . . Nationalist exaltation even aroused some new forces outside the January 2, 1956. Those small youth groups and veteran associations . . . virulent antiparliamentarianism, forms of agitation and taste for conspiracy . . . also multiplied . . . It was this current of national thought that weakened the regime and prepared its overthrow . . . It drew towards right-wing positions some men and groups that until this point were counted on the left . . . "

The tone of his didacticism makes Renoir look more like victim of his optimism, blind to the carnivorous nature of the tendencies culminating in the revolt of the generals, who, like Rollan, came from Algeria, and whose figurehead, Salan, was, also, originally a hero of the left. Its characteristic expression was not dancing in the streets but torture and terrorism à la OAS, and it took, not giddy dancing, but resolute marching, and striking, by, precisely, the *crowd,* to demonstrate to the generals, poised to invade metropolitan France, that invasion would initiate a civil war as bloody as the Spanish.

Thus the hopeful message of a Renoir film is, for the fourth time, belied. The Popular Front broke up while he was shooting *La Marseillaise*. Almost as he shot *Diary of a Chambermaid*, his American films were being booed in Paris. As he shot *The River*, after long preparation, the Hindu-Muslim massacres stained the end of a not quite idyllic imperialism with the blood of thousands. And yet, if we allow him the diadactic optimism of *La Vie Est à Nous*, of *La Marseillaise*, of *La Grande Illusion*, and of *Le Crime de Monsieur Lange*, the left's favourite Renoir film, then insofar as it is didactic, we cannot altogether condemn the "optimism" of *Elna et les Hommes*, nor even the—Gaullist?—combination of Tricolors and a Franco-Russian alliance in *French CanCan*. After all, Franju praised de Gaulle for having implemented so many aspects of Communist Party policy—asserting France against the Common Market, resisting American influence, arranging a *rapport* with Russia.

Although the political angle probably had little influence on its commercial success, the extent of the film's commercial failure is indicated by the fact that, for all its English version and its stars, it was never purchased, even for arthouse exhibition, in Britain. In view of his later evolution, Godard's comments on it are piquant. "If *Elena* is the French film *par excellence*, it's because it's the most intelligent film in the world." Pierrot Le Fou, Rollan le Fou . . .

Interlude: Family Albums

From the production problems of *Elena et les Hommes,* and after the failure of *The Golden Coach,* Renoir may well have drawn a moral about the difficulties inherent in elaborate, multilingual co-productions. His next feature films mark a decisive and indeed astonishing change of aesthetic strategy, and a reversion to what is not merely a national, but an intensely personal, focus.

Thus *Elena et les Hommes* concludes the "internationalist" era which began with *The River.* Despite all their visual and thematic differences, *The River* continues a spiritual theme of *Woman on the Beach.* Tod's dream links a past nightmare with a future dream. Losing both, he regains himself to live the reality of the present and its friendship. As he renounces the girl who infatuates him, so he ceases the projection of his own jealous paranoia, and is able to accept the loss of his dreamwoman made flesh. Freedom is won at a cost. Reconciliation and resignation are one.

The River picks up the same theme in another guise. Its rainbow surface conceals a certain pessimism. The rejection of paranoia in the previous film is followed by an acceptance of the snake—traditional emblem of treachery, i.e. suspicion. The link between the snake (which sheds its skin) and immortality had begun with Keefer in *Swamp Water.* In *The River* resurrection becomes reincarnation. That life goes on is both cruel and consoling.*

Several critics have commented that in *The River* the female principle seems invested with far more life-force than the male. Three young girls, a range of types entering their prime, feel strong passions. Yet the men are: two fathers of whom we see little, Bogey who never grows up; Captain John, on whom they lavish their fresh emotions, is crippled, pallid, learns resignation from his older namesake, and leaves them all. The forceful male principle appears only as a God, in a tale. Although Renoir's films have often

---

* Why the snake, in our mythology, should symbolise sexuality, treachery and wisdom is another question—but all three factors make it, in Freudian terms, a convenient substitute for the loved father.

contrasted the vamp, in one of her successive incarnations (Catherine Hessling, Janie Marèze, Simone Simon, Paulette Goddard, Joan Bennett) with weaker or handicapped men, *Diary of a Chambermaid* is the first Renoir film in which a woman is both the most vigorous character and our identification figure, and where the men are weak or ailing. In the earlier films we admire the vamp as her men do, and tend to judge her on their behalf; we are, so to speak, watching her from a kind of brotherly over-shoulder. Now woman is the centre; at once vamp, norm, and victim. *The Golden Coach* maintains this female predominance, contrasting one woman, who is our primary identification, with male satellites, each of whom is characterised by only one of her facets. *French CanCan* reverses the pattern; our identification is with Danglard, who is a male vamp. *Elena et les Hommes* returns to the pattern of *The Golden Coach,* but, like *French CanCan,* is comic. In all these films woman seems to possess the initiative, and men seem to refuse, or to prove inadequate. A woman's loneliness is tragic, and may be accepted as matter-of-fact; a man's loneliness is matter-of-fact or comic.

There had been premonitions of Renoir's sense of detachment: *La Petite Marchande d'Allumettes,* the baron in *Les Bas-Fonds,* Keefer's pseudo-death. *Woman on the Beach* is an entanglement of false suspicions, dreams, a verbalised past, an invisible sensuality, and blindness, as if a denial of immediate, palpable reality were operative. *The River* glories in the senses, but it is pantheistic, impersonal, told indirectly (flashback and commentary), and depends on a counterpoint of ellipses and asides. The very idea of *The Golden Coach*—Italian actors in 18th-century Peru—has a certain "unreality". It is followed by two nostalgic pictures of Paris just before their *auteur's* birth; the same theme is sustained and life seen as pivoting around false memories and a delusive shadow-play. Although each film asserts the sensual, it is as part of the spectacle; ironies undermine each human purpose, even when it is known to be delusive. The convergence of the real and the unreal, the spiritual and the spectacle, takes a startling turn in Renoir's subsequent phases. So, too, does the withdrawal from ideological commitment which characterises the period; for though each film becomes steadily more sceptical about politics, it is at the price of laying a sharper emphasis on politics than its predecessor. Surprisingly, *La Règle du Jeu* is less specific, less analytical, in its picture of French politics than *Diary of a Chambermaid,* and that is less specific than *Eléna et les Hommes*—which become quite as uncomfortably political as the first. Renoir's next two films, depoliticized, remain ideological and topical.

The River, followed by the rediscovery of *La Chienne* and *Boudu Sauvé des Eaux,* had re-established Renoir as a major director, and his status remained unaffected by the relatively reserved reception initially accorded to his next three films. Left-wing critics were much less enthusiastic over Renoir's "acquiescent" phase, but continued to hold him in respect till the sudden change provoked by *Elena.* By this time Renoir's whole career had been reviewed, and, via his appearance on TV, his celebrity reached the wider French public, a factor significant to the aesthetic strategy of his two next films. Since it also marks his turning from an international phase to a French and a personal genre once more, it is appropriate that we draw our dotted line between *Elena et les Hommes*, and a short film which was released as a supporting feature to it.

L'Album de Famille de Jean Renoir

In 1956 Roland Gritti filmed a short interview with Jean Renoir. Through paintings and photographs, it glances at the director's childhood, his father's work, and some of his own best-known films. He pays special attention to *Elena*, which he describes as a tribute to sincerity and to its (equally indispensible) counterpart, hypocrisy, and as a eulogy of laziness and a demonstration of the futility of human enterprises. Although it was produced by French TV, and is primarily televisual in style, it was released with *Elena et les Hommes* and is sometimes referred to as a prologue to it, although its correct description is presumably a "topical documentary", at least when shown on its own. The general approach is competent rather than inspired, but the film's evidence of Renoir's personal style in its less expansive key could hardly be other than fascinating to admirers of the director's work.

Le Grand Couteau

After *Elena*, Renoir thought of uniting Leslie Caron and Georges Simenon and shooting *Three Rooms in Manhattan* in the streets of New York; the subject and location were subsequently utilised by Jean-Pierre Melville. Another possibility was a development of *Paris-Province*, centering on a girl who has difficulty in adapting to Paris outside the village-within-a-city of booths and stalls near the Porte de la Chatillon.

In the event, Renoir again turned aside from the cinema. The *contretemps* over *Elena et les Hommes* may have given him pause, much as *La Règle du Jeu* preceded his departure for Italy, and the non-viability of his Film Classics project precipitated his return to Europe. Together with his gathering reputation, enhanced by the re-release of his pre-war features, his subsequent involvement with television encouraged him to take up new roots in Paris. Meanwhile the theatre renewed its call, offering both its less distraction-ridden interrelationship with actors and a more personal focus and scale. While concluding the writing of a still unperformed play in English, entitled *Calla Littles or the Heirs,* Renoir entered another theatrical enterprise.

Le Grand Couteau was a French adaptation of Clifford Odets' play *The Big Knife,* which had already been filmed in Hollywood by Robert Aldrich. Renoir's intimate knowledge of Hollywood qualified him for the subject which, from the point of view of his personal thematic, might be considered an extension of his quietly bitter asides about the relationship of commerce, art and friendship in *The Golden Coach* and *French CanCan.* Renoir also produced the piece, with Daniel Gelin in the principal role, and it was well received on its first night at the Théâtre des Bouffes-Parisiens on 30th October 1957.

Bande—Annonce

Bande-Annonce is a short introduction, written and spoken by Jean Renoir, to *La Grande Illusion* on the occasion of its third release (this time the definitive version) in France in 1958. Renoir shows snapshots and reminisces about the World War I background to the film. At this time Renoir was becoming well-known on French TV and these short films extend that relationship. They also institute that direct relationship between director and spectator which is to become a prominent factor in Renoir's evolving aesthetic.

Le Testament du Dr. Cordelier
(Experiment in Evil)

Renoir's next film, made at the same time as Godard's and Truffaut's first
features, parallels many *Nouvelle Vague* characteristics before they had fully
developed. At 65 Renoir had become a contemporary of his grandchildren's
generation.

French TV had long been soliciting his directorial talents and he now saw
a chance of outflanking some of the cinema industry's self-imposed restrictions. As new, lightweight film equipment, developed for TV, made it
possible for the *Nouvelle Vague* to renovate movie production and style, so
Renoir hit on an alternative employment of the same equipment.

Asked to direct a TV play, Renoir persuaded the producers to invest
instead in an "amphibious" production, which would, in his own words,
"prove that a television programme could quite well fill the cinemas. At this
period when the cinema faces great difficulties, and where it will soon have
to face the competition of the Common Market, what I propose could initiate
a renewal of the cinematograph industry . . . in shooting *Le Testament du
Dr. Cordelier* I tried to perfect a method (which is in no way claimed as
unique) allowing films to be produced at a cost which will put them on the
French market on level terms with dubbed films which, let's not forget, have
already covered their cost in their country of origin, at least as far as the USA
is concerned. . . . Otherwise, given the state of the market, there will, in
a few years' time, be no French films. . . . "

Renoir hoped to break down a boycott by which French film producers
intended to starve TV of product. Hollywood had tried the same strategy.
"Result: American TV made its own films, lived, triumphed, the studios
closed up or were sold to television . . . " Even if *Cordelier* was going
the other way (from TV studio to cinema) it would help to open producers'
eyes to the possibilities of collaboration, would remind exhibitors that the
showing of certain films on TV had doubled the expected attendance on sub-

sequent cinema showings, and would vindicate the national product against the "European-Hollywood" cosmopolitan tendencies of co-productions.

The film was shot in the Paris TV studios with a mixture of cinema and TV technicians. After pre-rehearsals with the actors alone, and technical rehearsals to ensure suitable lighting fields, a multiple camera and microphone system was brought into play. Between 5 and 13 microphones allowed a continuous sound "picture", while the number of cameras varied between 4 and 8, most often 5. Sometimes they picked up the actor in relay, sometimes they gave 4 or 5 simultaneous versions of a scene: for example, a general view, a tighter view, and a close-up of each of the principal actors' faces.

Multiple camera-coverage was not altogether new, and indeed far from rare in Hollywood films of the '30s. In many cases the director concerned himself only with the actors, and it was the producer and editor between them who decided which take of which view of which scene was to be used. What was new was the artistic spirit behind this battery of equipment. "I dreamed of a scenario written in such a way that I could shoot it in ten reels. No editing, only a little glue to join the reels end to end." Taken literally, Renoir's improvised statement might have described Hitchcock's ten-minute-takes, ten years earlier, rather than anything *Cordelier* could have been. For there is no continuity of image. Nonetheless the new camera set-up allows a continuity of action flowing throughout the scene—permitting therefore a structure based, as in the theatre, on the modulation and progression of the actor in himself, undisturbed by the discontinuity of set-ups which in the film studio trip him up and make him so dependent on the director. In this sense Hitchcock's ten-minute-take is somewhat constrictive. Throughout the long, complicated take the actor had to move, very meticulously, to just where the lens would find him. He had less autonomy than if he could be sure that whatever he did, the camera would follow him. It is this initiative which Renoir's procedures restored to him.

In the early '30s Renoir's acrobatic camera-movements and focal gymnastics had shown that temporary visual disruptions and imprecisions could be more than compensated by an inner, and theatrical, vivacity. Now came the possibility of an altogether new aesthetic idiom in which the actors became the *auteur*, the director acting as a sort of technical-grammatical midwife. Renoir indicated to the technicians that he would need certain shots at certain moments. Rehearsals permitted a general coordination, rather like the "head arrangement" of a jazzband. Thereafter it was up to the technicians to follow the actors, who had recovered their freedom of the stage. The new technique reverses the aesthetic of *French CanCan*. There, the actor seemed part of the usual surface; here, space is merely the—space!—through which the actor is unloosed. To shape the film around the actors in this way was to suggest a more complete coincidence of dramatic or apparent time, shooting time and performance time; and in the finished film this coincidence is maintained within the scene, although not between

scenes. In the event Renoir had the actors alone for a week, and actors and technicians together for a second. Exteriors took one week, studio work another. Venturing (before their American vogue) into an intriguing mixture of "happening" and cinéma-vérité, Renoir unleashed Barrault in his horrific make-up among unprepared passers-by, who studiously ignored him until his attack on a little girl, which they took for real and in which they intervened. "It was one of the few scenes I had to reshoot, for most of the film I needed one take only." The actors could, if necessary, walk from one setting to another, as in a "live" TV production: Severin's office was "continuous" with a landing, lifts, office and side-rooms.

"I had a desire to shoot something really mysterious in a suburb of Paris . . . the germ of *Cordelier* lies in those long walks of mine along walls moist under their prudish covering of moss. It lies in my stares, like a spy's, through rusty gates. It lies in my longing to guess the identity of the pallid inhabitants of those noble mansions, before they dissolve in the rain and draw all that remains as basis for our dream with them into their decomposition. . . . Then came the desire to lean on *Dr. Jekyll and Mr. Hyde,* to place those nicely modern and cemented streets of Paris in contrast with the old parks. *Cordelier* was born . . . "

Another aspect of the subject had haunted Renoir for some time: " . . . that of Good and Evil. But one doesn't tackle themes as important as that on one's own. I solicited the aid of M. Goethe, because there is something of *Faust* in my film . . . "

A fourth inspiration: "I am surrounded, and you are too, by people who take pills, who have themselves psychoanalysed, who live on couches . . . and unveil all the secrets of their soul. It has become such a mania that in basing . . . a film on discussions between such doctors, I felt that I was touching on many of our private lives . . . "

As the film begins, Jean Renoir, flanked by assistants, enters the TV studio to begin his broadcast. "We have just witnessed the conclusion of a remarkable adventure. So singular that it seems worthy to be the subject of tonight's programme. We begin from the beginning and go back several months in time . . . " Renoir's commentary continues over a shot of Cordelier (Jean-Louis Barrault) and his solicitor, Maître Joly, face-to-face in the latter's office. The voice-over explains Joly's surprise on learning that his old friend since regimental days has made a new will which will leave everything to a mysterious Monsieur Opale.

A few weeks later, a little girl is savaged in the street by an individual of dauntingly ugly aspect. Joly pursues him as far as a locked gate which gives onto Cordelier's back garden, and speaks to Cordelier's manservant, Désiré. Later Cordelier visits Joly to assure him that there will be no repetition of his protégé's crime. Joly tries to discuss Cordelier's researches with the latter's eminent but irascible and pettily jealous rival, Dr. Severin (Michel Vitold). The latter concedes that Cordelier had been a brilliant psychiatrist before giving up his practice to concentrate on a line of research which Severin considers pigheaded. After further attacks, whose victims include an old man, Opale is traced as far as a seedy Pigalle hotel. He has been terrorising a prostitute named Suzy, no doubt with the aid of the panoply of whips which adorn the wall of his room.

Cordelier asks Joly to negotiate a meeting with Severin, when he will offer his old antagonist a conclusive demonstration of his theories. But Opale appears in his place, and Severin is found dead, apparently of a heart attack inspired by Opale's revelations. Cordelier instructs his servants to block up the garden gate, and returns to his former social life. But an urgent midnight call brings Joly to Cordelier's, where Blaise (Gaston Modot) and other servants surround the laboratory. From behind its locked doors they hear the terrified voice of Cordelier, and break the door down—only to find themselves confronted by Opale, who quietens, and then insolently, only when covered by a revolver.

Opale shows Joly a scar on his wrist which proves that he is Cordelier and plays him an explanatory tape-recording of the latter's voice. Years ago, as a young, handsome doctor, he yielded to the embraces of an appetising young servant girl. But a fashionable lady called to discuss her son's "childish obsession" for their maid. Frozen by this mockery, Cordelier sacked his consort, and his sexual life thereafter took the form of anaesthetising his more beautiful patients and interfering with them as they lay unconscious. He renounced his practice and devoted himself to the problem of evil. A few months ago, he succeeded in developing a drug which directly influences the soul. Severin, his materialism outraged, refused to so much as listen. Too moral to experiment on others, Cordelier experimented on himself, and became Opale. Each tolerated the other's existence; but the transformation from Opale to Cordelier became progressively more agonising, and the transformation from Cordelier to Opale progressively more involuntary. Now, Opale can become Cordelier once more only by taking a dose whose strength will prove fatal. Convinced of immortality, he is prepared to take the step, heedless of Joly's kindly meant if somewhat confused pleas that suicide is a sin and that Opale ought to expiate his crime by surrendering himself to earthly punishments. The dialogue closes thus:

Désiré: "Our master is dead, but the other, the assassin?"

Joly: "He has dealt himself justice."

Voice of Jean Renoir: "As for Cordelier, who had paid with his life for the terrible frenzy of spiritual research, was it not he who had the finest part?"

Renoir's film retains from Stephenson's novel the form of the detective story, with flashbacks rather than the chronological order preferred in some screen adaptations. Cordelier's last words are, "I am sure that, separated from my double body, my soul will once again become immortal." Cordelier's earlier references to the soul's presence in man but not in animals (the orthodox Roman Catholic dogma), and the discomfiture of Severin's bigoted materialism, certainly bring Renoir's film very near a Christian frame of reference, and distinguish it from the Hindu spirit of *The River* (which involves pantheism and reincarnation).

But if Renoir approaches Christian theology, it is as constantly halved numbers approach zero, never to arrive. For Opale repudiates Joly's suggestion that he consider the remainder of his life as purgatory (a christian idea transposed into humanist terms) and instead commits suicide, in hope of immortality, i.e. a pantheistic, unchristian and indeed immoral, freedom. The idea that somehow after death something of oneself survives in some sort of form is a belief quite widely diffused among ordinary people, quite independent of any Christian attachments, or reactionary inclinations, and it's an almost instinctive attitude (no "primitive" people believes that the soul, or life-force, dies with the body). Opale feels he will survive *freed*. One can be quite clear that "l'ame", in *Cordelier*, carries a vitalist sense, and probably a pagan one, as distinct from a Thomist one.

Stephenson tragically acquiesces in the misanthropic view of certain tensions between Victorian materialism, Romantic optimism, and Puritanism. Renoir's attack is on a dominant form of 20th-century thought, an optimistic rationalism based on a hubristic assumption of mastery over nature. He appeals to a popular, generous, undogmatic and—moral, but indulgently moral—"folk" belief in the "immortality" (or transcendent value) of something in the human being somewhere. Apart from refusing to let Christian dogma hog the traditional phrases, his old-fashioned language has the additional advantage of expressing a working affinity with *many* kinds of spirituality only in what they agree in asserting against agnostico-technocratic "logic". But to say "many" is not to say "any", and if Cordelier shows so deeply the influence of an older-fashioned *bien-pensant* Christian rationalist consensus it is surely to arraign it for the deficiencies which produce the split between Cordelier and Opale. Renoir's sympathy with Cordelier's spirituality parallels Buñuel's reiterated preference for *Viridiana* over the engineer, and for St. Simon over the denizens of the discothèque, and it recalls a very pointed remark by a mysterious personage suddenly appearing in the tavern bedroom of *La Voie Lactée*, to the effect that the stupidity of this modern world will conclude in driving him to the folly of belief in God.

The theatre/life metaphysic so prominent between *The River* and *Elena et les Hommes* has yielded to a more traditional (and only in that sense reactionary) antithesis between spirit and matter. Untraditionally, though, Renoir refuses the rationalist view of intelligence as somehow equivalent to the soul, or *esse*, or "ending end" of man, and he places an impulsive sensuality on the spiritual side of the scale (the correspondence is confirmed by Ma Viper's paradoxes in *Orvet*). Renoir's anti-Platonic, Dionysiac spirituality, now recognises its principal enemy as a technocratic-rationalistic denial of vital satisfactions which, being badly misunderstood, have to be classified, if only temporarily, as "irrational". This Procrustean rationalism has its social, and therefore its political, aspects, summed up by "la planification" (the quiet but thorough reorganisation, under governments of right and left alike, of French society in the interests of French industry). If in the '30s Renoir espoused an egalitarian fraternity against the right-wing threat to liberty, the '60s see him turn, like Jacques Tati, against an industrial-bureaucratic complex which contrives to regiment lives and minds by methods whose intrinsic dangers, so long predicted by the traditionalist right, are at last being rigorously investigated by the radical left and by a wide range of the younger generation. His attacks on technocracy precede that of *Alphaville*.

"When for the first time I became Opale, I had succeeded in splitting open at one and the same time my body, and the framework of your society. I felt myself brusquely liberated from the heaviness which crushed me. I was light, light, light . . . " "Your" society is not specifically that of the left-wing's rationalist materialism. The personifications of the system are a lawyer, a diplomat, an alienist and a female snob whose hypochondria about her son's amours might have come straight from the files of R. D. Laing. Her conversation leaves Cordelier feeling "tarnished by my liaison which suddenly struck me as that of an immature and vicious student." Thus Puritan "immorality" has become rationalist "immaturity", and the last may be the more subtly destructive terminology. The liberty implicit in joyfully committed sin or crime is quite unlike that of Gide's *acte gratuite*, being neither undetermined nor gratuitous, but liberated from the ingrained guilt and shame which are the preconditions of bourgeois "permissiveness". The real

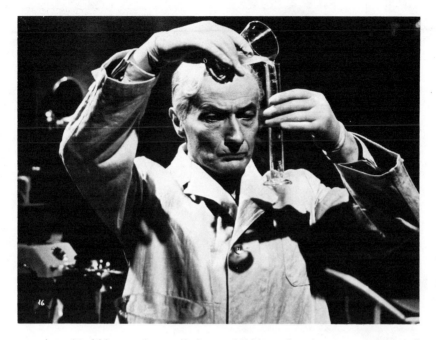

restraints should be not the mutilating prohibitions, but the counter-claims of moral pride and generosity. Opale's lightness represents the unleashing of an energy hitherto oppressed. Inertia becomes momentum. That it becomes destructive is tragic. But the reigning spirit, of a rationalist hypochondria, has prevented the creative acceptance of impulsive energy, of animal ignominy.

It is no longer progressive, but technico-bureaucratic, to see an anti-scientific attitude as the prerogative of reaction. Twenty years earlier, the Communist left had attacked Christianity and conservatism through Nicole Védrès's *La Vie Commence Demain* (whose title echoes that of Renoir's earlier movie). Jean Rostand and others seek to inspire a dejected French youth with such wonders of science as parthogenesis and genetic engineering. All of which alarmed me then, and alarms me now, even more. That film's prophets of progress spoke like so many Severins. Renoir's purpose might have been clearer, but he might have expected radical intellectuals to distinguish what was right from what was wrong in the confusions of Cordelier-Opale, Joly and their circle.

A second dimension of difficulties emerges from the psychological theories which Renoir expounds, and which are simultaneously muddled (in the manner of after-dinner discussion) and subtle. Renoir attacks modern psychology bag and baggage, attempting references to all its different schools, and failing to distinguish their liberating tendencies from their mystificatory ones. The attack is too indiscriminate, and Renoir's inclusive-

ness compounds the confusion. Philosophical ambiguities which can enrich a film when they emanate from a rich dramatic plane become infuriating when they comprise it—and disrupt it. Thus, Cordelier complains that "pour Severin, l'âme n'etait que la conscience." But French "conscience" can mean either conscience or consciousness, which makes quite a difference. Both Severin and Cordelier are described as psychoanalysts, although both express a variety of non-Freudian attitudes and not one single Freudian one*. Equally crucial and vague is the specific effect of the drug on Cordelier's psyche. Cordelier begins by seeking a purely physiological therapy, to cure "moral infections" just as materialistically as antibiotics cure physical ones. His compound is based on the principle of graduating the effects of certain

* The practice of psychoanalysis long remained rarer and more restricted in France than in Anglo-Saxon countries. French psychology had by and large remained more rationalist, in the pre-Freudian sense. The English nearest counterpart of Cordelier's mixture of puritanism and materialism would be found in the '20s generation (one of Julian Huxley's colleagues did in fact commit suicide as a result of the guilt he felt over his sexual desires for a housemaid). Severin might be paraphrased by H. J. Eysenck and Raymond B. Cattell, in their sceptical dogmatism. But Barrault's Cordelier seems more typical of a pre-1939 psychologist. He seems to me to call for a period setting; and I would concur with Poulle when he suggests that Renoir is deliberately, and provocatively, tackling the problems of the '60s with the ideas of 1910, and opting for the "senses" against "reason".

narcotics on the memory, the will, the association of ideas, "conscience" in both senses, and that something else which is "the soul". His medicine seems to leave the instincts untouched, however—or some of them. At any rate, "I had become a free being, free of all constraints, conscious of having every right. The profound change in my body was the transparent reflection of my instincts." In fact, Opale's liberation is highly selective; most conspicuously, anger turning violent, and sexual sadism. This very selectivity suggests that "soul" corresponds to something very different from "conscience", in the English sense, or "the good in man".

Does it, one may wonder, correspond to "the evil in man"? Is Renoir, like Stephenson in his Victorianism, equating freedom, eroticism, cruelty? But if so, one might expect Opale to do rather more in the way of leaping on women, children and probably men too. (Perhaps he might, when in his loving rather than his killing mood, embrace them with such selfish passion that if they offer any resistance he rapes them (like Boudu) and mangles them (like Mauger his pet squirrel). He would be a disastrous, and tragic, Marxist—*tendance Harpo*.

The liberation of the "soul" would suggest that Opale is the *full* man, whereas his incompleteness suggests that he is only a *partial* man, i.e. a *repressed* side of Cordelier. And Renoir carefully speaks of *graduated* effects. Without embracing Stephenson's puritanism, Renoir might still be observing that impulsive and heartless power is, not so much an instinct, as a radical tendency, that blocks off all others. And perhaps that childlike side of Opale, reminiscent of Harpo, or even of Charlie Chaplin in a certain mood, provides the clue. Opale is in a state of childish nature, without guilt, and without the social needs which in the child produce guilt. He is the irresponsible side of the child; man being a social animal, he is incomplete. Half of his "instincts" haven't stabilised out of his impulses. For such stabilisation to take place, he needs culture (in the broadest sense, of *formation*), which exists, precisely, to draw up the rules of the game—the game which isn't a game, and/can also generate its own dysfunctions (Schumacher is as randomly murderous as Opale). And what have the rules of Cordelier's world made of him? From the point of view of his animal soul—and even his soul as a social animal—his life is as incomplete as Opale's, for, through fear of ridicule, he dare love only unconscious bodies *(en-soi* not *pour-soi!)*. If anything, "soul" refers not to something moral behind and beyond the life-force, but the ability of the life-force to harmonise and maximise its various appetites. In this sense, it includes "conscience" and "consciousness," and philosophical anthropologists like Rollo May might claim the later Renoir for one of themselves. In the terms of *Love and Will,* Opale is Cordelier's "daimon." Cordelier's austerity and dedication are only sublimated counterparts of Opale's Dionysiac impulsiveness. Society prefers Cordelier, and we would probably agree with it that unconscious victims of rape suffer less than terrified victims of copulation-and-flagellation.* But Cordelier prefers to be Opale, and is delighted to become Opale so long as he can change back. Neither of his selves have synthesised their impulses and instincts properly. That is their *similarity*. Their differences could appear to be a trivial one. It's fear of disapproval (whether external or internal). Cordelier feels both guilt and shame. Opale feels neither. And here Renoir has certainly matched current preoccupations about the relationship of the two emotions. How far is shame guilt projected outwards, how far is guilt shame introjected, and are we shifting from a guilt culture (inner direction) to a shame culture (outer direction)? Such simple-sounding shifts would involve all sorts of complications, especially if we also accept Gordon Rattray Taylor's association of guilt with patrist (father-identifying) cultures and shame with matrist (mother-identifying) cultures. An intuitive awareness of shifting tensions in these areas may underlie the various '60s revivals of Stephenson's story: Terence Fisher's *Two Faces of Dr. Jekyll* (1960), Jerry Lewis' *The Nutty Professor* (1963), and, rather later, *Doctor Jekyll and Sister Hyde*. It's certainly interesting to apply Taylor's thesis to Renoir's world. Its conspicuously matrist features include an absence of guilt, a general sensitivity to others, an assertion of female sexuality over possessive monogamy, as well as of interpersonal relationships over prolonged introspection, and the "chameleonesque" fluidity of body- (and soul-) armour. Renoir's interest in shame culture may well have a second, anachronistic origin, however. Montesquieu had already characterised the feudal aristocracy as based on the code of "honour", i.e. fear of shame, as distinct from bourgeois-puritan-rationalist guilt. That contrast is quite clear as between William and Georges in *Orvet*. Renoir's alertness to it may have been triggered by his early access to circles where a bourgeois elite met the more affable elements of the aristocracy. And at the other end of the social spectrum are the maidservants—beloved of Octave, and paraphrased by Cordelier's attraction to his assistant—whose indulgence banishes guilt and shame alike.

Stephenson's Jekyll and Hyde story has a rather more complex, and grim, moral than, since Freud, is often supposed, and Renoir's talk of "soul" may be an attempt to evoke it. Jekyll isn't a product of simple "repression". He had a period of youthful wild oats. He is libidinously alive enough to be quite conscious of his strong sensuality, as well as of his exacting aspirations. He knows that each side of him torments the other. But he—and Stephenson—accept that *neither* should be allowed to get out of hand. It may be Jekyll's moral side which drives him to first take the drug, but thereafter his motive is less pure research than pleasure. And *Jekyll's* pleasure is

---

* It is very important that Joly, in contrast to the crowd's lynch-mob mood, manages to quieten the child attacked, and possibly sexually attacked, by Opale, by giving him a bar of chocolate (and his mother some money). The popular prejudice against child-molesters doesn't seem to correspond to the resilience of normally healthy children and if Joly's gesture seems idiotically "superficial" and 'materialist' he's probably nearer a true perspective than the outraged.

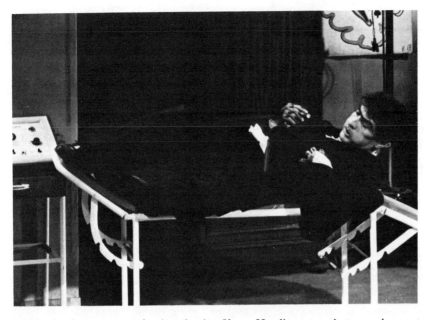

emphasised more strongly than in the films. He discovers that man has not one soul, but two, although the incipient Manicheanism shades back to the Calvinist notion of man as radically depraved. Nothing, says Stephenson, is sweeter than sin to "binary man", whose soul is a twin star, composed of an altogether fallen, and a less contentedly fallen, sphere. Jekyll likes Hyde (i.e. being Hyde), although Hyde increasingly resents Jekyll's obligations (including duty and guilt). But it is only when he is menaced with extinction that Jekyll fights back. He repents through fear, rather than disapproval. He commits suicide, not so much through repentance, as because he is cornered. By and large, Hyde wins. The Hollywood films lose most of the novel's intricacies, whitewashing Jekyll and giving him a much stronger redemptive side, and end.

Renouncing American optimism and Calvinism alike, Renoir turns to a more Goethean balance. It comes nearer a Freudian view, without really being related to it. The title-change expresses his altered perspective. Opale never renounces Cordelier's religious or moral beliefs. He knows that he needs him. It's not simply because his own crimes, the joy of committing which he can't resist, require Cordelier's protective respectability (this film is a *tragedy* of hypocrisy, counterbalancing *Elena*), and his income. Opale seems to sense that his own mind is too *unsynthesised* to be viable for long. He parallels the feeblemindedness of Boudu, by exaggerating the impulsiveness of Octave. So far as sexual relationships are concerned it would be difficult to decide whether Cordelier or Opale had the best of it. Cordelier's connivance is understandable, insofar as there probably is more, albeit malevolent, human contact involved in flogging a girl into acquiescence than in drugging one. It's Opale who has the ongoing, slightly stable, personal relationship. Not that one should overlook Suzy's real terror. And, while Cordelier drugs a woman who is clearly willing to accept him anyway, Opale terrorises a woman whom he could pay, so he's nobody's culture-hero either. For he too suffers from the taboo on tenderness—and reciprocation, i.e. respectability—which Cordelier has been unable to "synthesise". Hence his panoply of whips, as much evidence of fear of losing as of joy in dominating. In this respect he comes nearer Freud than recent assumptions that the less the guilt the fuller (more polymorphously perverse) the relationships, the greater the tenderness, and the more orgiastic the satisfaction. Nonetheless, the blame for Cordelier's, and therefore Opale's, repression is laid firmly on a compound of (1) bourgeois snobbery (the upper-middle-class lady) and (2) scientific rationalism (which pretending to clear away prejudice also devalues whatever is impulsive, subrational and natural in man). They combine in a view of 'normality' which in fact is extremely ascetic ('Cordelier' being a kind of monk)(*). From his vitalist angle, Renoir refuses to condemn a Bergsonian, or a Blakeian cruelty, (**) even if he regrets it for the victim's sake. Opale must die. But Renoir's own voice suggests that he has "the better part", that he remains his own master, in suicide, despite (1) the Catholic view that it's possibly the one unforgiveable sin, (2) the craving of a scientific society to learn everything, and (3) a general feeling that so quick, so clean an ending is insufficient expiation. But the difference between a guilty inability to kill, and a generous refusal to kill, is one with which conformist moralities have refrained from concerning themselves, and for obviously obscurantist reasons.

Carefully avoiding the Jekyll-and-Hyde antagonism on which other films climax, Renoir allows Cordelier to call on Severin in Opale's body. For Opale's mind, even if enfeebled, retains enough of Cordelier to function, if not too efficiently, for a while. Only a pharmaceutical misfortune renders their symbiosis unviable (science's short-term solutions tend to elevate problems to a higher level. And such misfortunes are another form of life's, nature's, chaos . . . and freedom). The first of the film's conflicts unite Cordelier and Opale in alliance against society. Its principal representatives

---

* Perhaps "Cordelier" also suggests "Cordonnier", i.e. "Schumacher", remembering Renoir's pronounced limp. Thus we have an Opale-Octave and a Cordelier-Schumacher . . . " Opale, as a gem, may suggest Symbolism, aestheticism, dandyism . . . all features of Zola's Paris. His is the world of irresponsible pleasure—in contrast to the pleasurelessness of Cordelier. Is it going too far to see the shoemaker-monk as a human relative of Renoir's automata, like the toys of *La Petite Marchande d'Allumettes?* In fairytales, cobblers abound. The cobbler is the artisan crouched, from dawn to dusk, in the window, over his toil, and all but deformed by it, with crossed legs and hunched back—for all his virtuous diligence he's in danger of becoming a grotesque—even if he's a capitalist cobbler, like the shoe-manufacturer who is Elena's caricatural suitor. Unlike Cordelier, Opale seems almost to *dance*. . . .

** Blake: "One law for the lion and the ox is oppression." And "Tiger, tiger . . . "

are Joly, the "man in the street", and he's not identified with his legal profession, since he's also Cordelier's old friend, who reacts with naive shock and very slowly comes to almost understand what's going on. He, rather than Cordelier, soothes the child, and keeps some sort of mediocre decency going, protecting Cordelier against the system and the system against Opale. The second conflict opposes Cordelier and Severin. To Cordelier's 19th-century reserve, Severin opposes a brasher, 20th-century bundle of nervous tics. As his succulent secretary watches him adoringly, he puffs nervously at cigarettes, runs his hands over his face, rambles on apoplectically, won't listen to Cordelier, and, when Opale forces him to *see*, promptly dies of a heart-attack, thus (a) making Opale seem far more wicked than he is, (b), depriving Cordelier of the confirmation which would have enabled him to end his double life, and (c) killing himself even earlier in the story than Opale. For Cordelier is no more Opale's victim, or his own, than he is Severin's. Severerin is fanatic and destructive (by suicidal shock) as well.

The same hysteria recurs at other social levels. One scene, sketching the mounting disquiet of simple folk before a mysteriously closed door, recalls a scene before the garage door in *La Nuit du Carrefour*. There, anxiety became xenophobia. Here, a manservant rushes to fetch the axe with which Opale, in self-defense, terrifies everybody—and again Opale seems guiltier than he is. At all social levels (Severin, Cordelier, ordinary folk) truth *disturbs,* truth is panic. And surely the thought that Opale is to Severin as Boudu is to Lestingois *ought* to disturb us considerably. But if Lestingois's nearest counterpart is Maître Joly, there's a little something of Octave in Joly also, enough to clarify Renoir's remark: "I made a noteable mistake over . . . the solicitor. I wanted to use the kindness and natural naivety of the actor . . . to make his personage ridiculous as one is ridiculous in life . . . "

Another source of confusion lies in the film's aesthetic experiments. Recalling the ironic prologue of *La Chienne*, Renoir gives a new twist to the paradoxical co-existence of Lumière illusion and Méliès spectacle. When shown on T.V., Renoir's prologue briefly makes the film look like a special news feature. And one can imagine a more opportunist director sedulously nourishing the illusion, in a manner to which Stephenson's detective story format would lend itself very well. As it is, Renoir no sooner inaugurates the illusion than he undermines it—so that the illusion/spectacle can continue on its two levels. Renoir doesn't compère a regular TV programme, and few if any spectators can fail to be dis-"illusion"ed when Renoir cuts to a private conversation, months previously, at which no TV camera would ever have been present. Renoir isn't groping for the new compound of "illusion" and of "spectacle" which was soon to be achieved, with more conventional techniques, by Peter Watkins's *Culloden*. But by transubstantiating TV "immediacy" into "spectacle", he converts an impersonal fiction, of whose illusions the spectator is usually supposed to be in some sense the victim, into a "ceremonial gift" by the creator to the spectator. "Let us, smilingly, agree to enjoy this fiction of the real." One remembers the paradox of the Cretan saying "All Cretans are liars", and its solution in terms of meta-languages, or, here, aesthetic levels. Renoir's discreet reminders as to the unreality of the illusion and the actuality of the spectacle go directly back to the '20s avant-garde, of which he and Gance were by now the only active survivors. Gance defied realism to enhance the illusion, Renoir, perhaps through his connections with painting, which had long ceased to be illusionistic, seeks another path, breaking, or rather bending, the illusion, to permit an "alienation effect", of continuity with *actuality*, i.e. the reality in which the spectacle exists and from which the spectator will emerge. In an intricate (lie-cut-lie) yet self-effacing manner, he parallels the "ultra-illusion" preoccupations of Shirley Clarke (in *The Connection*), the "anti-illusion" asides of Godard, and the fascinating mixture of the two in Peter Watkins. He is also enabled to conclude with an author's first person comment (his judgement of Opale), something rare and useful in *fiction* movies, though "arrière-garde" in the novel, except in ironic or solipsistic forms. Ironically, therefore, to dispense with the "illusion of an illusion" (which is considered avant-garde), as painting had done sixty years ago, restores that freedom to say "Dear Reader . . . " which the novel all but abjured.

That *Le Testament du Dr. Cordelier* requires a good deal of exegesis isn't evidence of artistic failure. We have seen how regularly Renoir's richest movies were seen back-to-front, inside-out and left-to-right-reversed. Yet, while one can respect the thought behind the film—and provocations analogous to Bunuel's—the aesthetic experimentation seems to me a failure in amost every way. Given the impossibility, in Victorian Britain, of clearly describing Hyde's pleasures, and of expecting the reader to identify with Jekyll's more-than-tolerance thereof, Stephenson's detective-story format offered an ingeniously "gradualist" approach. Today such considerations scarcely apply, and Renoir's heavy reliance on uninteresting inter-mediaries is so much deadweight, eclipsing even that poetry of bland, crumbling facades which was one of his inspirations. A certain aesthetic irony is created, no doubt. Cordelier's most intimate friends in real life know less of him than we, the anonymous mass audience; and that's not a McLuhanite paen of praise to the medium so much as a judgement on modern solitudes. (Foreigners in *Carrefour;* truth, here . . .). But from all angles, the minor characters remain uninteresting, and the "theology", however real-istically or spontaneously muddled, further clutters our view of the truth.

The film's loss of human substance is evidenced by the scar that proves Opale and Cordelier are one. Maybe Renoir's use of a hoary old contrivance expresses an ironic disdain of slicker modern contrivances, but how much richer are the human possibilities of, say, Joly (or even Cordelier, via videotape) interrogating Opale about a past they shared, even a girl they both loved, and lost, and learning from Opale how completely the truth differed from what the inhibited thought? Brilliant as Renoir's use of the ellipse was in *French CanCan*, the resultant extension of the *temps-mort* here inspires only a grey spider-web of words. Doubtless the dialogue has four theoretical justifications. (1) Renoir remembers a turn-of-the-century mixture of formality and warmth, attitudes now too often assumed to be antithetical, and sacrificed for an air of casual intimacy which is unrealistic and repressive. He showed his respect for such styles earlier—through Rauffenstein and Boieldieu, through Danglard and the bailiff's men. (2) These characters are *also* smothered in a humanly inappropriate culture. (3) Inexpressive dialogue may constitute an excellent scaffolding for eloquent acting—which Renoir clearly hoped he was going to have. (4) TV is more effortlessly close to filmed theatre than the big screen. Alas, the Pelion of *la parole morte* is piled upon the Ossa of *le temps-mort*, and what may well have been planned as a lyrically oppressive succession of non-contacts and even non-acts rarely rises above banality, admittedly relieved by an elaborate sidestepping of a dogturd just outside the great white clinic.

An emphasis on the trivialities of living had already half-paralysed the French cinema, from the mid-'50s on (bequeathed by Becker to crime dramas by Molinaro et al.), and there was no need for Renoir (who had sketched that waiter's astounding mixture of mental blankness and virtuosity, and gone on to make a gesturally fast and subtly inflected film like *Le Caporal Epinglé*), to sacrifice so much to an "actualist" tedium. Maybe yielding too much to a philosophy of acceptance, or to Bazin-*Cahiers* theories of reality revealing itself to the un-constructive eye (a vulgar phenomenonalism too frightened of positivism), or to a conjunction of the two, the dialogue and storyline suggest an unrevised first draft, while the actors seem uncriticised, uninspired, lost. Amidst uneasy mugging, Jean-Louis Barrault stands firm. As Cordelier, his countenance becomes a mask of gloomy fastidiousness, of crimped self-denial. Opale's animal joy triggers his swaggering, shambling, acrobatic movements. Swinging his stick like a propeller with joie-de-vivre, he abruptly accelerates into attacks dealt with dagger-and-rapier rapacity. Renoir's remarks about "inadequate rehersal time" suggest his own disappointment in the result, although the principle extends, surely, to "inadequate revision time". Chardère, aiming at Renoir's centre-right entourage, suggests that they praised him into critical complacency. But an excessive modesty, perhaps in reaction to it, is as much to the point. If we allow Bazin's use of "Franciscan" to mean the holy folly of inoffensive acceptance, then Renoir's pagan Franciscanism has an angelistic ascendancy over his Apollonian control. For acquiescence may be another mode of *hubris*. Dionysus won't come when called, or just because the studio door is left ajar.

The film was shown at the 1959 Venice Film Festival. Chardère: "We touch bottom. Nothing remains of craftsmanship, of simple *savoir-faire* . . . One seems to be dreaming . . . " Clément Cartier: "Now Renoir has his own company which he directs as he pleases. It plays with that touching application of troupes under patronage. Embarrassed, disordered, gesticulating. . . . '' Jean de Baroncelli made the kindest of the sensible comments: "One must be indulgent towards experiments".

The film's critical reception sealed the fate of its intended demonstration. The French film industry, still terrified of T.V., argued that since the film was subsidised by a government agency, it constituted unfair competition for its own product, and a boycott was arranged by the National Federation of French Cinemas. French TV refrained from showing it, perhaps to placate its critics, perhaps still hoping to secure the synchronised release originally planned. Disputes eventually resolved, it was released in May 1961.

57

Le Dejeuner Sur L'Herbe
(Lunch on the Grass)

Immediately after *Cordelier* Renoir rushed ahead with a variant of the same experience. Pre-rehearsals lasted a period variously described by its director as just over two, or three, or nearly four weeks. For the first week Renoir rehearsed the actors, then technicians joined in. Thereupon Renoir with his designer, camera operator and assistant sought out locations, whose outlines were chalked on the studio floor. Rehearsals with such indicated topography preceded departure for 21 days' shooting on locations at Auguste Renoir's house at Les Collettes and around Cagnes.

The nature of the action was such that the six cameras tended to surround the scene rather than be placed in relay along it; consequently there was more possibility for cutting within the scene. The presence of up to 12 microphones facilitated the direct recording of dialogue, even in exteriors. Because the long takes gave a "continuous" sound picture, Renoir could accept the irruption of extraneous noises (e.g. aeroplanes now came and went gradually instead of suddenly appearing and disappearing as they would have done with brief breaks between set-ups). Studio dubbing was needed for only twenty or so phrases, victims of technical accidents.

The director of photography's extensive experience in newsreel work facilitated rapid and sure response to improvisation or accident. Thus "I was able to shoot . . . with a substantially smaller budget that if I had employed normal methods. I tried to make a . . . sort of filmed poem. And I feel one musn't sleep on a poem, it's written at a sitting. . . . This rapidity brought me a certain style . . . allowing me to follow my impulsions, without reflection . . . I was seeking to put myself—and the actors, and the technicians—into a state of exaltation, almost at the threshold of trance . . . once the rehearsals were over, I hardly influenced the actors during shooting . . . when they're surrounded by five cameras, the actors have to forget there's a camera present, they have to play for themselves, or rather for the situation. . . . "

Renoir and Catherine Rouvel at the time of *Déjeuner sur l'Herbe*

The story is not so much science-fiction as future-history-fiction. In the elections which will decide the first President of the United States of Europe, the favourite candidate is Etienne Alexis (Paul Meurisse). An amiably glaciated biologist, he is dedicated to the cause of artificial insemination and biotechnology. He communicates with his fiancée, Marie-Charlotte, who leads an organisation akin to the Girl Guides, primarily through television. It's felt that a "lunch on the grass" would facilitate a more appealing image. But a sullen local, Gaspard (Charles Blavette), sitting with his goat by the ruined temple of Diana, summons up a powerful wind, which transforms their picnic, first, into an unwilling dance, as their limbs strain against and float upon the tumultuous air, and then into a Bacchanalia. Alexis is blown into the arms of Nenette (Catherine Rouvel), a peasant girl long eager to apply his eugenic innovations. Her experience of fickle and lazy men inclines her to want artificial insemination and a child which will be altogether hers. Alexis's genes have excited her admiration and her animal vivacity overwhelms his fastidious misgivings, leaving him spiritually very shaken. Her purpose accomplished, she allows his colleagues to persuade her to efface himself from his life, for the greater good of Europe, science and the species. Distractedly pursuing her, Alexis finally, in his distress, accepts Gaspard's instruction to consult his goat. As he kneels to hear the oracle, his bureaucratic friends seize him and carry him off.

Time passes. His "nervous breakdown" is almost forgotten, until, on the eve of his wedding to Marie Charlotte, he comes across Nenette, now chambermaid in this hotel, and resplendently pregnant. One wedding replaces another, and the President of the U.S.E. will proclaim a new, scientifically less fanatical policy.

If *Le Déjeuner Sur L'Herbe* briefly becomes a poem, it is more constantly an imaginative pamphlet, of a kind long familiar in literature. The values celebrated by the "holiday impressionism" of Renoir *père* are justified against the bureaucracy's version of utilitarianism. To borrow an antithesis from *Orvet*, the spiritual materialism of the first contrasts with the empty spiritualism of the second. Although Renoir might have touched on genetic engineering and its new problems of class and caste (for in the New Order's meritocracy, erstwhile illusions of inborn superiority will become realities), he limits himself to opposing *polytechnicien* and peasant, the old France and the new. *La Vie Commence Hier*.

Alexis, like Cordelier and Severin, typifies a kind of moralistic rationalism more common in French thought than in Anglo-Saxon. In England, the contradiction between Darwinism, fundamentalism, Burkean conservatism, and evangelistic and unitarian idealism forced evolutionary Darwinism, as a moral code, into a passive role, and in America it came to be overlaid by *either* Social Darwinism *or* individualistic or ethnic issues. Despite the efforts of the Huxleys (both Thomas and Julian), H.G. Wells and Olaf Stapledon, English scientists are less likely than French openly to propound the evolutionary moralism implicit in such phrases of Alexis's as "les esprits les plus nobles . . . " His mincingly complacent manner, cockier, brittler, more irritating than Cordelier's more sombre style, is an incarnation of a distinctly French cocktail of rationalist puritanism, intellectual narcissism, superior self-sufficiency, and what is not so much an absence of sexuality as a kind of lightness of emotion. Alexis's servants, aping their master, refer to themselves as "les purs", and the term's Manichean overtones mightn't be inappropriate for a master race—to which they won't belong. Maybe they feel disembodied; monks whose monastery is worldly vanity. Nenette's embrace is needed to mellow this evolutionary snobbery. Alexis wonders whether the dinosaurs didn't, after all, die happy, "indifferent to the fate of their species . . . " Their happiness honours, not the irresponsibility of "Après nous, le déluge", but his assumption that disinterested, i.e. self-sufficient, reason is the only moral, and vitalist, reason for living. Heretofore he has been satisfied with his TV courtship, a media asceticism whose peculiar mixture of public banality and specious intimacy, of voyeurism and non-tactility, expresses the dessication undergone by interpersonal contacts as the so-called "global village" takes the place of the cathedral. Alexis, emancipated from the illusions of this "society of the spectacle" by Nenette's physical spirituality, loses all sense of ideo-intellectual propriety, and relaxes into sympathy for a shabby priest and taking a goat as Diana's oracle.

If Alexis' equivalent of the Cordelier-and-Opale duality is a schizoid combination of self-sufficiency and public responsibility, Nenette has devoted herself, in the flesh, to "the happiness of others—in the plural—and not of one alone." Where sexuality is concerned, Renoir is fond of the ellipse, not because it leaves things out, but because it helps ensure that more is involved in sexual transactions than merely the contact of two epidermes. Diana was the Goddess, not only of chastity, but also of pregnancy, presumably because both are aspects of female self-sufficiency. Alexis wants to improve the race, Nenette wants her own child. Both are perfectionists, narcissists at one remove, as it were. This film is over-simplified if one sees its heroine as an earthy, traditional, uncomplicated peasant girl. For her interest in artificial insemination betrays an emancipated imagination. It is to the city that she comes to have her baby. Twice, it is her independence and her mobility which bring her into contact with Alexis. Thus Pan (with goat and pipes) and Diana (feminine independence) ally themselves against Western rationalism and manipulationism—perhaps a masculine vice, insofar as dogmatic rationalism used to be a masculine speciality, but common also in two forms of "Women's Lib", one represented by Nenette herself, the other by Marie-Charlotte, whose youth organisation sports an ever so slightly militaristic uniform. Leftwing criticism implied that the film's eventual acceptance of the U.S.E. advocated the Common Market (which the left opposed); and that Alexis's eventual reservations about it applauded General de Gaulle's con-

cept of "l'Europe des patries" (which the left also opposed). Nenette's peasant family evoked Poujadism, with its right-wing thrust. The priest's complaints about his church's leaking roof were an allusion to recently re-kindled controversies about state aid to denominational schools. The sun-bronzed workers, weaving happily in and out of the story on their Vespas, and arguing away like a Greek chorus, were untypically affluent and *embour-geoisé*. One line, "happiness is perhaps a submission to the natural order" justified the most conventional, even reactionary, views on birth control, abortion, etc.

Personally I fail to see how any honest celebration of the natural can escape a certain submission to it, and much sentimentality would be avoided if we ceased taking for granted that the ideal mixture of acquiescence and manipulation, nature and science, abandonment and prudence, were second nature, or just within our cultural grasp. On which point it's perhaps not too unkind to suggest that my left-wing colleagues were making their "lost leader" a scapegoat for the very real difficulties of the left itself—or should one say of the lefts themselves? Internationalist at heart, it found itself waving the Tricolor against the Common Market. Predisposed to rationalist planning, it increasingly feared the "state capitalism" of bureaucracy-and-big-corporations. Traditionally anticlerical, it saw Alexis' sympathy with the priest as uncriticised approval, whereas it's maybe a stage on the way to his resort to an oracular and pagan goat. The priest is out of favour with both his parishioners and his hierarchy, and while hardly progressive seems carved of the same stout wood as his spiritual forefathers in *La Marseillaise*. If it might be better if all the factory lads and girls struck their tents and erected barricades, their mobility is also an image for their existence as an independent and critical force, prisoners neither of state capitalism nor Stalinism. The permissiveness of Nenette's parents indicates their adhesion to traditionally anticlerical sections of the peasantry, and although, to be demographically typical, they ought to be poor peasantry possibly voting Communist, their prosperous villa, steeped in Impressionist associations, relates them to the peasant models of Renoir *père*, and a poetic, or rather mythic, relationship to the generous fertility of nature and of human nature. Here, where the principal labour of the men is doing justice to the cooking of the women, lieth the region of Arcadia, in the closest spiritual proximity to the village of *Under Milk Wood,* and Dylan Thomas's play isn't exactly a hymn to the happiness engendered by generations of Calvinism. The wind is raised by the piper, not the priest, and Renoir's natural order must be an orgiastic one, of which this peasantry lives a human, stable, decent form. Of course such stability involves compromise; only romanticism supposes otherwise. To liberate sexuality from marriage is one thing; to anathematize sexo-social commitment is another.

Renoir's film is certainly a provocative mixture of visual lushness, of overt argument, of cinéma-verité (one discussion certainly looks as if the actors are speaking their minds, inexpertly, no doubt, but with human conviction), of pagan myth, of tale, and of allegory (Nenette's influence on Alexis no more implies a boudoir view of history than Delacroix's Liberty on the barricades is one particular woman who happened to be there). It exists in a curious, awkward, and intriguing mixture of intellectual and narrative conventions, recalling the mixture of pictorial conventions in the Manet painting from which it takes its name. And these conventions jar, to much the same purpose as in Renoir's preceding film; to ensure that the "illusion", by its internal contradictions, doubles as a "spectacle".

Certain passages celebrate gold days and blue days; a midsummer day's dream. "In making this film I had no choice but to think about my father a great deal . . . All in all, this film is something of a homage to the olive-trees under which my father worked so much. I also shot on the banks of a little river called Le Coup, which he painted a great deal, and in a village called La Gaude, where he painted a great deal, so the film is drenched in memories of my father . . . "

Garry Broughton: "The first shot after the television prologue and the title is a beautiful axial pan showing trees against the sky (accompanied by a theme on a flute). Pure impressionism, one thinks, and then the camera comes to rest on the figure of a fat old farmer, stretched out, hat over eyes, fast asleep in the shade, an image straight out of Breughel. In the same camera movement, Renoir has created a synthesis of impressionism (nature) and realism (man)." In contrast, the corridors down which so much chaos and merriment flowed in *La Règle du Jeu* are as empty as the wings of an as yet unopened theatre. The *rats d'hotel* scene in *French CanCan*, with its miror, marked the turning-point towards this vacuumisation of city life.

Perhaps the film's most beautiful moments are those of transition. As the river of wind disrupts the counterfeit picnic, civilisation isn't too easily disrupted. It ebbs and flows; after the first shock comes a partial recovery, then the orgy (for there must be an assent of the mind), and, finally, the encounter of Alexis and Nenette, on a riverbank apart, in an apparent inter-lude which sows the seed of a more subversive permanence.

Of nature in man Nenette is an adorable incarnation: "a delicious pumpkin", Dilys Powell called her. If the film's underlying theme overlaps with that of *Et Dieu Créa La Femme* (rustic promiscuity upsetting order), so her animality rivals Bardot's, but generously rather than aggressively, sunnily rather than defiantly, welcoming rather than tragic. Her pride in her flesh and all that happens within it is neither egoistic, narcissistic, nor that of a sex-object. Her name evokes nénés, French slang for titties—and, of course, Nenette-Nini-Nana. . . . Ambiguously with his nonchalance, Alexis has a little dance in his walk. His *hubris* renders him vulnerable to the wind, whose magic is called forth by an earthy demiurge: Charles Blavette, who played Toni. One can imagine this emissary of divine disorder being incarnated by Pierre Renoir, whose Maigret sharpness of glance would suit a pagan context also. What is order but equal and opposite imbalances—impulses which *dance*?

The antagonism of intellect and sensuality is a new theme in Renoir's work, and to those whose thinking is post- (rather than, like Renoir's, pre-) Freudian, must seem, not so much reactionary, as anachronistic. Adopting, provocatively no doubt, the heartfelt naivety of the man-in-the-street, the film rambles on about the noise of vacuum-cleaners, a point in itself as uninteresting as, to cite a 19th-century equivalent, the clatter of iron-rimmed cartwheels over cobblestones in narrow streets. As with *Cordelier* Renoir's experimental pursuit of spontaneity has deprived him of a certain critical detachment. Magic moments, intriguing aspects, remain isolate. Yet the discontinuity deserves further commentary. Oscillating between an *illusion* and a *spectacle,* it strikes a new balance between *hallucination* and *communication,* and anticipates the filmed pamphlets of Godard, even if the latter's deadpan readings are more to a defensively cool taste than Renoir's gregarious discussions. This time his method is the implicit one, of jarring internal conventions, à la Manet, rather than its predecessor's virtual 1st person. Perhaps Manet's canvas seems internally more contradictory than in its time, while the contradictions in Renoir's films have a more immediate purpose. Seeing it for a first time, when it was new, it provoked in me a happy complicity, which became a strange, but intense, para-aesthetic exhilaration. The crudenesses seemed to matter less than a distinguished artist's deliberate abandonment of convention for the sake of a new kind of involvement (with his collaborators and his material) and with his audience. Renoir's acceptance of all risks had a beauty akin to that of Rouch and Morin's *Chronique d'un Eté,* a similar, although not identical, search for spontaneity and frankness, which concluded with the directors' autoconfession of semi-failure to the audience. Renoir's creative vandalism informed an incoherent, courageous, poignant bundle of qualities for which one felt grateful in a way which is probably historically unrepeatable, and which was certainly abused by young film-makers with no artistic talent to risk or renounce. As Shirley Clarke put it, Renoir's film "could only have been made by someone of 6 or 60." In contrast to the imputations of second childhood which Renoir's erstwhile supporters on the left had little scruple in making, the American artist celebrates a declaration of innocence of the middle-aged conventions around which her own *The Connection* sought its intelligent, painstaking way.

One may return to Bazin's distinction between "the spectator in the first degree" (who concentrates on the illusory reality) and the "spectator in the second degree" (who concentrates on the aesthetic spectacle and the artist's thought). Much of *Cahiers'* subsequent confusions, and dogmas, sprang from overlooking the fact that the traditional response of all aesthetically sophisticated spectators had long been to consider first and second degrees simultaneously and in inter-relation. Even the naive spectator is keenly

conscious of a film's *character* (first degree) as *star* (second degree), and very different responses to *Le Déjeuner Sur L'Herbe* often depend on the proportion of first and second degree responses. Either way one may appreciate the idea of Priap Boudu elbowing Octave-Oscar out of the directorial chair and producing a film which is indistinguishably, or by turns, innocent or infantile, or mellow or senile, or lunatic or inspired, unconvincing or so frank as to be "naked".

The trouble is that Bazin's account isn't complete, and I should prefer another description of the aesthetic process. Confronted with any representational artwork, the spectator is involved in (1) his actual reality (sitting in a cinema watching a spectacle) *and* (2) the illusory reality (patterns of light-and-shade are accepted as faces whose expressions reveal feelings), *and* (3) the creative reality (director, star). Most spectators compromise in a way which may seem "illogical" but which is psychologically real and structured and reasonably predictable, between these three levels, as seems to them likely to maximise their enjoyment (or minimise their discomfiture). The traditional view has it that a film communicates successfully insofar as the spectator's interpretations of (2), correspond as closely as possible (one can never exactly reproduce) whatever experiences of the artist's contributed to his sequence of cinematic choices, contributing to a correspondence on the level of (3)—the spectator shares the creator's thoughts, thus growing in wisdom, or at least enlarging his experience. Although this last element, of real, or apparent, experience, remains mysterious and imponderable, it is usually considered the deeper understanding, and spectators of the second degree may see the first as merely a means to its end. Art seems to me a valuable human communion (as distinct from entertainment, evidence of status, etc.) only insofar as both (2) and (3) make an effective, enriching and maturing contact with the spectator's experience-of-his-own-experience.

Although traditional aesthetics rely extensively on what Bazin calls second-degree awareness (which I call third-degree) this factor was often underestimated where movies were concerned, largely because of their reliance on photography*. Bazin re-emphasised second-degree aspects, but only at the expense of a curious metaphysic whereby what Renoir called external realism would of itself be transmuted into internal realism if only it were given enough spiritual rope. Those aesthetic theories which led the static visual arts towards minimalism and conceptualism represent a further hypertrophy of third-degree consciousness, a usually myopic or neo-Symbolist hypersensitivity to aesthetic actuality, and an absence of curiosity concerning the richness of reality. The poignancy of Renoir's movie, in its time, was that of a hybrid.

While film aesthetics have tended to run about seventy years or so behind those influencing the static visual arts (often to the latters' disadvantage), certain underground movies have adopted strategies akin to those of Renoir here. The wild generalisations of the workers' discussion of the TV programme they are watching constitutes a middle term between the mealtime discussion of malnutrition in *The Southerner* and the utterly vulnerable seduction of the cameraman and/or spectator unsuccessfully attempted by the heroine/actress of Steve Dwoskin's *Take Me*.

Renoir's error seems to me to be of a different order altogether. Poems, however short, are rarely written at one sitting, and if they are it is because the poet's problems are his life, have never ceased to preoccupy him, consciously or otherwise, and have ceaselessly been "revised" in his mind before he puts pen to paper. One cannot expect this from a troupe of actors, or only after an altogether exceptional preparation in the way of casting. Chardère may well be right to see Renoir's adulatory entourage as his false muse at this time. Yet there is, after all, a point at which aesthetically sophisticated audiences exploit stylistic excellence as a distraction from or consolation for urgent experience, rather than as, first, a means of sharpening and nuancing experience, and then "consoling" us for it only in ways which enhance our understanding of it. Had Renoir achieved the trancelike first-degree quality he sought, then the new mode of artist-spectator-reality contrast might indeed have had its special edge.

Released before *Cordelier*, the film was received very warmly by most press critics, primarily for its (supposed) overlap with impressionism (really restricted to subject matter), for its charm, and for Renoir's general reputation. Within the French film industry it was, one suspects, resented, and added to the impression of Renoir as a director who had lost all his touch.

---

* Hence film criticism limped along for years with lumbering versions of *auteur* theory, style-and-content issues, etc.

58

Le Caporal Épinglé
(The Vanishing Corporal)
(The Elusive Corporal)

Renoir reverted to conventional techniques for his film of Guy Perret's novel, for seven years a pet project of Guy Lefranc, a commercially well established film director, although never known to figure in any critical pantheon. Like most of its characters, he had been held as a prisoner of war throughout the Occupation. In the event, the subject was offered to Jean Renoir, who read the novel at one sitting and accepted it. He collaborated on innumerable revisions of the script, while Lefranc remained with the film as its "adjunct au réalisateur". Jean-Pierre Cassel stepped into a role intended at various times for Daniel Gelin, Robert Lamoureux and Jean Gabin. The film (105 minutes) was shot, mainly on location, in Austria for the very restricted budget of two million (new) francs during the winter of 1961 and had its Paris premiere on May 23rd 1962.

Superficially, the subject relates to André Cayatte's *Le Passage du Rhin* and Claude Autant-Lara's *La Traversée de Paris*. All three revive uneasy aspects of unity and disunity during the Second World War. The corporal (Jean-Pierre Cassel) and his fellow-soldiers find themselves herded into P.O.W. camps. A first attempt at regaining liberty is made with splendid ingenuousness. The (1940) Armistice means peace; and peace means the end of war; and the end of war means the end of prisoners of war; and one simply logical soul packs his bag forthwith and steps out, to be stopped, to his indignant surprise, by the guards at the gate. As they face their inner enemy, a soul-destroying stagnation, the men reminisce over their peacetime occupations. Penchagauche (Jacques Jouanneau) took pride in his skill as a waiter. Ballochet (Claude Rich) read gas meters, which one wouldn't guess from the aristocratic airs with which he has equipped himself. An electrician is nicknamed Caruso because he fancies himself as a tenor. Emile, a peasant, is steeped in anxiety about his farm. Le Begue (The Stammerer) punched tickets on the Paris Metro.

The Corporal, Pater and Ballochet team up to make the first escape attempt, an alfresco, improvised, up-over-the-wall-and-away affair. But with the other two already clear, Ballochet loses his spectacles. His brothers-in-arms hesitate before abandoning him to his fate, and everybody gets caught, although lessons are learnt. The second try is another spur-of-the-moment gambit (or gamble, or gambol) beginning when they lock their guard in the urinal. But the truck aboard which they scramble was merely on sanitary run, and dumps them amidst the refuse at their captors' feet. The third attempt is planned in a more orderly fashion. But while they're dyeing their uniforms black to look like civvies, they're caught by the order-loving collaborationist, Adjutant Dupieu. Nonetheless, they work on his— divided—sense of duty, and he can't bring himself to denounce them. Thereafter they can forgo secrecy, and call on the co-operation of their comrades. While a quarrel over soup creates a diversion, the Corporal and Penchagauche get as far as a passenger train bound for France. On board they encounter a compatriot in drag, who gives them not only identity papers but a great deal of valuable advice. Penchagauche tries his method of acquiring false identities, i.e., speaking like a German official and stealing the documents pushed under the loo door by the obedient German citizenry. Penchagauche is unlucky; a German security official emerges. The Corporal watches his friend hustled off, but is himself turned back at the frontier, gently, selfishly, impassively, by a French official. Then he's sent to the Punishment Camp, where they all but break his spirit. His soul is saved when he runs into Ballochet, now a "trusty" living a life of luxury as the Germans' Post Corporal.

Eventually he develops toothache and is taken to a civilian dentist in the town, where he flirts with the dentist's daughter-assistant, Erika. Their feelings, and the French poets on her mother's bookshelves, reinspire his quest for liberty. Returning to the camp, he deals a sound slap to Ballochet, suddenly absurd in his complacent, gourmet's fastidiousness. Sent to work on a farm, the Corporal meets Emile once more. Their escape attempt is frustrated when the latter's passionate attachment to his suitcase enables a flock of geese to give the alarm. It's back to the Punishment Camp, but this time his soul is strong, and he is overjoyed to see Ballochet now paying for his repentance by waddling around in the knees-bend, pack-on-back punishment drill. The Corporal hastily dons his pack, rushes into the circle of pain, and moves at double-quick speed till he can whisper to his old friend.

Ballochet outlines his scheme for the film's fifth escape. He will simply walk to the wire at night and use his stolen wirecutters, with no attempt at concealment. The Corporal warns him against it and waits, anxiously counting. He winces as the machine-guns snarl. The Corporal's next escape is with Pater and Le Begue, helped by civilian clothes found for them by Erika. Although Le Begue's incongruous garb arouses suspicion, the other two evade pursuit by mingling with a funeral procession, and make it to a

Renoir during the shooting of *Le Caporal Epinglé*

train aboard which two powers for chaos take a whimsical hand. The first
is an elderly drunken German (O.E. Hasse), of ex-military aspect yet
splendidly crotchety disposition. The second is a squadron of R.A.F.

bombers. Trekking cross-country, they encounter a French prisoner who works on a farm and plans to settle there with its German widow when the war is over. He gives them food and they make their way to Paris. The Corporal and Pater meet again in a bridge over the Seine, in a streetscape curiously cold and empty, not, it would seem, uniquely because of the Occupation . . .

Renoir's descriptions of the film before and during its production (throughout which the script was in continuous mutation) sit uneasily on the finished film. One wouldn't describe it as a "quasi-documentary", although it may have struck Renoir as such after his Technicolor nostalgias; the Corporal's separation from the group seems somewhat at odds with "the great solidarity which links men in the common crucible of despair". Certainly, though, Renoir has refused to lean on *La Grande Illusion*: "In matters of detail, my film will be gay", although "it will portray the daily reactions of all the individuals." Its gaiety is authentic (having known despair) but has a certain dryness which, if not misanthropic, yet involves detachment. The characterisation of *La Grande Illusion* is "fat" and has an obvious humanism to it; this film is "lean". One thinks of René Clair, or of the de Broca comedies from which Cassel came to Renoir, and one understands, even if one can't settle for, Pierre Billard's description of the trio of heroes as "the somewhat wearisome marionettes of a great, sad game; the game of escape . . . The failure of Jean Renoir to give life to his Corporal is amplified by the utilisation of Jean-Pierre Cassel . . . as soon as both Cassel and Brasseur are on the screen, or both Cassel and Rich, it's always Brasseur or Rich whom one is tempted to watch, never Cassel . . . " Yet by an equally strange phenomenon, the actor who for me doesn't exist, at least in retrospect, is Brasseur (Pater) and the actor who epitomises the film is Rich (Ballochet). The film's summarising after-image is, if anything, a longshot of cold grey camp with a figure running. It becomes the curious antithesis of the Technicolor tapestries; a dispersion of figures amidst a dank, chilly mist. The elusiveness of the "corporals" is of its essence.

Is the film serious, or comic, or becalmed between the two? Is it *La Grande Illusion* divided by *Tire Au Flanc*, or *Tire Au Flanc* multiplied by *La Grande Illusion*? There's no doubt that Renoir's plastic sensitivity flourishes as strongly as ever with the incidental characters, even if it's ironic rather than pathetic. The German C.O. inspects his prisoners on an old pushbike which an orderly takes to and from him. The Punishment Camp officer in his own callous way is a prisoner of *la ronde*. Another guard repeats his superior's gestures exactly but his heart isn't in it. And that alien escapee whose woman's shawl looks like a monk's cowl has a dark sinuous silhouette, a troubling glance. The real difference is, perhaps, that in *La Grande Illusion* all the characters want to expand out of their "role" and reveal their human fullness. Here they are content, more pessimistically,

to remain within it, to pass unobserved. At times, this *distanciation* is a matter of *reculer pour mieux sauter*. One lightens the mood to sensitise, when the sudden whiplash stings more sharply. The Corporal, accepting soup after his first bout of punishment drill, suddenly dissolves in tears. Curiously, this scene strikes me as true but doesn't move me, as in *La Grande Illusion* it might. Is it too easily confused with a simple reflex of weariness? Has the film accustomed us to a drier tone, so that we cannot suddenly plunge as rapidly as the *mise-en-scène* seems to expect? Is Dwight Macdonald right when he suggests that " . . . the mood is comic and *gemütlich* . . .maybe Renoir overdoes it . . . " Not so long ago my critical conferes were both baffled and disgusted by the cynical comedy of Billy Wilder's *Stalag 17*; Renoir's tightwire walk between pathos and *apathos* is equally unfamiliar. The softpedalling of the immediate emotion is as marked as that of Harriet's despair in *The River*; but there is no flashback-and-commentary to help out. There is instead the sceptical sympathy of an old man watching young men, Renoir is even more present throughout this film than in the prologue and epilogue of *Cordelier*. Given the current aesthetic hypertrophy of the notion of time, one might stress that Renoir's achronologism is an aspect of the irony that comes with experience. The greyness of *Le Caporal Épinglé* is not that of memory, but of a world in itself without meaning, through which we, valiant pinmen, dash. It is the hideously static equivalent of the subjacent nightmare, noticed by Agel. Only here it is erected around us, institutionalised, as quarries, as barbed wire and searchlight towers, and as latrines. This is a film of perimeters (laid out below us, under panning shots), tightened into the bent bowed hopping of prisoners under punishment packs.

Jean Douchet observes that the six escape attempts are not merely sequential but accumulative. What appears to be merely a picaro's random trajectory is a pilgrim's progress, but in laps. The Don Quixote of escape because the Pilgrim of liberty; the Corporal begins as body and concludes as spirit. We would trace the spiritual progression in a manner which differs from Douchet's, yet intertwines with it. We would begin, earlier, with the innocent who, maladjusted like Boudu, because he is straightforward in a devious world, wants to walk home. The second attempt, less naive, is hastily improvised and indecisive. Ballochet lost his spectacles on purpose— but impulsive, cowardly purpose—and the others who hesitate, to help him, are lost. The third attempt is more decisive, but opportunist, and suffers poetic injustice. Sanitation helps, sanitation hinders; thus coincidence takes with one hand what it gives with the other. Next time recourse to order provokes authority's order. But this order, being divided against itself, is paralysed, and anarchy opens the way to a larger fraternity of purpose. The advantages of the larger group bring in their train the problems of identity, identification, and solitude (Another prisoner poses as a woman, identity papers change hands, and when the Germans shoot at the nimble Corporal a complete stranger gets it in the kneecap). The P.O.W. in drag has mastered all the problems of identity, and of solitude. Douchet refers to him as Death, although I should first modify the notion of Death by the acceptance of the effacement of self. His "monk's cowl" evokes the dedication of monasticism, from *The Seventh Seal*. Primarily, however, this Prisoner suggests to me a noble willingness to accept any disguise, any transformation of his ego, any loss of self, to become free. He is to liberty as Keefer is to life. And,

like Keefer, he has his sinister aspect, and in this respect Death is the appropriate reference. Helpful to others as he is, he has escaped not just the camps, but dependence on others, and that is freer than a normal man should be. The next episode, therefore, confronts the Corporal with a duplicate of *himself,* equally selfish, and not at all helpful. It is a fellow-countryman, a Frenchman, a man anxious to *preserve* his own freedom, i.e., to 'escape,' who turns the Corporal back, to suffer, this time, punishment designed to break, not just himself, but his *spirit.*

Surviving it, he is rescued by Ballochet with his disorderly access to physical sustenance. Food, in its turn, becomes a temptation—to stay put in physical comfort, and spiritual ignominy. Its spiritual falsity is revealed by Ballochet's affectations of dandy finickeyness. The slap which the Corporal gives him repudiates both his weakness and his snobbery (Janus faces of spiritual mediocrity). The Corporal turns from Ballochet to the French poets on the German doctor's shelf, that is, to international culture, to the spirit, to another second nature, another, nobler, "affectation": what man *can* make of man. Appropriately, Ballochet's food gave him toothache. The dentist's surgery offers pain piled on pain, but there's pain and pain, especially if it's being inflicted by two women, of whom one is briskly compulsive (like a mother), and the other tender and beautiful (like the daughter). Trust and love replace bisexual chameleonism. But if the Corporal is to live up to the *true* culture, of medicine, poetry and woman, he must repudiate the false culture of dandy-snob-epicure. He considers escaping, with Emile. But maybe his egalitarianism is somewhat idealistic, for this stout earthy peasant is an impossible mate, being obsessed with the caseful of suits which are an ironic parody of the selftransformation which the Corporal has come to accept. Their escape route lies through the guard's cubicle, and they get caught by geese, which are suggestive of territoriality, property, and rustic suspiciousness.

For Emile as for Ballochet, the Corporal's friendship—or inspiration— brings strange rewards. Did that slap inspire Ballochet to martyrdom, or goad him to a task beyond his capabilities? Ballochet had long ago transformed himself: from meter-reader to aristocrat. But his disguise procures him only minor privileges. The slap shatters his game of individuation via pseudo-personality, of fraternity via ersatz condescension. We can't be sure why he decides to walk through the wire. Has he reacted to his glimpse of the truth (his helplessness) by losing himself in the illusion of straightforward audacity? Does his spiel about straightforwardness mask what he knows to be an expiatory suicide? If so, does he mask it so as not to embarrass his friends, so that pretence (art) appears as the redeeming nobility of the deeply injured? Or does he, or his art, involuntarily or otherwise, point the way to the next stage in enlightenment: the realisation that *real* liberty can take suicide, self-abandonment, in its stride. The Corporal feels in himself the bullets that rip Ballochet; he has "found" another, in his own responses, has "found" death of his exclusive self. The funeral corresponds to the monk's cowl, but extends it, socially, into a whole criss-cross of people, hypocrisies, purposes and pursuits. At last a French "peasant" (like Emile) who is trusty (like Ballochet), and about to become a German peasant, helps him across the border.

But in Paris the Corporal encounters the emptiness of modern life, the streets without perimeter. One meets, one parts. By the enterprise of escape, one could, briefly, bridge the gap between solitude and camaraderie (both well-assorted and ill-assorted). Now only an uncertain friendship distinguishes Paris from a prison with no *need* for wire . . . because there is no need for a deep camaraderie. Douchet: " . . . only Pater can and must achieve the escape with Caporal . . . . The reason is easily understood. Penchagauche, the café waiter, Emile the peasant, Ballochet the gas company employee, or the stammering metro-ticket inspector, all have a profession . . . Pater, the vagabond, deprived even of the notion of value, is content to exist in a natural state." The vagabond escapes, but without the spiritual pilgrimage, achieved the Corporal. Third in Douchet's hierarchy comes Le Begue, whose limitations are revealed by his underground profession, and, oddly, he gets no further than the funeral procession, which is another way of putting people underground. It is the nomads who can escape—the camps, society . . .

Granted the opposition of mind and body in Cordelier and *Dejeuner,* one may yet wonder whether Renoir really looks down on the body as Douchet's essentially Christian preference of spirit for matter implies. Certainly Douchet is absolutely right to stress the significance of that moment where the Corporal, shrinking from the pain of dental treatment, begins conjugating the past tense of the passive voice of "to humiliate". Thus word-mind overcomes pain-body, accepting the significance of the experience, but looking forward to its having been assimilated, that is to say, already learning the lesson (conjugation as schoolroom diligence). Inspiration begins in poetry (Ronsard) and concludes in grammar. Renaissance man erects the ideal of the "whole man", of which the aristocrat, the amateur-gentleman, are descendants. The Corporal, learning from Ronsard, becomes a poet and aristocrat, but humbly. He is the stoic counterpart of the whistling clown. And we remember, if we haven't before, the nickname of the ticket-inspector: Le Begue, The Stammerer; the man who can only begin to speak.

He suffers from a kind of mutilation, and his peacetime role places him. As ticket-inspector, he is on the side of the guardians, of the gamekeepers; he stops people travelling free. He's stunted; his civilian duty is a kind of parody of fraternity; he initiates a contact with one person after another, but never gets past punching their ticket, their identity paper, as it were. He is constricted by his job, as Ballochet, another inspector, is constricted by his attempt to escape from it. The identification—underground employee/working class—is more evident in French than in English, partly because the Communist Party used metro assassinations as a symbol for the Resistance, partly because of the frequency of metro-strikes.

Thus the themes of communication and fraternity are conjoined. Pater's affection for the Corporal is almost a dumb animal's, and one suggestion is that if he refuses to take part in certain escape attempts it is because the hazards of war, and the social barriers of peace, would make a continuance of their friendship impossible. In a sense, then, the Corporal is Nini, or Danglard, seeking freedom irrespective of their lover's feelings. He is *l'homme fatale,* and Pater, while he prefers to be with him, must also choose self-imprisonment. The Corporal seems to be more open in his feelings to Ballochet and, when he slaps him, he goads him to his best, most tragic "performance"—liberation by suicide—it is in an apotheosis of the mental-spiritual values which Douchet attributes to the Corporal. Ballochet over-reacts, or can't face reality, and prefers a suicide which the Corporal feels and which helps its empathising spectator on the road to altruism. In a curious way, Ballochet is Nana—the selfish child who goads the realist to transcend himself, to become others. "L'enfer, c'est les autres", says a character in Sartre. In Renoir, the others is a reality which lies on the other side of a purgation, both of oneself, and of the one particular being whom one loves exclusively, in whom one seeks to localise and to limit one's unselfishness. Pater, unselfish in one way, is selfish in another. He doesn't seek to possess, he doesn't seek to identify with, he just likes to be with. Maybe he doesn't ask enough—like Felipe, the "chameleon" in *The Golden Coach.**

The film's crux is the terrible problem: liberation from boredom by liberation from self. It's no surprise that the faces of the principals, vivaciously delineated as they are, fade into greyness. It affects even their names. Douchet calls the Cassel character Caporal as if that were his surname. And then again *Caporal* is the name of a cheap, eminently expendable cigarette.

The first and the third escapes are made with three people (three, that

---

* Probably, in the last analysis, the name *Pater* isn't an accident, or it's a happy one. August Renoir was a great escaper—during the siege of the Paris Commune, he was given a pass by both the attacking and defending forces, and painted while the slaughter went on around. If one accepts a Freudian interpretation in other cases, there seems no reason to reject it here. The name reverses the roles. But Pater is Jean, and the Corporal is Auguste. The son loves the elusive father-brother. Ballochet is the artist as child, pretending to be a kind of super-father (the aristocratic role).

unstable number, the number which, more than company, is an intimate crowd). Ballochet, the eloquent, is replaced by the stammerer. Perhaps the friendship of the binational "peasant" is the Corporal's reward for taking the gross Emile along. But never in Renoir is a symmetry exact. The "peasant" will never go back to his nation, his land and his family, for the very good reason that his nation gave him neither land nor family. Being only a day labourer on other people's land, he couldn't even afford a family. And this detail isn't a contrivance: demographers seem agreed that the age of marriage was traditionally higher in the English lower classes than now because of economic impediment. The enemy country is this man's country, and the film doesn't blame him, given his proletarian generosity to the fugitives. His antithesis is the German aristocrat, whose jingoistic bonhomie all but exposes the Frenchmen to capture. But when he decides that the R.A.F. bombers are Wotan banishing the impure Nazis from Germany's sacred soil, he makes confusion worse confounded and gives them a chance to get away. He oscillates between being agent of doom and agent of salvation. His visionary absurdities also act as link between the fictional story and those newsreel inserts which, so thoroughly out of key in their irruption, so thoroughly humiliating (for the French) and depressing (for our characters) in their context, here turn about, establishing the need for a sustained, massive and free purpose which only feels like fate. Escape is, in the end, a collective effort—French poets, a German dentist's daughter, British bombers . . .

Douchet also poses the film's fundamental polarity: liberty versus excrement. It's no accident that latrines figure so largely in the action, and the precise contents of the sanitary truck no doubt approximate to those of the climactic tank in *The Magic Christian*. The equation of imprisonment and stagnation with excrement is a motif which no ex-inmate of English barrack-rooms will find obscure; a man who curries favour with those set over him is called a "brown-noser", and the wartime slang for "bored" was "browned-off". Here a prisoner, resentful of emptying the Germans' cesspool, adds to it so as to feel he's working for himself, at least. The Corporal observes, "If you live in *merde* (shit) you'll die in it". If the Corporal's buoyancy is appropriate for comedy, the excremental notations, emollient, by exaggeration, of the states of mind they signify, also contribute a quality which one might define as Rabelaisian pessimism. We are not so far from Huxley and Céline (once named by Renoir as a favourite author) or from the blackness of *La Chienne. On purge le Caporal.*

After two avant-garde experiments, *Le Caporal Epinglé* is impeccably professional, despite a double generation gap (the director old enough to be the grandfather of leading players too young by a generation for the events they re-enact). Is this that rarity in Renoir's career, a perfect, minor film? One can, after all, justify even Ballochet's dialogue, which several critics found "too literary". Ballochet constructed his fastidiousness from books, taking to an extreme the Corporal's more cursory indebtedness to Ronsard. Certainly, Ballochet's archaic, incongruous style, links with the dessicated formality of the dialogue throughout Cordelier, and the mincing affectation of Alexis in *Déjeuner*. But if this film is minor, it is so only insofar as its characters are unaware of the moral patterns which they live out. It is just this closure of consciousness, this insouciance, which renders this film so right, lean, dry. For it is also the film's spiritual mainspring. Integrity is liberty is duty, and the film's affinities are with existentialism; as also is its sense of solitude. Yet it alters existentialism's, or rather Sartre's, tone in the hopefulness which accompanies its regret that society, less free than atomised and alienated, offers so little chance for travelling companions to achieve a deep fraternity. The Corporal is as unaware of his morality or his "motives" as Camus's Outsider, like whom he finds a philosophical liberty, although it lies through fellow-travelling, not its negation (murder).

In *The River* Renoir invited us to watch a woman reviewing her girlhood, in a new perspective. In *Le Caporal Epinglé*, a man matures, morally, on the level of his reflexes, with none of the usual detours through self-consciousness, self-justification, or willed (or faked) self-realisation. Cassel's essentially comic style is swift, light and lively as a jumping flea. He would shrug off all notions of salvation, moral beauty or elitism. In asserting the comic as a vitalist response to life's radical futility—or sadness—Renoir pulls the rug from under the romantic cliché of the tragic clown, and offers us an anti-Hamlet. If *The River* is Hindu in its sensuous acceptance, *Le Caporal Epinglé* is athletic and Buddhist in its ascetic evasiveness, except that it won't renounce fraternity. The laughter in Buddhism is that of a tolerant immunity, and is satirical, and this film's cold, chastened, smiling humanism seems to me at once moving and frightening, deft, perfect and profound.

59

Renoir Mon Père
(Renoir My Father)

Renoir's biography of his father had matured in his mind many years before its publication in 1962. Biographies of great men by families or intimates are numerous enough, and scarely exempt from the prejudices and loyalties which infiltrate every human relationship. The mere project of writing a biography is apt to freeze souvenir into cliché, just as the amateur's old Box Brownie freezes its subjects into their only too appropriate attitudes.

Renoir's mixture of observations, anecdotes and speculations reveals not only the man but the sensibility in which both the man's actions and the painter's work were rooted. A thematic which some have thought narrow through myopia is revealed as a conscious choice, related to a world which Renoir *père* saw with the caustic clarity of innocence. There is little or no attempt at psychological analysis, and the father's moral and other strategies are indicated but not schematised. The biography remains within the Boswellian mode, an inspired reportage tracing a sensibility throughout dimensions which the work reveals without defining.

In a sense, the book is itself impressionist. If Renoir observes time carefully (we always know just when we are), he altogether fragments normal narrative structure. The temporal kaleidoscope paraphrases the impressionist moment, and Renoir thus follows the natural flow of the literary medium, and its evolving tradition from "the story" to the "stream of conciousness". His fidelity to sensibility allows him to succeed in evoking a Paris he cannot himself have seen, through stories, and details, in those stories which he remembered, just as he presents and absents himself with the serene and sensible convenience of the third-person narrative. The book exists in a mode between the eternal present of impressionism and the encyclopaedic nostalgias of Proust—both being dependent on a kind of discriminatory omniverousness over atoms and chronons of detail. This responsiveness becomes the antithesis of modern alienations. Immersed in the subject, one forgets oneself; responsive to others, one sees them from a variety of viewpoints, even when the subject is oneself. The integration of these processes is infinitely more demanding than stylised reductionisms which, supposedly rigorous, are in fact only too systematic and impoverished. Renoir's book is thus diametrically opposed to a post-humanist Western Europe culture whose thought tends to polarise between a tight introversion and an impersonal rationalism. Through father and son alike, it asserts the gentle, yet often scathingly disinterested, wisdom of sensitised extroversion.

Freud once remarked that it had been his fate to discover what every nursemaid knows about childhood sexuality; Auguste speculates on the influence of bottle-feeding on adult character as nonchalantly as if middle-class rationalism and illiterate wisdom had never gone their separate ways, nor intellect split intelligence from intuition. The sensuous and the sociological are similarly linked. "In Paris the steam from the casseroles still gives the passers-by a clue as to whether a Burgundian is stewing kidneybeans with bacon or a Provençal is preparing a dish heavily flavoured with garlic." Renoir's sense of class is as natural, as sensuous, as his sense of region; hence, too, his sense of the individual and the collective as interpenetrating and interdependent.

He begins with the period when his contact with his father was closest, because both continuous and adult; the crippled soldier convalesced alongside the crippled widower. With his father's respect for the eighteenth century as a cultural watershed, he evokes, anticlockwise, his great-grandfather's death (1845), his brush with Louis XVIII (1815), his marriage (1796) and birth (1773). This recalls his father's views on heredity, and enables him to slide smoothly up the branches of the family tree to return to the year of his own father's birth. Later, his great-grandfather's death introduces a panorama of the Paris in which his grandfather was reared, and of those surviving inns as the author found them. It's only apparently paradoxical that as our historical senses (our senses of the past as different) has improved, our sense of our own roots has lost in emotional force. Renoir's temporal flexibility restores both the past to itself, and the past in ourselves.

While, obviously, the son has stressed in the father that which he took from the father, one cannot but be struck by the light which the father's personality throws on his son's films. Bazin's remarks on the river as the film-maker's motif are anticipated in a reiterated image of the painter's: "One is merely a cork", and "You must let yourself go along in life like a cork in the current of a stream." He indicates the general strategy of Renoir's career: "You go along with the current . . . Those who want to go against it are either lunatics or conceited; or, what is worse, 'destroyers'. You swing the tiller to the right or left from time to time, but always in the direction of the current." There is a constant fascination with the culinary arts, "a deep respect for what was still left of the 18th-century way of life in France". A suspicion of man's derangement of nature re-echoes certain caustic remarks of Renoir *père*. "It's all Pasteur's fault. With his vaccine, and all the children who have been saved by it, this planet is getting dangerously over-populated.

Perhaps God has sent us pederasty to keep things in balance." The balance in such remarks between peasant conservatisms and urban tolerance, between a reverence for the natural and a bracing heartlessness, between an "aristocratic" indifference and a "democratic" concern, is a fine one.

" . . . to express himself well, the artist should be hidden . . . The trouble is, that if the artist knows he has genius, he's done for. The only salvation is to work like a labourer, and not have delusions of grandeur." Jean, also, carefully speaks of his craft, and effaces himself behind his actors, or his theme, or the requirements of commerce, or collaborators, including Beaumarchais and Vivaldi. Both father and son were cavalrymen, and Gaston Modot's description of Jean's *dréssage en douceur* paraphrases a cavalry officer's testimony as to Auguste's skill with horses: "He lets them do what they want, and finally they do what he wants." Father and son began their careers in related media, Auguste as a porcelain-painter, Jean in ceramics. The son analyses an aesthetic choice of his father's in terms reminiscent of his own: "One would be forced either to work from Nature, with all the uncertainties that implied, including the tricks played by the sunlight; or else to work in the studio under the cold precision of controlled light." How the impressionists converted those difficulties into opportunities is a matter of art history. Throughout his career the son frequently swung the tiller between those alternatives. Maybe Renoir's sense of the significance of the *commedia dell'art* was sparked off by his father's enjoyment of the knockabout shows staged outside the theatres of "Le Boulevard du Crime." *Les Enfants du Paradis* opens with Prévert's hero performing in just such a show.

Auguste, as a child, played marbles under the trees past which Louis XVI walks to his eventual execution in *La Marseillaise*. That monarch's defense of toothbrushes echoes a discussion between the director's grandparents. The cobra with whom one can co-exist was a companion of Jean's uncle Eugene. Boudu and the poachers have something of a common model in one Baudry, "an old curmudgeon who had broken for good with civilization and the law." To his mother's gifts (which weren't so cold as Lestingois' charity, since she meant him to spend them on drink, because it made him happy), Baudry would reply, "You are more beautiful than *Madame des Etangs*" (The Lady of the Ponds). "We never learned who the lady with the poetic name was", but we might recognise something of her in *La Fille de l'Eau*, played by Catherine Hessling, the father's last model and the son's first wife. Auguste, too, was "attracted by the 'cat' type of woman." La Belle Abbesse may have been inspired by Gabrielle's anecdote of how Jean himself, when very young, was introduced to Toulouse-Lautrec and his "two female friends of the moment; two Montmartre women in Algerian dress with exotic names. They did the belly-dance at the *Moulin-Rouge*."Auguste, like Danglard, was frequently inspired by the "working girls he stopped on the street. And how often those casual encounters developed into warm friendships!" Their technique is identical: "Introduce me to your mother!" Even *On Purge Bébé*, apparently Renoir's least personal film, correspond to a chapter which begins, "Renoir was opposed to all efforts to train young children," and includes father and son discovering a common propensity to involuntary relaxation of bladder control on tense occasions.

The transportation of showbusiness and church was also a common theme. Jean describes Auguste's evocation of his youthful success as a singer. "'I was concealed behind the great organ', he said. 'I was alone, yet at one with them.'" As is Danglard, behind his feminine musical-box. Renoir found "my brother Pierre playing with a miniature altar equipped with the necessary accessories for playing Mass. 'What are you going to be when you grown up?' My father asked Pierre. 'An actor', came the quick reply. Renoir meditated on this for a moment, then said to his friend, 'Perhaps you are right; an actor and a priest are pretty much the same.'" If, in *Le Carosse d'Or*, showbusiness shades into the sacrament at one end of the spectrum so, in *Nana* and *French CanCan*, it shades into prostitution at the other. "Sometimes we got on the subject of whores. . . . Everyone had a role to play in life, and that was all."

One speaks of a spectrum, not a hierarchy. Auguste's often scathing but basically affectionate interest, perhaps even fascination, in ladies of easy virtue culminated in a platonic and possibly apocryphal friendship with two beautiful whores each of whom offered to keep him in idle ease. Yet Renoir believed in faithfulness, and, in the films as in the home, there is a distinct reticence or reserve. François Poulle points out how rare, in Renoir's films, is the sensual or passionate kiss; indeed, the one conspicuous exception, in *Partie de Campagne*, becomes a big close-up of a trapped, dilated, tragi-ecstatic eye. "I never saw my father kiss his wife in public, or even in front of us children, though I except the conventional goodbye kiss in railway stations." A married couple or a pair of lovers showing their feelings too openly in public made Renoir uncomfortable. "It won't last," he would say, "They're waving it about too much." Renoir's sensuality is more deeply interfused, and his films do not have that curious coldness, that air of general repression, which so often goes with the idealisation of erotic spontaneity. Douchet's canine comparison for Pater's love for the Corporal has a precedent in the director's own imagery. Recalling his friendship with Cézanne's son he writes "I liked to be with Paul simply for the mental and physical pleasure of being with him, just as a dog likes the company of another dog. And I know he felt the same way about me. In India you find this silent appreciation of another's presence . . . "

The father's vision might be likened to a narrow-angle lens, the son's to a wide-angle. The father's might seem merely hedonistic, perhaps self-indulgent, in its insistence on the pleasing; the son's self-effacing in a flexible acceptance of other interests, of the "big" problems, of the social network. The father's seems more tenderly self-imposing, a beautifully controlled infatuation, the son's more receptive, even maternal, and more complex. The father was presumably aware of having found for himself an artistic mode to which civil wars and commitments were not relevant; and the son's biography reveals Auguste's anti-intellectualism as a lucid, intelligent position, quite distinct from a "know-nothing" brutishness. The paintings are its fruit, nurtured not by a mindless innocence but by a fully matured wisdom whose display was reserved, ironically, for the dinner-table.

Correspondingly, the son turned to the cinema at first for its relaxed poetry and its technique—analogous to his father's "sport" and "craft". Gradually he found himself caught up in the dramatic and the social. All that the father carefully excludes from his art (which is a homage to life at its most indulgent), is admitted and explored by the son, but with a characteristic impersonality: via friends, influences, collaborators, requirements, accidents. Whence the grain of truth in the *Premier Plan* image of a Jean Renoir who is well-meaning, merely responsive, and non-existent—a helpful nonentity, like the deathlike escaper in *Le Caporal Épinglé*. But Renoir is dependent in a way which ought perhaps to be second nature to more 20th-century artists. Ours is, after all, an era of outer-direction, of multi-media, of one hundred and one forms of social interaction and teamwork, not all of which are as debilitating as critical theories, hankering after romanticism, too easily imply.

Les Cahiers du Capitaine Georges (The Notebooks of Captain Georges)

Renoir's long-standing interest in more personal creative forms continued with a novel, published in 1966, whose full title in English is *The Notebooks of Captain Georges: Memories of Love and Warfare 1894-1945*.

His choice of a verbal medium represents the natural accomplishment of the reflectiveness, the self-communion, evident in his work from *The River* on. For while movies, for Renoir, are the medium of creative interaction and exchange, of spiritual commensalism, the solitude of the writer's study intensifies self-awareness and self-detachment.

Furthermore, personal expression and incessant revision ("improvisation") aren't caught in the gears of an expensive organisational machine, whose physical conditions are sufficiently taxing for a man of Renoir's years. And most important, event and commentary quite naturally intertwine. Despite a recent evolution, and liberation, the film medium is still influenced by the convention of agreed illusion, and it would be difficult even today for a director to comment on his own film, in the straightforward way in which a novelist may, if he wishes, insinuate comment, by his choice of word, or third-person intervention. The first person hero can say "I felt that . . . .", whereas a film's facial expressions are often overlooked or misread. Renoir's overlaid voice at the beginning and end of *Cordelier* comes near an author's first person. (Chris Marker and later Godard took matters further—although at the expense of transforming film-fiction into film-essay.) More usually, films rely extensively on the affective, evaluative and moral overtones of physiognomy ("generous" or "mean"). If the printed word is less intensely tactile and sensuous than images, it still permits a more rapid, evocative and complex interaction between mental sensations of heterogeneous kinds—

particularly abstractions, invisibles, and generalisations.

Renoir's first novel features two narrators, both elderly, writing what is, in effect, their first novel. The solitude which is the writer's creative situation is continuous with their plight. Insofar as this "Chinese box" structure suggests isolation and alienation, it might seem rather avant-garde, but it is also, of course, archaic and common enough in the "tale" from which the novel historically evolves (e.g. *The Thousand and One Nights, The Decameron*). It becomes particularly elaborate just before the "tale" turns into the novel (e.g. *Melmoth, Frankenstein*). It persists in, for example, Stephenson, Conrad, and particularly the detective story.

The friendship of Richard Hartley and Captain Georges is re-echoed in the ambiguous, far from simple, pattern of tolerance and concessions between Georges and Emilien. Hartley, the shy passive man with very little experience of women, discovers his affinity with Georges, the man with a privileged experience of them. The man of the world, at home with aristocrats, demi-monde and barrackroom alike, is confounded by the curious alliance of materialism and religion in the peasant soul. His idyll with his one love, Agnes, recalls the theme of purely physical infatuation projected for *Woman on the Beach*, but transposed into the pinks and pastels of *French CanCan*. Georges's military camaraderie, his easy involvement with women of all kinds, assort intriguingly with his solitude and self-sufficiency.

Hartley and Georges come to like each other through a common interest in breeding dogs; Georges's relationships with his mare, *La Joconde*, constitutes a conspicuous sub-theme. On the subject of man as animal, Renoir's views are in complete contrast with the assumptions of "Nature red in tooth and claw" or the Social Darwinist view of society as a jungle in which almost every man's hand is against every man's. Relationships between human beings are largely a matter of grooming, of taking care.

As Cordelier is to Opale, so Georges is to Boudu: complementary characters coming to a similar solitude. Boudu epitomises impulse and irresponsibility without concern; Georges epitomises another kind of promiscuity, that of detachment and friendly responsibility without passion. His profounder attachments are subject to reincarnation: Nancy, Agnes, Hartley's unmarried mother.

Georges's willingness to pay for his pleasure has nothing sordid to it. Money plays an essentially similar role in another kind of companionship, that of the barrackroom. It is merely an expression of friendship, more respectful even, for it allows the recipient to choose what use he will make of it. It is a more generous giving of oneself than the most "unmercenary" declarations or subtleties. It is a crutch for the nervous soul, and when accompanied with a real respect, can free the irresponsible from guilt. It is that form of taking care which least binds its beneficiary. Fidelity is another mode of relationship, and here reveals its feudal aspects. Agnes is faithful to her husband and her code, her fidelity matching that of Rauffenstein, and as destructive of herself and of others. Her fidelity takes a living death silently in its stride. In our minds' eye, we can all see Émilien: less sneaky than Michonnet, less pompous-cum-affable than Dufour, far less kind than Maigret. On the autobiographical level, barrackroom comradeship, the mulling wine round the stove, comes very close indeed to the unit of *La Nuit du Carrefour*.

Renoir Mon Père recalls a man whose personality was the centre of a family, yet who retains a nimble elusiveness. The novel which follows it evokes a man without a family, but with a hundred half-families (nurse and major-domo, Wuillaume and his horses, his barrackroom comrades, the Colonel and Lucie, Agnes and the avuncular Marjeulin, Agnes and Emilien, even, most bizarre of all, the homosexual Russian prince who meets Georges on a train and wants him to marry his handsome sister). Finally, post-humously, comes the link, through Hartley and a slut, between Georges and Agnes. Small wonder, given this family theme, that the possibilities of incest are nonchalantly evoked. Georges at fifteen: "The only desirable member of the household was my mother, but I felt that I had no talent for playing the hero of a Greek tragedy. I was afraid to tackle any of her women friends. Some were decidedly possible, but they were not to be trusted. It would have to be a prostitute," perhaps one of those creatures mentioned in the tabletalk of Renoir *père*. Long before Freud, Stendhal blandly recalled quite unsublimated incestuous desires. Even after Freud, by whose theories Renoir has never shown any trace of influence, these brisk, nonchalant references suggest a similarly natural sophistication—like his father's observations on bottle-feeding, or on overpopulation in relation to personality disorders.

The novel has many cross-references to Renoir's other works. *Orvet* has a servant called William who lacks respect for his merely bourgeois employer, a writer also called Georges, until the latter threatens to trounce him. The play and the novel share an interest in the English aristocracy. Both William and Wuillaume (an explicitly Anglo-Norman name) appear lost within the functional convention of their role (impeccably correct); both turn out to be influential and individualistic; both establish standards by which their middle-class employer feels judged. By comparison with the French aristocracy's emphasis on court, etiquette and system, the English aristocracy retained closer links with the country gentry and with middle-class mercantilism. Its apparently unbending snobbery, its "stiff upper lip", is also utilitarian and realistic. The affinities and contrasts between the French, German and English aristocracies have fascinated many writers: the theme is a "public" one. Yet, like any artist's chosen themes, it has a private aspect: "My grandfather was thus able to live a life of leisure. Making his wound an excuse for his natural indolence, he never left his armchair . . . " One thinks of Auguste and Jean together during the latter's convalescence—as of Captain John.

Vivid as Renoir's cinematographic tactility is, the prose of *Les Cahiers du Capitaine Georges* permits a sensual intelligence whose movie equivalent would have required a complete transformation of cinematic style and basic syntax, a recourse to means since indicated in the occasional underground film. Georges evokes his nurse: "Today, more than forty years later, Nancy still lives on for me. I never attempted to see her again. She married Corneille and they went to New Zealand. Except for the odour, the scent of her flesh mingled with the scent of violets, my physical recollections of her are vague. She was blonde, but the word is now no more than an adjective. I evoke her, not in human shape, not in any definite shape, but rather a very soft cushion, soft but firm, wholly enclosing me. It is not silk or hay or cloud, but a cushion of living matter."

And of Agnes: "What best reminds me of the velvet texture of her breasts are the lobes of my own ears. All I hope for, in faithfully and truthfully compiling this personal memoir, is that it will bring her back to me, to the point where I can recover the sensation of her breasts beneath my finger-tips."

Renoir's sensuousness, as fine as Colette's, is less tense, less cryptic, more freely extended to reflections and associations—canine rather than feline. Within a few years, perhaps, the stream-of-conciousness cinema, adumbrated by certain films of Mary Ellen Bute, Conrad Brooks and Carl Linder, will have achieved an equivalent flexibility and precision. The visual equivalent of the above memory of Nancy is very near that jelly-like consistency of female flesh so often to be found in the paintings of Renoir *père*— and, in a different emotional key, the distensions of flesh in Francis Bacon. The play of tactile sensation within visual images indicates the other new dimension through which such a cinema might move. It is the "natural"— yet infinitely difficult—development of the "pictoriality" of *French CanCan*.

The novel can easily be misread as a minor, moving, sentimental piece. The second world war and its spiritual aftermath has rendered even the tolerant or affectionate accusation of sentimentality so lethal that it's tempting to take a critical line of relatively little resistance and claim merely that in the context of Renoir's whole work his novel becomes something more than that. Yet its equipoise of discipline and openness, of loneliness and friendship, of mellowness and pessimism, of forgiveness and cynicism, of loss and reparation, with feelings as water into which pebbles are thrown— always patterned, always unstable—seems to me to assert a well-tempered-ness, in the profound sense, of having been through fire, which is very far from minor. In its biological vitality, the book matches Lawrence while never evoking him. In its sense of decorum, of calculation, of appraisal and restraint, it matches Jane Austen without ever reminding us of her. Once put in this perspective, Renoir's novel is one of the few French novels to relate closely to what F. R. Leavis rightly or wrongly designates as "The Great Tradition". I should prefer to reverse the argument, and suggest that the novel transcends the petty and narrow aspects of both Lawrence and Austen and reveals itself as quite as important as either.

The "nostalgic" films are dominated by women (with Nini as the middle term between the three adolescent girls of *The River* and the mature courtesans, Camilla, Elena; one might well imagine the incarnation of Nini, Françoise Arnoul, as George's Agnes). The novel, comparing two apparently opposed kinds of male sensibility, concerns itself with the tensions of solitude and self-discipline, of a disappointed emptiness, endless, and yet bravely borne. Georges is one of Renoir's solitaries, like most of his aristocrats, like the creator of *Orvet,* like Cordelier, like Alexis, like Jurieu, like the vanishing corporal. Boudu's and Danglard's are two kinds of solitude, the nomad's and the promiscuous impresario's—both easier to vindicate in the '70s (after *The Dharma Bums* and the "permissive society") than in their time. But there are also his less fashionable solitaries, those of the study, whose relationships are fulfilled only vicariously, or outside the normal orders of time and reality. The girl whom Hartley adopts is "little better than a prostitute", i.e. than Georges's Agnes. Georges, very much a man of the world, has Danglard's affability. Hartley, paralytically shy, is the linking term between Renoir's machine men, valorous, dutiful, defeated (the wooden soldiers of the little waif, dying one by one like the matches she strikes), the cossacks of La Belle Catherine, Rauffenstein and Boieldieu, the "bons petits soldats" of *French CanCan,* and even, in his way, Ballochet, so disciplined, so fossilised, in his aristocratic play-acting that it is easier for him to march calmly towards certain death, in the full glare of the *spotlights,* than to become what he does not wish to admit he is.

Given the conviviality, the sense of flow and fickleness, of his earlier films, it is perhaps unexpected that Renoir's later work should celebrate reflection, separateness, a stoic solitude, a hopeless loyalty. Yet solitude is not loneliness. And to be free is to discipline oneself.

"Life is a state, not an enterprise." Renoir's "soldiers" are those who are prepared to discipline and sacrifice themselves to an enterprise. But to refuse all enterprises is to drift, and to seek one state rather than another is itself an enterprise. What is a film director, but an artist who engages himself in a series of enterprises, each of which he pursues, like a Don Juan, not simply for what he can reveal of himself, but rather for what he can find to admire in his quarry?

If the fundamental "psychodrama", or Ur-theme, of Shakespeare's plays is "order", and the many and varied threats to it, whether from impiety, severity or wilfulness, so Renoir's is "disorder", and liberation from a narrow stagnation by some lord or lady of misrule, or by life's ungrateful fluidity. Yet this liberation is a state and not an aim, i.e. not on object of enterprise. Whence the paradox: one is free, but only if one chooses to be a "bon petit soldat". The films of pure freedom have a paradoxical air—Boudu is both subnormal and touched by God, *Le Caporal Épinglé* ends almost desolately.

Conversely (from the point of view of the individual), enterprises tend to be meaningless in themselves. Often they are commanded by some categorical imperative, issuing, not from some rigid Kantian prescription engraved in the tablets of human nature, but from some vitalist instinct or intuition—or from human gregariousness (not "the herd instinct", as liberal individualism so scathingly misnamed it, but, "the tribal instinct", where one's loyalty is to others rather than, or inclusive of, oneself). The Renoir hero seeks freedom to choose his enterprise and not an absolute freedom à la Gide. Often the enterprise itself is a pretext; for the purpose of the enterprise is to be a joint enterprise. The aim of participation in a joint enterprise is no more the aim of the enterprise itself than the pleasures of love-making are identical with the reproduction of the species. The word "tribal" may under-emphasise the high degree of individuality within Renoiran groups.

There is the anti-enterprise, the Dionysian "panic". Renoir, it seems, welcomes it, though with chastened respect, rather than fears it. It replaces the narrow enterprises set by social convention, reason or complacency with instinctual ones. Even Legrand's and Lantier's lives, ending in actual or virtual suicide, are richer than they would have been without the vamp. Nana's victims are their own as well as hers; Lulu and Dédé are Legrand's victims rather than he theirs. The Dionysian end may or may not be terrible, but that is a matter of fate rather than control.

There is always someone left out, left over—like Hartley throughout most of his life, like Georges after Émilien's return, like the stumbling drunk who accidentally bows to the cinema audience, like Danglard, banished from the stage, moving from his chair backstage through an audience which doesn't want to see him, only his show. Rauffenstein has his intimate steel sarcophagus, and his geranium. One outlives oneself.

There remains stoicism: the soldierly, the aristocratic qualities which need neither war nor hierarchy, and without which one cannot join the dance, but will either be trodden over, or left outside, as too grasping. The wooden soldiers die; it is the more dashing supple officer who stays, for a while, ahead in the race with death. As the two horses fly across the clouds, their manes and tails with Karen's hair and dress flowing in the wind, all together take on a rhythm, a sort of convulsive undulation which is the exaggerated equivalent of the sinuousity of a snake; as if the orgasmic struggle against death were the ambivalent ferocity of a life-force in its human form*.

* A far-fetched interpretation? Of course. But no more far-fetched than this. Renoir recalls his visits to the Paris *Guignol* with Gabrielle: " . . . the director of the *Guignol* came out in front . . . and played a little tune on the accordian; it was also an instrument which terrified me when I was small . . . It's rather like a serpent . . . There was always a little trembling before the curtain went up, and I remember that, at just that moment, very often I peed in my pants. . . . The curtain rising, it's always given me that mixture of anguish, of infinite joy, and of fear, rather like love, like the act of love . . . "

The act of love as the possession of the waif-mother (who, in her use of her soldiers to die for her, is rather like the cruel Gods of Anger's *Inauguration of the Pleasure Dome*) and the struggle against the "other's" father, Death, appears in other permutations. Bogey offers a saucer of milk to a cobra, and is reborn, as his posthumous sister, in his mother. Renoir's camera is baffled by the serpentine concertina of M. Oscar in *La Nuit du Carrefour*—Oscar being the name of a fatherly musician who plays to conciliate a crowd which is impatiently waiting for curtain up—whereupon a squadron of high-kicking females attack them, from every other direction. . . .

Fringe Theatres

Les Cahiers du Capitaine Georges opens a great deal of new creative ground, although its elegaic quality suggested that it also marks the end of a spiritual phase. If it prefaced a long interval before another work, it was largely for reasons of *force majeure*.

It was a major misfortune for Renoir—and for the cinema—that the ill-success of his two television films should have eclipsed the viability of *Le Caporal Epinglè*, and that that in turn should have seemed, quite wrongly, a pallid remake of *La Grand Illusion*. His attempts to reverse the French cinema's attitude to television had not exactly earned him the industry's good-will. Even the stress on his distinguished past probably did him harm, since he had reached an age film producers had come to find suspect.

Though now in his seventies, he was far from inactive. Travelling between California and Paris, he arranged the repurchase and reissue of several of his earlier films, made public appearances and gave innumerable interviews, having become one of France's cultural father-figures. The peasant ancestry evident in his physique blended impressively with his artistic background, his cosmopolitan experience, his sense of tradition, the straightforward humility of his style, and the evident affection of the *enfant terribles* of the New Wave. He could switch, with sensitivity and warmth, from provocatively reactionary remarks to an acceptance of change. He seemed almost the incarnation of a "middle France" which, with all the fallibility which Renoir defended, and displayed, could somehow come to terms with change without losing its own essence. The texts of his interviews coarsen and conceal meanings which can only be "read" from the vocal intonations, from the facial inflections and gestures.

Television strangely completed the circle between nostalgia and reality when, for a television programme about his career, he and Simone Simon consented to show viewers how they collaborated on the set of *La Bête Humaine*. Reasonable as this limited purpose is, it almost wilfully runs the danger of a crude forgery, exposed by time. Here, with a vengeance, is spectacle without illusion. Yet Renoir warms to his task, forgets the television cameras, and generates a powerful current with his collaborator once more. Another strange throwback between public and private faces occurred when, in the first of Jacques Rivette's three one-hour programmes about Renoir's work, his old collaborator and *Doppelgänger,* Michael Simon, relished in such mischievously indecent sentiments that the entire programme was banned. Boudu lives.

Meanwhile, Renoir never ceased nursing the idea of a return to the studios in a directional capacity. In 1969, after failing to find backing from other sources, he submitted a project entitled *C'est la Revolution* to the Centre Nationale du Cinéma, an organization set up by the French government to subsidise films which promised to be of exceptional artistic quality. Its officials created something of a sensation by rejecting Renoir's proposals as "idiotic and obscene". One might have expected certain sectors of right and left alike to have resented Renoir's candid declaration that he now felt closer to the direct and ingenuous Americans than to the hyper-cunning French; and not only film people but war heroes know just how little the most lavish encomiums for one's past achievements mean in terms of present situations. But the officials' unusually derisive language suggests that something in the film's subject had jabbed a nerve hard.

At that stage the film was to consist of seven sketches. As Renoir continued to search for backing and the ideas developed, their number was reduced to five, all linked by the proverb whose English equivalent is "the last straw breaks the camel's back." It doubtless contains an allusion to the events in Paris in May 1968. The cast was set to include Simone Signoret, Paul Meurisse, Pierre Olaf, Robert Dhery, Colette Brosset and Oscar Werner. One of the stories may indicate what infuriated the artlovers of the Centre National. Two corporals from opposing armies are trapped in a farmhouse between the lines. They change uniforms so that each can surrender to his own side, spend the duration as a P.O.W. amongst familiar food, language and customs and enjoy all the little privileges which familiarity might bring. Of course, one has to masquerade as an alien; so that "patriotism" acquires a new, derisive meaning, compatible with treason, even though it is better to transform oneself than to lose home comforts. The sketch is an ironic counterpoint, rather than contradiction, to *Le Caporal Épinglé.* Its moral is guaranteed to infuriate everyone; patriots, revolutionaries, lovers of freedom, despisers of all the little pleasures—of habit, of familiarity, of a chimney-corner, *pantouflard* existence. If those ignominious pleasures are so thoroughly despised by everyone, it is for an obvious reason. They are amoral, basic, ineradicable, and extremely powerful. Only an extremely tactless person would vindicate them.

Other projects included a remake of *Le Systeme du Docteur Goudron et Professeur Plume,* as one episode in an Edgar Allan Poe trilogy, alongside contributions by Vadim and Fellini; but eventually a third section was directed by Louis Malle. Another project, *La Clocharde*, was set to star Jeanne Moreau, whom Renoir had wanted to use ever since he saw her in *Jules et Jim*. "She will play a prostitute. The other main character is an aristocrat of about forty. In the end she murders him with a kitchen knife." The film was to celebrate "that desire for liberty by renunciation which contrasts with the belief that happiness resides in profit."

Eventually, however, Renoir found financial backing from French television and four sketches were filmed, for broadcast in France and for theatrical release in the U.S.A.

62

Le Petit Theatre du Jean Renoir (The Little Theatre of Jean Renoir)

Beside a toy, or puppet-, theatre, Renoir introduces each sketch. The first is entitled *Le Dernier Reveillon* (The Last Christmas Eve), and dedicated to Hans Christian Andersen. A beggar (Nino Formicola) is paid by a band of revellers to stand outside a restaurant window and stare at them with his hungry eyes. His longing will sharpen their enjoyment of their feast. He does his job only too well; they are unable to eat; and the management have to make the beggar a Christmas box of their uneaten repast, for him to go away. He takes the food to a beggar-woman (Milly) whom he has loved for many years. Reminiscing about the good old days, they fall asleep in each other's arms. Two other beggars find them frozen to death, and make off with the meal.

The second episode is entitled *La Cireuse Electrique* (The Electric Floor-Waxer). Emilie (Marguerite Cassan) is obsessed with gleaming parquet floors, and when her husband (Pierre Olaf) obtains promotion, she presses him to buy such a machine. Finally he yields, only to slip on the highly polished surface, strike his head and die. An old flame (Jacques Dignan) takes his place, and detests the machine's noise, which he ruefully discusses with the (animated) photograph of the dear departed. Eventually the new husband throws the machine out of the window, Emilie leaps after it.

The third episode is "an excursion into the past", a song about *la belle epoque*, sung by Jeanne Moreau. A song also lends its title to the fourth episode, *Le Roi d'Yvetot*. Duvallier, a prosperous landowner (Fernand Sardou), is married to a beautiful wife (Françoise Arnoul) while his young maid has dreams of being a courtesan. He seems blessed with everything, including prowess at bowls. His rivals, clinging for consolation to the proverb "lucky at games, unlucky at love", decide, with hopeful vindictiveness that he must be a cuckold. Their supposition is realised by the local vet, who expects a violent reaction when his adultery is discovered. But Duvallier aspires to peaceful co-existence—that revolutionary notion. . . .

The first episode, evoking *La Petite Marchande d'Allumettes*, is a tragedy treated in the key of sentimental farce, and a frankly theatrical stylisation of that. Yet "tragedy" is a misnomer; it's too derisive; it's an atrocity, like the death of two (human) animals, as the end-product of theatrical circumstances. Life is a game, but the game's end is death—as a rule. The diners who want to see a hungry man are like those who want, not just neo-realism, but cinéma-vérité, from their comfortable cinema seats. Like the American public watching Vietnam War newsreels, they're upset by what they see. Yet their squeamishness isn't pity, and though the beggar turns his apparent "tragedy" into comedy, his triumph leads him straight to a real, and double, tragedy. He seems to get everything he's wanted—the meal, the woman, the solace of memories. But that's another mode of "theatre," i.e., deception. Those souvenirs of the "good old days" don't quite ring true. His and his beloved's double death may look like the togetherness which it isn't. There memories, foreshortening time, suggest that human life is, in essence, no longer than a sparrow's Summer. Man flies, and dies, as briefly as a bird.

This derisive comedy of subsistence, not unrelated, in spirit, to the cutting edge of the Spanish picaresque, is followed by a tragi-comedy of affluence. A meal is at least an animal obsession. Now we turn to the bourgeois apartment. In this Garden of Eden, the role of the serpent is played by the floor-waxer, which is the antithesis of the musical box and the apotheosis of the machine. (It is effective only because the couples have ceased to love one another; a young couple don't notice the noise from a building site). Renoir describes the episode as an "opera"—an opera for *musique concrète*. Both husband and wife are killed by the machine, but at different times, and with rather more distance between them than the beggars of *Le Dernier Reveillon*. The theme of an asynchronous relationship recurs in the conversations between the second husband and an animated photograph of the first. The second, apparently triumphant, has to endure the noise which the other evaded by dying. The animated photograph, parodying the cinematograph, is another machine—a time-machine. Its presence is unexpected, given Renoir's latterly declared disinterest in camera-tricks and effects. There is, after all, something self-mocking in the device long associated with barrel-scraping comic effects and to which Renoir has never before made reference.

The beggars had their memories, the husbands their "two-way cinema" through time. Now the past consolingly fills the screen, incarnated by Jeanne Moreau, "our guide on this excursion into the past to which with infinite grace she agreed to lend her beauty and her talent." Her song is an "opera-cabaret" performed by a beautiful woman in a flamboyant period dress, and its theme is: "Quand l'amour meurt." Which is honest enough. But these "touching elements", celebrating a myth, merely "put on a show." "Infinite

grace . . . beauty and talent" are only *lent* to us, and to the film. A little
more honestly, the song evokes the doubly delusive tour of the nightclubs
in *French CanCan*. Is there a hint of irony in the star's performance? At any
rate, Renoir, the director, has gone through the motions of deceiving himself. . . . Floorpolisher, photographs, cinema—three gadgets, useful,
sustaining, delusive. . . . The fourth episode contrasts with all of its fore-
runners. Unlike the revellers and the beggars, Duvallier enjoys life with
impunity. Unlike the singer, he is not immune. His wife isn't a slave of a
gadget, a housewife merely. And he is not long deceived. Shaken by the
truth, he does not allow his neighbours' envy to infect him, and since his
wife's lover increases her happiness, invites him to join the family. "But
what of convention?" the lover hesitates. "Blast convention! Life is made
bearable only through little revolutions—in eating habits, in the bedroom,
in the public square. . . . " The Duvalliers' maid dreams of being a rich
courtesan; she'll learn, and yet there is a certain sympathy between Duvallier's mellowed realism and her fresh, proud hopes. They almost make a pair:
the Cuckold and the Courtesan; or, of course, Father and Daughter, like
Hartley and his "almost a prostitute".

Renoir is sufficiently celebrated to put his name in his film's title, but the
effect is more a parody of the notion of director as Superstar. For the Cinemascope of "Fellini-Satyricon" he offers his "little theatre"—which the
simplest camera-illusion (e.g. an apparent track in) makes large enough for
us, i.e. larger than life.

His "little theatre" might almost have been called "Creature Comforts,"
or, better, "Home Comforts," for home is what the beggars call their patch
of embankment under a Seine bridge; and Jeanne Moreau's song recalls the
epoque Renoir glimpsed from his childhood home. One says "home comforts" but not *"le confort bourgeois."* Its anti-heroism is not an inert assent.
Complacency, a good conscience, property rights, vanity are not among
them. The first episode undermines any sense of security, the second the
uniqueness of the couple. The third, a cabaret icon, substitutes a courtesan
for a madonna. The protagonist of the fourth jettisons vanity and prefers an
unusually honest fraternity to patriarchal tyrannies or self deceptions. As
befits the summarising episode, the last is the most realistic in setting and in
tone. Its predecessors correspond to the fairytales, the fetishes, the automata,
the dreams; the last enfolds, and transforms, them into hopes, half-tones,
mellow uncertainties, as life should enfold, and transform, such psychic
absolutes as death, fear, loss, nostalgia.

At the time of writing Renoir plans a second collaboration with Jeanne
Moreau, called *Julienne et Son Amour*, "the story of a prostitute and the rich
man who discovers that he can fall asleep only when he is in bed with
her" (sleep, sister of death, and rebirth, and humblest of creature comforts . . .). Meanwhile he has approached the conclusion of his auto-
biography, which promises to be a third major literary work.

Renoir Times R

With *The River*, the elevation of Renoir to the critical pantheon began, and an affectionate reverence for a lifelong career was independent of, or biased reactions to individual work. But there was also a swelling counter-chorus of criticism from the left, whether a younger generation, or those who, like Sadoul and Brunius, had been among Renoir's most trenchant colleagues and champions.

As early as *The River*, both Satyajit Ray and Jacques Brunius had sensed, and regretted, the change in Renoir, to little themes, to nostalgias, to inoffensiveness and acquiescence. *Elena et les Hommes* unleashed a sharper tone. The ideological issues were compounded by the aesthetic ones. Marcel Martin spoke, regretfully, of "the collapse of Renoir, who, with Vigo, was our greatest cineaste," as "a veritable tragedy for the French cinema . . . " Ado Kyrou: "The Renoir whom I loved has become a sickeningly indulgent old man, a boy scout of the camera, an admirer of bungled work, and what's worse, he has repudiated some of his best films. But I shall remember only the pre-war Renoir." If we overlook the productorial imbroglio of *Elena*, perhaps the unkindest way of putting the truth is to identify its director's position with that of Mauger, the soldier-turned-affluent-Boudu of *Diary of a Chambermaid*. He throws dirt at the right but has no basically opposed stance and doesn't bargain for the unexpected "terrorist," Joseph, i.e. the OAS. The political issue makes a bittersweet comedy of a double renunciation of public life (by Elena, by Rollan) look like a declaration of acquiescence, a Ship-of-Fools complacency. And the confusion colours *Le Déjeuner Sur l'Herbe*, also, in its way, a fable of socio-political renunciation.

François Poulle develops an ingenious, sensitive, and almost unavoidably *ad hominem* argument to account for Renoir's evolution. Renoir, throughout his life, had been a lost soul, looking for the comradeship exemplified in the barrackroom life and the cavalry charge of *Les Cahiers du Capitaine Georges*. He had sought that companionship in 1913 as a simple soldier in the barrackrooms; in 1919 in his family's pottery enterprise; in 1923 in the cinema; in 1935 in the Popular Front; from 1949 in an acquiescent mysticism; from 1955 in memories of his father's Paris. With *Renoir Mon Père* he achieves a kind of communion with and recreation of his father in himself, and from then on, he sees the modern world only through his father's eyes. Alongside Poulle's scenario, frequently intertwining with it, one may posit another possibility. Auguste, deciding that the world was intrinsically bewildering and contradictory, carefully restricted his art to exploring, offering, the intimate, sensuous, bountiful world of his paintings. His tabletalk is sage, ironic, truculent. In a sense, his impressionism parallels the spiritual hermetism of Symbolism—although its subject matter is not artifice and its preciosity, but nature and her fertility, a contrast which entails a great many others. From another angle, this careful "privacy" can be seen as a venerable peasant strategy. But Jean was tossed into another epoch, another vocation, another formative class. Armed with his father's truculent ironies, as well as his generous curiosity, he was drawn into the greater issues, and found aother greatness, never quite abandoning, nonetheless, the sense of an independent world—whether that of the entirely artificial studio of *La Petite Marchande d'Allumettes,* or that of *La Compagnie Jean Renoir.* Certainly the yin and yang of fraternity and solitude, commitment and liberty, enterprise and flight, aristocracy and ignominy, concur with theories of artistic creation as "the wound and the bow". But one should not underestimate that *absence* of alienation which generates, not a lost soul, but a divine discontent.

Poulle clearly sees Renoir as an uncertain, fickle child, and certainly such an *anima* is incarnated by his vamps, until *La Règle du Jeu,* when they are replaced by a maturer female figure (Christine, Elena). Nenette, perhaps, synthesises the two. Finally, almost desperately (Poulle goes on to suggest), Renoir finds solace, and solidity, by re-creating his own father in himself (and introjecting the goodness of Pierre?). It's only a psychoanalytical hypothesis, and must be flanked by caveats of every kind. Perhaps the simplest indication of certain necessary reservations is by positing a counter-pointing psycho-scenario, itself open to an infinity of questions. The director of a film unit is the father of a family, with its "models" (who are encouraged to think, after being stopped from thinking!), its "domestics" (or technicians), its "friends". And if we apply certain stock interpretations to *La Petit Théâtre de Jean Renoir,* we find that, far from being merely four episodes without a linking theme, it suggests four stages of this double process.

The beggars in their second childhood are covert children, their infantile sexuality linked with food. The meal which the beggar/son is condemned to envy is the family meal, specifically, the mother. By succumbing to memory-fantasy-art, the beggar/child loses everything. The second episode expresses the sterility of duty, the shiftingness to which the impossibility of exclusiveness in human relationships condemns them. If it's not a vamp's other men, it's houseproud gadgetry. One's beloved is always elsewhere, i.e. herself, and to destroy her totem is to lose her too. The grotesque, atemporal fraternity of the rivals leads to the third episode, also a relationship with a "picture" from another time. Renoir's fatherly courtesy frames an actress with whom he never got to work because, despite the demonstration of *Le Caporal Epinglé*, he was thought too old. The director ironises over his own exclusion from his major projects by appearing within his own, little, theatre, i.e. film. The fourth, and most realistic episode expresses the wisest solution to the persistence of division and illusion within the closest possible relationships.

Truffaut, like Poulle, imputes an ironic significance to some second-degree family relationships in Renoir movies. He suggests that Pierre Renoir's Louis XIV is the director's auto-portrait, through his elder brother, thus implying that Renoir is really on the side of reaction and against revolutions. There are only the little revolutions—offering messengers legs of chicken. But the reference may be both autoportrait and autocriticism. For there are other, incompatible, autoportraits in the movie. The artist in the film provides a "middle term", a more affable view of Renoir's own stance, his own gifts, his own contribution. Already he sees himself—not altogether seriously—as preserving an older order, an academic aesthetic (and the French film avant-garde was certainly academic). But we can't exactly dismiss as merely factitious Renoir's affinities with the feminist Bonnier and with the sharper Arnaud. The film's heroes represent the militant Renoir, who arranged for the bloodthirsty speeches of the time to be spoken, who made the film, and whose "civilized", 18th-century reservations are expressed through Roederer. With *Elena et les Hommes,* and not until, the film director is a Jean Renoir who has become *one* Pierre Renoir—Louis XIV—and ceased to be his vigilant, and scathing, "brother"—Maigret.

Renoir's biography of his father is followed by a novel whose underlying theme is, perhaps, what the son might have become had he remained (as he was briefly tempted to remain) within the military world, and if, unlike so many of his young contemporaries, he had not been liberated from the social world of his youth by his father's household, the enfranchisement of art, the cinema, and the Popular Front. After Hollywood, and the continuing bitternesses of post-war, Cold War, France, the hopes, and the reflux, begin. The two ultra-spontaneist films celebrate the middle-aged, the old-fashioned.

Without their constraining and constricting setting Renoir's continuing modernity might have been more evident. *The River* celebrates two drop-outs with Indian inclinations (Mr. John, Captain John), and honours the Hindu sense of sexuality as divine. The Viceroy in *The Golden Coach* is a model of cool; Felipe seeks a tribal togetherness. *French CanCan* celebrates living in the present, not the future, the state against the enterprise, Women's Lib, and non-possessiveness in love, in everything. It desolemnises art into whistling clowns, and substitutes a Dionysiac, audience-participative "happening" for showbusiness. *Le Testament du Dr. Cordelier* focuses on the liberation of personality by drugs from a technological culture. Given Renoir's anticipations of avant-garde aesthetic, one needn't labour the extent to which his ethos overlaps with that of a generation which, five years later, went as far as rediscovering Vivaldi—to dance to.

Leaving France for America in 1962, Renoir commented: "The Americans now correspond to the French of 1910 . . . That's my period. It's sad, a world where one can't remain ingenuous . . . "*. The assumption that ingenuousness and wisdom are interimpregnated by each other recalls Renoir *père*: "Never trust a man who doesn't get excited at the sight of a pretty breast", "My models don't think"—alongside his multiplicity of artistic and intellectual friends. The experience of a large household, with a multiplicity of comings and goings, is surely the original for the master-servant *chasséss-croisées* of so many Renoir films, as of Renoir's characteristic asides (whatever's happening, someone's getting on with something else). Self is both a part of a collectivity, and a "vanishing corporal". Poulle's "lost child" is also a *maitre-d'hotel,* trying to give a chaotic film unit, and later a divided world, the cohesion, or the illusory example of cohesion, of a "family of man". The child runs eagerly after the cook, the gardener, the painter—and "in pursuit of his craft", writes Modot of Renoir, "his insatiable curiosity leads him to an unusual range of knowledge; it's a pleasure to hear his colourful dissertations on the cylinders of an automobile engine, Lavater's theories of physiognomy, the different types of movement in timepieces, the sense of direction in migrating birds, the revolutionary theories of the Jacobins . . . and he listens, as well as speaks, with the concentration of a neophyte, avid for discovery and served by astonishingly rapid powers of assimilation."

In the intellectual world of Renoir's youth, the exuberance of *art nouveau* co-existed with a cubo-futurist élan, automobiles and aviation enjoyed their halcyon days. Leisured youths could turn mechanic for the sake of hobbies which they knew would make history, and the cavalry's simple pride co-existed with the frail, infinite promise of the spruce-and-linen aeroplane. Renoir is also, as Leprohon defines him, "a Parisian from old rural roots." Where so many French artists sought in Paris a refuge from rural or bourgeois suffocation, and paid for their freedom with urban alienation, Renoir had to renounce no aspect of his complex and supple inheritance. Devoid of complacency, he took risks, and ranged across dreams, peasantry, the workers, America, India. . . .

Alexandre Arnoux emphasises his debt to a double current of late 19th-century culture; impressionism on one hand, and literary realism on the other. He is also the cinema's child, of both its mainstream (Chaplin, Stroheim)

---

* Yet it's as well not to equate *la belle epoque* too closely with the Edwardian high summer, at least in its Gilbert-and-Sullivan or Korda versions. In France particularly, it was an open season for anarchist subversions of every kind, and bitter political strife.

and of the avant-garde movement with which his smaller early films are usually grouped and of which, in 1949, *Sequence* reported that he "spoke in glowing terms".

When Brunius compares his "cloister and the hearth" policy, after the failure of *Nana,* with that of Cavalcanti and René Clair, he is undoubtedly right to imply that the "small" films are those which Renoir felt to be his personal ones. Yet, from another angle, Renoir's "free" or "parallel" or "underground" cinema films don't belong to the avant-garde in any more specialised or precise sense. His first three films, of which he was also the producer, are aimed at the widest possible public. In his smaller films he is unconcerned with "Art" in the spirit which inspired, and misled, so many other avant-gardists. His own approach is usually frivolous, simple, or child-like. Even the Dadaist *Entr'acte* is formally elaborated, sophisticated and socially critical, whereas Renoir's smaller films, experimental in technique, are more lightly so. Only *La Petite Marchande d'Allumettes* is authentically impressionist (in the film sense) and avant-garde, and even there Renoir describes its truquage as "sport" and it turned out to be almost the rearguard of 100% *un*realism, at least for thirty years or so.

Renoir's avant-garde connections resemble Claude Beylie's description of an eternal amateur whose enthusiasm enables him to continue taking professionalism seriously long after the merely professional has contentedly deteriorated into hacks. Nothing if not contradictory (or dialectical) Renoir, later at least, compared himself to a prostitute, although, no doubt, a prostitute à la Renoir—that is, another kind of courtier, of dancer . . . Sport, craft and vocation alike are all humbler than Art-with-a-capital-A, more agreeable to compromise and subterfuge. But they can also be more relaxed, and more sensitive, and maybe that explains why *Charleston* and *La Petite Marchande d'Allumettes* flow so smoothly and compel admiration while touching the heart—in contrast to all those contemporary artistic efforts which reek less of real experience than of theory's midnight oil—even on location in the sun. Given Renoir's response to the opportunities of the mid-'30s, one can complement Beylie's thesis with the proposition that public, and collective, feelings and issues didn't just permit the fusion of Renoir's initial amateurism and accumulating professionalism, but enriched an initial fusion of both beyond itself. Which isn't to go as far as the other extremes, represented by *Premier Plan's* impressive compendium of interviews and criticisms, which constitutes something of a war-machine designed to reduce Renoir to "simply the gifted mirror which reflects at one moment the Art Film, at the next the Popular Front, then America, then India, and finally an arrivist and insincere entourage in which he can see nothing reflected but his own myth."

Of all celebrated *auteurs,* Renoir has most consistently insisted on his debt to his collaborators, to his audience, and to the crises of an epoque by which so many other artists were enriched—or broken. By and large, I feel that the influence of epoques on artists is stronger than that of any individual artist—or all artists—on epoques, and that varieties of collective factors go deeper than specifically individual ones. Nonetheless, *La Chienne, La Nuit du Carrefour* and *Madame Bovary* leave little doubt that Renoir's work had been steadily accumulating spiritual depth and social breadth. It is with a real pang that one wonders how Renoir might have influenced the French cinema (and vice versa) had he returned to France and made *Diary of a Chambermaid* there. But one may also speculate how the Communist Party might have influenced Renoir, and France, had it been less thoroughly Stalinised as to turn, not Renoir alone, but half a generation of artists and intellectuals away from left-wing aspirations altogether. No doubt an American perspective had worked on Renoir also, but it is precisely because Renoir was more "committed", and more responsive, than Clair and Duvivier that it was more difficult, more painful, for him, to return, and see his friends of Popular Front days tearing one another apart, and no doubt also tearing at him, whichever option he chose.

Anglo-Saxon critics, far from France, free from ideological choice, and given to considering art as "above" politics, religion, society and everything but individual lyrical or vaguely philosophical experience, saw nothing controversial in Renoir's work at all. Gaven Lambert aligned him with a "humanist" tradition, along with "Ford . . . Chaplin, de Sica, Dovzhenko, Donskoi, Flaherty and Jennings". Nowadays one would have to puzzle over what common ground existed between Jennings's Timothy and Renoir's Boudu (whom Lambert hadn't had a chance to see), or why Vigo, for example, didn't merit inclusion. Today Renoir is often described as a "humanist", as if no qualification or reservation were required. Yet his films abound in the fauns and satyrs which are not all as easily lovable as those of Renaissance canvases and often recall the gargoyle faces outside cathedrals. On the one hand, the fauns—Boudu; Brunius's satyr in *Partie de Campagne;* the homage paid to Kali in *The River*; Pan's set, merciless eyes in *Le Déjeuner Sur l'Herbe*—and on the other, the puppets—like the commedia dell'arte, the marionettes which, like *Punch and Judy,* relate to folk irresponsibility, not to say brutality, and gainsay all that "humanism", unqualified, implies in the way of rationalist decorum and its New Testament inheritance. One wonders, indeed, how far "humanism", with its assumptions of human worth, can accommodate Renoir's sense of life as theatre—not quite real, not quite earnest, yet all there is. Can we claim, as "humanist", ideas which "vary between Hinduism and Sartre"? Perhaps we can speak of a Rabelaisian humanism, founded less on reason, virtue and good order than on the senses, fraternity and stoicism; always conscious of the presence of Dionysus, and of his ambivalence; and so of a subjacent chaos. The steady flowing of Renoir's river is a compromise between the jerkiness of his puppet-fauns and the courtly evolutions of his "Mozartian" protagonists. It evokes both a Bergsonian vitalism and a Heraclitean sense of flux—with eddies, whirlpools, weirs replacing the latter's *sturm und drang*. As Octave-Renoir's wearing of the bearskin (from which only a friendly vamp can tug him free) implies, Renoir's characters shade into animals, and the courtiers into musical-box figurines. The bear and the snake balance the soldiers and the dolls. Boudu, Mauger, and some others complete the circle, being simultaneously part-human, part-animal, and, by their jerkiness, part-puppet.

Renoir Américain found his first defender in Maurice Scherer (=Eric Rohmer), who saw in it a movement towards the traditional virtues, social stability, a sense of God, and the Gospel according to Roberto Rossellini. Henri Agel, retaining certain moral reservations, felt that "one of the multiple interests of his American period is its offering us, through such films as *Woman on the Beach* and *Diary of a Chambermaid,* a fascinating expression of the dematerialization of reality, of the Dream." Yet even if Agel's response has spilled from the *qualities* of the French films to the *minor flaws* of the American ones, it's altogether valid when Renoir comes nearest film noir expressionism with *Woman on the Beach*. And, given narrow *auteur* theory, there is a sense in which *Diary of a Chambermaid* is to *La Règle du Jeu* as a dream is to a reality (a little blurred, distending into an expressionist caricature . . .). *This Land is Mine* can be seen as "a dream of Europe" and even *Swamp Water,* which after *The Southerner* is Renoir's most realistic Hollywood film, has its dreamlike resurrection. Its mists recall those of *La Nuit du Carrefour* and of *La Bête Humaine.* Ironically, Agel's acute insight into an underlying sense of "disembodiment" is not contradicted, but counterpointed by, the themes which endow Renoir's Hollywood period with its new stabilisation between optimism and pessimism, effort and chaos, criticism and acceptance. *Woman on the Beach* ushers in Renoir's "philosophical" period, and it's a characteristic artistic paradox that a philosophical detachment should accompany an intensification, through colour, of sensory impressionism. The detachment is from intensities of anger (the sexual murders), emotion, perhaps even desire; the world remains philosophical, fraternal, corporeal.

Simultaneously, André Bazin, celebrating *The River*, made his valiant, ingenious and tactfully oblique bid to claim Renoir's Heraclitean paganism for a Christian Franciscanism. The river which flowed through so many of Renoir's films, delving its course in conflict and in complicity with the lie of the land, usually gentle, occasionally torrential, ran, not to be lost in the wide salt sea of death, but to unite itself with a transcendental pantheism which, for Bazin, was an unconscious Christian's apprehension of God.

Agel, sentinel of a sterner Christian strain, wisely sounded a warning against the equation, Renoir=love=Christianity, a warning equally pertinent against the subsequently popular Anglo-Saxon equation, Renoir=love= humanism. "The attraction of water for Renoir so pertinently analysed by Bazin . . . corresponds no doubt to the author's obsession with the feminine . . . nonetheless water, which is also present in Epstein, Vigo, and Gremillon, proffers itself as the privileged element for self-loss and for cosmic dissolution . . . Renoir, 'witness and friend of men,' I will grant you—although that will require closer examination—but also Renoir possed of a cosmic instability . . . we are nearer with him to a certain aspect of Lucretius than to the eighteenth century. A Dionysian instinct, a Panic impulse . . . explains Renoir's detachment and what is a little too quickly called his goodness . . . "*

If Bazin and Agel both opened different perspectives into Renoir's spirituality, Anglo-Saxon film criticism laid an increasing stress on Renoir's earlier films as a source of neo-realism. In 1951 neo-realism could seem to have begun with Rossellini's *Open City* in 1945. But at London's Institut Français in 1957, Thorold Dickinson and Jacques Brunius, introducing Jean Renoir and *La Chienne*, emphasised the continuing influence of its concern with external realism through to Visconti and *Ossessione* in 1942.

The December 1957 issue of *Cahiers du Cinéma* comprises the first extended review of Renoir's entire career, and the signatures of directors-to-be loom large (Godard, Truffaut, Rivette, Rohmer, Claude de Givray). A variety of approaches create an overall emphasis on Renoir the *auteur*, the "calligraphist" whose nonchalant genius amiably expresses itself through, and impresses itself on, every element of a film. The camera movements (or their lack) are the subject of special attention, and there lingers more than a little of the "Bazinian" Renoir, the loving observer in whose presence nature exudes her essence. The unwary might suppose that Renoir's mixture of theoretical beginnings and incessant revisions is some sort of "native woodnotes wild," that the Renoir of 1924 is exactly the same man as the Renoir of 1954, and that such unresponsive inertia is a touchstone of artistic integrity. A pernicious glamourisation began. Interviewed, Renoir unaffectedly confessed his miseries during the shooting of *Elena et les Hommes* and stressed the extent to which he was obliged to resort to a structure of contrivances. (Not many directors would speak so frankly to critics about their current work.) But he finished with the word "pirouettes," which in its context, means simply, a "switch," and, by implication mechanically contrived. His interviewers exclaim: "It's that abundance of pirouettes which delight us!" Which is the exact converse of what Renoir began by telling them.

Truffaut, implicitly, and truculently takes one extraordinary argument to its extreme. (1) Because Renoir's work sympathises with so many people it must be impartial. (2) Because it is impartial it cannot protest against the *status quo*. (3) The *status quo* is defined by its traditional elements. (4) Any

---

* One may, in turn, query Agel's talk of *Obsession* with the feminine—after all, half the human race is feminine, so one might speak of *interest* rather than obsession. It's not as if Renoir only had heroines. To say Renoir has a feminist streak is rather truer. Agel's equation of the fluid, the feminine and the contradictory, betrays that Christian patriarchal longing for moral dogmatics which slurs over its own inconsistencies by seeing woman as "illogical" while talking of "man's tragic paradox" and the "Christian mysteries."

radical elements in it don't balance it but threaten it. This ideological sleight-of-hand explains Truffaut's interpretations of *Tire Au Flanc*, of *La Marseillaise* and of *This Land is Mine*.*

Apart from the Cahiers subgroup, a wider section of the *Nouvelle Vague* generation adopted as their spiritual godfather an aesthetic rather than a philosophical Renoir. His diffuseness and awkwardness of emphasis, his technical unconventionalities, his virtuoso camera-movements, all encouraged their flight from the idiom predominant since 1935. Influenced, for the good, by Hollywood, that idiom was characterised by crisply edited tempi, non-discursive plots, and "tennis-rally" reverse angle close-ups. Almost alone among his generation, Renoir matched its pace, yet an aesthetic conservative, continued, right through to *La Règle du Jeu*, to keep his cameras mobile. Although his principal reason was to follow the actors, and his younger admirers were interested in camera movements for reasons of "pure" visual style, their reasons certainly revealed aspects of Renoir's thought. His cameras rivalled the mobility now made easier by the modern equipment derived from lightweight TV gear, and his films anticipated innovations on everyone's agenda. Similarly, the new equipment facilitated new possibilities of improvisation, and improvisation was much more conspicuous in Renoir's films than in those of, say, George Cukor or Gregory La Cava. Thus Renoir seemed the only director to conjoin the neo-realistic and the calligraphic, the literary and the visual, the social and the metaphysical, the artificial and the natural. His long creative evolution, the breadth and diversity of his *oeuvre*, his rich mixture of cultural relevances, and his personal presence, placed him, given the young Turks' anxious need for handy ancestors, in a unique position. One could approach him from almost any angle and every approach led steadily and agreeably to every other angle.

Through Renoir more than anyone else, the cinema's past reflected its

---

* Truffaut's drift is confirmed by the reasons he gave for refusing to collaborate with Resnais, Godard, Varda, Marker and Lelouch on *Loin de Vietnam*. First, he admired the exemplary restraint shown by the humiliated party, which in his opinion was the American military machine. Secondly, he thought films ought not to diverge from "public opinion." Where Renoir is anarchist, Truffaut is defeatist; and the individual's weakness renders vengeance, whether female or authoritarian, perfectly right and proper. In fact severity strengthens the individual. His best defence against war is to admire its beauty. About class barriers it's futile to complain. From his columns in *France-Observateur* Truffaut requested the Parisian police to stop young students offering radical literature to passers-by in the smarter Paris streets. He cites the Fascists Bardèche and Brasillach *approvingly* when they smile at the Declaration of the Rights of Man in *This Land is Mine*. *Les 400 Coups* mainly criticises parents who fail to provide a proper bourgeois order within the home for their child. The sexually unfaithful parent is also the cruellest to the child. *Fahrenheit 451* affirms learning-by-rote against, ironically, the audio-visual media. One hardly dares believe that the "firemen" represent a self-criticism of Truffaut's own appeal to the police. Truffaut's detestation of anarchism and feeling for impulse as *hubris* in *L'Enfant Sauvage* affirms old-fashioned severity as against an exploration of the mind. The highest Doinel can hope for is a contented, orderly, boring existence. It's an artistically authentic pessimism, like a latter-day Duvivier's, and imbued with intense sense of tragic weakness and hopelessness in his best films. But his ideological prejudices are central to his comments on Renoir.

future. Like the genial Méliès in a trick-film, the same friendly figure waved from a sunrise in the East and a sunset in the West. He was the solution for which a generation was groping. He offered the example of his instinctive balance to the stiffness of alienation, all the more fraternally in that he had constantly made mistakes, admitted them, and learned how to learn from them. Even his mistakes revealed the structure of his thought so helpfully that one wanted to defend them, almost against the possibility of happier and richer solutions.

This defensible enthusiasm was compounded by certain optical illusions, engendered by the inadequacies of film history—inadequacies inevitable given the short release-pattern of films, their unavailability in archives, two world wars linked by a slump, the paucity of funds for scholarship, and so on and so forth. Narrow *auteur* theory ensured that once Renoir had come into the critical spotlight, his earlier films would attract filmgoers and enjoy the newer, more sophisticated kinds of exegesis for which few of his contemporaries could hope. He could seem more unique than he was. Thus critics who only became aware of camera movements as content in the '60s were naturally excited by their high degree of elaboration in *Boudu Sauvé des Eaux*. It was difficult not to think of Renoir as ahead of his time. Yet directors as diverse as F. W. Murnau and Harry Langdon had already made extensive use of camera movements, and cameras around 1930 moved fast and often. It's true that Renoir's camera movements have their own characteristics, e.g. a "wayward" relation to architecture (because he's chasing the actors and their groupings). But the younger, more sophisticated critics couldn't notice the differences because they'd seen too few older films; and the older critics, who'd seen them, had had different criteria, had looked for different things, and either forgotten how much cameras moved, or insisted it didn't matter.

The general lack of cultural prestige from which the cinema has suffered, and the propensity of, if not need for, young critics to make bold and simple claims, i.e. exaggerations, to arouse any interest, have induced a runaway inflation of critical vocabulary. Thus any film to which any coherent message can be imputed, whether by fair means or foul, tends to get described as a hitherto neglected masterpiece. How much more prestigious, and, in a real sense, hard to handle, were such connoisseurs' items as Renoir's lesser movies, briefly drawn forth from the archives, like the most fragile of jewels. Isolated from their contemporary idioms and preoccupations, they bred a kind of wonderment which is undoubtedly a rich and necessary stage of aesthetic receptivity but only one stage in the process of aesthetic response.

Renoir's "second birth," in '40s America, to a feeling that the world needed love rather than sarcasm, and the presence, within his sarcastic films, of that feeling that "everyone has his reasons," seemed to cast a soft veil over all Renoir's films. All was acquiescence, impartiality, tolerance: "All that Renoir signs is love." (Claude Beylie). In reaction to this new consensus, a new asperity was introduced by French left-wing critics. First a mammoth issue of *Premier Plan,* edited by Bernard Chardère, seeing Renoir as little more than a lucky mirror, and then a partial but incisive study by Francois Poulle, seeking in Renoir in his prime the seeds of his decay.*

Truth, as usual, falls between two stools. The best in Renoir comes from others through him as well as from him and his ability to elicit and accept the best of others is a *positive* capability. So far as his less successful films are concerned, Renoir himself intimated a useful critical perspective. " . . . a bad conversation with Mozart, if you love him, is more interesting than a good conversation with a composer to whom you're less attached." One might add that an artist's blindnesses may, by their relation to his insights, teach more about human possibilities than the successes of competence, and therefore do become positive sources of profound insight to those sufficiently interested to think out the connections. Which turn of thought might have saved *auteur* theory from a pervasive lack of realism.

With new techniques, new awarenesses, for which Renoir himself is partly responsible, it is theoretically quite possible that the qualities which made his films so precious will become commonplace. Let us, indeed, hope that our children will take for granted those truths which in our day, only his real spiritual penetration could sense. Perhaps they will enjoy art, and criticism, and culture, as self-sacrificial—potlatch rather than competition. We're putting our game in a common pot, not staking claims to property-rights on Parnassus.

Renoir's films will endure as testimonies to a unique—because historically unique—juncture of sensibilities: his, his actors', his collaborators', his times'. They are unrepeatable, neither replacing, nor being replaceable by, the most authentic and sensitive of those movies which resemble them, but corroborating them, communicating with them. Their perennial freshness may be suggested by a comparison with *cinéma-vérité,* apparent apotheosis of the "realism" or "spontaneity" or "multi-sensibility" to which Renoir's films can be too easily reduced. The latter's syntax will ensure a sense of each touch or gesture having been, not merely *caught* by a nimble and observant deployer of easily expendable emulsion, but having been observed, savoured, remembered, recreated by a *conspiracy* of artists. This reverence will be counterpointed by an irreverence at once robust, fickle, tender and scathing. Renoir's realism will remain as distinct from *cinéma-vérité* as the painting of Degas from the polyfoto.

---

* Surprising it may be to find the Fascist critics of the '30s forgiving Renoir his errors, as those of a good man fallen among Jews, while left-wing critics of the '60s are enraged by his "defection". But the Fascists were finding reasons not to have to imprison him, and so they smiled, they forgave, as Goebbels smiled at Lang, at Pabst, etc., etc. If *Premier Plan's* indispensible symposium occasionally verges on character assassination, that is, at least, a *crime passionel,* by no means the least sympathetic of crimes. It leaves Renoir much more alive than *auteurist* hagiography or *l'ennui mortel de l'impeccabilité.*

Renoir Renoir

Let us ungratefully take for granted the Renoir who feels he can bring his fellowmen only his love, and approach his films' philosophy from another quarter. Let us take as our text Agel's already quoted antithesis between Renoir as "witness and friend to men" and his sense of "the universal instability". It isn't at first clear whether this last phrase implies that no universal stability exists, or that no areas of stability exist, and it's the difference between a nihilism which Agel might want to attribute to agnosticism, and the belief that befriending one's fellowmen isn't quite so easy to do. But Agel seems to imply that Renoir's world allows agonisingly little solid ground for fraternity. "What links *La Règle* with *Eléna* is "not love, but rather a sort of sarcastic compassion for these puppets which 'seem ridiculous in their lives, in their struggles and their sufferings because the mechanism of their sentiments is dismantled by an ironist devoid of pity' (Leprohon). Not devoid of pity but liberated, perhaps, from certain attachments which permits him to see his fellowmen through a *different* lens . . . Whereas nature is true—let us remember the long tracking shots along the river at the end of *Boudu*—the human world is only a spectacle. Not a ballet, as in René Clair; a spectacle, a comic opera. And it's to the extent that this spectacle can, in certain circumstances, attain that degree of paroxysm at which the tragic and the burlesque dissolve into each other *(La Règle, Diary, The Golden Coach, Eléna)* that the observer attains beatitude . . . " The dichotomy remains true, even if other observers, like this one, may prefer those films in which the "puppets" are as lifelike as those of *La Règle*, where the tragic is not mitigated by the burlesque, which thus remains, in the tragic sense, "absurd". From this angle, *Charleston* has an "interior realism" which *Eléna* lacks, and Agel's preferences seem to me motivated by his own Christian, and differently derisive, view of, and detachment from, worldly vanities and the foibles of the flesh. For Renoir's preference for caricature regularly has another motive—a moralizing one. Juliana is perfectly realistic, and a caricature only in the sense that we don't share his attitudes.

The family of *Partie de Campagne* is another example, although here the "caricature" borders on caricature in the usual sense—alas. Mauger isn't so much a caricature as a grotesque (although the same character could have been handled more conventionally). Frequently, Renoir resorts to caricature (used broadly, to cover all these senses) whenever he wants, not just to criticize, but extensively to discredit or demolish attitudes with whom one would expect his film's audience to feel a strong human and moral affinity. In contrast, criminals, aristocrats, and outsiders tend to be treated with more sympathy, and seriousness, thus generating complexity and tension (and, incidentally, questioning the association of the inadaptive and the comic suggested by a fellow vitalist, Bergson). Muffat and Legrand aren't caricatures, but tragic grotesques—and in a sadder version of *Diary of A Chambermaid*, Mauger might have had their timbre.

If caricature is the predominant form of Renoir's attack on the bourgeoisie, it isn't a foolproof method (ah, if only art disposed of foolproof methods . . .). If the halfway-enlightened spectator recognises, or responds to, the implicit moral ("these attitudes render one absurd, diminished, dehumanised"), others may see the caricatures as criticisms of their neighbours only, or of excess only, or see only the distinguishing absurdity, not the significant similarity. The caricaturisation of Mauger seems to have an opposite source. He's a character with whom American audiences, then very rigid, would have had great difficulty in identifying in any case. The conventional Hollywood wisdom would have made him more "reasonable," i.e. colourless. Renoir takes the other option, and, thinking perhaps of Chaplin, of Groucho, and of critically less fashionable "grotesques," e.g. S. Z. "Cuddles" Sakall, allows him to retain most of his excesses. He becomes a "high speed" grotesque.

Thus Renoir's moral caricaturisation has many modes, but shouldn't be confused with a fundamental cruelty. Nor is a sense of cruelty, merely cruel; it also requires an honesty which refuses the edulcoration of pathos. (This isn't to deny that that honesty might be reinforced by *Schadenfreude* of one kind or another, and Renoir understands Opale; don't we all?) Detachment, and *truancy*, may go hand in hand; and truancy is a participation: in *something else*. . . . When we speak, as Renoir did in 1951, of his "love of atrocious situations," we are speaking of the sensitive, and ruthlessly honest, "cruelty" which Renoir shares with Chaplin and Shakespeare, and which comes closer to, while remaining distinct from, Buñuel's "philosophic Sadism". Ready access to a fellow feeling is checked for the sake of lucidity, which gives whatever pleasures truthfulness can give; and the spectator may smile, gratefully, with a sense of *rightness*, as an artist, telling, for whatever reason, the truth, liberates us from sentimental lies. Otherwise, tragedy would be either sado-masochistic, or unbearable. But telling the truth, also, is involvement.

Perhaps the least reassuring part of Renoir's vision is that, despite a lack of emphasis on malice, it pivots on disorder: rape, murder, and revolution. "What is really terrible, is that everyone has his reasons. . . . " From this sympathetic involvement with the "reasons" of the destructive victims who are rarely also "villains," spread the black and chaotic vibrations on which Agel so rightly insists. If Renoir's vision often entails a tragic or a stoic view of life, yet curiously eludes our usual classification of tragedy, it isn't because optimism, sensationalism or sentimentality dilute it. It is because that very sense of "orderly" accumulation which is characteristic of conventional tragedy is shaken by his sense of a "transformability" of ego, and of certain "absurdist" conjunctions. The criticism of paranoid, righteous "scapegoating" in *The Woman on the Beach* comes from deep roots. Renoir doesn't need Iagos, Edmunds, Lady Macbeths . . . which is not say that they don't exist: the valet, Joseph, is one such. But most murderers are . . . Legrande, Lange . . .

Those who preach amorality may do so out of accommodating dispositions which are masochistic rather than sadistic, although the terms aren't mutually exclusive, and one might find that in Renoir's films generally more people are killed by those who are consistently victims than vice versa. Similarly, the man who can forget his own ego and welcome others' is quite likely to be correspondingly fickle, and therefore dangerous. The turnabouts fascinate Renoir, perhaps because of the inexorable logic which underlies them. Boudu the ungrateful rapist is as ready to jump into the Seine as Georges to lose his life in the disciplined and fraternal communion of a cavalry charge. A "weak ego" may also be a divine carelessness. Legrand and Lantier qualify, at least in theory, as classical tragic heroes (being simultaneously victims of their own tragic flaws, of fate and/or its modern equivalent, the social order) and of their own conscious volitions. But far from being the 'highest' kind of tragedy (i.e. the most truthful and interesting), it's only one kind of tragedy among others which are equally interesting because the sudden reflex, instinct or illchance is counterpointed by everyday emotion, or no particular emotion. If Bonnier and Boieldieu, who die, aren't tragedians it's because they're comedians. That's the only difference, and all the difference. Beckett & Co. have since taught literary critics what Renoir said so often; that the comic and the tragic spirit are not antithetical. Each can sense, and acknowledge, the other, and a certain "stereoscopy" is perhaps the characteristic sign of a life lived fully. Comedy itself has a tragic lashback, since it makes light of human seriousness. And tragedy has a comic aspect, since earnestness may be absurd. Perhaps the product of this "stereoscopy" is a certain emptiness. Life remains a game, that one must play with dignity, with consideration, with melancholy—i.e. with grace. After Lulu dies, Legrand lives on—derisorily. After Jurieu dies, life is a . . . commedia dell'arte . . . a cancan . . . Without Agnes, it is . . . a solitude. It isn't as one might expect, a boredom, like Madame

Bovary's (though that has lately become a common theme). Georges' life, like the life which she doesn't see, is rich, varied, fruitful enough. It is the emptiness at the heart of things which generates the sense of—*only* a game, *only* a theatre. This sense of inauthenticity never becomes numbness, or loss of nerve, or fear of sacrifice. In the '30s, Renoir was both tragic and absurdist; his later work substitutes tragic absurdity, or the acceptance of ignominy—with courtesy. His 'instability' is a pagan matter. The Greeks followed their tragedies with a "goatplay", a Dionysian farce, as if to celebrate the rebirth of the slain god, spring after winter. Of this comic epilogue, our suspense-with-a-happy-end is a degenerate form, degenerate because it denies both tragic death and comic rebirth alike. Renoir paraphrases this double ruthlessness by his love of mixed emotional tones, of aesthetic impropriety. Conventional tragic, and dramatic, clashes and choices are extremely intense certainly, but pixilated by another opposition. Boudu is Nietzsche's Dionysian phase while Renoir's officer-aristocrat is his Apollonian. Nietzsche, reared in a guilt-inducing and patriarchal culture, constructed from an essentially tragic life a philosophy of pagan vitalism, of joyful sacrifice, which he warned his readers was a mask, but which he insisted was a human possibility. Renoir's work offers another perspective on that pagan world; flowing, like a woman's draperies, or a cavalry charge; guiltless but not without violence; and restrained from killing, not by guilt but by shame and sympathy. If we hadn't seen the rest of the film, we might think that the suddenness with which Lange kills Batala was that of a snake. The camera *uncoils,* the revolver *strikes,* and Batala dies near his holy-water fountain just like Bogey dies near his saucer of milk. Did we really think Renoir's Great God Pan was just St. Francis in disguise?

"My ideas vary between Hinduism and Sartre." If towards any ideology Renoir is something of a vanishing corporal, it is because his true allegiance is to a balance between a generosity which draws him towards involvement and a liberty which is by no means egoistic, which entails enterprises and commitments, but which exists at a point, for which we have no name, between alliance and conversion.

Agel speaks of *devenirs*; of becomings, of transformability. The interchange of identifications, of sympathies, may be either shallow and reassuring, or profound and disturbing, depending how far one's love and sympathy extend to all that in man is tragic, animal, selfish and evil. Henri, in *Partie de Campagne,* has a code, which he betrays, thus generating a mere moment of pleasure which is a lifetime's unhappiness and a divine discontent. So much for that humane morality which depends on a realistic sense of human consequence. But to lack any code would be to oscillate helplessly between Boudu and Opale. The puppet play framing *La Chienne* doesn't ridicule the characters, and if it ridicules the censor's moral code in particular, it ridicules by implication, any moral code which depends on dogmatics or generalities, i.e., has a puppet stiffness.

It's not that Renoir is a moral solipsist. It's simply that life isn't very moralistic. "Consideration for others" is no answer, since we can't know their real needs or wishes any better than we can apply any code to particular circumstances. If Renoir's existentialism is more amiably vitalist in tone than Sartre's, it's morally no less unnerving.

Morally, Renoir's films can be grouped as "contradictory" pairs. *Nana's* theme is its heroine's chastening, *Charleston* is her triumph. *Marquitta* is contradicted by *La Petite Marchande d'Allumettes*. In *La Chienne* the bourgeois is humiliated; in *La Nuit du Carrefour* he is vindicated. *Les Bas-Fonds* emphasises despair and evasion, *La Marseillaise* despair and revolution. A trio is formed by *The Golden Coach*, *French CanCan* and *Eléna et les Hommes*. Show-business is sad because a concomitant of stardom is the renunciation of life; show-business is happy because it's an apotheosis of life; politics is only a very dangerous form of show-business.

The "incoherence" of Renoir's moral code isn't a philosophical defect; it indicates an acceptance of the arbitrary which idealistic rationalists vainly strive to schematize away. Since guilt and injustice are inevitable, and self-centredness, even without malice, which also exists, is cruel, the best one can be is generous, resilient and stoic. Moral codes, being the product of obsession, harbour and complicate the cruelty which they limit. The real morality can only be indicated—by the escapees of *La Grande Illusion*, the mountain outlaws of *La Marseillaise*, and the moral emancipation of *Le Caporal Epinglé*. Enterprise, mutual aid, and inner freedom, generate a mixture of self-expenditure and responsiveness which is neither love, nor morality, nor fraternity, but somewhere between the three. Love is not so very different; there is something sisterly, or brotherly, or motherly, in the natural style of Christine, of Elena. If infatuation looms so large in the passional world of Renoir's films, it is precisely because it comes so close to that fatherly tenderness which, fatally weak, takes another's instabilities (whether impulses or lies) for its own ego. It is Dionysian, and if the communal lunch on the grass is liberating, loss of ego is often a collusion, such that the victim is as guilty for his deception as the vamp. (Walter is a cut above Legrand.) Often the beloved is simply the lover's *anima*, releasing, or enacting what he has repressed; and in that sense infatuation is a form of transformability which resembles the "negative capability" of Keats. Keats, too timidly, described it as merely playful (i.e., below serious consequence) and sublimely poetic (i.e., above serious consequence). Renoir's position is more complex. Less romantic than classical, it is classical in the pagan sense, whereby the "romantic" is incarnated by Dionysus—the male vamp who has many incarnations and moods, ranging from Octave (a male Elena) to Dangland (a male Camilla). There are some stable households too. But Renoir's view of love radically differs from that bourgeois interpretation of Freud which restricts sexually mature fulfilment to the nuclear family of suburban life.

The theme of transformations is balanced by that of solitude and self-sufficiency. While its fauve aspect is conspicuous (Boudu), its dominant mode is represented by Renoir's aristocrats (Andersen, Jouvet's Baron, Rauffenstein, the Viceroy, Prince Alex) and by their servants (the two Williams). Aristocratic castes have long provided the popular arts with a symbol for (among other things) a quiet self-control, for that civilized irony which doesn't weaken one's strength. In Renoir's work an aristocrat is an aristocrat in the sense that Dangland is "un Prince." In a real aristocrat, the natural consequence of the aristocratic virtues is abdication. His only exception is Rauffenstein, who, though conceding to Boeildieu that the day of his caste is done, prefers to die at his post. Georges, the "absolute monarch" of *Orvet*, abdicates, as Louis XVI should have abdicated, but to the common people, not to his courtiers. Abdicate one should, but with good judgment: not irresponsibly. The baron turned bum has his destructive side.

Abdication isn't an aristocrat's duty only. Boudu, Nini, Rosenthal all *abdicate* in their various ways. In this *moralistic* use of the notion of aristocracy, Renoir probably isn't just using a familiar metaphor, but also remembering the impressions made on him in his young manhood by aristocratic acquaintances or officers. From another angle, Renoir, selling his father's pictures to finance a film, or "picking up the bills" in the barrackroom, or mucking in with the film unit, is the privileged youth who has abdicated for the sake of his fraternal family. The solitude of the aristocrat modulates into that of the two narrators of *Les Cahiers du Capitaine George*.

Renoir's respect for impulse and for stoicism alike results in the dissolution of almost all temptation situations. In an altogether un-Thomist (and un-common sense) way Renoir's personages have character but no will. Of all the facilities, intelligence has the least hope of foreseeing or controlling relationships. Will is the *whole* character *in its response* to situation. "Resignation" in *The River* is not the antithesis of resistance in *The Southerner*. The cruelty of Nature infiltrates human nature and refers us back to Renoir's celebrated renunciation of sarcasm: " . . . the only thing I can bring to this illogical, irresponsible and cruel universe is my love . . . Obviously, there is in my attitude the egoistic hope of being paid in return. I am as wicked as anyone else and have the same need as they of a smiling indulgence."

It is easy to remember from this passage only the words: "love . . . hope . . . smiling indulgence," to make light of "illogical, irresponsible, and cruel," or of "egoistic . . . wicked" and to forget that the indulgent smile may very well have a very sharp edge of stoic irony which is not at all, but not at all, a wholehearted approval.

Certainly there is all the difference in the world between Renoir's contemplative view of Bogey's death and that apparently instinctive (but also paranoid) animosity towards snakes which looms so large in European iconography. Yet this "smiling indulgence" ceases to seem so easy when one thinks of Prunelle's old age, of the fates of Legrand and Opale, of the murders which Lange and Pépél oppose to the injustices of society, of Joseph's viciousness.

Hence Renoir's respect for the spiritual liberty which certain murders may imply. Several of the revolutionary speeches in *La Marseillaise* display a jocose ferocity, and Opale's violence has at least the integrity of a force of nature. This liberty is quite unlike the "liberty" of Gide's *acte gratuite*, and little closer to that of Camus's *The Outsider*. It corresponds to the wild beast's pounce—after, sometimes, "premeditatively" stalking its prey. When Renoir's murders involve the equivalent of a psychological convulsion, a spiritual explosion, blankness, or amnesia, it is not simply by way of apologetic rhetoric (although, of course, it is partly that). The eruption of animal vitality in Lange and Pépél allows one to speak of a Bergsonian or Blakeian cruelty. They don't feel remorse, and if they had had proper possession of their nature from the beginning they might have been able to kill without that "convulsion" which, far from confusing them, liberates them, leaves them with the grace of a well-balanced mind. Nearer the other extreme (Opale), Boudu asserts his liberty first by an attempt at suicide and then by an impulsive rape. Clearly he holds neither his own life nor anyone else's personality particularly sacred, nor, since the object of his rape is the wife of the man who saved his life, does he possess a highly developed sense of interpersonal relationships. What preserves Renoir's "black vitalism" from any stronger affinity with Sade (and Céline, for whom he has declared a certain admiration) is that generosity, which, because it includes hypocrisy, renders him deceptively acceptable to Christians and humanists alike, counterpointed with that worldly, rather than moral, side which takes pride in the self-control, the "good grace," of a dancer, courtier, or soldier. If Renoir's "fauve" side links with certain animal-emblems (in ferocity: bear, and snake), his "classical" figures could, if they were not careful, turn into puppets, or toy soldiers—and there are curious metamorphoses between them (there are animal victims (pigeons, geese) and two murderous puppets: Death, and Joseph . . .).

So complex is the knot of tensions in Renoir's work that one wonders whether it is not permissible to classify certain traits within it as a special kind of baroque: the ambiguities of generosity and fickleness, the interplay of a humanist fullness with that *other* classicism, over which Dionysus presides, that unpredictable mixture of drama and aside. Romantic assumptions may present Renoir as the great lyricist; family connections may remind us of Renoir the impressionist; but one should not forget that, in *La Règle du Jeu* and *La Tosca,* there is an approach to the baroque, defined by Victor L. Tapié as "art whose lines intercross, twist or break". One may contrast the irregularities, the sense of fleeting, in Renoir, with the regular, rotatory baroque of Ophuls. But there is the light baroque of Venice as well as the heavy baroque of Rome. It is the Venetian Vivaldi whom Renoir calls as collaborator. Since we allow a Dionysiac classicism, why not *une baroque fauve?* A baroque without monumentality?

If the phrase seems paradoxical it is because one habitually associates baroque with courts, just as in English we associate neo-classicism with the heroic couplet. But English neo-classicism is notoriously narrower in register than its European counterpart, lacking its links with both the baroque and the popular arts. The links between neo-classicism and slapstick are established by Renoir's own reference to Goldoni, the Venetian playwright whose career constitutes the historically very concrete link between Molière and the *commedia dell'arte*—which provides the allegory for art as life in *The Golden Coach*, whose derisive spirit frames *La Chienne*, jets forth in the incongruities of *Charleston*, and takes on a tragic cast in so sophisticated a film as *La Règle de Jeu*. The quality of a baroque lies less in the contrasts and more in the turbulences engendered by all the polarities which we have noticed: between evasion and commitment, between Boudu fauvism and the Viceroy's dignity, between state and enterprise, between the household and the group ("tribe"). Of all film directors, perhaps the closest to Renoir is Fellini—with his more extensive repertoire of "toys" (his *ronde* of circus characters), his nostalgias, his more internal, less social, yet less lonely world. *The Golden Coach* must remind us also of Von Sternberg (both are tapestries, and one can imagine Sternberg's frostier icon, and version).

Renoir's mixture of vitalism and acquiescence betray a tribal temperament which has neither been uprooted nor crushed by the arid alienation of our era. Thus the *commedia*, the classical, the baroque and the fauve shade gradually into one another, the first and the last joining in the image of the pantomime bear to complete the circle: clown-actor-man-and-beast. One might define Renoir's art as a classicism which is sufficiently realistic to grant that its formality is a continuously shifting balance of impulses. Or as a realism sufficiently sophisticated to grant that masks, games, dreams and polite hypocrises are not only an evasion of life, but that part of it which we create. Or as a romanticism which accepts and understands that the truth of a feeling lies not primarily in a first fine careless rapture which time or compromise dilute and debase, but equally in a certain contemplation, dissimulation, detachment, and even convention, provided that withdrawal, whether weak or ironic, leaves one as generous towards others as towards oneself and as astringent towards oneself as towards others. For life is a continuing dance, not one simple saving or damning leap.

"Life is a state, not an enterprise." But there are always enterprises in Renoir—the co-operative's, Chotard's, Lange's, Tucker's, Danglard's. Hence Renoir's sense of life as a stream of states doesn't conclude in stream of consciousness (despite its impressionist tendencies) and never abandons narrative (which is the natural expression of enterprise). Even Renoir's most "pointilliste" work, *Renoir Mon Père*, with its extreme disintegration of normal continuity, retains a strong sense of relationships. It remains within a sophisticatedly humanist tradition (the atemporality of Sterne, Carroll and Proust), and remains aloof from that alienation and exasperation of sensitivity which begins with Virginia Woolf and trickles, through the *nouveau roman*, in to various avant-garde avenues and cul-de-sacs. Renoir's manipulation of time and significance adheres to the complexities of *La Jour Se Lève,* of *Citizen Kane* and of *Je t'Aime, Je t'Aime.*

The "baroque" element of Renoir represents, then, a disruption of conventional perspectives—insofar as film "families" are transient, and everyone's reasons terrifyingly reasonable. But the continuous effort of re-integration, is expressed by Renoir's "traditional" elements.

Hence it is that (astonishing as it may seem) there is in the amoralist Renoir something of Tolstoi. Not only in artistic stature, nor in the coincidence that both became army officers out of conformism or aimlessness. Both in different ways, are feminists. Both are realists, of rare diversity, energy and breadth. Both imbue with spiritual warmth the prosaisms of social and peasant life. For both, the individual is fully himself only in belonging to a group: Tolstoi more rigidly centering on the extended family and on the spiritual corporality of the Orthodox tradition; Renoir, with his greater variety of more loosely knit groups, inspired by the permeability of his ego-armour. Tolstoi's noble, primary moralism indicts over and over again an easy, often apparently generous thoughtlessness, which is also callousness and impulsiveness. Its consequence is not punishment in the Dostoievskian sense but a process of redemption. That impulsiveness, even in callousness, Renoir feels one must be prepared to accept, and in Boudu and Opale, even to respect, as integrity. In both artists, the characteristic "shots" are of families, of groups, or of long "travellings"—journeyings. Who can doubt but that the author of *War and Peace* would have recognised in *La Grande Illusion* an epic by a fraternal spirit, or that the author of *The Devil and Family Happiness* would have thundered against the author of *Boudu Sauvé des Eaux* and of *Partie de Campagne* as being of the devli's party, and, what's worse, knowing it?

Tolstoi's evangelistic concentration contrasts with all which in Renoir is not so much amoral as partly moral. In Renoir, morality is orbital. Tolstoi's thought works steadily towards a reduction of human nature to a peasant simplicity; all happy families resemble one another. Renoir acquiesces in a diversity typical of a bourgeoisie which is richly specialised but not yet alienated. Yet Renoir, with his deep peasant roots, often used the peasantry as a reference point for a warm human simplicity (in *La Grande Illusion,* in *Le Déjeuner Sur L'Herbe*) thus allowing a certain idealism which, as in the latter film, can become almost evangelistic in spirit—but an evangelism of pagan vitalism. Conversely, Tolstoi, as an anarchist, derives from his peasant connections a stress on "mutual aid", akin to Renoir's co-operatives. Renoir's premature revolutionaries take to and return from the mountains, where they find fraternity; Tolstoi returns from a solitude with God. The latter's bouts of Hebraic prophecy contrast with Renoir's Parisian paradoxes of engagement and fickleness, of real involvement and ulterior liberty. It is arguable that if both artists evade the full atrocity of classic tragedy it is for complementary reasons. Tolstoi prefers the Christian pattern of sin and redemption, while Renoir prefers a noble sophistication. Tolstoi's dislike of aestheticism contrasts with Renoir's delight in the *truquage*; yet both are wary of high culture as idolatry, and if Tolstoi prefers the piety of simplistic art Renoir prefers street-music, barrel-organs and the cancan. Tolstoi often overmoralises (one need only compare certain ruinous passages in *Anna Karenina* with Renoir's more diffuse but maturer *Madame Bovary*). Tolstoi stresses the prostitutes's repentance, Renoir the matter-of-factness of her profession (compare *Les Cahiers du Capitaine Georges* with *Resurrection*). Tolstoi's breadth of vision forces onto his moral single-mindedness the complex structure of *War and Peace*; Renoir imbues intimate narratives with the unpredictable spaces, the irregular *expansions* of his interjected asides. Moral pattern and purpose drive Tolstoi's characters on their epic pilgrimages; Renoir's characters find life only as they assent to the river flow. Yet something about Tolstoi's death evokes the quality of stoic futility in the Renoir world. "After having renounced his aristocratic origins, his literary glory, and his artistic gifts, he had still to sacrifice that which was dearest to him, and his family. At the age of 82, Tolstoi fled from his home, Death overtook him in the little station of Apostouro. After falling ill in the train which was taking him away, Tolstoi, this pilgrim of the Absolute, dies in a station-master's office, stretched on a simple iron bed." The scene might have been written for the cameras of Jean Renoir, that pilgrim of the relative . . .

Bibliography

This bibliography aspires to be helpful rather than exhaustive, even within its sphere of competence. With a few exceptions, it is restricted to post-war articles in French and English. It gives some idea of the intellectual background within which the present book was written. Pierre Leprohon's *Jean Renoir* and the Premier Plan *Jean Renoir*, edited by Bernard Chardère, are particularly useful for their bibliographies and citations from pre-war French writers. The interviews are arranged chronologically.

BY JEAN RENOIR

ARTICLES, INTERVIEWS

"Souvenirs" in *Le Point* No. 18, December 1938, and in *Chardère* (op. cit.).

"Jean Renoir Discusses His Work, Present and Future" in *Ciné-Technician* March-April 1939.

"Charlie Among the Immortals" in *Screenwriter* July 1947

"Renoir, Passim" (by Satyajit Ray) in *Sequence* No. 10, New York 1950

"On Me Demande" in *Cahiers du Cinéma* No. 8, January 1952, and as "Jean Renoir—I Know Where I'm Going" in *Films in Review*, March 1952, and as "Personal Notes" in *Sight and Sound*, June 1952.

"Quelque Chose M'Est Arrivé . . . " in *Cahiers du Cinéma*, No. 8

"Entretien Avec Jean Renoir" (by Jacques Doniol-Valcroze) in *Cahiers du Cinéma* No. 8

"On Limelight" in *Cahiers du Cinéma* No. 18, 1952

"Entretien Avec Jean Renoir" (by Jacques Rivette and François Truffaut in *Cahiers du Cinéma* No. 34 April 1954 and No. 35 May 1954, and (abridged) in *Sight and Sound* July-Sept 1954 and in *Films in Review* in November 1954

"Mes Rêves" in *Cahiers du Cinéma* No. 38 Aug-Sept 1954

"Le Public A Horreur de Ça" in *Cahiers du Cinéma* No. 42, December 1954

"Sur Hollywood" in *Cahiers du Cinéma* No. 54

"Toni et le Classicisme" in *Cahiers du Cinéma* No. 60 June 1956

"Slanting Films for the U.S." in *Today's Cinema*, 9.8.1956

"La Chienne" in *Film* No. 9, Sept-Oct 1956

"Ce Bougre de Monde Nouveau" in *Cahiers du Cinéma* No. 78 Christmas 1957 and as "Devil of a New World" in Whitebait, William, ed., *International Film Annual No. 2*, John Calder, 1958.

"Nouvel Entretien Avec Jean Renoir" (by Jacques Rivette and François Truffaut) in *Cahiers du Cinéma* No. 78.

"On Films and TV" (by André Bazin, with Roberto Rossellini) in *Sight and Sound* January 1959

"Jean Renoir Parle . . . " in *U.R.C.J. Information*, Numéro Speciale, 1961

"Conversation with Jean Renoir" (by Louis Marcorelles) in *Sight and Sound* Spring 1962

Selections from Renoir's interviews and articles in Chardère, 1963, q.v.

"Jean Renoir on Love, Hollywood, Authors and Critics!" in *Cinema* (U.S.A.), Feb 1964.

"J. R. via Paris" in *Cinéma 65* No. 97, June 1965

"Mes Prochains Films" (by Jean-André Fieschi, Michel Delahaye) in *Cahiers du Cinéma* No. 180 July 1966 and as "My Next Films" in *Cahiers du Cinéma in English* No. 9, March 1967

"Hommage à Von Stroheim" in *Études Cinématographiques* No. 48-50, 1966

"Renoir le Patron; Propos de Renoir" (by André Labarthé and Jacques Rivette) in *Cahiers du Cinéma* No. 186 January 1967

"How I Made Boudu" in *Film Society Review* Feb 1967

Selected extracts, 1948-1967 in Leprohon, q.v. 1967

Interviews With Film Directors (by Andrew Sarris) 1967

"Jean Renoir", (by Gideon Bachmann) in *Contact* No. 4, Sausalito, California.

"La Marche de l'Idée: Entretien Aven Jean Renoir" (by Michel Dalahaye and Jean Narboni), in *Cahiers du Cinéma* No. 196 December 1967

"Foreword" to *What Is Cinema* Vol. 1, by André Bazin (ed. Hugh Gray), University of California Press, 1967

"Interview With Jean Renoir" (by Rui Nogueira and François Truchaud), in *Sight and Sound* Spring 1968

"Meanwhile in London . . . " (Anon) in *Sight and Sound* Spring 1968

"Farthingales and Facts" in *Sight and Sound*, Summer 1968.

"Hommage to Albert Lewin" in *Action* August 1968

"Dreyer's Sin" in *Carl Th. Dreyer; Danish Film Director*, Ministry of Foreign Affairs, Copenhagen, 1970.

SCRIPTS

(Asterisk = full-length script. Others listed are extracts only.)

La Bête Humaine, in Leprohon, Pierre, (op.cit.)

Carola et les Cabotins in *Cahiers du Cinéma* No. 78, Christmas 1957

C'est la Révolution in *Cahiers du Cinéma* No. 200, April 1968 and No. 201, May 1968

Le Déjeuner Sur L'Herbe, in Leprohon, (op. cit.)

French CanCan, in Leprohon, (op. cit.)

French CanCan, in *Cinéma 55* No. 2, December 1954

French CanCan, in *Cahiers du Cinéma* No. 47, May 1955

**La Grande Illusion*, in *L'Avant-Scène (Cinéma)* No. 44, January 1965, and Lorrimer Press, 1968.

Paris-Province, in *Cahiers du Cinéma* No. 35, May 1954

*Partie de Campagne, in *L'Avant-Scène (Cinéma)* No. 21, 1962

Partie de Campagne (missing scenes), in Leprohon, 1967 (op. cit.)

La Règle du Jeu, in *Cahiers du Cinéma* No. 38, August-Sept 1954

*La Règle du Jeu, *L'Avant Scène (Cinéma)*, No. 52, 1965, and *The Rules of the Game*, Lorrimer, 1970.

*The Southerner, in Gassner, Ernest, and Nichols, Dudley, ed., *Best Film Plays 1945*, Crown, 1946.

*Le Testament du Dr. Cordelier, in *L'Avant-Scène (Cinéma)* No. 6, 1961.

*This Land Is Mine, in Gassner, Ernest, and Nichols, Dudley, ed., *Twenty Best Film Plays*, Crown, 1943.

La Vie Est à Nous, in Chardère, Bernard, (op. cit.)

ABOUT RENOIR

BOOKS, PAMPHLETS AND SPECIAL ISSUES OF MAGAZINES

Anon., The Film Society Programmes 1925-1938, Arno Press, 1972

Agate, James, *Around Cinemas: First Series*, Home and Van Thal, 1945.

Agee, James, *Agee on film: Reviews and Comments*, Beacon Press, 1958.

Agel, Henri, *Miroirs de L'Insolite dans le Cinèma Français*, Éditions Universitaires, 1954

Agel, Henri, *Les Grands Cinéastes*, Editions Universitaires, 1955

Agel, Henri, *Les Grands Cinéastes que Je Propose*, Éditions Universitaires, 1967

Bardèche, Maurice, and Brasillach, Robert, *Histoire du Film*, André Martel, 1948; Le Livre de Poche, 1967; (expurgated), Allen & Unwin.

Barkan, Raymond, in Leprohon, 1967, op. cit.

Bataille, Sylvia, in Leprohon, 1967, op. cit.

Bazin, André, Doniol-Valcroze, Jacques and Duca, Lo, eds., *Cahiers du Cinéma* No. 8, January 1952.

Bazin, André, Doniol-Valcroze, Jacques and Rohmer, Eric, eds., *Cahiers du Cinéma* No. 78, Christmas 1957.

Bennett, Susan, *Study Unit 8: Jean Renoir*, British Film Institute Education Dept., 1967.

Beylie, Claude, *Jean Renoir: Films 1924-1939*, *L'Avant-Scène du Cinéma*, 1969 (120 slides and commentary).

Braudy, Leo, *Jean Renoir: The World of His Films*, Doubleday, 1972.

Brunius, Jacques, in Manvell, Roger, ed., *Experiment in the Film*, Grey Walls Press, 1949.

Burch, Noel, in *Praxis du Cinéma*, Gallimard, 1969.

Cauliez, Armand-Jean, *Jean Renoir*, Editions Universitaires, 1962.

Celine, Louis-Ferdinand, *Bagatelles pour un Massacre*.

Chardère, Bernard, ed., *Jean Renoir: Premier Plan* No. 22-24, S.E.R.D.O.C. Lyons, 1963.

Clair, René, cited in Ajame, Pierre, *Le Procés des Juges: Les Critiques du Cinéma*, Flammarion, 1967.

Davy, Paul, *Jean Renoir*, Club du Livre du Cinéma, Brussels, 1967.

Dickinson, Thorold, *A Discovery of Cinema*, Oxford University Press, 1971.

Durgnat, Raymond, *Films and Feelings*, M.I.T., Faber and Faber, 1967.

Federazione Italiana del Circoli del Cinema, *Jean Renoir*, 1952.

Griffith, Richard and Rotha, Paul, *The Film Till Now*, Vision, 2nd ed., 1951.

Institut des Hautes Études Cinématographiques, *Analyse des Films de Jean Renoir*, 1966.

Jacob, Guy, in *Jacques Prévert: Premier Plan* No. 14, S.E.R.D.O.C., Lyons, 1960.

Jacobs, Gilles, *Le Cinéma Moderne*, S.E.R.D.O.C., Lyons, 1964.

Kael, Pauline, *I Lost It at the Movies*, Little Brown, 1965.

Kyrou, Ado, *Le Surrealisme au Cinéma*, Eric Losfeld, 2nd ed., 1963.

Kyrou, Ado, *Amour-Erotisme au Cinéma*, Eric Losfeld, 2nd ed., 1965.

Leprohon, Pierre, *Presence Contemporaines: Cinéma*, Nouvelles Éditions Debresee, 1957.

Leprohon, Pierre, *Jean Renoir*, Editions Seghers, 1967.

Mauriac, Claude, *L'Amour du Cinéma*, Editions Albin Michel, 1954.

M.D. and J.B., *The Golden Coach*, Information Sheet No. 61 (New Series), C.F.F.S.

Il Nuovo Spettatore Cinematografico No. 26, November 1961 (Turin).

Poulle, François, *Renoir 1938 ou Jean Renoir Pour Rien?*, Éditions du Cerf, 1969.

Sadoul, Georges, *Dictionnaire des Films*, Editions du Seuil, 1965.

Siclier, Jacques, *La Femme dans le Cinéma Français*, Editions du Cerf, 1957.

Tele-Cine, No. 36-37, March-April 1953.

Thomson, David, *Movie Man*, Secker and Warburg, 1967.

U.R.C.J. Information, *Numero Special: Jean Renoir Parle . . . .* , Ciné-Club des Jeunes de l'Académie de Toulouse, 1961.

ARTICLES IN PERIODICALS

Alpert, Hollis, "The New Classic Renoir" *(The Golden Coach)* in *The Saturday Review* 23.1.1954.

Andrey, Roger, *"De Bonne Guerre . . . ? Jean Renoir Fait Son 'Testament'"* in *Cinéma '60* No. 51, Nov-Dec 1960.

Anonymous, *"La Vie Est à Nous"* in *Cahiers du Cinéma* No. 218, March 1970.

Anonymous, *"Encyclopédie Permanente du Cinématographe: Truffaut (Constantes)"* in *Positif* No. 94, April 1968.

Aristarco, Guido, *"Le Grandi Illusioni di Renoir"*, in *Cinema Nuovo* No. 163, May/June 1963.

Audiberti, Jacques, "Note Sur *The Woman on the Beach"*, in *Cahiers du Cinéma* No. 40, 1954.

Auriol, Jean-George, *"La Nuit du Carrefour"*, in *La Revue du Cinéma* No. 31.

Bachmann, Gideon, *"Le Déjeuner Sur L'Herbe"*, in *Film Quarterly*, Winter, 1960.

Barkan, Raymond, *"Un Des Plus Grands Auteurs de Films"*, in *Ciné-Club* April 1948.

Barr, Charles, *Le Crime de Monsieur Lange*, in *Movie* No. 13, Summer 1965.

Bataille, Sylvia, in, Philippe, Pierre, *"Ombres Dans l'Ombre: Sylvia Bataille Ou l'Absence, ' . . . absence, abominable absence de la guerre'"*, in Cinéma 61 No. 58, July 1961.

Bazin, André, *"Renoir Français"*, in *Cahiers du Cinéma* No. 8, January 1952.

Bazin, André, "Petit Journal Intime du Cinéma *(Jules César)"* in *Cahiers du Cinéma* No. 38, Aug-Sept 1954.

Bazin, André, "Portrait d'Auguste Renoir *(French CanCan)*" in *Cahiers du Cinéma* No. 47, May 1955.

Bazin, André, "Renoir *(Le Crime de Monsieur Lange, Journal d'une Femme de Chambre)*", in *Cinéma '56,* No. 12, Nov. 1956.

Bazin, André, Doniol-Valcroze, Jacques, Givray, Claude de, Godard, Jean-Luc, Marcorelles, Louis, Rivette, Jacques, Rohmer, Eric, Truffaut, François, "Bio-Filmographie de Jean Renoir" in *Cahiers du Cinéma* No. 78, Christmas 1957.

Beranger, Jean, "The Illustrious Career of Jean Renoir" in *Yale French Studies* 1965.

Beylie, Claude, "Renoir le Constructeur", in *Cahiers du Cinéma* No. 80, February 1958.

Beylie, Claude, "Où Est la Liberté *(La Grande Illusion)*" in *Cahiers du Cinéma* No. 89, November 1958.

Beylie, Claude, "Cette Male Gaieté" in *L'Avant-Scene (Cinéma)* No. 21, Dec. 1962.

Beylie, Claude, "Jean Renoir Ou *La Règle du Jeu*; Des Mécanismes de la Representation Aux Mécanismes de la Création" in *Cinéma 69* no. 140.

Billard, Pierre, *"Le Testament du Dr. Cordelier"* in *Cinéma 62* No. 62, Jan. 1962.

Billard, Pierre, *"Le Caporal Epinglé",* in *Cinéma 62* No. 68, July-August 1962.

Braudy, Leo, "Zola on Film" in *Yale French Studies* No. 42, 1969.

Broughton, Garry, "Reviews: Le Déjeuner Sur L'*'*Herbe" in *Oxford Opinion* No. 31, May 1960.

Brunelin, André-G., in *Cinéma 55* No. 2, Dec. 1954, and in Leprohon, 1967, (op. cit.)

Brunelin, André-G., "Histoire d'Une Malédiction: *La Règle du Jeu*" in *Cinéma 60* No. 43, January 1960.

Brunelin, André-G., "Jacques Becker Ou La Trace de l'Homme" in *Cinéma 60* No. 48, July 1960.

Brunelin, André G., "Au Temps du Vieux-Colombier De Jean Tedesco—*Suite et Fin"* in *Cinéma 61* No. 52, Jan. 1961.

Brunius, Jacques, "Footnotes to the Film *(La Chienne)*" in *Film* No. 9, Sept-Oct 1956.

Callenbach, Ernest, and Schuldenfrei, Roberta, "The Presence of Jean Renoir" in *Film Quarterly,* Winter 1960.

Cameron, Ian, and Shivas, Mark, "Two Views of Jean Renoir's *Le Caporal Epinglé*" in *Movie* No. 4, November 1962.

Chardere, Bernard, *"French CanCan"*, in *Positif* No. 14-15, Nov. 1955.

Cohn, Bernard, "Trente Ans Après", in *Positif* No. 93, March 1968.

Collet, Jean *"La Bête Humaine"*, in *Télérama*, 28.5.1968.

Collins, Richard, *"The Notebooks of Captain Georges/Renoir My Father"* in *Monogram* No. 2, Summer 1971.

Comolli, Jean-Louis, "Des Migrations Exemplaires" in *Cahiers du Cinéma* No. 196, December 1967.

Conrad, Randall, "Diaries of Two Chambermaids", in *Film Quarterly,* Winter 1970-1

De La Roche, Catherine, *"The River"*, in *Picture Post*, 1.3.1952.

Delmas, Jean, Otchkovsky-Laurens, Pierre and Mohr, François, *"La Règle du Jeu"*

Demonsablon, "À propos du *Caresse d'Or*", in *Cahiers du Cinéma* No. 38, Aug-Sept 1958.

Desnos, Robert, "Pages Retrouvés Sur *Les Mystères de New York*" in Jeune Cinéma No. 23, May 1967.

Doniol-Valcroze, Jacques, "Une Esquisse", in *La Revue du Cinéma* No. 4, January 1947.

Doniol-Valcroze, Jacques, "Camilla et le Don", in *Cahiers du Cinéma* No. 21, March 1953.

Douchet, Jean, "Naissance d'Un Soleil: *Le Caporal Epinglé*" in *Cahiers du Cinéma* No. 133, August 1962.

Durgnat, Raymond, "Symbolism: Another Word For It *(Boudu Sauvé des Eaux, Le Testament du Dr. Cordelier, Le Déjeuner Sur L'Herbe)*" in *Films and Filming*, April 1962.

Fauchois, René, "Réconciliation Auteur de Boudu", in *Cinéma 56* No. 7, November 1955.

Florelle, cited in Phillipe, Pierre, "Ombres Dans L'Ombre: Florelle, ou Les Mouettes Meurent Au Port", in *Cinéma 61* No. 55, April 1961.

Fofi, Goffredo, *"La Vie Est Á Nous"*, in *Positif* No. 113, February 1970.

Gauteur, Claude, "Pour les 75 Ans De Michel Simon", in *Cinéma 70* No. 146.

Grahame, Virginia, *"La Règle du Jeu"* in *The Spectator*, 2.2.1951.

Greene, Grahame, *"La Bête Humaine"*, in *The Spectator*, 5.3.1939.

Harcourt, Peter, "Jean Renoir" in *The London Magazine* December 1962.

Hennebelle, Guy, *"La Vie Est À Nous"* in *Jeune Cinéma* No. 37, March 1969.

Hessling, Catherine, cited in Philippe, Pierre, "Catherine Hessling, Ou Retouches A Un Renoir", in *Cinéma 61* No. 57, June 1961.

Jacob, Gilles, *Le Cinema Moderne*, Serdoc, 1965.

Joly, Jacques, "Between Theatre and Life: Jean Renoir and *The Rules of the Game*," in *Film Quarterly* Winter 1967-68.

Kerans, James, "Classics Revisited: *La Grande Illusion*" in *Film Quarterly* Winter 1960.

Lambert, Gavin, "French Cinema: The New Pessimism" in *Sequence* No. 14 Summer 1948.

Lambert, Gavin, *"La Règle du Jeu"*, London Film Society Notes, 8.11.1949.

Lambert, Gavin, *"The River"*, in *Sight and Sound*, March 1952.

Leenhardt, Jean, "Jean Renoir et la Tradition Française", in *Intermède* Spring 1946 and in *Premier Plan* (op. cit.)

Lejeune, C. A., "The Man Who Came Back," in *The Observer*, 1942.

McCarten, John, "Jaunty Colombine *(The Golden Coach)*" in *The New Yorker* 30.1.1954.

Madsen, Axel, "Renoir Américan (bis)" in *Cahiers du Cinéma* No. 191, June 1967.

Madsen, Axel, "Renoir at 72" in *Cinema* (U.S.A.), Spring 1968.

Martin, Marcel, *"Elena et les Hommes"*, in *Cinéma 58* No. 27, May 1958.

Mayoux, Michel, "Renoir Parmi Nous", in *Cahiers du Cinéma* No. 8, January 1952.

Millar, Daniel, "The Autumn of Jean Renoir", in *Sight and Sound*, Summer 1968.

Milne, Tom, "The Two Chambermaids", in *Sight and Sound*, Autumn 1964.

Mirande, Pierre, *"Elena et les Hommes"*, *Fiche Télé-Cine* No. 284

Modot, Gaston, in Leprohon, (op. cit.)

Nichols, Dudley, *"The River"*, in *Cahiers du Cinéma*, No. 8, January 1952.

Niderste, R., "Jean Renoir, Cinéaste du XVIIIe Siècle" in *Jeune Cinéma* No. 14, April 1966.

Philippe, Pierre, "Catherine Hessling" in *Cinéma 61* No. 57.

Phillips, James E., "A Commedia dell'Arte *(The Golden Coach)*" in *Hollywood Quarterly of Film Radio and Television*, Fall 1954.

Powell, Dilys, "The Man Who Came Back", in *The Sunday Times*, 1942.

Prévert, Jacques, *"Le Crime de Monsieur Lange,"* in *Arts et Essai* No. 1-3.

Ray, Satyajit, "Renoir in Calcutta," in *Sequence* No. 10, New York 1950.

Renoir, Claude, "Problèmes d'Operateur Ou Écrire Pour Ne Rien Dire." in *Cahiers du Cinéma* No. 8, Jan 1952.

Resnais, Alain, "Memories of Renoir", in *Sight and Sound* Summer 1968.

Rohmer, Eric, "Les Singes et Venus *(Elena et les Hommes)*" in *Cahiers du Cinéma* No. 64, November 1956.

Rohmer, Eric, "La Jeunesse du Jean Renoir", in *Cahiers du Cinéma* No. 102, December 1959.

Russell, Lee, "Jean Renoir", in *New Left Review* No. 25 May-June 1964.

Sarris, Andrew, *"Boudu Saved from Drowning"*, in *Cahiers du Cinéma in English* No. 9, March 1967.

Scherer, Maurice, "Renoir Américain" in *Cahiers du Cinéma* No. 8, Jan. 1952.

Scherer, Maurice, "La Robe Bleu d'Harriet *(The River)*" in *Cahiers du Cinéma* No. 8, January 1952.

Scholsberg, L., (in Poulle, op. cit.)

Selz, Thalia, "Swing Low Sweet Chariot *(The Golden Coach)*" in *Hollywood Quarterly of Film Radio and Television*, Fall 1954.

Shorter, Eric, *"Woman on the Beach"* in *Daily Sketch*, 21.3.1948.

Sibirskaia, Nadia, cited in Philippe, Pierre, "Ombres Dans L'Ombre: Nadia Sibirskaia Ou Un Certain Fluide" in *Cinéma 61* No. 60, Oct. 1961.

Simsolo, Noel, *"La Règle du Jeu,"* in *Image et Son* No. 244 1970/1.

Stroheim, Eric Von, "Ma Première Rencontre Avec Jean Renoir", in *Cinémonde* 1937 and in *L'Avant-Scène (Cinéma)* No. 44, January 1965.

Tedesco, Jean, See Brunelin, 1961, (op. cit.)

Tournier, Jacques, in Leprohon, 1967, (op. cit.)

Truffaut, François, "Orvet Mon Amour" in *Cahiers du Cinéma* No. 47, May 1955.

Venturini, Franco, "Apunti Sul Renoir Americano," in *Eco del Cinema*, 15.1.1953.

Weinberg, Herman G., "Reflections On The Current Scene: *Le Petit Théâtre de Jean Renoir*" in *Take One* Spring 1971.

Whitebait, William, *"The River,"* in *New Statesman*, 3.5.52.

Whitehall, Richard, "Painting Life with Movement," in *Films and Filming*, June 1960.

Whitehall, Richard, "The Screen Is His Canvas," in *Films and Filming*, July 1960.

Winnington, Richard, "Films: *The Woman on the Beach*" in *News Chronicle*, London, 1949.

Zeman, Martin, *"The Little Theatre of Jean Renoir"*, in *Film Quarterly*, Spring 1971.

ADDENDA

Beylie, Claude, *Jean Renoir: Films 1924-1939*. Slide Album. L'Avant-Scene du Cinema, 1972.

Fofi, Goffredo, *The Cinema of the Popular Front in France (1934-38)* in *Screen*, Winter 1972/3.

Renoir, Jean, and Sesonske, Alexander, *Renoir: A Progress Report* in *Cinema* (U.S.) Vol. 6. No. 1.

OTHER REFERENCES

Arvon, Henri, *L'Anarchisme*, Presses Universitaires de France, 1968.

Baylis, Claude, in Runes, Dagobert D., *Dictionary of Philosophy*, Philosophical Library 1942, Peter Owen, 1950.

Bergler, Edmund, *Counterfeit-Sex*, 2nd ed., Grove Press/Evergreen Books, 1961.

Brogan, D. W., *The French Nation*, Hamish Hamilton, Arrow Books, 1961.

Brown, J. A. C., *Freud and the Post-Freudians*, Penguin Books, 1961.

Caudwell, Christopher, *Illusion and Reality*, International Publishers, N.Y., 1970.

Cobban, Alfred, *A History of Modern France, Volume Two: 1799-1945*, Penguin, 1961.

Dagobert, D., *Dictionary of Philosophy*, Philosophical Library, 1942; Peter Owen, 1950.

Fauvet, Jacques, *The Cockpit of France*, Harvill Press, 1960.

Maurois, André, *A History of France* (3rd edition), Jonathan Cape, 1960.

Pickles, Dorothy, *The Fifth French Republic* (2nd edition), Methuen, 1962.

Prévert, Jacques, *L'Orgue de Barbarie*, in Prévert, Jacques, *Paroles*, N.R.F., 1961, Le Livre de Poche.

Remond, René, *The Right Wing in France: From 1815 to De Gaulle*, University of Pennsylvania Press, 1966.

Tapié, Victor L., *Le Baroque*, 3rd ed., Presses Universitaires de France, 1968.

Tawney, R. H., *Religion and the Rise of Capitalism*, Penguin, 1970.

Taylor, Gordon Rattray, *The Angel-Makers*, Thames and Hudson, 1958.

Taylor, Gordon Rattray, *Sex in History*, Thames and Hudson, 1958.

Werth, Alexander, *France 1940-1945*, Robert Hale, 1956.

Wilenski, R. H., *The Modern Movement in Art*, Phaidon, 1957.

Index